The Open University

Science Short Course

Understanding the weather

Shelagh Ross, Stephen Lewis and Nicholas Braithwaite

This publication forms part of an Open University course S189 *Understanding the weather*. Details of this and other Open University courses can be obtained from the Student Registration and Enquiry Service, The Open University, PO Box 197, Milton Keynes MK7 6BJ, United Kingdom: tel. +44 (0)845 300 60 90, email general-enquiries@open.ac.uk

Alternatively, you may visit the Open University website at http://www.open.ac.uk where you can learn more about the wide range of courses and packs offered at all levels by The Open University.

To purchase a selection of Open University course materials visit http://www.ouw.co.uk, or contact Open University Worldwide, Walton Hall, Milton Keynes MK7 6AA, United Kingdom for a brochure. tel. +44 (0)1908 858793; fax +44 (0)1908 858787; email ouw-customer-services@open.ac.uk

This course was produced in partnership with the Royal Meteorological Society.

The Open University
Walton Hall, Milton Keynes
MK7 6AA

First published 2008. Second edition 2009

Edited and designed by The Open University.

Typeset by SR Nova Pvt Ltd, Bangalore, India.

Printed and bound in the United Kingdom by Halstan Printing Group, Amersham.

ISBN 978 1 8487 3211 7

2.1

Contents

Chapter 1
Weather contexts

Weather is important to everybody, and it is therefore natural to view it first in the context of its impact on our own daily lives. We have all been directly affected by major weather events, such as a big storm that has resulted in flooding, disruption to public transport, or damage to buildings. The repercussions of an event like this may also spread far beyond the area in which it occurs, with crop damage causing increases in the price of certain foods and insurance claims resulting in a rise in insurance premiums for everyone. In less developed parts of the world, the consequences of weather events can be even more serious. If houses are poorly constructed, a severe flood can destroy whole villages. In places where many people farm at subsistence level, a long dry spell can result in famine. Although it is extreme events that make the news, the weather impacts constantly on everyone, wherever they live. At a personal level, the weather may determine what clothes you wear, how you spend your free time, whether you heat or air-condition your home, or whether your area is subject to restrictions on your use of water. At local or national level, the weather governs agriculture, building design, water supply, power generation, transport, tourism, sport and leisure activities.

1.1   What will the weather be like?

Much of the interest of 'weather watching' lies in the sheer variability of the weather from day to day, season to season, year to year and place to place. Whatever the weather is like today, the one certainty is that it will change – if not in the next few days, then in the next few weeks. And there are always surprises in store.

Summer conditions in southern England and parts of France over the years 2003–2007 vividly illustrated how different the weather can be from one year to the next. Although England does not suffer the kinds of extreme weather events that can be experienced in some parts of the world, the story of these five summers is still full of contrasts. In 2003, the summer months of June, July and August were all very warm in England, and a notable ten-day heat wave during August brought a new high temperature record for the UK of 38.5 degrees Celsius (or centigrade). Further south in France it was even hotter and a large number of deaths were attributed to the heat. In 2004, summer temperatures in England never came anywhere near the record set the previous year and August was a very wet month, with the village of Boscastle in Cornwall being devastated by a flood. By the summer of 2005, there were concerns about drought (Figure 1.1a). In 2006, there was again very hot weather, though this time it came earlier, setting a new UK temperature record for July of 36.5 degrees Celsius. The long-range seasonal forecast for the summer issued by the UK Meteorological Office (usually simply called the Met Office) at the end of May 2007 and covering the next three months stated that there were likely to be fewer occurrences of very hot weather than in the previous few years, and indicated that rainfall would be average or below average in the southern part of the UK. In the event, things turned out very differently. While the predictions proved correct in respect of temperatures, they were quite at odds with the exceptionally high rainfall experienced that summer. There was severe flooding in a number of areas of England in June and July (Figure 1.1b), yet no excess rain in France. As you progress through the course, you will find out why some of these weather events and patterns occurred.

(a)   (b)

Figure 1.1 Contrasting images of summer weather in England. (a) The Weir Wood reservoir in Sussex, which is one of the main sources of water supply for southeast England, drying out in 2005. (b) Tewkesbury (Gloucestershire) during the summer floods of 2007.

The story of the 2007 summer illustrates the unreliability of long-range seasonal forecasts. However, all the heavy rainfall events of that summer *were* accurately predicted by professional forecasters several days in advance. An amateur observer without access to the technology that underpins modern-day forecasting but with experience of 'weather watching' would also have been able to tell that wet weather was coming, though probably not until 4–6 hours before the event. Certainly the careful observer can pick up many clues by watching the sky and the environment, and make quite accurate short-range forecasts as a result. This skill used to be more widely practised than it is today, and it gave rise to a rich folklore of weather-related sayings. Many of these pieces of weather lore have little basis in fact, but others have some validity, and are worth adding to one's personal store of weather wisdom. You will find a few of the more useful sayings scattered through subsequent chapters. However, weather lore is no substitute for informed observation and scientific insight. This course aims to help you in developing your own observational skills as well as equipping you with the scientific understanding that will enable you to use your observations to the full.

Activity 1.1 Heat, drought and flood

The estimated time for this activity is 40 minutes.

In this activity you will be able to watch a compilation of some television coverage of a number of weather events that occurred in England during the five summers of 2003–2007. The compilation itself is on the DVD. If you have not already checked the instructions in the *Study Guide* on how to run this you should do so now.

The detailed instructions for all the course activities are on the course website. Access the site, find the section called Activities and follow the guidance for Activity 1.1.

1.2 The science of the weather

The science of the weather is essentially the science of the atmosphere, a layer of air surrounding the Earth. As Figure 1.2 illustrates, the atmosphere is very shallow indeed in comparison with the diameter of the Earth. Yet as a result of the heating of the Earth by the Sun, the large amount of water on the surface of the planet and the nature of the atmosphere itself, this shallow layer of air produces winds, clouds, snow, storms, tornadoes, and all the other forms of weather with which we are familiar. The composition of the atmosphere is discussed in Box 1.1.

Study comment

The diagrams and photos are important parts of the course material. You should make sure that you read the figure captions carefully. They often contain a lot of information! Check that you can identify in the figure all the features mentioned in the caption and/or discussed in the text.

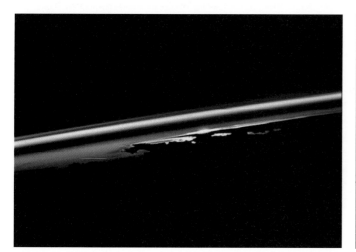

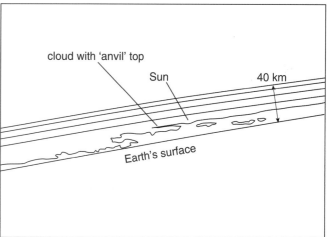

Figure 1.2 Sunrise over the southwest Pacific, photographed from a satellite. Notice how shallow the atmosphere is: the top of the dark-blue layer in this photograph is about 40 kilometres above the Earth's surface. (Compare this to the diameter of the Earth which is about 12 800 kilometres.) All the familiar weather phenomena are generated in the lowest layer of the atmosphere, up to about 15 kilometres above the Earth's surface. Here you can see silhouetted against the red of the sunrise several very large thunderclouds with 'anvil' tops.

Box 1.1 What is 'air'?

Near the Earth's surface, if the air is perfectly dry it is made up of approximately 78 per cent nitrogen (by volume), 21 per cent oxygen, and one per cent argon, with just traces of other gases. One of those other gases is carbon dioxide. As you will be aware, the increasing level of carbon dioxide is a cause for concern in terms of its effect on the global climate. Nevertheless, the total atmospheric contribution by volume of carbon dioxide is very small: roughly one-thirtieth of one per cent. There is, however, another atmospheric gas that is present in highly variable quantities and in much higher concentrations than carbon dioxide. This gas is water vapour. Close to the surface over a large desert like the Sahara in Africa or over a very cold polar region there may be almost no water vapour at all in the air. In hot tropical rainforests the air may hold up to 4 per cent water vapour by volume. The behaviour of water vapour in the air is a vitally important factor in weather systems.

The study of atmospheric phenomena and processes is called meteorology, a term from the Greek word 'meteoros' meaning 'high' or 'raised up'. In about 340 BC Aristotle wrote a treatise entitled *Meteorologikon*, in which he put forward ideas about things that could be seen in, or fell from, the sky. The latter category included rain, hail, lightning and meteors. Some of the subjects Aristotle covered in this work are now regarded as part of astronomy, and meteors from outer space are studied by planetary scientists. Meteorology has narrowed to become the science of the atmosphere, but that still encompasses a complex mixture of topics. Meteorologists study the physical and chemical properties of the atmosphere, large-scale circulations within it, and the ways in which it interacts with the Earth's land and ocean surfaces. Both climate and weather are manifestations of the properties and behaviour of the atmosphere, so meteorology is also concerned with short-range weather forecasting and the study of longer-term changes in climate. Although this course focuses on weather rather than on climate, the distinction between them will be explored in Section 1.4.

Many of Aristotle's ideas were erroneous, yet they remained unchallenged for the best part of two thousand years. It was not until the seventeenth century, when instruments such as thermometers and barometers were invented, that measurements of a number of the physical properties of the atmosphere could be made and a genuinely scientific approach to weather phenomena began to emerge. By the nineteenth century, the science of meteorology was really developing, as observations, measurements and physical laws were coming together to form a more coherent picture of atmospheric phenomena and processes. From the middle of the nineteenth century, when observations and data could be transmitted by telegraph, the movement of storms could be followed. But it was not until the twentieth century that balloons and aircraft allowed measurements to be made high above the ground, giving a three-dimensional view of the atmosphere. Now weather satellites observe the state of the atmosphere from positions out in space, and computers process vast amounts of data to provide weather forecasts days or even weeks ahead.

In your study of this course you will follow a rather similar chronology of scientific discovery, looking first at individual elements of the weather as you might experience and measure them at a particular place on a particular day. Then the picture will widen to encompass the large-scale processes within the atmosphere that generate the variation in weather patterns around the Earth. In subsequent chapters you will be able to apply your understanding of these processes in considering a wide range of weather phenomena in many different parts of the world. You will also find out how weather data are collected at the Earth's surface, by instruments sent up through the atmosphere and by satellites that look down on the atmosphere from vantage points in space. You will begin to appreciate how this vast amount of data is processed to generate forecasts, and should therefore better understand the successes and limitations of the forecasts you access. The final chapter of the course returns to the comments that opened this chapter, briefly examining some of the impacts that the weather has on human lives and activities.

Activity 1.2   Obtaining meteorological data

The estimated time for this activity is 30 minutes.

During your study of the course, you will need to download from the internet various types of weather data and forecasts for your local area. This information, coupled with your own observations, will be required for part of the assessment. The purpose of this activity is for you to find and bookmark the websites you will use most frequently.

You will find the detailed instructions for the activity in the Activities section of the course website.

During your study of the course you should make a regular practice of checking a local weather forecast. Chapter 6 discusses measures of forecast reliability and includes an activity that requires you to monitor the forecast for seven consecutive days and to compare the predictions with what you observe. You might like to start this activity sooner and could then keep records of the forecasts for a longer period. If you want to see what is involved, go to the instructions for Activity 6.1 on the course website now. (You do not need to have read Chapter 6 in order to make sense of these instructions.)

1.3   An introduction to the Earth's atmosphere

The atmospheric processes that show themselves through the weather are powered by the energy delivered by the Sun. The sunlight falling on the atmosphere and the Earth's surface starts a complicated sequence of processes that determine the ways in which the air, the oceans and the land heat up or cool down and what temperature they therefore reach. Figure 1.3 illustrates three ways in which heat can be transferred from place to place.

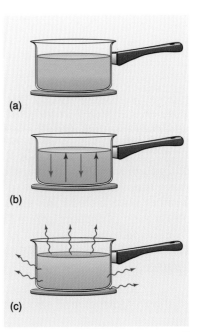

Figure 1.3   Three ways in which heat may be transferred. (a) Heat from the hotplate is transferred directly by conduction to the base of the pan, and hence to the water in contact with the pan. (b) Water at the bottom of the pan initially gets hotter than water higher up. In a process called convection, the hot liquid rises. Cooler liquid sinks to replace it, and the cooler liquid then gets warmed in its turn. (c) The heat from the hotplate, the pan and the warm liquid can be felt if you put your hand near them, with the heat being transferred through the air by radiation. Air very close to the hotplate, the hot pan, or the hot liquid surface will be warmed by conduction and will then rise by convection.

5

- Heat can be transferred from an object at one temperature to an object at a *lower* temperature when the two objects come into contact with each other, as illustrated in Figure 1.3a. This process is called thermal conduction. Metals are particularly good conductors of heat (which is why they are used for saucepans). Air is a poor conductor of heat, but heat is nevertheless transferred by conduction *to* the lowest layer of the atmosphere where it is in contact with hotter ground and *from* the lowest layer of the atmosphere where it is in contact with cooler ground.

- Convection is a process whereby heat is transferred from one part of a liquid or a gas to another by movement of the liquid or gas itself. In the situation illustrated in Figure 1.3, heat is transferred first by conduction from the hot base of the pan to the liquid that is in contact with it. Hot liquid then rises, carrying heat away from the original hot area (Figure 1.3b). Cooler liquid sinks towards the bottom of the pan thus coming into contact with the hot base of the pan, so the process continues. Convection is an important mechanism for heating gases as well as liquids and plays a crucial role in the behaviour of the atmosphere and in the formation and development of clouds.

- All warm objects emit radiation, some of which we feel as 'heat'. If the hotplate in Figure 1.3c were glowing, that would mean it was emitting visible radiation in the form of red light. But even if the plate were not hot enough to be glowing, as soon your hand got close to it you would still be able to feel the heating effect of 'invisible' infrared (IR) radiation that was being emitted. The warm surface of the Earth also emits IR radiation. The heat from the Sun is transferred to the top of the atmosphere by both visible radiation ('sunlight') and invisible radiation, including IR and the ultraviolet (UV) radiation that causes sunburn.

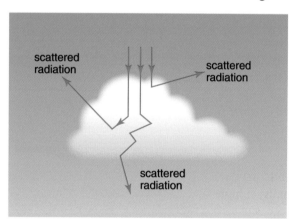

Figure 1.4   Radiation from the Sun is scattered by clouds and a proportion of it is returned to space. Radiation redirected into space is no longer available to drive the Earth's weather systems, but it is what allows satellite observation of the atmosphere from above. Satellite pictures of weather systems, using both visible and IR radiation, will be discussed in Chapter 5.

The ways in which radiation from the Sun interacts with the atmosphere are numerous and complex, but one basic principle underlying the interactions is that anything that absorbs the radiation heats up. Thus the atmosphere can acquire heat directly, by absorbing some of the solar radiation. The radiation absorbed directly by the atmosphere never reaches the Earth's surface, nor does the substantial proportion of the incoming radiation that is scattered in all directions as it travels through the atmosphere. Clouds are particularly good scatterers of radiation, as illustrated in Figure 1.4. Clouds occupy on average about half the global sky, so a large amount of incoming solar radiation is scattered by them. As Figure 1.4 shows, a proportion of this scattered radiation may take an indirect route through a cloud and then reach the Earth's surface, but a lot of the radiation will be redirected back into space. Thick low clouds are more efficient at scattering solar radiation back into space than thin high clouds which are more transparent to the Sun's rays. Overall, about a third of the incoming solar radiation is scattered away from the Earth. Of the radiation that does reach the Earth's surface about a tenth is 'reflected', that is in effect scattered straight back upwards into the atmosphere. Fresh snow and ice reflect particularly well. The rest of the solar radiation reaching the Earth's surface is absorbed, with the result that the surface heats up.

As a 'warm object' the Earth emits IR radiation from its surface. This radiation travels back into the atmosphere where some of it is absorbed, thus heating the atmosphere from below. However, this heating from below by radiation is just one of the ways in which the lower atmosphere warms up. As you have seen, cool air very close to the surface can also be heated by conduction if it is in contact with warmer ground, but because air is a very poor conductor of heat this process only affects the first few centimetres of air above the surface. The main heating process for the lower atmosphere is convection, whereby heat is carried upwards as hot air rises through colder air. Convection is a particularly important process because, as well as transferring heat from rising warm air to colder air further up, it also moves water vapour, in the form of moist air, around in the atmosphere. The evaporation of water from the Earth's surface, its movement as water vapour within the atmosphere, and its eventual return in the form of rain (or snow) play a crucial role in transferring heat between the Earth and the atmosphere. You will find out a lot more about the mechanisms by which heat is transferred and redistributed within the atmosphere as you study Chapters 2–4.

1.4   Climate and seasons

We know that the weather of western Europe is very different from that of southern India, that the temperature in Paris will not be the same in December as it is in July, and that there is a particular hurricane 'season' in the Caribbean. All these statements are expressions of the fact that the weather at a particular place and time is always set in the broader contexts of climate and the cycle of the seasons. This section explores the climatic and seasonal factors that underpin variations in the weather.

The climate of a particular place depends on many complicated and interlinked factors. However, there is one geographical factor that underlies all others: latitude. Box 1.2 explains how any location on the Earth's surface is pinpointed by its latitude and longitude.

Because of the curvature of the Earth, the share of solar radiation that a place receives depends on its latitude. Figure 1.5 shows that there are two reasons for the heat provided by the solar radiation being generally lower at high latitudes than on the Equator. Near the Equator, the Sun's rays are almost perpendicular to the Earth's surface. At high latitudes, on the other hand, they strike the surface at a glancing angle (i.e. the Sun is always low in the sky), so the incoming radiation is effectively 'spread' over a wider area than at the Equator. Additionally, at high latitudes the radiation has to travel through more of the atmosphere to reach the Earth's surface and the chance of it being scattered away from the surface is proportionately increased. Also, as you have already seen, the atmosphere absorbs a proportion of the incoming radiation, so the greater the distance within the atmosphere that the radiation has to travel, the smaller the proportion of it that will be available to heat the ground.

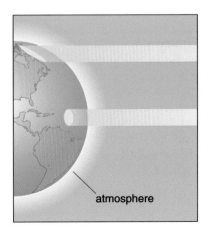

Figure 1.5   Schematic diagram of two identical beams of solar radiation reaching the Earth's surface at different latitudes. (Not to scale: the thickness of the atmosphere is greatly exaggerated.) At high latitudes the Sun's rays travel a longer distance through the atmosphere, and strike the ground at a more glancing angle, than is the case near the Equator. The extent to which the radiation reaching the Earth is 'spread' across the surface is indicated by the yellow areas.

Box 1.2 Latitude and longitude

As illustrated in Figure 1.6, latitude is a measure of distance north (N) or south (S) of the Equator. The units of measurement of latitude are the degree (symbol °) and the minute (symbol ′), where 1° = 60′. The Equator has a latitude of 0°, the North Pole has a latitude of 90° N and the South Pole has a latitude of 90° S. If you were to walk in a straight line due northwards from 0° to 1° N, you would cover the same distance (about 111 kilometres) as you would walking between 89° N and 90° N. Figure 1.5 also shows longitude, which is a measure of how far east or west a location is from the Greenwich Meridian. This is a line which passes through London and defines the zero of longitude 0°.

In discussing weather systems, it is quite common to think in zones of latitude. Latitudes north of 60° N or south of 60° S are referred to as the 'high latitudes'. Latitudes either side of the Equator between 30° N and 30° S are described as 'low latitudes'. It is worth noting that the low latitudes cover half the entire surface area of the Earth. In between the high and low latitudes are the so called mid-latitudes, spanning the regions between about 30° and 60° in each hemisphere. In the Northern Hemisphere (i.e. the half of the Earth that is north of the Equator), the mid-latitudes include most of Europe (south of Iceland), most of the USA and Japan. In the Southern Hemisphere the mid-latitudes are largely covered by ocean, with New Zealand, the extreme south of Australia, the tip of South Africa and the southernmost third of South America being the only land masses.

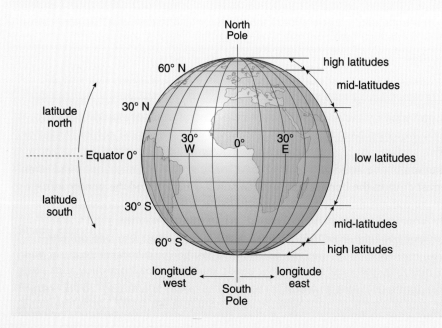

Figure 1.6   A view of the Earth as seen from above the Equator. The blue lines parallel to the Equator are lines of latitude, and the red lines that connect the poles are lines of longitude. Lines of both latitude and longitude are shown here at 15° intervals.

Study comment

You will learn best if you study 'actively', and interact with what you are reading. To help you do this, you will find a lot of short questions, indicated by ■, where you should stop and think. The answers follow immediately, marked by □. You will gain most benefit by covering the answer while you think carefully about your own response to the question, and then checking to see whether you are right. In most cases, you will not need to write anything down.

■ If there were no other complicating factors, what would be the effect of this uneven distribution of incident solar radiation on the ground-level temperatures at equatorial and high latitudes?

□ It would result in there being a greater heating effect and hence in higher temperatures near the Equator than at higher latitudes.

As you will see in later chapters, it is this uneven heating of the Earth's atmosphere that is mainly responsible for the movements of air and water in the atmosphere that we see manifested as 'weather'.

Superimposed on the general decrease in temperature from the Equator to the poles are the effects of the seasons. The Earth rotates once a day about an axis (an imaginary line through the centre of the Earth joining the poles) and also orbits the Sun once a year. Seasons occur because the axis is tilted with respect to the orbit. This means that the poles spend part of each year tilted towards the Sun and part of it tilted away from the Sun. When a hemisphere is tilted towards the Sun it receives more sunlight, in the sense of having more hours of daylight; this corresponds to summer. When a hemisphere is tilted away from the Sun, it experiences winter.

Figure 1.7 shows a schematic view of the Earth's orbital path round the Sun. How do we experience this from our Earth-bound viewpoint? One thing we notice is the height of the Sun above the horizon in the middle of the day. The latitude at which the noonday Sun is overhead migrates between 23.4° N (the Tropic of Cancer) and 23.4° S (the Tropic of Capricorn) and back again during the course of a year. The Sun is overhead at the Equator only twice a year, at the equinoxes, at which times the lengths of day and night are equal.

When the Sun is overhead at one or other of the Tropics, it is the summer solstice (the longest day) in the hemisphere experiencing summer, and the winter solstice (the shortest day) in the other hemisphere. Polewards of the Tropics, the Sun is never directly overhead. It is common for the regions between the Tropic of Cancer and the Tropic of Capricorn to be referred to as 'the tropics' (with a lower-case, rather than a capital, letter) or 'tropical'.

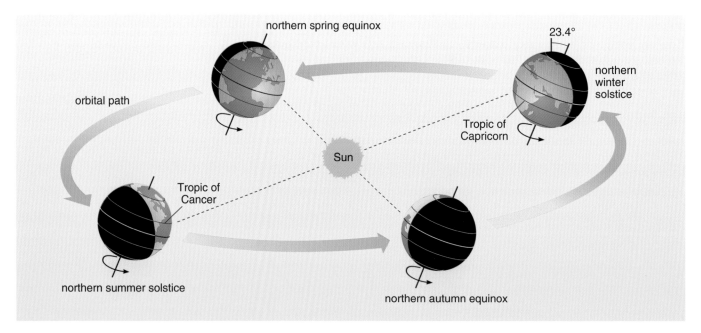

Figure 1.7 The four seasons for the Northern Hemisphere, in relation to the Earth's orbit round the Sun. The Earth's axis is tilted at approximately 23.4° to a line at right angles to the plane of its orbit around the Sun. This angle of tilt determines the latitudes of the Tropics (23.4° N and 23.4° S), where the Sun is overhead at one of the solstices, and of the Arctic and Antarctic circles (66.6° N and 66.6° S, i.e. 90° − 23.4°), poleward of which there is complete darkness for part of the year. (This figure is not to scale. The size of the Earth is greatly exaggerated in relation to both the size of the Sun and the size of the Earth's orbit.)

Activity 1.3 Locating unfamiliar places

The estimated time for this activity is 30 minutes.

The course covers weather phenomena in many different parts of the world and you will probably need to find out where some unfamiliar locations are situated. This activity allows you to check that you have a means of doing this, and at the same time gives you some practice in using latitude and longitude.

You will find the detailed instructions for the activity in the Activities section of the course website.

Study comment

As well as the short 'stop and think' questions, there are also numbered questions like the one that comes next. These numbered questions will take longer to answer, and you should always try to write out your answer, rather than just thinking about it. It is worth keeping all your answers together in a notebook or a folder. Full specimen answers are provided, but don't be tempted to look at an answer until you have made a genuine attempt at writing your own. Then compare your answer carefully with the one at the back of the book, noting any differences. If there are some differences make sure you understand the reason(s) for them. You may have said the same thing, but simply phrased it differently, which is fine. But if you have omitted or misunderstood something then you should go back and study the relevant part of the text again. Making use of specimen answers in this way, rather than just reading them, is another element of active study. The questions also allow you to measure your progress towards achieving the Learning Outcomes for the course and comments below the answers will help you to do this. You will find a list of these Learning Outcomes near the back of the book, just before the answers to the numbered questions.

Question 1.1

Briefly explain three reasons for the North Pole still being very cold in summer, despite receiving 24 hours of sunlight. (One or two sentences per reason is sufficient.)

In the high and mid-latitudes, the winter and summer seasons are quite distinct in terms of both temperature and length of daylight: summers are warmer than winters and have more hours of daylight. Places in the low latitudes are always warm unless they are in the mountains, and day and night are of more similar length. In many of these locations, seasons are defined by patterns of rainfall. For instance, there may be a wet season and a dry season. In some areas near the Equator, there are two wet seasons, which may be of different lengths (for example, the 'long rains' and the 'short rains' in Kenya). The climates of the world are classified on the basis of their average seasonal patterns of both temperature and rainfall (or snowfall), but there is no exact matching of climate zones to latitude because the distribution of climates is complicated by many other geographical factors. Altitude is just one such factor: even near the Equator, it can snow, as illustrated in Figure 1.8.

Figure 1.8   Mount Kilimanjaro (in Tanzania) is only a few degrees south of the Equator, but because of its height (5896 metres), it is often snow-capped. However, this sight may become less common in the future. A report published in 2007 by the Intergovernmental Panel on Climate Change (IPCC) noted that if the climate conditions that were then current were to persist, snow might permanently disappear from the summit of Kilimanjaro some time in the period 2015–2020.

In general terms, the climate of a region may be thought of as the average conditions that are experienced in that area over a long period of time. Climatic changes occur relatively slowly – over decades, or hundreds to thousands of years. The weather, on the other hand, is determined by the precise state of the atmosphere at a particular time and place. The weather can change from month to month, week to week, day to day or even hour to hour. This distinction is neatly encapsulated in the saying:

Climate is what you expect on the basis of previous averages. Weather is what you actually get.

Question 1.2

Read the following sentences and explain, in one or two sentences each, whether they are descriptions of weather or climate.

(a) At the time of writing in 2008, the highest temperature ever recorded in the UK is 38.5 degrees Celsius.

(b) Between May and September the average daily temperature in Mecca (Saudi Arabia) is about 38 degrees Celsius.

(c) Between May and December Trinidad (in the Caribbean) experiences showers on most days.

(d) Between 20 and 31 July 2003, bands of showers, some heavy and thundery, moved across Northern Ireland.

1.5   Summary of Chapter 1

Meteorology is the science of atmospheric phenomena and processes.

The Earth is surrounded by a thin atmosphere, and the weather arises from movement within that atmosphere caused by the Sun's uneven heating of the Earth's surface. Heating can take place by the processes of conduction, convection and absorption of radiation.

The Earth's environment is quite literally solar powered. Because the Earth is a sphere, on any given day places at different latitudes receive different amounts of sunshine and heat up to different extents. Differences in latitude play an important role in determining zones of climate, although many other factors also have an influence. Seasonal variations within climate zones occur because of the orbital and rotational motion of the Earth. Seasons may be defined in terms of temperature, hours of daylight or patterns of rainfall (or snowfall).

The average conditions that are experienced in a region over a long period of time define its climate. The weather is determined by the precise state of the atmosphere at a particular time and place and is therefore inherently variable.

Chapter 2
Weather elements: Part I

In general conversation, we usually describe the weather in terms of the particular features or 'weather elements' that seem most obvious to us on that particular day. We might say it's hot or cold, sunny or cloudy, dry or pouring with rain, without a breath of wind or blowing a gale. Depending on where we are in the world, our descriptions will be coloured by what we know to be typical for that place and that time of year, and by what we are used to: for example, temperatures that are normal on the coast of Kenya would be considered exceptionally hot for an English summer day. A day considered to be very wet in Ireland would not see anything like the dramatic amount of rainfall associated with a tropical storm in Hong Kong. Descriptions such as 'hot' and 'wet' may be meaningful in the context of a *local* weather forecast, because everybody in the audience shares the same experience and expectations of hot or wet weather in that area, but scientists need consistent ways of communicating their understanding of the weather across countries and continents. The focus is on six main weather elements: temperature, humidity, pressure, clouds, precipitation (e.g. rain and snow) and wind. These elements can combine in a very large number of ways, and change over periods ranging from minutes to weeks, giving the weather its inherent variability. This chapter and the next one will introduce you to some of the technical terms and measurements that meteorologists use to give precise descriptions of the weather elements, as well as covering some important scientific concepts that govern the behaviour of the atmosphere.

Some of the material in Chapters 2 and 3 may already be familiar. Other parts, especially the more theoretical sections, may be new to you. However, it is all worth studying carefully, because it lays the foundation for the rest of the course. Time spent mastering the concepts in these two chapters will pay dividends later on.

Study comment

One of the most useful study skills to acquire is a reliable method of keeping track of information, so that you can locate it again when you need it. When you are working on later chapters, you might want to check up on something you read in an earlier part of the course. You might also need to keep track of any queries you have until such time as you can return to them. You will probably want to refer back to several parts of the course in order to complete the assessment. So it is important to develop a way of managing information. For material in this book there are two main methods of doing this: making notes or highlighting the text. In this chapter you will have a chance to practise both techniques and decide whether one works better for you than the other.

You will find references to many different geographical areas in this course. You will certainly know where many of the locations are, but probably not all. At the beginning of each chapter, you will find a list of all the locations mentioned in that chapter. If you think you are likely to find it disruptive to have to research these places individually when you come to them in the text, you might find it convenient to look up any unfamiliar ones before starting work on the first section. As with Activity 1.3, you can use any 'atlas' resource you find convenient. The full list for Chapter 2 is:

- Countries and land areas: Kenya, Ireland (both mentioned above), Antarctica
- Cities/towns: Hong Kong (China, mentioned above), Edinburgh and Oxford (UK), Moscow and Verkhoyansk in Siberia (both Russia), Ushuaia (Argentina), Vancouver (Canada), Browning in Montana and Spearfish in South Dakota (both USA), Al Aziziyah (Libya)
- Deserts: Sahara Desert (north Africa), Arabian Peninsula (Saudi Arabia and the Gulf States), Thar Desert (Rajasthan, India), Atacama Desert (Chile), Kalahari Desert (Botswana).

2.1 Temperature

Temperature is one of the most obvious weather features and is crucial in planning many aspects of daily living, from what clothes we will wear tomorrow to the probable electricity demands for a city. Heating and cooling processes within the atmosphere, which are manifested as temperature changes, are key drivers for weather systems. For both these reasons, the careful measurement of temperature is therefore a vital part of meteorology.

Study comment

As you study Section 2.1, make notes of what you see as the important points. Writing in the margin of the text or using 'Post-it' stickers is one way of keeping everything together. This is a *work*book and you should feel free to annotate it. Alternatively you could use a notebook or even single sheets of paper, though if your notes are loose leaf it's a good idea to file them immediately in a ring binder, so they don't become jumbled or get lost. Remember to mark them clearly with section/page/figure numbers, so you can relate them to the text at a later stage. Your aim is to record what you regard as important points in any format that you find helpful – full sentences, short phrases, lists or diagrams. You may also want to write down any queries you have, so that you can return to them later or maybe discuss them with a Study Adviser.

2.1.1 Measuring temperature at the Earth's surface

We are all familiar with temperature as the extent of hotness or coldness of a substance, as measured by a thermometer. Temperature is just one of the so-called 'physical properties' of an object, which is the term scientists use to refer to properties that can be precisely measured. Box 2.1 gives more detail about how the values of these kinds of quantities are reported.

Temperatures are nowadays often measured with electronic instruments, but the archetypal kind of thermometer shown in Figure 2.1 is still in widespread use. In this basic thermometer, a change in temperature results in a detectable

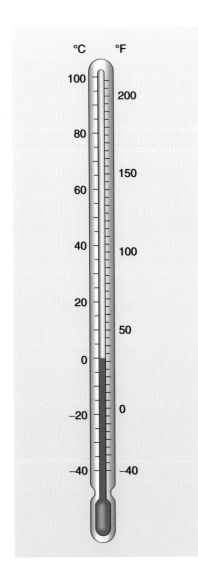

Figure 2.1 Liquid-in-glass thermometer, marked with Celsius and Fahrenheit scales. The temperature shown by the height of the liquid column in this example is that at which pure water freezes: 0 °C or 32 °F.

Box 2.1   Measuring physical quantities

Meteorologists deal in quantities such as temperature, pressure and wind speed, for which units of measurement are crucial. Generally speaking, a 'physical quantity' consists of a number multiplied by a unit of measurement. For example, a distance of 3 kilometres is the result of multiplying the number 3 by the unit of distance measurement called the kilometre, i.e. 3×1 km. When you state the value of a physical quantity, the unit is at least as important as the number!

There are recognised abbreviations for nearly all the units: for example, those for the metre, the kilometre and the second are respectively m, km and s. The abbreviations for some units, like these three, are written in lower-case letters; others, like °C , which is the abbreviation for degrees Celsius, have a capital letter. The conventions regarding capitalisation must be adhered to, if abbreviations are to be correctly interpreted. With only 26 letters available, some are used in lower case for one quantity and in capital format for an entirely different sort of quantity. (For example, the abbreviation Km could certainly be a valid abbreviation for the units of some physical quantity, but the quantity would *not* be a distance measured in kilometres.) Abbreviated units must always be written in singular form. So 3 kilometres must be written as 3 km, never 3 kms, which could be interpreted as 3×1 km $\times 1$ s.

Units can be multiplied and divided just like numbers. The result of dividing 8 m by 2 s may be written as 4 m/s; this is said as '4 metres per second'.

If you want to know more about scientific units of measurement, you will find further information in the Maths Skills ebook on the course website.

change in the length of a column of liquid, often alcohol coloured with a dye. The temperature is determined by reading the length of the column against a scale. The Celsius scale, which is the one most widely used in meteorology, is fixed by two points: the freezing temperature of pure water, which is assigned a temperature of zero degrees Celsius (written as 0 °C), and the boiling temperature of pure water under standard atmospheric pressure, which is assigned a temperature of one hundred degrees Celsius (100 °C). (You will understand why the conditions of standard atmospheric pressure are important when you have studied Section 2.3. For the moment you can take this to mean 'at sea level'.) The scale between these two fixed temperatures is then divided into 100 equal units, called degrees. As noted in Chapter 1, the word 'centigrade' is sometimes used instead of 'Celsius'. In some parts of the world, most notably the USA, the Fahrenheit scale is in widespread use. On this scale, the freezing temperature of pure water is 32 degrees Fahrenheit (written as 32 °F) and boiling temperature of pure water under standard atmospheric pressure is 212 °F.

You can see approximately how the Celsius and Fahrenheit scales compare in Figure 2.1, but this diagram wouldn't provide an accurate way of converting a given temperature from one scale to the other. A more precise conversion can be made using the graph in Figure 2.2. If you are unfamiliar with graphs, study the material in Box 2.2 now, as it picks out some important features of this figure, and of graphs in general.

Figure 2.2 Graph showing the relationship between temperatures on the Celsius and Fahrenheit scales.

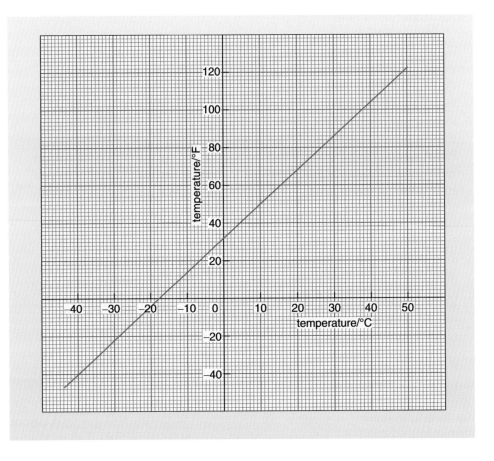

■ What is the Fahrenheit equivalent of 28 °C? (You may need to draw some lines on Figure 2.2 in order to answer this question.)

☐ 28 °C is equivalent to 82 °F.

We all make our own estimates of outdoor temperatures in the sense of how hot or cold we feel, and we are usually aware of some of the factors that influence our estimates, including where we are and what objects are around us. On a warm sunny day by a lake, sand at the water's edge may be too hot to walk on comfortably in bare feet, yet the water will seem comparatively cold. If we start to feel hot in the sun, we might move into the shade, knowing that will be cooler. If a chilly wind is blowing, we are likely to feel less cold where we are sheltered from it in the lee of a wall. Meteorologists need to eliminate all these kinds of complicating factors, so as to ensure that the temperatures they measure are those of the *air*. Measurements must also be made in a standard way at all observing

Box 2.2 Understanding graphs

Graphs are essential tools in scientific work, and being able to use and interpret them is an important skill that is one of the Learning Outcomes for this course.

A graph shows how one quantity depends on another. These quantities and their values are displayed on two reference lines, called the axes, at right angles to one another. The axes are marked to show the range of possible values of the quantities, scaled in equal divisions: for example, in Figure 2.2 the horizontal axis is scaled from −40 through zero to +50 and the vertical axis is scaled from −40 to +120. (The positive sign is normally assumed and need not be written.) Whatever the variable you want to display on a graph, you have to take account of the units of measurement in such a way as to plot a *pure number* (i.e. a number *without* units) on the graph. The horizontal axis in Figure 2.2 could have been labelled as 'temperature measured in °C', but a more succinct form 'temperature/°C' has been used. This indicates that the temperature values have been divided by their units (°C) to give pure numbers:

For example: $\dfrac{27\,°C}{°C} = 27$

It is conventional in science to use 'quantity divided by its units', in the form 'quantity/units', to label the axes of graphs.

A graph can be used to find corresponding pairs of values for the two quantities that are plotted. For example, to find the temperature in degrees Fahrenheit corresponding to 40 °C, start by finding the point on the horizontal axis representing 40 °C and draw a line vertically upwards until it meets the plotted line. Then draw a line horizontally from that intersection to meet the vertical axis and read off the corresponding temperature in °F. *Draw these lines directly on to Figure 2.2, using the grid lines of the graph to help you.* You should find the equivalent of 40 °C to be 104 °F.

Now apply the reverse process to find the Celsius equivalent of 10 °F. Draw a horizontal line corresponding to 10 °F until it meets the plotted line. Then draw a vertical line from the intersection to meet the horizontal axis. You should find that the equivalent of 10 °F is −12 °C (actually −12.2 °C, but the graph cannot be read to that precision).

If you are not sure how to read the divisions on the scales, or feel you need more practice at using graphs in this way, you should now work through the appropriate section in the Maths Skills ebook.

stations, anywhere in the world, if meaningful comparisons are to be drawn between data gathered in different places. There are therefore strict conditions laid down for the way in which all weather-measuring instruments, not only thermometers, are sited, set up and read. Later in the course you will find out more about how weather data are collected at meteorological stations.

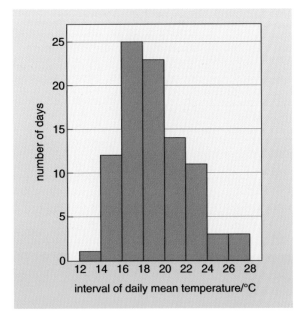

interval of daily mean temperature/°C

Figure 2.3 Histogram of the mean daily temperature at Oxford (UK) for the months of June, July and August 2003. Temperature is plotted along the horizontal axis. The vertical axis shows how many times the mean daily temperature was within a particular 2 °C interval during this three-month period. For example, the longest column shows that the mean daily temperature was either exactly 16 °C or between 16 °C and 18 °C on 25 occasions during this period. By convention, a value that corresponds exactly to the boundary between intervals is counted as part of the interval to the right of the boundary.

2.1.2   Temperature variations, averages and extremes

In many parts of the world, temperatures fluctuate considerably, with nights significantly cooler than days, winters very much colder than summers, and heat waves or cold snaps occurring every so often. With all this variation, meteorologists have to find ways of organising and summarising temperature measurements. Figure 2.3 illustrates one way in which temperature data can be usefully displayed: a histogram. (If you are unfamiliar with histograms or bar charts, these ways of presenting data are explained in Box 2.3 on p. 20.) To understand Figure 2.3, it is important to realise that the quantity plotted on the horizontal axis refers to average temperatures. Everybody is familiar with the word 'average' as used in ordinary language, but in science and statistics there are actually several different kinds of average, which are used for different purposes. In meteorology the sort of average that is commonly used is the 'mean' and the terms mean and average are often used interchangeably in weather reports. For a set of measurements, the mean is defined as the sum of all the measurements divided by the total number of measurements made. For example, if the temperature is recorded at the Oxford weather station once an hour (which is normal practice at UK stations), then the mean daily value for a particular date is the sum of the 24 readings taken on that date, divided by 24.

■ You may remember from Chapter 1 that 2003 was a very hot summer in England, with a record high temperature of 38.5 °C. Why are there no readings in excess of 28 °C on Figure 2.3?

☐ The temperatures plotted on the figure are average values over 24 hours. Night-time temperatures will have been lower than daytime ones, and the average for each 24-hour period will lie somewhere between the maximum and minimum values recorded during that period.

In the case shown in Figure 2.3, it is the temperature readings that are averaged over a set period of time, with mean temperatures being plotted on the horizontal axis. However, it's possible to take averages in a different way, as illustrated in Figure 2.4. Here, the same 2 °C interval of temperature as before is used on the horizontal scale, but what is plotted are actual minimum temperatures instead of daily means. However, on this occasion the vertical scale records the average number of days *per year* on which the minimum temperature was within a particular interval, with the period of observation extending over 21 years.

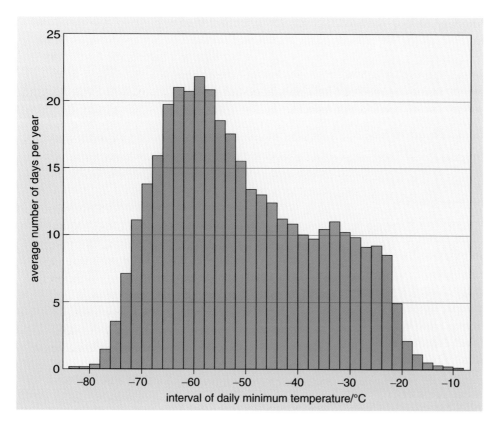

Figure 2.4 Histogram representing the results of measuring the daily minimum temperature at a weather station on the high plateau of Antarctica between January 1984 and December 2004. The columns show the average number of days annually over a 21-year period in which the minimum temperature was within each 2 °C interval. For example, over this period there were on average 10 days per year on which the minimum temperature was either exactly –40 °C or between –40 °C and –38 °C.

■ How would this average (i.e. mean) number of occurrences per year have been calculated?

☐ The total number of days with a particular minimum temperature would have been found for the whole time period of 21 years, and this total divided by 21 to give the mean number of occurrences per year.

The shape of the histogram in Figure 2.4 is worth examining in some detail for what it can reveal about the weather in Antarctica. Three obvious features are:

• There is a cluster of high values on the histogram corresponding to minimum temperatures of between about –50 °C and –68 °C. This shows that there are a lot of days on which minimum temperatures in this range occur. These are the typical winter days.

• There is another cluster of high-ish values rising from a flatter portion of the histogram corresponding to the minimum temperatures of between –28 °C and –36 °C. These are the typical summer days. It is noticeable that there are many fewer days in this temperature range than there are with colder temperatures, which shows the brevity of the Antarctic summer!

• Days with minimum temperatures below –78 °C or above –16 °C are very rare. In weather terms these are extreme events.

The kind of long-term averaging over time illustrated in Figure 2.4 comes close to representing the *climate* of the recent past on the Antarctic plateau, as far as temperature is concerned. Displaying weather data as a histogram in this way serves as a useful reminder that some kinds of weather are more likely than others, that some may be likely only at certain times of the year and that extreme events always occur every so often.

Box 2.3 Histograms and bar charts

Histograms are used to show how data are distributed into groups across a continuous range. Temperature is a good example of a quantity with a continuous range: this simply means that it can take any value. So temperature can be plotted along the axis of a graph, as was the case in Figure 2.2. Alternatively, temperatures can be considered in groups or intervals spanning a particular range. In Figure 2.3, the horizontal axis is divided into equal temperature intervals of 2 °C and the vertical axis is scaled to show the number of occasions on which the mean daily temperature was within a particular interval. Notice that because the entire range of values of the mean temperature is covered, the columns touch.

Bar charts are used to summarise data in discrete categories. The categories are listed along the horizontal reference line, and the data for each category are represented by a vertical bar. In the case of Figure 2.5, the categories are the months of the year, and the data are the mean temperatures. The scale for the bars is given on the vertical axis, using the same conventions as for the graph of Figure 2.2. The bars in a bar chart usually do not touch, emphasising the fact that each bar relates to a distinct and individual category. However, in Figure 2.5, there are two sets of data (maximum and minimum temperatures) for each category, and the bars for the same category *do* touch.

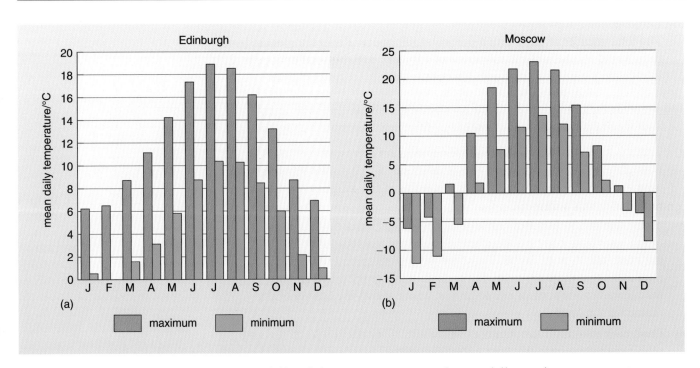

Figure 2.5   Bar charts showing the mean daily minimum temperature and mean daily maximum temperature for each of the 12 months of the year for (a) Edinburgh, UK (latitude 55° 55′ N) and (b) Moscow, Russia (latitude 55° 45′ N). Note that the vertical scales on these two charts are not identical. February data for Edinburgh are not missing: the mean daily minimum temperature is 0 °C.

Chapter 2   Weather elements: Part I

Temperature data can be summarised in a slightly different way by using a bar chart. Figure 2.5 shows mean daily maximum and minimum temperatures for Edinburgh and Moscow for each month of the year.

■ If you were asked to gather data and work out the mean daily maximum temperature for July next year in your own home location, how would you do it?

☐ You would have to record the maximum temperature on each day of the month, add the 31 values together and divide the total by 31.

The values in Figure 2.5, however, are not those for just a single year. The July value in Figure 2.5 is a mean calculated from temperature records taken over many Julys. The number of Julys used to determine such a mean is not arbitrary: there are standards for statistical weather reporting, which are laid down by the World Meteorological Organisation (WMO). This is a United Nations Agency set up in 1948 to coordinate the exchange of meteorological data and services worldwide, for the purposes of research and weather forecasting. The WMO rules stipulate that averages must be calculated using data accumulated over non-overlapping set periods of 30 years. The most recent such period covered the years 1961–1990, so many averages you will see relate to this timeframe. When, in the current concern over global warming, we are told that 'temperatures in April were nearly 1 °C above average' the average used in the comparison will usually be that for 1961–1990. Under this system, data being collected now will contribute to the 1991–2020 averages. However, many WMO members, including the UK Met Office, additionally update their averages at the end of each decade, so for many locations averages are also available for the 30-year period 1971–2000, and those for the period 1981–2010 will be published in 2011. It is possible that the WMO system may change to ten-year updates in the future. If you are using averaged data to make comparisons, it's worth checking that the averages all cover the same period. Those in Figure 2.5 are for 1961–1990.

Question 2.1

A weather presenter on a local television news programme for the East Anglian region of the UK summed up the month of August 2007 by saying: 'the temperature in August has actually been pretty much average, but it has been the coldest August in our region since 2002'. Explain briefly whether or not there is a contradiction in this statement.

There are some obvious similarities in the mean daily maximum and minimum temperatures for Edinburgh and Moscow shown in Figure 2.5. In both places the mean daily maximum and the mean daily minimum have their highest values in July (summer) and their lowest in January or February (winter).

■ How do the highest mean summer temperatures and the lowest mean winter temperatures compare between the two locations?

☐ On average, Moscow is hotter than Edinburgh in the summer and much colder in the winter.

You saw in Chapter 1 that one of the main factors determining how temperature varies from place to place is latitude. Yet although Edinburgh and Moscow are at almost the same latitude, Moscow experiences a much wider range of temperatures. Clearly there must be other factors involved. One reason for the difference between the seasonal temperature variations in these two locations is the fact that Moscow lies deep within a large continent, whereas Edinburgh is on an island on the western fringe of the continent. The distance of a location from the sea plays a large part in determining its typical temperature variation, because there is a contrast in seasonal temperature changes between land and sea. This is due in part to the high 'specific heat capacity' of water. (The specific heat capacity of a substance is the amount of heat required to raise the temperature of one kilogram of the substance by 1 °C.) On average it takes about three times more heat to raise the temperature of a body of water by 1 °C than to raise the temperature of an equivalent quantity of dry rock or soil by 1 °C. Consequently, the oceans act as huge heat stores and warm up (or cool down) much more slowly than the land. This has a strong influence on temperature: places deep inside continents typically have hotter summers and colder winters than places at the same latitude but nearer the sea. Indeed any large body of water will moderate the temperatures of adjacent areas.

Another way in which oceans affect temperatures can be exemplified by comparing the mean daily maximum and mean daily minimum temperatures for Edinburgh with those for Ushuaia, Argentina, which are shown in Figure 2.6. Ushuaia is the most southerly city in the world, near to the tip of the South American continent. It is much the same distance south of the Equator as Edinburgh is north of it. Like Edinburgh, Ushuaia is not far from the sea; in fact it is close to both the Pacific and the Atlantic Oceans.

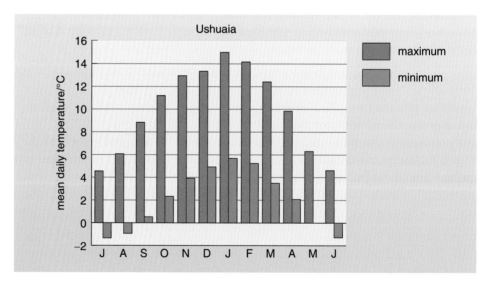

Figure 2.6   Mean daily minimum and mean daily maximum temperatures for Ushuaia, Argentina (latitude 54° 58′ S) over the 12 months of the year. Note that the months are listed on the horizontal reference line starting in July, so that the winter months are at the ends of the line and the summer months in the middle. This facilitates comparison with Figure 2.5. May data are not missing: the mean daily minimum temperature is 0.1 °C, which does not show on the scale of this histogram.

■ Compare Figures 2.5a and 2.6 closely. Does Ushuaia have higher or lower mean temperatures in the Southern Hemisphere winter months than Edinburgh does in the Northern Hemisphere winter? (Note that the vertical scale in the two bar charts is not the same.)

☐ Both the mean daily minimum and mean daily maximum temperatures are lower in Ushuaia in June, July and August than they are in Edinburgh in December, January and February.

■ Does Ushuaia have higher or lower mean temperatures in the Southern Hemisphere summer months than Edinburgh does in the Northern Hemisphere summer?

☐ In the hottest months of the year in Ushuaia (December, January and February), both the mean daily minimum and the mean daily maximum temperatures are lower than they are in Edinburgh during the summer months (June, July and August).

A major reason for Edinburgh being warmer year round on average than Ushuaia is the North Atlantic extension to the Gulf Stream, an ocean surface current that carries warm water from tropical latitudes northwards and eastwards across the Atlantic. This has a benign influence on the climate of Britain (even the eastern side of Britain, although the effects are more marked on the western side) and northwestern Europe in general, making it warmer than it would be otherwise, especially in winter. Ocean surface currents near the tip of South America are cold rather than warm, making Ushuaia colder on average than Edinburgh, even though the two cities are at almost the same latitude south and north of the Equator. Ocean currents play important roles in both climate and local weather along coasts. Whereas on land the heat from the Sun is absorbed in just a thin surface layer, the oceans can absorb this heat into deeper layers and distribute it through convection and the movement of ocean currents.

Figure 2.5a gives the mean maximum daily temperature for Edinburgh in July at about 19 °C. Yet if you were to be in that city in July you would not expect the maximum temperature necessarily to be close to 19 °C on any one day, let alone day after day. The main thing to remember is that when meteorologists talk about mean or average values they are referring to averages calculated for a period of 30 years. Because the data are accumulated over such a long time, extremely unusual weather events as well as more typical conditions contribute to the average. This means that the average does not necessarily correspond to what is typical; indeed the average on its own does not give any information about what is typical. An example may help to make this last point more obvious. Imagine a ten-day period consisting of 7 days on which there were 8 hours of sunshine each day and 3 days with no sunshine at all. There would have been 7×8 hours = 56 hours of sunshine hours in total. The daily average would have been:

$$\frac{56 \text{ hours}}{10 \text{ days}} = 5.6 \text{ hours per day.}$$

But this average does not correspond to what actually happened on any one of those ten days. Nor does it represent what was typical during that period, which was to have either 8 hours of sunshine or none at all.

Having focused on averages for much of this section, it may interest you to see a few of the extremes of temperature that have been measured around the world.

- The highest land surface temperature ever recorded was 58 °C on 13 September 1922, at Al'Aziziyah in Libya, and the lowest was −89.2 °C on 21 July 1983 at the Vostok research station in Antarctica.

- The place with the greatest ever recorded range of temperature is Verkhoyansk in Siberia with 105 Celsius degrees: from a low of −68 °C to a high of 37 °C.

- One of the greatest temperature changes in a 24-hour period was recorded in the USA at Browning, Montana, where on 23 to 24 January 1916 the air temperature fell an incredible 56 Celsius degrees: from 7 °C to −49 °C. The most rapid temperature rise was also recorded in the USA, at Spearfish, South Dakota, where on 23 January 1943 the temperature rose from −20 °C to 7 °C in just 2 minutes!

The fact that all these records have stood for so long suggests that they represent very rare events.

2.1.3   Temperature and human comfort

Air temperature plays a big part in how comfortable we feel, although the temperatures at which particular individuals begin to be adversely affected does depend on whether they are involved in physical activity, on what clothing they are wearing, on their age and state of health, and also on what they are used to. People do become acclimatised: if you normally live in a hot climate you will probably be more comfortable at higher temperatures than someone who usually lives in a colder climate.

Countries in which very warm or very cold conditions are rare often have a system that triggers some sort of official alert if a heat wave or an exceptionally cold spell is forecast. For example, in England a 'Heat Health Watch' is maintained during the summer, to ensure that social and healthcare services are suitably prepared for a potential heat wave, which could be particularly dangerous for the very young, the very elderly and people with chronic illnesses. If a heat wave is really severe and/or lasts for a long time, then even the fit and healthy can be at risk, especially if they are engaged in vigorous exercise. The temperatures at which a heat wave is declared are slightly different in different areas of England; in London the threshold is a maximum daytime temperature of 32 °C and a night-time minimum of 18 °C reached on at least two consecutive days and the intervening night. Yet these kinds of temperatures are routine in many parts of the world!

Many people use the temperatures given in weather forecasts as their main guide for how comfortable they are likely to feel, and this is often an adequate measure. However, comfort sometimes depends on how other elements of the weather combine with temperature. People travelling from warm dry climates to warm humid ones tend to complain more about the heat even if the air temperature is much the same in the two places. If the temperature is low, it can feel pleasant in a sheltered spot in the sun and bitter if it is cloudy and windy. These factors will be examined further in subsequent sections.

2.1.4 Temperature and altitude

Anybody who has climbed a mountain will have experienced the way in which temperature changes with height: the higher you climb, the colder it gets. On average, the temperature decreases by about 6 °C for every 1000 metres of increase in elevation above sea level, though values vary considerably with location, season and time of day. This steady reduction in average temperature with increasing altitude continues up through the atmosphere long after the top of the highest mountain has been left behind, until a temperature of about −57 °C is reached. The 'layer' of the atmosphere in which this steady reduction in temperature with increasing altitude occurs is called the troposphere. As discussed in Chapter 1, the lower part of the atmosphere is mainly heated from *below*, and heat is mostly redistributed to higher levels by convection. The result is that the temperature of the troposphere decreases with increasing distance from the Earth's surface. Above it is a region called the tropopause, where the temperature remains roughly constant with increasing altitude and above that is the stratosphere, where the temperature *increases* with increasing altitude. The tropopause marks the height at which convection ceases. In the stratosphere the main source of heat is radiation entering the atmosphere from above.

Figure 2.7 shows this 'layering' of the atmosphere as defined by the way in which temperature changes with altitude. There are a number of further layers above the stratosphere, but in this course you will be concerned almost exclusively with the troposphere. In terms of the weather, the troposphere is where the action is. It contains virtually all the clouds and moisture in the atmosphere. The term 'troposphere' is derived from the Greek work 'tropos', meaning 'turn' or 'churn': the troposphere is the layer in which the greatest amount of churning or mixing of air occurs and vertical churning is a crucial driver for weather systems. You will find out more about how this churning takes place in Chapter 4. So when 'the atmosphere' is mentioned in discussions of weather phenomena, you can take it that it is only the troposphere that is being considered. The altitude to which the troposphere extends is significantly dependent on latitude and time of year. For example, the top of the troposphere is at a maximum (15–20 km) over equatorial regions and lowest near the poles (about 10 km).

Although the *average* temperature of the troposphere decreases steadily with increasing altitude there are often areas where there is an *increase* in actual air temperature with increasing height – in other words where warm air overlies cold air. This frequently happens in the lowermost layers of the atmosphere at night. As discussed in Chapter 1, one of the ways in which heat can be transferred from place to place is by radiation. The warm Earth constantly emits IR radiation. When heat is transferred from an object at one temperature to an object at a lower temperature, the initially cooler object warms up, and the initially warmer object cools down. An object that is emitting radiation therefore gradually cools

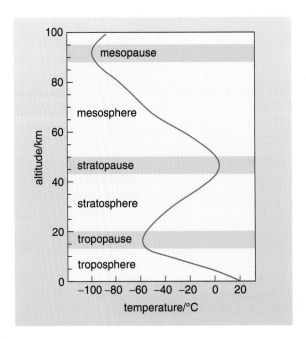

Figure 2.7 Changes in the average temperature of the atmosphere with height above sea level. The successive 'layers' or 'spheres' (i.e. concentric shells around the Earth) are separated by 'pauses' where the change in temperature with altitude switches from increasing to decreasing or vice versa. The blue line shows how the average temperature changes within each layer. The outermost reaches of the atmosphere extends up to about 100 km. The height shown for the top of the troposphere is about 13 km, corresponding to a mid-latitude location.

25

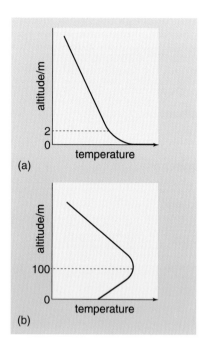

(a)

(b)

Figure 2.8 Development of an overnight temperature inversion. (a) In the afternoon on a calm sunny day in the mid-latitudes, the air temperature decreases with increasing height above the ground. Air in contact with the ground has been heated by conduction, so is particularly warm, but this effect fades rapidly with height because air is a poor conductor of heat. (b) On a calm dry night the ground cools more rapidly than the air and by the end of the night the air near the ground is colder than that just a little higher up. An inversion has formed. Note that, in both cases, the lack of wind means that there is almost no mixing of surface air with air higher up. Notice also that the vertical scale on the two diagrams is not the same. There is no scale on the horizontal axes, but the arrows show the direction in which the temperature is increasing.

(unless it has a power source like the hotplate in Figure 1.3). When at a particular place the Sun has set, there is no incoming solar radiation to heat the air or the ground there, but the ground continues to emit IR radiation. As a result the ground cools overnight. Throughout the hours of darkness the ground and the air that is touching it cool more quickly than the air a little bit higher up which is not in contact with the cold ground. This process is slow but it does result in successively higher layers of air gradually cooling down. Consequently, by the end of the night the coldest air is nearest the ground and the air temperature gradually increases with height for a short distance above the surface. This situation is called a temperature inversion, because it is the opposite of the normal overall decrease in temperature with elevation. Figure 2.8 illustrates possible variations in temperature slightly above the surface.

■ Why are inversions more common on winter nights than on summer ones?

☐ There are more hours of darkness in the winter, so the cooling goes on for longer.

In the mid-latitudes the depth of the nocturnal inversion (i.e. the vertical distance over which the temperature increases with height) is usually less than 100 m. Near the poles, where the winter darkness lasts for months, the inversion is frequently 1000 m deep and may sometimes extend to a depth of 3000 m. Other factors also affect the development of inversions: for example, wind tends to mix the air layers and inhibit the formation of an inversion. As you will see in later parts of the course, inversions may form through mechanisms other than nocturnal cooling, and they may occur at any height in the troposphere, with major consequences in terms of the weather.

Study comment

Look back at the notes you have made while studying Section 2.1. Are there points you want to go over again? Would the notes help you to recover information at a later stage in the course? Are there any loose ends you need to follow up before you move on, perhaps by discussing them with a Study Adviser? Refining the way in which you keep track of information and ideas is an important aspect of developing your own learning strategies (Learning Outcome KS3), so you should now decide whether you want to make adjustments to your note-taking technique for the next section.

2.1.5 Key points of Section 2.1

Chapter 1 finished with a summary of the whole chapter, and this style will also be followed in Chapters 4–9. In Chapters 2 and 3, which cover particularly important meteorological principles, a slightly different system is used. Each *section* of these two chapters ends with a set of key points to help you keep track of the most crucial concepts. You will need to apply your understanding of these concepts frequently in later parts of the course.

Average temperatures vary from one place to another due to a combination of four main factors: latitude, the distribution of land and water, the influence of ocean surface currents, and altitude.

Average (i.e. mean) temperatures are usually calculated using data obtained over 30-year periods. These data will include both 'typical' and 'extreme' temperatures, so the average does not necessarily reflect what is typical. The average does, however, represent the climate of the recent past.

The average temperature falls steadily with increasing altitude through the troposphere, the layer of the atmosphere in which weather occurs. When the temperature in a portion of the troposphere increases with height, this is known as a temperature inversion.

2.2   Humidity

Our perception of temperature, particularly in hot weather, is quite strongly influenced by our perception of humidity. Conditions that are both hot and humid – the kind of weather that is often called 'muggy' in the mid-latitudes – can be very uncomfortable. Humidity is related to the amount of moisture in the air, but that is far from being the whole story and meteorologists measure humidity in several different ways. These kinds of measurements may seem difficult to follow at first, especially as some are not always aligned with intuitive ideas about what constitutes 'dry' and 'moist'. However, the concepts developed in this section are crucial in understanding how the weather works, so it is worth studying the explanations slowly and carefully. The starting point is to think about how moisture gets into the atmosphere in the first place.

2.2.1   Water in three phases

You have already seen that water vapour is one of the 'variable' gases in the atmosphere, being present in different amounts at different times and places.

■ Roughly what percentage of the air may be water vapour?

☐ It was stated in Box 1.1 that water vapour is present in the atmosphere at local concentrations of between 0 and 4 per cent by volume.

This variability indicates that there must be mechanisms by which water can enter and leave the atmosphere. These mechanisms hinge on the fact that, within the range of temperatures found in the troposphere, water can exist in three different 'phases' or 'states': solid (ice), liquid (the usual interpretation of the word 'water') and gas (water vapour).

The smallest particles of water that exist are called water molecules. To understand how water behaves in its three phases, it's necessary to know a little about how these molecules behave. All molecules are attracted to one another, but this attraction decreases sharply as they move further apart. Molecules are always in motion, and the average speed at which the molecules of a substance move depends on its temperature: the higher the temperature, the higher their average speed. The way in which the molecules move also depends on the phase of the substance, as illustrated in Figure 2.9.

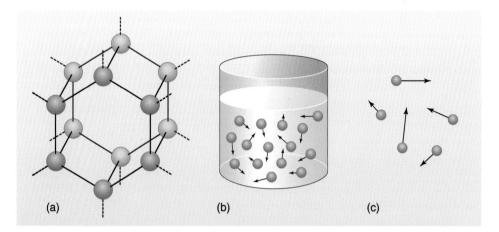

(a)   (b)   (c)

Figure 2.9 Schematic diagram of the behaviour of water molecules in the three phases of water. The molecules are represented as blue spheres. When the water is frozen solid (a), the molecules fit together in a rigid structure. In liquid water (b), the molecules move randomly in different directions, as shown by the arrows. They also move at different speeds; this is indicated by the arrows being of different lengths, with longer arrows corresponding to faster-moving molecules. In water vapour (c), the molecules are further apart than in the liquid and on average they are moving more rapidly.

In the solid phase (ice), the water molecules are locked together in six-sided structures (Figure 2.9a). Their mutual attraction is strong and this holds them in fixed positions relative to one another. Each molecule vibrates around its position, but doesn't move far enough to break away from its neighbours. The lump of ice therefore holds together and keeps its shape. In liquid water, the molecules are moving more freely. They are still close enough to be attracted to one another, but the regular arrangement of the solid has broken down (Figure 2.9b). The molecules move in all directions and at different speeds, often colliding with one another. As a result, liquid water flows, taking up the shape of its container. The attraction between molecules is strong enough for them to cluster together, resulting in the water settling in the lowest part of the container. When the water is in vapour form, the molecules are even further apart than in the liquid and their average speed is greater, so there is less attraction between them (Figure 2.9c). In a sealed container, molecules of water vapour would spread out evenly through the space. In the atmosphere, molecules of water vapour intermingle freely with the molecules of the other atmospheric gases such as oxygen and nitrogen. Because the molecules in a gas are a large distance apart on average, it is relatively easy to push them closer together (think of a bicycle pump). This is expressed in scientific terms by saying that gases are compressible.

Weather phenomena provide obvious examples of water in its three phases. There is nearly always some water vapour in the air and when there is a lot we may notice the humidity. Liquid water is seen as rain and dew. Solid water falls from the sky as hail or snow and forms on surfaces as frost. However, the phase changes of water are meteorologically important for another reason as well. They play a vital role in transferring heat to and from the atmosphere and in redistributing heat within the atmosphere, processes that drive the Earth's weather systems.

2.2.2   Phase changes and latent heat

When a solid melts, the ordered arrangement of molecules breaks down: there is a transition from a phase in which molecules occupy nearly fixed positions in a rigid structure to one in which the molecules are moving fairly freely. This transition requires that the molecules be given enough energy to break up the solid structure. This energy is supplied in the form of heat. Even when an ice cube is at 0 °C, further heat is required to make it melt into liquid water at 0 °C. This heat doesn't just disappear when all the ice has been turned into water. It is stored in the moving water molecules themselves, as so-called 'latent' heat. (The term latent just means hidden.) This 'latent heat of melting' is released when the water refreezes. So in order to turn water at 0 °C into ice at 0 °C a refrigerator must pump away the latent heat that is released when the phase change occurs.

The phase change of a substance from liquid to gas (vapour) is termed evaporation, and also involves latent heat. The molecules in the gas are much further apart, and moving on average much more quickly, than they are in the liquid. So energy in the form of heat is required for evaporation to occur, energy that the molecules in the gas then carry with them and which is termed the latent heat of vaporisation.

■   On hot days, drops of water (e.g. perspiration) can evaporate from our skin. How does this help to cool us down?

☐   Heat is required to convert a drop of liquid water into water vapour. This heat is taken from the skin and carried away by the vapour as latent heat, thereby cooling the skin.

This example illustrates that water does not have to be boiling in order to evaporate. The molecules in liquid water are moving with a range of speeds, and there are always some that are moving quickly enough to shake off the influence of their neighbours and enter the air from the water surface. At the same time, other water molecules are undergoing the reverse process, moving from the air into the water. This transition from a vapour into a liquid is termed condensation.

Under some circumstances, it is even possible for water molecules in a solid to have enough energy to shake themselves free of the attraction to their neighbours and enter the air as water vapour without having first passed through the liquid phase. Such a solid-to-gas transition is called sublimation. The reverse process, whereby molecules of water vapour attach themselves directly to solid ice is called deposition.

The key factor that determines how the molecules in a liquid or a gas behave is temperature: the higher the temperature, the greater the average speed of the molecules. If the temperature remains constant, the average speed of the molecules also remains constant (although the speed of *individual* molecules will keep changing as they continually bounce off one another). If the temperature falls, the molecules will on average move more slowly. So as water is heated a larger proportion of the molecules will have speeds high enough to enable them to shake themselves free from one another. Hence, the warmer the water (all other conditions remaining unchanged), the more molecules will move from the liquid to the vapour above it, i.e. the greater the rate of evaporation from the water surface. Conversely, as air is cooled the average speed of the water molecules in the vapour decreases and condensation is more likely to occur. Slowly moving water molecules in the vapour come under the influence of water molecules that are near the surface of the liquid, to the extent that they are attracted into the liquid itself.

However, condensation can also take place another way within the air itself. Essential to this process are tiny solid particles of ash, dust and salt which are normally present in the atmosphere. When the air is warm the water vapour molecules are moving quickly and they just bounce off these solid particles. When the air is cooled the molecules of water vapour move more slowly on average and the most slowly moving among them may stick to the surface of the solid particles. Further water vapour molecules can then condense onto these surfaces, until eventually droplets of liquid water form. For this reason the solid particles are called condensation nuclei. In a similar way, minute solid particles can promote the formation of ice crystals from water droplets and these are called freezing nuclei. Although the freezing temperature of water is usually stated to be 0 °C, water can remain liquid at much lower temperatures than this if there are no freezing nuclei. A substance that is liquid at a temperature below its normal freezing temperature is said to be supercooled, and supercooled water is common in the atmosphere. Supercooling is a particularly important process within clouds, where in the absence of freezing nuclei liquid water droplets may exist at temperatures down to −40 °C.

2.2.3   Saturated and unsaturated air

Knowing that the temperature of liquid water affects its rate of evaporation into the air, the next step is to look at the issue from the other side and investigate how the temperature of the air affects the amount of water vapour within it. Everyday experience gives some clues about this. If the air is fairly dry, and the weather is warm, then water will evaporate readily; this is the kind of weather in which washing hung on a line outside dries quickly and puddles disappear. On the other hand, if the air is moist and the overnight temperature is fairly low, water condenses out of the air to form dew on the grass. The first situation is an example of conditions in which more molecules are evaporating into the air than are condensing out of it. The second situation is an example of conditions in which the reverse is true. There is also a third kind of situation, in which the same number of water molecules are leaving the air as are entering it. Under these 'balanced' conditions, the air is said to be saturated with water vapour. When the air is saturated, no more water vapour can enter it through evaporation unless at least an equal amount leaves it by condensing. In other words, saturation describes the situation in which the amount of water vapour in the air is at its maximum possible level for the prevailing temperature.

The temperature is important because the warmer the air, the greater the proportion of water vapour molecules that are moving quickly enough to avoid condensation. Thus the warmer the air, the more water vapour molecules can be present in a given volume (for example a litre) of air.

■   What does this imply about the relative likelihood of saturation in still warm air above a pond and in still cool air above the same pond?

☐   It implies that (provided all other conditions are the same) saturation is more likely to occur in the cold air.

Now imagine what happens if instead of the air being still, a wind were blowing across the pond. This would continually remove some of the moist air from above the pond. The air above the water would no longer be saturated and more evaporation could take place. Thus wind enhances evaporation. This is why washing hung outside dries more quickly on windy days than on still ones with similar temperatures.

Suppose you want to determine just how much moisture there is in the air. What kind of measurements could you make? One method would be to take a sample of air, weigh it, extract the moisture from it using a chemical drying agent, and weigh the amount of water extracted. You could then describe the moisture content of the sample by stating the number of grams of water vapour per kilogram of air in the original sample. This quantity is called the specific humidity and it is useful in that it provides a measure of the actual amount of water vapour in the air.

The way in which the average specific humidity changes with latitude is shown in Figure 2.10. This graph shows that in the regions between the Tropics and the Equator (i.e. between 23.4° N and 23.4° S), which are generally described as 'hot and humid', the average specific humidity is indeed very high. On the other hand, most people think of desert air as 'dry'. Many of the major deserts of the world (e.g. in the Northern Hemisphere the Sahara, the Arabian Peninsula, the Thar Desert of Rajasthan, parts of the southwestern USA; in the Southern Hemisphere the Atacama, the Kalahari and the central area of Australia), are centred around a latitude of about 30°.

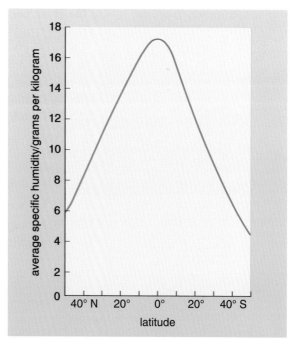

Figure 2.10 The variation in average specific humidity with latitude. The highest average value is recorded at the Equator. The lowest average values in each hemisphere correspond to the highest latitudes shown on the graph.

■ According to Figure 2.10, how does the average specific humidity at a latitude of 30° N compare with that at 50° N (roughly the latitude of Cornwall in the UK and Vancouver in Canada)?

☐ The value at 30° N is approximately double that at 50° N.

On this measure, desert air is certainly very far from being 'dry': there is plenty of moisture in the air over the Sahara.

Although the specific humidity gives a measure of the actual amount of water vapour in the air, you will not find values of specific humidity reported on the weather forecast. However, in places where humidity is high forecasters do often give a value for the 'relative humidity'. This quantity, which describes how close the air is to being saturated, is meteorologists' preferred measure of how much moisture there is in the atmosphere. The relative humidity is defined as the ratio of the amount of water vapour actually in the air at a given temperature to the amount that would correspond to saturation at that temperature. Put another way, it is the ratio of the actual moisture content of the air to the maximum amount of moisture the air could possibly hold at that temperature. Relative humidity is expressed as a percentage. Thus, if the relative humidity is 50 per cent (usually written as 50%), the air is holding half as much water vapour as it would if it were saturated. (If you are not familiar with calculations involving ratios and percentages, you will find it useful to work through the sections of the Maths Skills ebook that cover these topics.)

■ If air has a relative humidity of 100%, what does this imply?

☐ A relative humidity of 100% implies that the air contains the maximum possible amount of water vapour; in other words it is saturated.

■ What fraction of the water vapour required for saturation is present if the relative humidity is 25%?

☐ One-quarter. (25% means 25 parts in 100 or one part in four.)

■ If more water molecules evaporate into unsaturated air, does this correspond to a rise or a fall in the relative humidity?

☐ Water vapour has been added to the air, so it is closer to being saturated. Hence the relative humidity has risen.

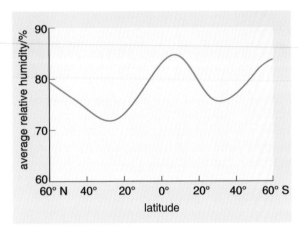

Figure 2.11   The variation in average relative humidity with latitude. Compare the shape of this graph with that of Figure 2.10.

The way in which average relative humidity varies with latitude is shown in Figure 2.11. The shape of this graph is very different from that of Figure 2.10. Very low latitudes near the Equator have high relative humidity as well as high specific humidity. High relative humidity is also found at latitudes of about 60° in both hemispheres. The relative humidity is on average at its lowest around latitude 30° in both hemispheres, corresponding to the bands in which the major deserts are located.

You have already seen that the temperature affects saturation, and that saturation is more likely to occur in cold air. Temperature therefore also affects the relative humidity. If the temperature of unsaturated air is lowered and there is no condensation (i.e. the total amount of water vapour in the air remains the same), the air approaches more closely to saturation.

■ What is the resulting change in the relative humidity?

☐ The relative humidity rises, because the air is closer to being saturated.

In summary then:

• If the air temperature doesn't change, the relative humidity rises when water vapour is added to the air and falls when water vapour condenses out the air.

• If the amount of water vapour in the air doesn't change, the relative humidity falls when the air gets warmer, and rises when the air cools.

Question 2.2

Figure 2.12a shows a pattern of temperature variation in a mid-latitude garden during 24 hours of warm still weather.

(a) Sketch on Figure 2.12b the corresponding way in which relative humidity will change over these 24 hours, assuming that the *total amount* of water vapour in the air doesn't change over the period.

(b) Some of the plants in the garden were starting to wilt during this period. If the gardener had wanted to revive them by spraying them with water, at what time of day would this have been most effective and why?

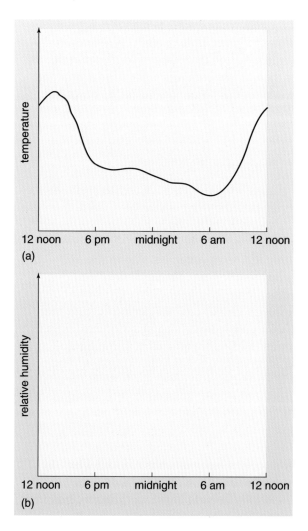

Figure 2.12 (a) A pattern of temperature variation over a 24-hour period. (b) Variation of relative humidity over the same period (to be completed for Question 2.2). The vertical axes are not scaled, since the purpose is to show changes and comparative trends in temperature and relative humidity, not actual values. However, the arrows on the axes show the direction in which values increase.

Study comment

You will almost certainly find some sections of the course harder than others. When you hit a difficult section, the most important thing is not to give up entirely. Make a serious attempt to understand the material, but if you are still struggling then make a note of the problem and move on. You may find it all seems clearer if you come back to it later. Alternatively, you could discuss the problem with a Study Adviser.

If you have found Section 2.2 rather hard going so far, then be reassured that Sections 2.2.4 and 2.2.6 are an easier read. Also, Chapter 2 as a whole is probably the most theoretical of the whole course. Some of the concepts discussed here will seem much easier once you have repeatedly seen them used in later chapters, in the context of a variety of weather situations.

2.2.4 Humidity and health

Most people feel more uncomfortable when the weather is hot and humid (e.g. in a tropical rainforest) than when it is hot and dry (e.g. in a desert). The main way in which our bodies regulate their temperature in hot weather is by evaporation of perspiration. If the relative humidity is low, evaporation is rapid and the cooling mechanism is efficient. If the relative humidity is high (i.e. approaching saturation), there is little evaporation and hence little cooling. We therefore feel more uncomfortable in the humid situation than the dry one, even if the air temperature is identical in both. In extreme conditions, the heat-regulating mechanisms of the body may fail, and serious illness can result, as described in Box 2.4.

Box 2.4 Health problems in hot and humid weather

The normal temperature of the human body is 37.5 °C. Body temperature is regulated by a region in the brain called the hypothalamus, which triggers perspiration when the temperature of the body rises above normal. As perspiration evaporates from the skin, more is produced. Eventually, continual sweating results not only in loss of water, but also in loss of essential salts from the body, giving rise to heat cramps. This kind of problem commonly besets athletes during long periods of exertion in hot weather. If evaporation of perspiration cannot cool the person enough, their body temperature will rise, and this, coupled with dehydration, can result in 'heat exhaustion', with symptoms of fatigue, headache, vomiting and even loss of consciousness. The most serious hot-weather illness is 'heat stroke', which occurs when body temperature exceeds about 41 °C, and is associated with failure of circulatory functions. Heat stroke can result in death, even among otherwise fit and healthy people.

Because the efficiency of the body's cooling mechanism is reduced when the relative humidity is high, temperature alone is not a reliable guide to how comfortable one is likely to feel, especially in parts of the world where humidity can vary considerably from day to day. The idea of 'apparent temperature' has been developed to provide a single quantity indicative of possible effects of the weather on people's comfort and health. The apparent temperature is a measure of how hot (or cold) the weather 'feels' to an average person outdoors. Although it is quoted in degrees Celsius, it is not a *measured* temperature but a value calculated from a combination of factors. The high end of the apparent temperature scale is often called the Heat Index. (The low temperature end will be discussed in Section 3.3.) Table 2.1 shows how the Heat Index combines the effects of both air temperature and humidity, rating the apparent temperature according to the potential dangers posed to health.

2.2.5   Dew point

A quantity that is very important in understanding how clouds form, and whether dew or frost will be deposited on lawns overnight, is the 'dew point'. This is the temperature to which air would have to be cooled (without changing its total moisture content or any other conditions) for it to reach saturation. For a given sample of air, the difference between the actual air temperature and the dew point is therefore an indication of how close the air is to being saturated. For example, if the air temperature is much higher than the dew point, the air is nowhere near being saturated.

Table 2.1 (a) The Heat Index, showing how air temperature and relative humidity are combined to give an apparent temperature. Notice that the labelling of the column showing the air temperature and the rows showing the relative humidity both follow the same conventional layout of 'quantity divided by units' as the axes of graphs. The 'apparent temperatures' in the coloured boxes are in °C. Categories of hot weather health risks are indicated by the coloured tones; the darker the tone, the higher the risk to health. (b) The health hazards associated with the four categories of the Heat Index, corresponding to the four coloured tones in (a).

Temperature/°C	Relative humidity/%												
	40	45	50	55	60	65	70	75	80	85	90	95	100
47	58												
43	54	58											
41	51	54	58										
40	48	51	55	58									
39	46	48	51	54	58								
38	43	46	48	51	54	58							
37	41	43	45	47	51	53	57						
36	38	40	42	44	47	49	52	56					
34	36	38	39	41	43	46	48	51	54	57			
33	34	36	37	38	41	42	44	47	49	52	55		
32	33	34	35	36	38	39	41	43	45	47	50	53	56
31	31	32	33	34	35	37	38	39	41	43	45	47	49
30	29	31	31	32	33	34	35	36	38	39	41	42	44
29	28	29	29	30	31	32	32	33	34	36	37	38	39
28	27	28	28	29	29	29	30	31	32	32	33	34	35
27	27	27	27	27	28	28	28	29	29	29	30	30	31

(a)

Category	Heat Index	Possible heat disorders for people in high-risk groups
Extreme danger	54 °C or higher	Heat stroke or sunstroke likely.
Danger	41–53 °C	Sunstroke, muscle cramps and/or heat exhaustion likely. Heatstroke possible with prolonged exposure and/or physical activity.
Extreme caution	32–40 °C	Sunstroke, muscle cramps and/or heat exhaustion possible with prolonged exposure and/or physical activity.
Caution	27–31 °C	Fatigue possible with prolonged exposure and/or physical activity.

(b)

■ If the air temperature is 4 °C and the dew point is also 4 °C, what is the relative humidity?

☐ The air does not have to be cooled at all to reach saturation. It is already saturated, so the relative humidity is 100%.

The value of the dew point is determined by the total moisture content of the air. The higher the dew point, the more water vapour there is in the air.

■ When evaporation increases the amount of water vapour in the air, will the dew point increase or decrease?

☐ It will increase. (Conversely, when water vapour condenses out of the air, this lowers the dew point.)

The differences between Figures 2.10 and 2.11 make more sense if viewed with an understanding of dew point. Like specific humidity, dew point is related to the total amount of water vapour in the air. Figure 2.10 shows that on average there is more water vapour in the air at a latitude of 30° N than there is in the air at a latitude of 50° N. At higher latitudes, the average specific humidity falls even further. Polar air can in this sense be described as 'dry'. Hence the dew point is higher in the Arizona Desert (which is at roughly 30° N) than in the Arctic. However, the air temperature is *much* higher in Arizona, so there is a much bigger separation between the air temperature and the dew point in Arizona than in the Arctic. This means that the air in Arizona would have to be cooled much more than Arctic air in order to reach saturation. The warm air in Arizona is thus a long way from being saturated so it has a low relative humidity, as shown in Figure 2.11. The cold air in the Arctic is much closer to saturation so it has very high relative humidity.

2.2.6   Dew and frost

What do you expect to observe when moist air cools from just above to just below the dew point? You know that the relative humidity will rise as the air cools, until the air temperature reaches the dew point, which corresponds to the air being saturated with a relative humidity of 100%. As the air cools further, water vapour must condense out of it. This is a weather situation that is commonly encountered. On cool nights, the ground rapidly loses heat, often becoming significantly colder than the air. The lowest layer of air, which is in contact with the ground, cools by conduction. If the temperature of this layer falls below the dew point, then water vapour condenses from it. Small droplets of water form on objects at ground level: these droplets are what we call dew. Figure 2.13a shows dew on a low-growing plant. You may have noticed that dew forms more readily on grass or low vegetation than on bare earth, stones or a brick surface. One reason for this is that these substances warm up more than the grass during the day and take a long time to cool down at night, so the air just above them remains above the dew point for longer than air just above the grass. The second reason is that grass, like all plants, 'transpires', i.e. produces water vapour.

(a)

(b)

(c)

Figure 2.13 Dew and frost: (a) dew on leaves in the early morning; (b) frozen dew; (c) hoar frost on trees and bushes.

■ What effect does this have on the dew point of the air in contact with the grass?

☐ It raises it (because the amount of water vapour in the air has increased).

As a result, the air temperature does not have to fall as low for dew to form on grass, compared to brick, rock or soil.

As discussed in Section 2.2.2, water may remain liquid at temperatures below 0 °C if there are no freezing nuclei. It is common for dew to remain in a supercooled liquid state even though the temperature drops a few degrees below 0 °C, but at a temperature somewhere between −3 °C and −5 °C it will freeze into nearly spherical beads of ice called frozen dew or silver frost. Frozen dew, which is shown in Figure 2.13b, is quite different in appearance to the more common feathery soft ice called hoar frost illustrated in Figure 2.13c. Hoar frost forms by deposition on plants and other objects when they cool below 0 °C, i.e. water vapour from the air in contact with the cold surface changes directly to the solid phase without first condensing to a liquid.

Study comment

Did you persist with note-taking as you studied Section 2.2? If so, review your notes now and think about how well your system of writing things down is working. The next section suggests an alternative technique for you to try.

2.2.7   Key points of Section 2.2

This has been a long section, containing a lot of detail. However, the key ideas from it that you will use again and again in later parts of the course can be summarised quite concisely.

> Water vapour enters the atmosphere by evaporation or sublimation and leaves it by condensation or deposition.
>
> The amount of water vapour in the air is variable. When it reaches its maximum possible value for the prevailing conditions the air is said to be saturated.
>
> Relative humidity is a measure of how close the air is to being saturated, but does not indicate how much water vapour is actually in the air. Relative humidity increases if evaporation increases or if the air is cooled.
>
> The difference between the air temperature and the dew point is a measure of how close the air is to being saturated.

2.3   Air density and air pressure

Atmospheric pressure and air density are the least obvious of the weather features discussed in this chapter, in the sense that we cannot see them and can feel them only in exceptional circumstances. We can in fact feel a pressure change via our ears, but only when the change is very considerable and fairly rapid: most people encounter changes like that only in aeroplanes on take-off and landing. However, air pressure and density are both crucial elements in the weather story, because air movement is associated with pressure difference and density changes. Air temperature, pressure and density are all related to one another. Together with humidity, they largely determine the weather.

Study comment

If you have been using written notes so far, experiment with a different technique in this section, by using highlighting to mark important words or ideas. You can use a 'highlighter pen' or simply underline words with a pen or pencil. You need to be selective and avoid highlighting huge chunks of text, so this method requires active reading and understanding *before* you wield the highlighter.

2.3.1   The density and pressure of the air

The density of a substance is related to the number of molecules of the substance in a given volume: the greater the number of molecules in a particular volume, the greater the density. As discussed in Section 2.2, the molecules in a gas move quickly and freely. Because of this freedom of movement, if a gas is given more space the molecules will spread out through the whole of the available volume; in other words the gas will always expand to fill the available space. If a gas expands so that the molecules occupy twice the volume they did originally, then the density of the gas will have halved. Conversely, it is relatively easy to compress a gas (i.e. to restrict the molecules to a smaller space).

■ If a gas is compressed into half the volume it occupied originally, what effect will this have on its density?

☐ The density will be doubled.

Near the surface of the Earth, there are many more molecules in a given volume of air than there are higher up in the troposphere. In other words, air density decreases as the altitude increases. The summit of Mount Everest is higher than nearly 70% of the molecules in the atmosphere and the air density there is only about a third of what it is at sea level. Mountaineers and other people who travel to places that are at high altitude often describe the air as being 'thin'. There are fewer oxygen molecules in a lungful of air than at sea level (as well as fewer molecules of all the other atmospheric gases), so people who are not acclimatised feel short of breath.

As well as taking up space, air molecules (i.e. the molecules of all the atmospheric gases including water vapour) have weight. The weight of the atmosphere presses down on the surface of the Earth and the push exerted over a fixed area defines the atmospheric pressure. You may sometimes come across the synonymous term 'barometric pressure', which is derived from the Greek word for weight. You probably already know that atmospheric pressure is measured using instruments called barometers or barographs. Slightly confusingly, there are various systems of units in use to measure atmospheric pressure. The simplest is the 'atmosphere' (abbreviated as atm). Old barometers record pressure in inches of mercury. The unit most commonly seen on weather maps is the millibar (abbreviated as mb), although this is gradually being replaced by the hectopascal (abbreviated as hPa) which is essentially equivalent to the millibar. The average value of the air pressure at mean sea level is called 'standard atmospheric pressure' and defined as 1 atm:

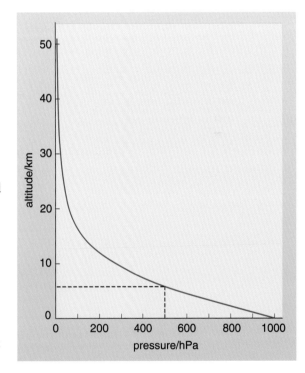

Figure 2.14 Change in average atmospheric pressure with altitude. The pressure at sea level is approximately 1000 hPa. At an altitude of 5.5 km, it is half that.

1 atm = 29.92 inches of mercury
= 1013.25 mb = 1013.25 hPa

The pressure at a point in the atmosphere depends on the number of molecules above that point. The higher the point is, the fewer molecules there are above it, so the lower the weight of air pressing down from above, and therefore the lower the atmospheric pressure. Figure 2.14 shows how rapidly the average atmospheric pressure drops with increasing altitude. For the first 1000 m above sea level, the pressure decreases by about 10 hPa for every 100 m of height gained.

The dependence of the pressure on altitude is a major issue when meteorologists want to compare pressure measurements from weather stations that are situated at different heights above sea level. To avoid the problem, weather-station readings are adjusted to the value they would have at mean sea level by adding 10 hPa for every 100 m the station is above sea level. When maps are drawn up to show pressure patterns across a wide geographical area, these corrected readings are the ones that are used, and the maps are therefore called mean sea-level (MSL) pressure charts. An example is shown in Figure 2.15. Pressure patterns change and move over time, and have a profound influence on the weather, which is why these kinds of charts are probably familiar to you from daily weather forecasts. Among other features, they show areas of low or high pressure (usually called just 'lows' and 'highs'), which are marked on Figure 2.15 as L and H respectively. However, because these maps also contain a lot of other information, they are quite complicated and their interpretation won't be explored in detail until Chapter 7. Meanwhile a much simpler representation of highs and lows will be perfectly adequate, as illustrated in Figure 2.16.

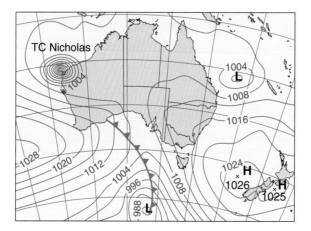

Figure 2.15 'Weather map' for the Australian region on 19 February 2008, marked with areas of low (L) and high (H) mean sea-level (MSL) pressure. The other features marked on this kind of map will be discussed in Chapter 7. The abbreviation TC stands for tropical cyclone. You will find out more about tropical cyclones (also called hurricanes) in Chapter 4.

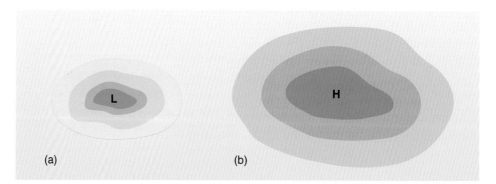

Figure 2.16 Schematic representation of (a) a low (L) and (b) a high (H) as seen from above. In (a) the pressure is lowest where the blue tone is strongest. An observer moving in any direction away from the centre of the low would see the pressure gradually rising; this is indicated by the paler blue tone. In (b) the pressure is highest where the red tone is strongest. An observer moving in any direction away from the centre of the high would see the pressure gradually falling; this is indicated by the paler red tone.

Activity 2.1 Weather data round the world (Part 1)

The estimated time for this activity is 30 minutes.

In this chapter you have seen that both temperature and pressure are measured in a variety of units, and that humidity is more relevant to comfort levels in some parts of the world than others. In this part of this activity, you will look at weather forecasts from meteorological services in a number of countries to discover how temperature, pressure and humidity are reported. (You will carry out Part 2 of the activity during your study of Chapter 3.)

As usual, you will find the detailed instructions for the activity in the Activities section of the course website.

2.3.2 Variations in air pressure and air density

Temperature, air pressure, air density and altitude are all interconnected; if one of them changes, the others usually change also. Having so many variables to contend with can make it hard to work out what is happening, and the best way to think through the consequences is to imagine changing just one variable at a time.

Consider first the situation in which the pressure is constant but the air temperature changes. If the air is warmed, the molecules will move more quickly on average, which results in them spreading out; i.e. the air expands and its density decreases. Thus if the pressure is constant, the air becomes less dense as the temperature increases. Conversely, it becomes more dense if the temperature decreases. In other words, at a given pressure, cold air is more dense than warm air.

Now consider situations in which the pressure changes. As you have seen, there must be more air molecules above a region of high pressure than above a region of low pressure. A change in the number of air molecules is accomplished if there is an imbalance in the amount of air moving into and out of the region. One way in which this can happen is by a horizontal inflow of air into the region from opposite directions. This process is called convergence and is always accompanied by some compensatory vertical motion. The opposite process, whereby there is horizontal outflow of air from a region, is called divergence.

Figure 2.17a illustrates the convergence of surface air that always occurs in the mid-latitudes at an area of low pressure (you will discover the reason for this in Chapter 4), with the associated divergence of air higher up.

- If the amount of air that is leaving through divergence exceeds the amount entering through convergence, then the density of the air above the region will be reducing (because there will be fewer molecules occupying the same amount of space) and the pressure at the surface will be falling even further.

- Conversely, if the amount of air leaving through divergence is less than the amount entering through convergence, then the density of the air above the region will be increasing and the pressure at the surface will be rising.

- If the divergence and the convergence exactly balance, then the pressure at the surface will maintain the same (low) value.

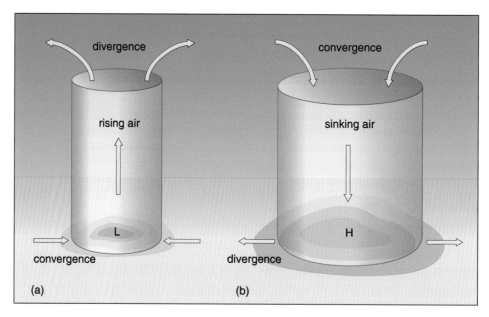

Figure 2.17   Schematic illustrations of convergence and divergence of air in the mid-latitudes. (a) Near a low, there is convergence of air near the surface and divergence at altitude. (b) Near a high, there is divergence near the surface and convergence at altitude.

Figure 2.17b shows the opposite situation, that near to an area of mid-latitude high pressure, where there is always a divergence of air near the surface (again, you will find out in Chapter 4 why this is the case).

■   What will happen to the pressure in an already high-pressure area if the amount of air entering the region through convergence at altitude exceeds the amount leaving through divergence near the surface?

☐   The density of the air above the region will increase (because the molecules will be pressed more closely together) and so the pressure will increase still further.

The horizontal movements of air, such as those shown in Figure 2.17, are of course what we normally call 'wind'. A wind is associated with a pressure difference. (You can observe this on the small scale if you open the valve on a pumped-up car tyre. The pressure in the tyre is greater than the atmospheric pressure outside it so when you open the valve the air rushes out.) The pressure differences in the atmosphere usually have their origin in differences in air temperature (and hence in air density) in different regions.

2.3.3   A refreshing breeze off the sea

A common experience during summer afternoons in many parts of the world is the onshore wind (i.e. a wind blowing off the sea towards the land). On the basis of what you have read so far, you can explain this weather phenomenon. First, recall what you know about the speeds with which land and water heat up.

- If a large body of water and an adjacent area of land receive identical amounts of sunlight, which will warm more quickly? (Check back to Section 2.1.2 if necessary.)

☐ The land will warm more quickly than the water.

This situation is shown in Figure 2.18a. During the day, the land heats up more quickly than the sea. The air becomes warmer (and less dense) above the land than above the sea. This warm, less dense, air will tend to rise and spread out to replace the cooler air at altitude, so there is an influx of warm air at altitude over the sea. At the same time, cooler air is moving in the opposite direction at the surface, and it is the latter that is experienced as an onshore wind that is often called a sea breeze. This cool air moving in at surface level from the sea warms once it is over the land, becoming less dense. Once it is warm enough, it rises until it reaches the altitude at which it moves out over the sea again. There it cools and sinks, completing a circulation loop, as shown in Figure 2.18b. Because this movement of air has been brought about purely by differences in air temperature across the sea and the land, it is termed a thermal circulation. For a noticeable sea breeze to develop, there must be a distinct temperature difference between the land and the sea. This condition is met year-round in many tropical areas, but only in late spring and summer in the mid-latitudes.

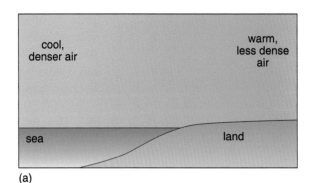

Figure 2.18 Development of a sea breeze. (a) The air over the land warms up more quickly than the air over the sea. (b) A thermal circulation loop operates.

At night, the land cools more quickly than the sea and the air becomes cooler (and more dense) above the land than above the sea. The winds in the thermal circulation loop therefore reverse, and the surface wind blows offshore. This wind blowing *from* the land is called a land breeze. In most parts of the world the temperature difference between land and sea is greater during the day than at night, so land breezes are not as strong as sea breezes.

2.3.4   Stable and unstable air

The example of thermal circulation on the coast is just one illustration of the way in which air moves vertically as well as horizontally. Clouds are the most visible evidence of this vertical movement. Before considering cloud formation, however, it's important to understand the processes that lead to air rising, sinking or staying put at a particular level above the ground. Imagine a 'parcel' of air filling a tiny, invisible, infinitely expandable, insulated balloon that doesn't weigh anything when it is empty. The balloon is so small that its movement won't substantially affect the air around it. (Such a balloon cannot exist of course, but it's a very convenient fiction and doesn't invalidate the conclusions that can be drawn about the behaviour of the air inside it.) The balloon keeps the air together and prevents it from mixing with the air outside. It also stops any heat entering or leaving the air parcel. Suppose that the parcel contains perfectly dry air and starts off at the Earth's surface where it has the same temperature and pressure as the air all around it. What would happen if the parcel were to be lifted? (Again, as part of the fiction, the actual lifting mechanism is irrelevant.) You know that pressure falls as the altitude increases, so as the parcel moves upwards, the pressure of the air surrounding it will decrease. This is illustrated in Figure 2.19. The air in the parcel will therefore expand until the pressures inside and outside the parcel are equal. In order to push the parcel walls outwards, the air molecules have to use up some of their own energy, and end up moving more slowly on average than they were originally.

■   What does this imply about the temperature of the parcel?

☐   A reduction in the average speed of the molecules corresponds to a reduction in the temperature of the air in the parcel.

Thus as the parcel of dry air is lifted, it expands and its temperature drops. If the parcel were to be lowered back to ground level again, it would be compressed to its original volume and regain its original temperature. This process is also shown in Figure 2.19. In summary then:

Rising air expands and is cooled; sinking air is compressed and warmed.

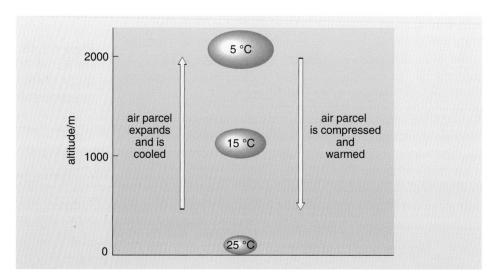

Figure 2.19   A lifted parcel of dry air expands and is cooled by about 10 °C per 1000 m of height gained. A lowered parcel of dry air is compressed and is warmed by about 10 °C per 1000 m of height lost.

Although the air in the parcel of Figure 2.19 was imagined as being perfectly dry, the rate of cooling and warming as the air parcel moves up and down is actually the same whether the air is dry or moist. *Provided it is not saturated*, rising air always cools by about 10 °C per 1000 m of height gained, and sinking air warms by about 10 °C per 1000 m of height lost. However, if the parcel consists of moist, rather than perfectly dry air, it may approach saturation simply because of being lifted.

■   What happens to the relative humidity as the moist parcel rises?

☐   The rising parcel is cooled, so the relative humidity increases (as you saw in Section 2.2.3).

If the parcel cools to its dew point, the relative humidity will be 100%: the air will be saturated. If the parcel is lifted further and cools still more, condensation will occur and a cloud will form.

■ If the parcel then remains at the same height, what happens to its temperature as a result of condensation having taken place? (Check back with Section 2.2.2 if you need a hint.)

☐ Its temperature increases, because latent heat of vaporisation is released within the parcel when water vapour condenses.

As a result, a lifted parcel of saturated air cools less than a parcel of unsaturated air for the same increase in altitude: saturated air cools by about 6 °C for every 1000 m of height gained. This is illustrated in Figure 2.20. Now compare the temperature of the surrounding air in this figure to the temperature of the parcels.

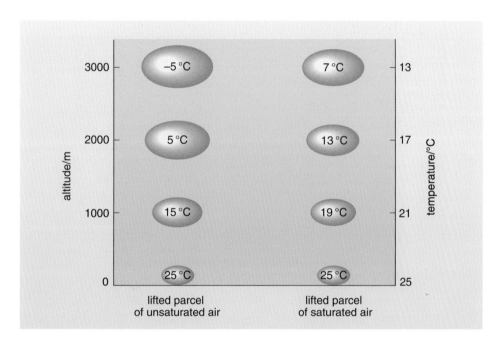

Figure 2.20 An example of a stable atmospheric environment. A lifted parcel of unsaturated air (cooling at 10 °C per 1000 m of height gained) and a lifted parcel of saturated air (cooling at 6 °C per 1000 m of height gained) both always remain colder than their surroundings. The temperature of the surroundings is shown on the right-hand axis. The natural tendency of both air parcels is to sink.

■ Are the parcels warmer or colder than their environment?

☐ At all the heights shown, both parcels are colder than their environment.

These parcels are therefore always more dense than the air surrounding them, and would have a natural tendency to sink back to their original level. An air parcel that naturally resists being lifted is described as stable. The atmosphere can be imagined as being made up of a very large number of individual parcels, so in a region where all the parcels are stable, the air and the local atmospheric environment can both be described as stable.

Completely *un*stable conditions arise when a lifted parcel of air is always warmer, and therefore always less dense, than its surroundings. This is illustrated in Figure 2.21. Once they had been lifted just slightly, both the air parcels in Figure 2.21 would naturally continue to rise. Instability occurs when the air aloft is relatively cold. Completely unstable conditions hardly ever occur, except at very low levels. However, *conditional* instability is common. This situation is shown in Figure 2.22 and occurs when the atmospheric environment is stable for unsaturated air, but unstable for saturated air.

Figure 2.21   An example of a completely unstable atmospheric environment. A lifted parcel of unsaturated air (cooling at 10 °C per 1000 m of height gained) and a lifted parcel of saturated air (cooling at 6 °C per 1000 m of height gained) both always remain warmer than their surroundings. The temperature of the surroundings is shown on the right hand axis. The natural tendency of both air parcels is to rise.

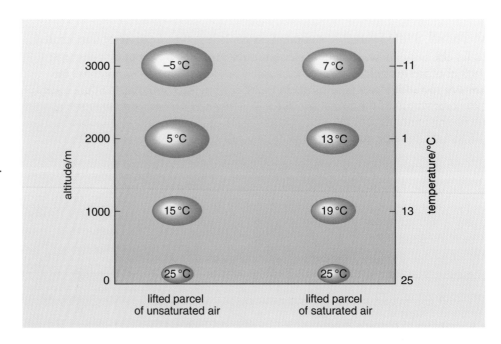

Figure 2.22   An example of a conditionally unstable atmospheric environment. A lifted parcel of unsaturated air (cooling at 10 °C per 1000 m of height gained) always remains colder than its surroundings and would have a natural tendency to sink. A lifted parcel of saturated air (cooling at 6 °C per 1000 m of height gained) always remains warmer than its surroundings and would have a natural tendency to rise.

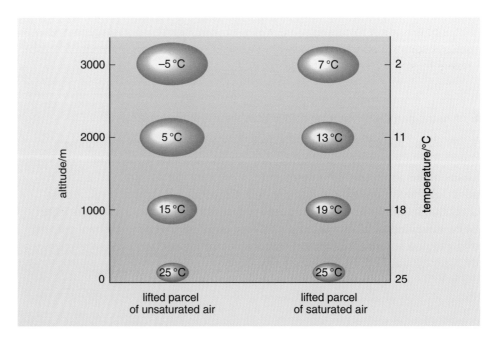

Clouds are the visible sign of vertical air movement and of condensation. The extent to which the atmospheric environment is stable or unstable with respect to saturated air determines whether clouds will form and what they will be like. Chapter 3 examines cloud formation in more detail.

Question 2.3

Why does an inversion put a 'lid' on rising air, preventing it from rising any further?

Study comment

Look back over the words and ideas you highlighted in this section. Does this method of active study work better or less well for you than note-taking? From now on, you should use your preferred method – or you might like to devise your own combination of the two techniques! By trying out various ways of studying and finding methods that suit you, you are working towards Learning Outcome KS3 and the development of your own learning strategies.

2.3.5   Key points of Section 2.3

This section contains a number of ideas that you will put to immediate use in the next chapter, but will also apply frequently in subsequent chapters.

Air density, air pressure and air temperature are interconnected.

Rising air expands and is cooled; sinking air is compressed and warmed.

In a stable atmospheric environment a parcel of air that is lifted is always colder than its surroundings and will tend to sink back to its original level. In an unstable atmospheric environment, a lifted parcel of air remains warmer than its surroundings and will continue to rise. The most common state is conditional instability, in which the atmospheric environment is stable for dry air, but unstable for saturated air.

Chapter 3
Weather elements: Part II

Chapter 2 discussed three of the six main weather elements: temperature, humidity and atmospheric pressure. This chapter covers the other three – clouds, precipitation and wind. The concepts in these two chapters lay many of the foundations for understanding weather phenomena, and you will use them repeatedly as you progress through the course. It is therefore worth investing study time at this stage, as it will make things much easier later on.

If you would like to check up in advance where the places mentioned in this chapter are located, the list follows. For the UK locations, it is sufficient to know where the counties are. It is not necessary to be able to locate the Matterhorn precisely within the Alps.

- UK locations: Boscastle (Cornwall), Horsham (Sussex) and Wattisham (Suffolk)
- Continental European locations: the Matterhorn (a mountain in the European Alps), the Salento Peninsula (Italy; the cities of Brindisi and Taranto mark the edges of this peninsula), the upper Danube valley (Germany)
- State within the USA: Florida
- Countries: Bangladesh, Guadeloupe (Caribbean)
- Ocean: the Gulf of Mexico.

Study comment

Another useful study technique is 'scanning' material before starting to study it more thoroughly. Scanning involves a *very* quick read through, during which you ignore questions and activities, and simply try to identify the main topics and the new concepts. This chapter, like Chapter 2, lists key points at the end of each section, which give good indications of the most important ideas. Include the diagrams in your scan, just to get an idea of the relative numbers of simple and complex ones. Try scanning Section 3.1 now. To make sure you don't get bogged down in detail, allow no more than 20 minutes for this. Don't make notes or do any highlighting while you are scanning. When you have finished, make a quick note of any parts that you think will be straightforward and any parts that you feel will require particularly careful study. Keep these notes safely until you have finished studying the section properly.

3.1   Clouds

Clouds are the most obviously varied of the weather elements. For the careful observer, they also provide the most important clues as to the weather that might be expected in the short term. Learning to read the 'cloudscape' is therefore a vital step in understanding and predicting your local weather. The wide variety of clouds can initially make this seem a rather daunting task, but with practice you will be able to identify different types of cloud and appreciate what kinds of weather they are likely to bring.

3.1.1   What are clouds?

What we see as a white or grey fluffy cloud is in fact a collection of tiny water droplets or (at very high altitude) minute ice crystals suspended in the air. For this collection of droplets or crystals to qualify as a cloud, its base must be above the ground. A similar collection of droplets in contact with the ground is called mist or fog. Cloud droplets are extremely tiny: the largest ones are no more than a tenth of a millimetre (0.1 mm) across and the smallest are a hundred times smaller than that. A cubic metre of cloud (i.e. a cube-shaped 'piece' of cloud one metre in each direction) contains many hundreds of millions of droplets suspended in the air, although the droplets are nevertheless very thinly distributed.

Clouds are formed when rising air cools below its dew point. Water vapour condenses producing the cloud droplets. These are so small, and hence so light, that even very gently moving air is enough to keep them aloft against the pull of gravity and they remain suspended in the air. As mentioned in Chapter 1, clouds scatter incoming sunlight in all directions. No particular colour of light is preferentially scattered or absorbed by cloud droplets, so clouds generally appear to be white. Scattered light can penetrate all the way through thin clouds and thin clouds therefore look white all over. As a cloud grows vertically, less and less scattered light penetrates all the way to its base, so less light emerges through the bottom of the cloud. In fact, the taller the cloud from top to bottom, the greater the proportion of the incoming light that is scattered back towards space, so the brighter the cloud appears from above and the darker it appears from below. 'Threatening black clouds' are thus often the tallest and these are indeed very likely to produce heavy rain.

3.1.2   Observing clouds

In describing clouds, there are two main aspects to be covered: how much cloud there is and what sort of clouds can be seen.

It's fairly easy to work out how much cloud there is. Meteorologists measure cloud amount in oktas (eighths), where 0 oktas corresponds to completely clear sky and 8 oktas to complete cloud cover, but simplified descriptions are usually used in forecasts. For your own observations it will usually be sufficient to record cloud cover in just four categories:

- clear: no cloud
- partly cloudy: less than half the sky covered
- mainly cloudy: more than half the sky covered but with some breaks visible
- overcast: whole sky covered with cloud.

Identifying the clouds you see is more of a challenge. Every cloud is unique: you will never see two that are identical in every respect. However, they do fall into recognisable groups on the basis of their appearance from ground level. Figure 3.1 shows two contrasting examples: wispy high cloud and a tall puffy cloud.

(a)   (b)

Figure 3.1   (a) Wispy high-level cirrus clouds. (b) Towering cumulus cloud above the Matterhorn.

Luke Howard, an English naturalist, devised the first generally accepted cloud classification system in 1803, and the terms he chose to describe the clouds are still employed today. Howard's scheme involved just four basic cloud forms, to which he gave Latin names:

- cirrus ('a curl of hair') for wispy clouds
- stratus ('layer') for horizontal sheet-like clouds
- cumulus ('heap') for puffy clouds
- nimbus ('rain') for rain-bearing clouds.

Other cloud types could be described by combining these terms: for instance, stratocumulus is a puffy cloud that shows horizontal layering. Nowadays, nimbus is not used on its own, but only in combination with two other component names, giving cumulonimbus and nimbostratus. In 1887, a further refinement was added, whereby clouds were classified according to the height of their base above ground level. The middle level clouds were given the prefix 'alto'. The resulting classification scheme of ten cloud types is shown in Table 3.1. By analogy with the way in which biologists classify plants and animals, these basic types of cloud are called the cloud genera (singular genus). The genera can be further subdivided in two ways – into species and varieties. Cloud 'species' are defined in terms of details of their shape and structure. For example, a low, layered cloud with a ragged appearance is a species called fractostratus (i.e. 'broken stratus'). Cloud 'varieties' are defined by their transparency and by the way in which their elements are arranged. For example, a cloud that is thin enough for the position of the Sun or the Moon to be apparent is a variety called translucidus ('transparent'); a layer cloud with fairly regular holes is a variety called lacunosus ('with gaps'). You do not need to worry about the names of species and varieties; the Learning Outcome for this course is that you should be able to identify only the ten genera.

Table 3.1 The ten cloud genera. The altitude of cloud base is given here in both metres and feet (abbreviation ft) for mid-latitude regions. In general, the altitude range is greater in the tropics and less near the poles. Cloud base is still reported in feet in many parts of the world.

Genus	Altitude of cloud base	Shape	Colour	Other visible features
Cirrus	High: above 5000 m (16 000 ft) in mid-latitudes	Delicate and fibrous clouds, in patches or bands	Mainly white	Popularly called 'mares' tails' because of their appearance
Cirrostratus		Thin veil of cloud with some fibrous structure	Transparent white	The Sun is visible through the cloud and casts shadows. There are often halo effects round the Sun or a full Moon
Cirrocumulus		Thin patch or sheet of more or less separate, rounded cloudlets in ripples	Mainly white	Extensive cirrocumulus is popularly described as a 'mackerel sky'
Altostratus	Medium: 2000–7000 m (6500–23 000 ft) in mid-latitudes	Sheet cloud with a fairly uniform appearance	Greyish	Often cover the entire sky. The Sun may be visible as if through ground glass, but no shadows are cast. No halo effects
Altocumulus		Broken, patchy clumps of cloud, often in ripples or bands. Thicker altocumulus can have a 'quilted' appearance	White or grey	With the arm extended at least 30° above the horizontal, altocumulus cloud elements appear to be 2 or 3 fingers' width across
Cumulus	Low: below 2000 m (6500 ft)	Puffy, cauliflower-shaped detached cloud, with a flat base and sharp outlines	Base is white or pale grey, top is often brilliant white	Usually well-separated, with a lot of blue sky between individual clouds
Stratocumulus		Sheet-like, but composed of rounded, lumpy individual cloud elements that may form in rolls	Light to dark grey	With the arm extended, stratocumulus cloud elements appear roughly fist sized
Stratus		Uniform, featureless cloud with a level base, often covering the entire sky	Grey	No accompanying precipitation, or only a light drizzle
Cumulonimbus		Very tall giant cloud, often with an anvil-shaped top	Dark grey base and white sides and top	Associated with heavy showers, hail and thunderstorms
Nimbostratus		Featureless thick layer of cloud	Dark grey	Associated with continuous steady rain or snow, and poor visibility

Nimbostratus clouds are the tallest of the layer (i.e. 'stratus') clouds and can show a range of base heights. This can lead them to be classified with altostratus and altocumulus as mid-level clouds. However, the base of nimbostratus clouds is usually considerably lower than 2000 m, so they appear in the 'low' category in Table 3.1.

Activity 3.1   Identifying clouds

The estimated time for this activity is one to one and a half hours.

In this activity you will look at many images of individual clouds of all the different genera. You will then be able to test your skill in cloud recognition by trying a quiz. Being able to recognise different types of cloud will be important for some of the observational work you will carry out later in the course.

You will find the detailed instructions for the activity in the Activities section of the course website.

3.1.3   Cloud formation

Clouds form when air rising through the atmosphere cools below its dew point, and the kind of cloud that results depends to some extent on the way in which the uplift of air occurs. Figure 3.2 illustrates how cumulus clouds form by surface heating and convection. You saw an example of convection in Chapter 1, whereby heat could be transferred through a liquid contained in a pan sitting on a hotplate. Hot liquid rises, with cooler liquid sinking to take its place. Similar vertical movement of air can take place in the atmosphere. If a small area of the Earth's surface absorbs more sunlight than surrounding areas, a 'hot spot' forms, as shown in Figure 3.2a. Air in contact with this hot spot becomes warmer than the surrounding air. A warm parcel of air called a thermal can then break away from the surface and rise spontaneously, as illustrated in Figure 3.2b. When many such parcels rise in a continuous stream they form an ascending current of air called an updraught. The air within the updraught will continue to rise, expand

Figure 3.2   Formation of a cumulus cloud. (a) A bubble of warm air grows at a hot spot on the ground; (b) the parcel of warm air rises; (c) condensation produces a cloud. Around the cloud, air sinks; (d) a big cloud is built by continuing updraughts, but downdraughts also occur within a big cloud.

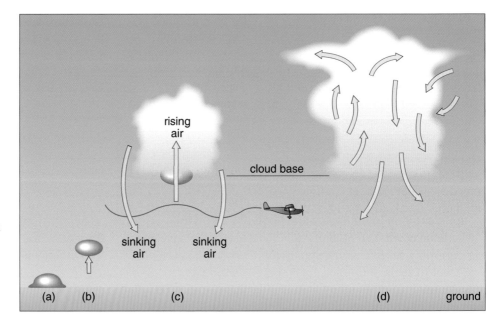

and cool until it reaches its dew point, whereupon condensation occurs and the cloud begins to form. The base of the cloud therefore marks the level at which condensation starts. Clouds formed directly as a result of rising thermals are the product of the process of convection and are therefore collectively known as convective clouds.

■ Suppose the ground temperature at sea level is 30 °C and the dew point is 20 °C. At what height would you expect the cloud base to be? (Hint: you may want to check back to Figure 2.20.)

☐ The cloud base will be at the level at which the air is at the dew point. Air rising from sea level must be cooled by 30 °C − 20 °C = 10 °C to reach this temperature. Since unsaturated air cools at 10 °C per 1000 m of ascent, the cloud base will be at 1000 m above sea level.

The stability of the air above the cloud base determines how the cloud subsequently develops. Once condensation occurs, latent heat is released, and the rising parcel can remain warmer than the air surrounding it. If the atmospheric environment between the cloud base and much higher levels is conditionally unstable, the cloud will continue to grow vertically into a tall billowing cumulus or even a cumulonimbus cloud. The total vertical extent of the cloud is usually called its depth. In the mid-latitudes, cumulonimbus clouds can be 10 000 m deep, but in the tropics they can approach a depth of 20 000 m, rising to the very top of the troposphere. Convective clouds do not build vertically much beyond the top of the troposphere because within the tropopause the temperature ceases to fall with increasing altitude, as was shown in Figure 2.7. A region in which the air temperature does not change with height corresponds to a stable atmospheric environment. The tropopause therefore acts as a 'lid' on the development of convective clouds.

If on the other hand there is a stable atmospheric environment just above the cloud base, air cannot rise much beyond this level and only small 'fair weather' cumulus clouds develop. The drier the surrounding air that mixes into the cloud at its edges, the more rapid the evaporation, and the less the cloud builds. As shown in Figure 3.2c, air directly below and within a developing cumulus cloud is rising, but around it air is sinking. Evaporation round the edges of the cloud cools the air there, making it denser so that it sinks. The alternation between rising air immediately below the clouds and the sinking air around them can result in a bumpy ride if you are flying below the cloud base. This is illustrated in Figure 3.2c. Cool sinking air impedes the development of thermals beneath it, so small cumulus clouds usually build up individually, with lots of blue sky visible between them.

When drier air from outside the cloud is drawn into it, evaporation of cloud droplets can significantly cool a section of the cloud. The colder, denser air then falls through the cloud, as illustrated in Figure 3.2d. This descending current of air is called a downdraught. Downdraughts may also be initiated or enhanced by heavy raindrops falling through the cloud and dragging air with them. The appearance of downdraughts is characteristic of mature thunderstorms, which will be covered in more detail in Chapter 8.

Figure 3.3 Cumulus clouds above an island in the Dry Tortugas, west of the Florida Keys.

Question 3.1

Figure 3.3 shows a cloudscape above an island off the coast of Florida.

(a) Why has cumulus cloud formed directly above the island but not over the sea?

(b) Explain why the bases of these clouds are flat and all at roughly the same height, whereas their tops are rounded and at different heights.

The development of cumulus or cumulonimbus clouds can be enhanced by uplift resulting from the convergence of two moist streams of air at the surface, as shown diagrammatically in Figure 3.4a. This is most likely to happen regularly on a peninsula, where winds blow in off the sea from opposite directions. Where the two airstreams meet they are forced upwards. This situation occurs regularly in Florida during the summer, when sea breezes from the Atlantic and the Gulf of Mexico converge there. As a result, Florida has a high level of summer rainfall. The uplift from convergence, added to the effect of strong heating of the land, produces showers and thunderstorms along the spine of the state during the afternoon. Another example, this time from Italy, is shown in Figure 3.4b.

Figure 3.4 Uplift produced by convergence. (a) Diagram showing how two opposing airstreams cause a lifting of air. (b) Satellite picture of convective clouds over the Salento Peninsula in southern Italy: sea breezes from both sides of the peninsula result in convergence in the central part of the peninsula.

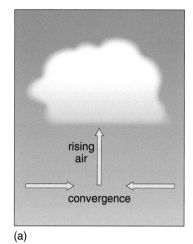

(a)

(b)

Clouds arising from convection, convergence or both develop rapidly, mainly vertically and depend for their growth on unstable conditions aloft. In the absence of such rapid uplift and in more stable air, clouds tend to form in sheets or layers. In stable air, lifting does not occur spontaneously, but must be 'forced', for example by moving air being pushed upwards by the physical barrier of a mountain, as shown in Figure 3.5. The upward movement of air when it encounters rising terrain is called orographic lifting. The kind of cloud that results from orographic lifting depends on the conditions, particularly the humidity of the air and the stability of the atmospheric environment. In cool damp conditions, moist air lifted in this way in a stable atmosphere condenses to form a stratus cloud, often with its base partway up the slope.

(a)

(b)

Figure 3.5   (a) Air forced to rise by the presence of a mountain. (b) Orographic stratus cloud.

In this section you have met three ways in which air can be lifted to form clouds: convection, convergence and orographic lifting. There is also a fourth mechanism, which you will meet in Chapter 4.

3.1.4   Mist and fog

When a collection of minute water droplets is suspended in the air at ground level, the visibility drops: fog has formed. Clouds, fog and mist are all manifestations of the same situation – air reaching its dew point and water vapour condensing from it to produce tiny droplets that are so small and light they remain suspended in the air. The only difference between cloud and fog is that a cloud has its base above ground level. In terms of the processes involved, fog is just a 'cloud on the ground'. There is no real difference between mist and fog, apart from the distance it is possible to see through them. When the visibility is reduced to less than 1 km, the suspension of droplets is classed as fog.

Fog can form in several different ways. One of the most common occurs when moist air at ground level is overlain by a layer of drier air. On a clear cool night, the ground rapidly loses heat and the lowest layer of air cools more than the air higher up, so an inversion forms as described in Section 2.1.4. If the temperature of the moist lowest layer falls below the dew point, the air becomes saturated and fog forms. Since this type of fog forms from the ground upwards, it tends to get denser as the night goes on. The coldest (and hence densest) air naturally settles in valleys, so the fog frequently forms in river valleys, especially as evaporation from a river can increase moisture levels in the valley air. An example of fog in a valley is shown in Figure 3.6. In Chapter 8 you will meet fog that arises in rather different circumstances.

Figure 3.6   Fog that has formed in a valley overnight. (This photograph was taken in the Upper Danube Valley.)

The water droplets in fog often coalesce to form larger drops on plants and other surfaces. An example is shown in Figure 3.7a. If the surfaces are at sub-zero temperatures, then a transparent layer of ice, called glaze, is deposited; for this reason the fog is then called 'freezing fog'. When glaze forms on tarmac or other dark surfaces it can be very difficult to see, which is why it is commonly known as 'black ice'. If the water droplets in the fog are supercooled, then when they come into contact with cold surfaces they freeze into rough crystals of ice, giving a deposit called rime, which is illustrated in Figure 3.7b.

Figure 3.7 (a) Water drops on a spider's web, following overnight fog. (b) Rime on vegetation in freezing fog. Tiny bubbles of air are trapped within the ice crystals and scatter the light, making rime look opaque and white.

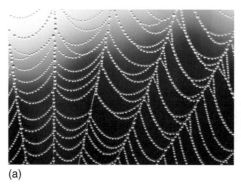

(a)   (b)

3.1.5   Key points of Section 3.1

As in Chapter 2, each section in this chapter will conclude with a list of key points. These summarise the concepts that you will use again frequently in explaining weather phenomena.

> Clouds result from the condensation or freezing of water vapour to give minute water droplets or ice crystals that are suspended in the air above the ground. The cloud base corresponds to the lowest level at which condensation occurs.
>
> Clouds may be classified according to the height of their base, their appearance and whether or not they produce rain.
>
> Cloud formation requires lifting of air. Three ways in which this may occur are surface heating and convection, convergence of air at the surface, or forced (orographic) movement over a barrier.

Study comment

Now you have finished studying this section, look back at the quick notes you made after your initial scan and think about whether the scan helped you in your more detailed study of the section. For instance, was it helpful to have an idea of the 'storyline'? Were you correct in your identification of the parts that were straightforward and those that you had to work through more slowly, and was it useful to know this in advance? Decide whether you need to approach the scanning process any differently and then try scanning Section 3.2. This is slightly shorter than Section 3.1, but it is also slightly more theoretical, so give yourself the same 20-minute limit for the scanning process. At the end of the time, again write very brief notes about how you think you should apportion your study time for the section.

3.2 Precipitation

Of all the weather elements, rain and snow are often the ones we care about most. We need rain for crops to grow and to ensure that we have enough water for domestic use. On the other hand, we hope that special events won't be spoiled by wet weather, that transport won't be disrupted by snow, and certainly that there won't be flooding of homes and businesses. An appreciation of how precipitation is formed in clouds and then released is therefore a particularly important part of understanding the weather.

3.2.1 Types of precipitation

Precipitation is the meteorological term for water in any solid or liquid form that falls from a cloud and reaches the ground. Rain, drizzle, hail and snow are thus all forms of precipitation. Phenomena like dew and frost, which are deposited directly on the surface, and mist or fog which consists of water droplets suspended in the air, are not classed as precipitation, even though they may result in objects at the surface getting very wet.

Many people would say 'it's raining' if any liquid water were falling from the sky, but the drops reaching the ground have to be at least 0.5 mm in diameter for a meteorologist to class them as rain. Most raindrops are between 1 mm and 2 mm across. Precipitation drops smaller than 0.5 mm in diameter are classified as drizzle. In distinguishing rain from drizzle, the amount of water coming down is irrelevant: it is drop size that matters, not the intensity of the precipitation. In fact you will get considerably wetter in 'heavy drizzle' than you will in 'light rain'. You will also be able to see less far. The many small drops of drizzle can have a significant effect on visibility, just as fog droplets do. Visibility is used as a measure of the intensity of drizzle, whereas the intensity of rain is classified by the total amount of water deposited. Drizzle usually comes from shallow stratus cloud, whereas rain is more likely from deeper clouds. However, if small raindrops emerge from a cloud and fall through unsaturated air their size may be reduced through evaporation, so that by the time they reach the ground they constitute drizzle.

Snow is the most common type of solid precipitation. Snowflakes are formed when many tiny ice crystals suspended in clouds collide and stick together, a process called aggregation. Water droplets can also freeze on contact with the ice crystals. Because large snowflakes involve the aggregation of many ice crystals, they form into beautiful patterns, just a few of which are illustrated in Figure 3.8. Note that all snowflakes have the hexagonal (i.e. six-fold) symmetry of the individual ice crystals shown in Figure 2.9a. It only snows when the weather is cold, but air frost (i.e. an air temperature of 0 °C or lower) is not a requirement for snow. Although the edges of a flake will begin to melt at any temperature above 0 °C, if the surrounding air is unsaturated the water will evaporate, cooling the air around the flake. The drier the air, the longer the flake can persist. In the comparatively dry downdraught from a big cumulonimbus

Figure 3.8 Computer-enhanced images of individual snowflakes. Notice that these all have hexagonal symmetry.

cloud, there may be snowflakes even when the air temperature approaches 10 °C. In the UK, heavy snowfall is usually associated with air temperatures between 0 °C and 2 °C. At slightly higher temperatures, a mixture of rain and melting snow may fall; this is called sleet.

Hail is solid precipitation in the form of lumps of ice. For falling ice pellets to be classed as hail they must be at least 5 mm across, but in fact they can be more than ten times this diameter. The largest authenticated hailstone in the UK fell in Horsham on 5 September 1958 and weighed 142 grams, but this is dwarfed by the records in other parts of the world. The North American record stands at 757 grams for a hailstone measuring 14 cm across. Such large lumps of ice can cause considerable damage and 92 people were reported killed in a hailstorm in Bangladesh on 14 April 1986.

3.2.2   Precipitation processes

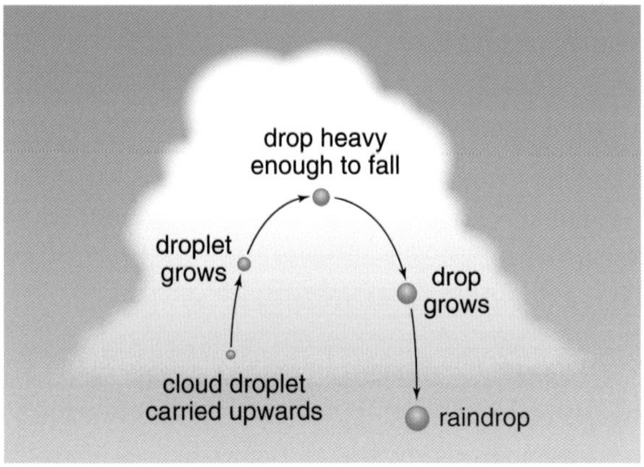

Condensation alone is not sufficient to produce rain. Cloud droplets are so tiny that they mostly remain suspended in the air and any that do fall quickly evaporate once they reach the warmer air below the cloud. The rain-producing mechanism was originally thought always to be one of colliding droplets merging together (a process called coalescence) to give larger, heavier raindrops that could fall to the ground. In a 'warm cloud', i.e. one that has temperatures greater than 0 °C at all levels, rainfall is indeed produced by condensation and coalescence, as shown in Figure 3.9. Droplets of different sizes are swept up or fall at different speeds. It turns out that a rain drop with a diameter of 3 mm will fall at over twice the speed of a rain drop with a diameter of 1 mm, and at four times the speed of a large drizzle drop of diameter just under 0.5 mm. A large drop will therefore fall through areas containing very many small drops, and collide with a lot of them, rather as a runner would barge through a group of slowly moving pedestrians. These many collisions result in the large drop continuing to grow as it falls. Extremely large drops usually disintegrate though, so there is a constant supply of new smaller drops. The size of the raindrops that emerge from this process depends on the nature and depth of the cloud. Shallow stratus with slow updraughts does not allow the drops enough time in the cloud for them to grow much, so produces only drizzle, whereas deep warm cumulonimbus clouds with vigorous updraughts can generate large raindrops.

Figure 3.9   A cloud droplet in a warm cloud rises on the updraught, growing by coalescence until it becomes heavy enough to fall. It grows further by the same process as it falls through the suspended cloud droplets, eventually leaving the base of the cloud as a raindrop.

In the late nineteenth and early twentieth centuries, meteorologists began to realise that mid- and high latitude clouds extended into regions in the atmosphere where the air temperature is well below 0 °C. Such clouds are called 'cold clouds'. It then became apparent that although the simple coalescence idea worked for warm clouds it could not apply universally. The mechanism for the formation of precipitation in cold clouds is usually called the Bergeron process, after the Swedish meteorologist who first suggested in 1933 that raindrops derived from ice crystals.

A typical mid-latitude cumulonimbus cloud is shown in Figure 3.10. A large section of this cloud is colder than 0 °C, but it contains supercooled liquid water droplets as well as ice crystals. Only at the very top of the cloud are there ice crystals but no liquid droplets. The reason for this lies in the conditions necessary for ice to form. As discussed in Section 2.2.2, water droplets form on condensation nuclei, and freezing nuclei are required for ice crystals to form. Freezing nuclei work best if their geometry is hexagonal, like that of an ice crystal, but such particles are rare. A cold cloud thus contains many more condensation nuclei than freezing nuclei, and therefore there will be more liquid droplets than ice crystals, even at temperatures well below 0 °C. In the portion of the cloud that contains both water droplets and ice crystals, water molecules can escape more easily from the liquid droplets than from the solid crystals. The air in the cloud is saturated, so if water vapour is to be added to the air by evaporation from the droplets, an equal amount of water vapour must be removed from the air by condensation or deposition. The water vapour condenses or freezes most readily onto the ice crystals and the crystals therefore grow at the expense of the droplets.

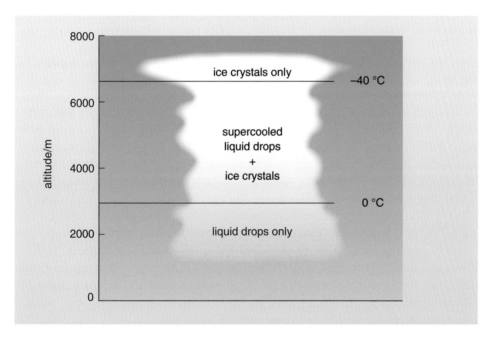

Figure 3.10   The distribution of ice and water in a cold cloud in the mid-latitudes.

Once the crystals are large enough that they can no longer be held aloft by the updraughts, they start to fall through the cloud of supercooled droplets. Various things can then happen to them. If the cloud contains many ice crystals, some may break up as they fall through the cloud, producing tiny 'secondary' crystals. Small falling crystals may collide with and stick to one another. As described in Section 3.2.1, this process of aggregation forms snowflakes. Nimbostratus clouds often have the high number of ice crystals required to produce snow. If the snowflakes melt in the lower, warmer parts of the cloud they will emerge from the base of the cloud as rain. Figure 3.11a shows these processes schematically.

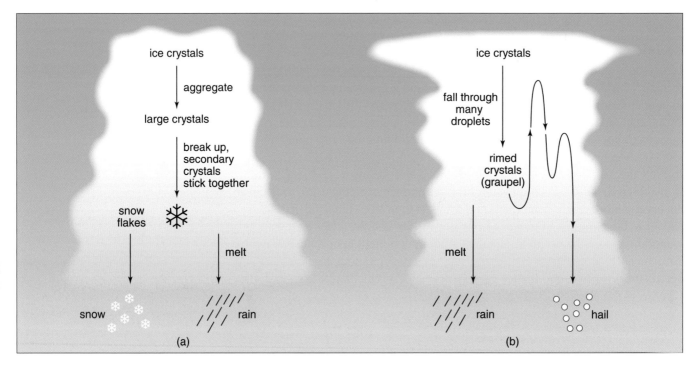

Figure 3.11 Precipitation produced by the Bergeron (ice-crystal) process in (a) a cloud with a lot of ice crystals and (b) a cloud with a lot of liquid droplets.

On the other hand, if the middle levels of the cloud contain more water than ice, falling crystals will collide with many droplets, which will freeze on contact with the crystals and stick to them. This process is known as riming, and the resultant icy material is called graupel. The way in which graupel moves within the cloud determines whether or not hail is formed. Graupel may be carried upward on an updraught, be pushed sideways out of the updraught by the wind, fall a short distance and then encounter another updraught. If the updraughts are strong and the cloud is a deep one, graupel may go up and down through the cloud a number of times, accumulating sufficient ice to fall as hail. This process is shown schematically in Figure 3.11b. The up and down motion through the cloud means that the ice will be deposited on the growing hail pellet under a number of different temperature conditions. As a result, hailstones are often 'layered', with some transparent ice (glaze) and some opaque ice (rime).

The form of precipitation that is finally observed at ground level depends on the conditions at the base of the cloud and below it, although hail emerging from a cloud usually reaches the ground as hail because there isn't time for it to melt completely even if it falls through air that is well above 0 °C. Snow falls more slowly than hail, so snow emerging from the base of a cloud and falling through air that is above freezing may have turned to rain by the time it reaches the ground. It may at first seem surprising that hail is much more common in the summer than in the cold months of the year, but Figure 3.11b gives the clues to explaining this fact.

■ What causes the updraughts in convective clouds?

☐ Rising air (thermals) resulting from heating of the ground.

■ In the mid-latitudes at what time of year are these thermals most likely to form?

☐ In the summer, when the ground is strongly heated.

■ In the mid-latitudes at what time of year will convective clouds build to the greatest height?

☐ The strong updraughts result in clouds building to their greatest height in the summer.

■ Will a deep cloud be more likely to be warm or cold?

☐ The deeper the cloud, the colder it is likely to be at upper levels.

■ Why is the air likely to be particularly humid in the summer?

☐ Humidity is the result of evaporation, and evaporation is higher in summer because the temperature is higher.

The conditions of strong updraughts, a deep cold cloud, and more water drops than ice crystals in the middle portion of the cloud, which are the requirements for the formation of hail, are therefore all more likely to be met when the ground is strongly heated by the summer sun.

Question 3.2

Figure 3.12 shows a weather phenomenon that you may have observed: a trail of rain falling from a cloud but not reaching the ground. This is called virga. Explain briefly how the phenomenon might be brought about.

Figure 3.12   Virga below a cumulonimbus cloud. Virga, sometimes called 'fallstreak', is a trail of rain or snow that can be seen below a cloud but tapers off and does not actually reach the ground. (You may also have seen another rather similar phenomenon, called 'praecipitatio' in which a dark 'curtain' of rain, snow or hail can be observed descending from a distant cloud all the way to the ground.)

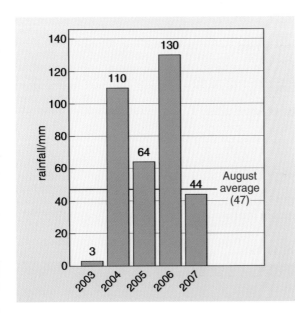

Figure 3.13   Bar chart showing the rainfall totals for the month of August at Wattisham (Suffolk, UK) over the period 2003–2007. The August average for this location is 47 mm. The totals for each August are written above the corresponding bar. Note that the amount of rain that has fallen is measured by recording the depth of water that accumulates in a flat-bottomed gauge, and is conventionally measured in millimetres. To determine a monthly total, the rainfall will have been measured on a daily basis and the readings added up at the end of the month.

3.2.3   How much rain has there been?

Compared to the temperature statistics for the UK shown in Figures 2.3 and 2.5a, UK rainfall statistics show considerably more variation. Rainfall amounts are determined by collecting the water in a flat-bottomed container, and measuring the depth of water that has accumulated. Figure 3.13 shows the August rainfall at a weather station in eastern England for the five summers discussed in Chapter 1. Only in two of these years was this rainfall close to the August average. In 2003, it was about a fifteenth of the average, and in 2004 and 2006 it was more than double the average.

Question 3.3

(a) Use the values noted above each bar of the chart in Figure 3.13 to calculate the mean August rainfall at Wattisham over the five years 2003–2007.

(b) To what do you attribute any difference between your value and the August average given in the figure caption?

You may have remembered that August 2004 was noted in Chapter 1 as the month of the Boscastle flood. Boscastle is on the southwest side of the UK, and has higher average rainfall in August than Wattisham, which is near the east coast. In 2004, the *total* August rainfall in Wattisham was 110 mm, a bit more than double the monthly average for that location. In Boscastle on the day of the flood 75 mm of rain, which is roughly the monthly average for August there, fell in *two hours*. Just imagine then what it must have been like on the island of Guadeloupe in the Caribbean on 26 November 2007 when 38.1 mm of rain fell in just one minute! This is the record for the most intense rainfall ever measured.

3.2.4   Key points of Section 3.2

Although this has been quite a complicated section, the key points that you need to carry forward into subsequent chapters can be summarised quite simply.

Precipitation is water in any liquid or solid form that reaches the ground after falling from a cloud.

In warm clouds, larger water drops fall through areas where smaller ones are suspended, and grow by successive collisions and coalescence into raindrops.

In cold clouds, the precipitation process is initiated by ice crystals. Cold clouds with more ice than liquid drops produce snow and rain. Hail comes from clouds with more liquid drops than ice and requires conditions in which strong updraughts produce a deep cloud.

Study comment

Now you have finished studying this section, look back at the quick notes you made after your initial scan and think again about whether the scan helped you in your more detailed study of the section. Do you think that spending time on the scan made your study time for the material longer or shorter overall? Decide whether you are going to continue using this approach for subsequent sections and chapters.

3.3   Wind

Wind may be invisible, but it is a weather element of which we are all aware, because its effects are so obvious at ground level. A gentle breeze may make a hot day more pleasant, while strong winds add greatly to the chill of cold weather. The winds associated with storms or hurricanes can cause widespread damage and sometimes loss of life. Winds also play a huge role in the global sense, transporting heat and moisture (and pollutants such as dust) between different regions of the Earth.

3.3.1   Wind speed and direction

From the point of view of forthcoming local weather, there are three things we want to know about the wind. How strong will it be? This is the colloquial way of asking what its speed will be. Will it be steady or gusty? And from which direction will it come? Wind speed is traditionally measured in knots, meaning nautical miles per hour. A nautical mile is slightly larger than a land mile.

$$1 \text{ knot} = 1 \text{ nautical mile/hour} = 1.15 \text{ miles/hour} = 1.85 \text{ kilometres/hour}$$

Precise measurements of wind speed are made using an instrument called an anemometer. However, it is possible to make good estimates of wind speed by simple observations of the wind's effects. This is the basis for the Beaufort scale, which was devised in 1805 for his own private use by a Royal Navy commander Francis (later Sir Francis, hydrographer to the Navy and Rear Admiral) Beaufort. The scale was originally based on the effect of the wind on the sails of a large naval ship, and was introduced on all Royal Navy vessels in 1838. A number of subsequent modifications have been made to base the scale on the appearance of the sea surface, and to adapt it for land-based observation. A simplified version of the current scale is shown in Table 3.2. You may find these land-based indicators of wind speed are a useful guide to what you might expect from the wind speeds predicted in routine weather forecasts. The Beaufort scale is still in widespread use, including in the UK shipping forecast and in the Far East where it has been extended with Forces 13–17 to describe the winds associated with typhoons. In the USA, however, hurricane winds greater than Force 12 are described on a separate five-point scale that relates to their hazard level (e.g. of flooding and property damage).

Table 3.2 The Beaufort wind scale.

Beaufort number ('Force')	Beaufort name	Wind speed/ miles per hour	Wind speed/ kilometres per hour	Sea conditions	Land conditions
0	Calm	Less than 1	Less than 1	Surface like a mirror	Calm; smoke rises vertically
1	Light air	1–3	1–5	Ripples, but no foam crests	Wind direction shown by smoke drift, but not by weather vanes
2	Light breeze	4–7	6–11	Small wavelets, with glassy crests that do not break	Wind vanes move; wind felt on face; leaves rustle
3	Gentle breeze	8–12	12–19	Larger wavelets, with scattered whitecaps	Leaves and small twigs move
4	Moderate breeze	13–18	20–28	Small waves (height 0.3–1.2 m), numerous whitecaps	Small branches move; wind raises dust and loose paper
5	Fresh breeze	19–24	29–38	Moderate waves (height 1.2–2.4 m), many whitecaps, some spray	Small trees begin to sway; crested wavelets form on inland waters
6	Strong breeze	25–31	39–49	Large waves (height 2.4–4 m), whitecaps common, more spray	Large branches on trees move; overhead wires whistle; umbrellas become difficult to use
7	Near gale	32–38	50–61	Moderately high waves (height 4–6 m), with sea heaping up and foam streaking off breakers	Whole large trees move; walking against the wind is difficult
8	Gale	39–46	62–74	Moderately high waves (height 4–6 m), with edges of crests breaking into spindrift, and foam blown in streaks	Twigs break off trees; moving cars may be pushed off course
9	Strong gale	47–54	75–88	High waves (6 m) with sea beginning to roll and visibility reduced by spray	Slight structural damage occurs (e.g. to roof tiles, signs and aerials)
10	Storm	55–63	89–102	Very high waves (6–9 m), with overhanging crests and rolling sea	Trees uprooted; considerable structural damage occurs
11	Violent storm	64–72	103–117	Exceptionally high waves (9–13 m)	Widespread structural and environmental damage
12	Hurricane	In excess of 72	In excess of 117	Waves over 14 m, sea completely white with driven spray, very poor visibility	Extensive structural and environmental damage

Meteorologists have to be quite unambiguous about the wind direction: this is always stated as the direction *from* which the wind is blowing. An easterly wind is thus a wind that blows from the east. A south-southwesterly blows from a direction between south and southwest. Figure 3.14 shows the 16 compass points used to describe wind directions.

■ If you turn your back to a west-southwesterly wind, in what direction will you be facing?

☐ East-northeast.

Because winds are associated with pressure differences and because pressure patterns are constantly evolving and moving, winds are subject to frequent changes in direction. A wind that is changing direction clockwise is said to be 'veering'. A wind that is changing direction anticlockwise is said to be 'backing'. Thus a wind that was blowing from the north and shifts to blow from the east has veered. A southerly wind that is expected to shift to easterly is predicted to back. However, a forecast that predicts only typical wind speeds and directions may not tell the whole story, especially if the winds are fairly strong, as air turbulence may result in sudden increases in wind speed over short periods of time. A significant increase in wind speed that lasts only a few seconds is termed a gust. A similar increase that lasts for over a minute is called a squall. Both gusts and squalls are often accompanied by sudden changes in wind direction, which can increase their damaging effects.

■ In the UK shipping forecast the expected winds are described in the format 'southerly, backing southeasterly'. How would the following predictions be formulated? (i) A wind blowing from the southeast is expected to shift through south to blow from between the south and the southwest. (ii) A wind blowing from the northwest is expected to shift through south to blow from the southeast.

☐ (i) Southeasterly veering south-southwesterly. (ii) Northwesterly backing southeasterly.

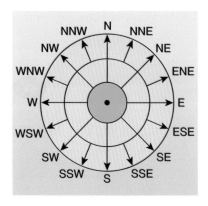

Figure 3.14 Compass divided into 16 points. The points are indicated by capital letters; for example, SW stands for southwest and ENE for east-northeast.

Activity 3.2 Weather data round the world (Part 2)

The estimated time for this activity is 30 minutes.

In Activity 2.1, you looked at weather forecasts from meteorological services in a number of countries to discover how temperature, pressure and humidity are reported. Now you should return to the same websites to see how they show cloud type, cloud cover, precipitation, wind direction and wind speed.

You will find the detailed instructions for the activity in the Activities section of the course website.

3.3.2   Wind chill

Just as the apparent temperature rises with increasing humidity, so it falls in windy conditions. In cold air, the human body loses heat to the air by conduction and convection. However, air is a poor conductor. If the air is still, then the thin, warm layer of air very close to the skin loses heat only slowly. If the skin or clothing is wet, we often feel colder, because water is a better conductor of heat than air, and heat is therefore lost more quickly from wet skin. Additionally, the latent heat required to evaporate the water must be supplied by the body, and its loss makes us feel even colder. Windy conditions also make us feel colder, because the thin layer of warm air next to the skin is constantly blown away, and heat is quickly lost. This cooling effect is called wind chill. The apparent temperature then depends on how rapidly the insulating layer of warm air is lost, and this in turn depends on the wind speed.

Table 3.3 shows apparent temperatures corresponding to various combinations of air temperature and wind speed, based on the loss of heat from the face, since that is the part of the body most likely to be exposed in very cold weather. For example, if the air temperature were −1 °C and the wind speed 25 kilometres per hour (which is only a moderate breeze), the combination would feel like −7.2 °C.

Table 3.3 Apparent temperatures for a range of air temperatures and wind speeds. (These apparent temperatures are also called the 'wind-chill effective temperatures'.) The apparent temperatures in the body of the table are how cold it *feels*. In other words, they are still-air temperatures that would result in the same heat loss from exposed skin as the combination of actual air temperature and wind speed read from the row and column headings.

Wind speed/ kilometres per hour	Air temperature/°C														
	10	9	8	7	6	5	4	3	2	1	0	−1	−2	−3	−4
5	9.8	8.5	7.5	6.4	5.2	4.1	2.9	1.8	0.7	−0.5	−1.6	−2.7	−3.9	−5.0	−6.1
10	8.6	7.4	6.2	5.0	3.9	2.7	1.5	0.3	−0.9	−2.1	−3.3	−4.5	−5.7	−6.9	−8.1
15	7.9	6.7	5.4	4.2	3.0	1.7	0.5	−0.7	−2.0	−3.2	−4.4	−5.6	−6.9	−8.1	−9.3
20	7.4	5.1	4.9	3.6	2.3	1.1	−0.2	−1.5	−2.7	−4.0	−5.2	−6.5	−7.8	−9.0	−10.3
25	6.9	5.7	4.4	3.1	1.8	0.5	−0.8	−2.1	−3.3	−4.6	−5.9	−7.2	−8.5	−9.8	−11.1
30	6.6	5.3	4.0	2.7	1.4	0.1	−1.3	−2.6	−3.9	−5.2	−6.5	−7.8	−9.1	−10.4	−11.7
35	6.3	4.9	3.6	2.3	1.0	−0.4	−1.7	−3.0	−4.3	−5.6	−7.0	−8.3	−9.6	−10.9	−12.2
40	6.0	4.6	3.3	2.0	0.6	−0.7	−2.0	−3.4	−4.7	−6.1	−7.4	−8.7	−10.1	−11.1	−12.7
45	5.7	4.4	3.0	1.7	0.3	−1.0	−2.4	−3.7	−5.1	−6.4	−7.8	−9.1	−10.5	−11.8	−13.2
50	5.5	4.1	2.8	1.4	0.0	−1.3	−2.7	−4.1	−5.4	−6.8	−8.1	−9.5	−10.9	−12.2	−13.6

■   Suppose you were riding a bike at 20 kilometres per hour straight into a gentle breeze blowing at 15 kilometres per hour. If the air temperature were 4 °C, what would be the apparent temperature?

☐   The combined effect of the wind and your speed through the air would correspond to an effective wind speed of (20 + 15) kilometres per hour. The combination of this wind speed and the air temperature of 4 °C would make it feel like −1.7 °C.

The range of air temperatures shown in Table 3.3 is not extreme; it is what might be expected in the daytime during the course of an average winter in southern England. The more extreme the winter temperatures, the more important it is to have a version of the table that alerts people to the dangers of wind chill. If the body is losing heat faster than it is producing and absorbing it, hypothermia sets in. This is a potentially fatal condition. Many cases of hypothermia occur even when the air temperature is above 0 °C, due to a combination of wet clothing and the effect of wind chill.

3.3.3   What determines wind direction and speed?

You have already seen that wind is a horizontal movement of air associated with a pressure difference. Figure 2.17 illustrated how net convergence or net divergence of air can affect changes in pressure at the Earth's surface. Look back at this figure to remind yourself of the principle.

■   Does the wind on the surface blow towards or away from an established area of high surface pressure?

☐   It blows away from it.

Surface winds move air horizontally away from an area of high pressure, and this divergence of air at the surface is compensated to a greater or lesser extent by colder air converging aloft and slowly sinking. The high will be maintained at the same pressure if the amount of air that converges aloft exactly matches the amount that moves away at ground level.

However, the direction of the winds is complicated by the fact that we live on a rapidly rotating planet. If you were to stand on the Equator you would be travelling eastwards at about 1670 kilometres per hour. We are largely unaware of this rotational motion of the Earth because objects around us travel with us at the same rotational speed as our own. Winds are a rather different matter though. We do notice that they are affected by the Earth's rotation, because they blow across large distances. Wind speeds and directions are measured relative to the ground (which to Earth-bound observers appears to be stationary). Because of the rotation of the Earth, an observer in the Northern Hemisphere will notice that horizontal winds appear to be continuously deflected to the right of their direction of motion, whereas an observer in the Southern Hemisphere will notice that horizontal winds appear to be deflected to the left. Observation also shows that the magnitude of the deflection depends on latitude, being greatest at high latitudes and decreasing to nothing at the Equator. It also turns out that the higher the wind speed, the greater the deflection. Conversely, the lower the wind speed the smaller the deflection. Any freely moving object, starting off in any direction, is in fact subject to this effect, but the deflection is only noticeable if the object travels over very large distances (as winds and ocean currents do) and/or if it moves extremely quickly. The phenomenon is known as the Coriolis effect, after a nineteenth century French scientist who worked out the details of the underlying physics. A full explanation of the reason for the apparent deflection requires mathematics beyond the scope of this course, but no discussion of wind and weather can ignore the Coriolis effect because it profoundly affects the way in which we see the movement of air within the atmosphere.

From our Earth-bound viewpoint, horizontal winds therefore do not blow straight out of the middle of a high-pressure area, but are deflected. In the Northern Hemisphere, horizontal winds are deflected to the right, resulting in an apparent clockwise movement of air around the high-pressure area as seen from above. Conversely, there is an apparent anticlockwise movement of air around an area of low pressure. These movements are illustrated in Figure 3.15. Note that Figure 3.15 refers only to winds in the Northern Hemisphere. An observer in the Southern Hemisphere would see the winds being apparently deflected to the *left*, so would see winds blowing anticlockwise around areas of high pressure and clockwise around areas of low pressure. The situation shown in Figure 3.15 is a simplified representation, but it is a useful approximation. It is a particularly good approximation at high latitudes, and a reasonable one in the mid-latitudes, but poor in the tropics where the Coriolis effect is least noticeable.

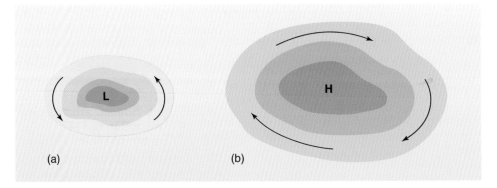

Figure 3.15   Winds aloft (i.e. a few kilometres above the Earth's surface) appear to be deflected to the right in the Northern Hemisphere. As seen from above, horizontal winds appear to circulate anticlockwise around areas of low pressure (a) and clockwise around areas of high pressure (b).

The wind speed depends on the associated pressure differences but near the surface it is also affected by friction. You will be aware that friction slows moving objects down. You can slide further on ice than on grass because grass exerts more friction than ice. The amount of friction between the wind and the Earth's surface also depends on the terrain. A wind blowing over a calm sea is not slowed down as much as one blowing over hilly land and forests. In general, high-level winds, which are less affected by friction with the ground, tend to be stronger than winds at the surface.

The fact that winds very close to the ground are slowed down by friction with the surface means that while Figure 3.15 is a good representation of air circulation aloft (i.e. a few kilometres above the surface), the situation near the ground is slightly different. The winds are slowed down by friction, and the Coriolis deflection decreases. As a result, surface-level winds spiral into areas of low pressure. Conversely, surface-level winds spiral out of areas of high pressure, as shown in Figure 3.16. The exact angle at which the winds emerge from highs and enter lows depends on the wind speed.

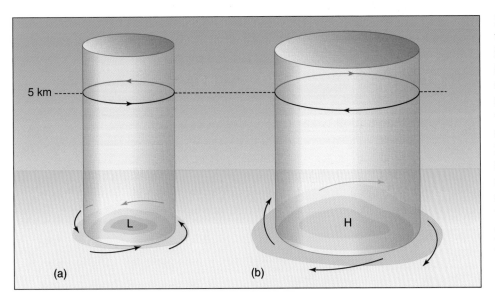

Figure 3.16 Circulation of winds around highs and lows in the Northern Hemisphere. (a) Horizontal winds aloft circulate anticlockwise around areas of low pressure, and winds close to the surface spiral anticlockwise inwards into the low-pressure area. (b) Horizontal winds aloft circulate clockwise around areas of high pressure, and winds close to the surface spiral clockwise outwards from the high-pressure area.

Study comment

It is often useful to draw rough sketches yourself, as an aid to visualisation and understanding. The two questions that follow give you the opportunity to practise this skill.

Question 3.4

Suppose you are in the UK and see high clouds moving from south to north. What is the high-level wind direction? Draw a sketch to show whether the nearest centre of low pressure is to the east or west of you.

Question 3.5

Draw a sketch to show the direction of horizontal *surface-level* winds near (a) a low and (b) a high in the Southern Hemisphere, as seen from above.

Wind is a very powerful element of the weather. This section has been concerned with wind at a local level, but on much bigger scales winds move whole weather systems. There are also air circulation patterns that span the globe. The next chapter looks at these large-scale movements of air and the ways in which they determine the weather.

3.3.4 Key points of Section 3.3

Wind and air circulation are extremely important in explaining how weather systems develop and change. In subsequent chapters, you will repeatedly apply the first and third of the following key points, and you will make use of the second one when you carry out your own observations of the weather.

Wind is the horizontal movement of air associated with pressure differences. Wind direction is the direction from which the wind is blowing.

The Beaufort Scale gives an estimate of wind speed on the basis of the observed effect of the wind on the sea or a land environment.

Horizontal winds aloft circulate around areas of high pressure, clockwise in the Northern Hemisphere, anticlockwise in the Southern Hemisphere. Winds close to the surface spiral outwards from high-pressure areas. Horizontal winds aloft circulate around areas of low pressure, anticlockwise in the Northern Hemisphere and clockwise in the Southern Hemisphere. Winds close to the surface spiral inwards into low-pressure areas.

Chapter 4
Weather regimes

In Chapters 2 and 3 the weather was considered on a fairly local scale, in terms of individual properties of the atmosphere that can be monitored at any given spot on the Earth. However, the atmosphere is constantly in motion and constantly changing. Both weather and climate are determined by large-scale processes, in which many factors operate simultaneously. Moreover, the whole of the atmosphere and the whole of the planetary surface are inextricably linked: there are a multitude of interactions between the atmosphere and the Earth's surface, whether that be land or water, mountain or valley, lake or ocean, covered in vegetation or buried under snow and ice. This chapter looks first at the way in which air circulates round the planet, and then at some major weather systems associated with large-scale movements of air.

If you would like to check up in advance where the places mentioned in this chapter are located, the list follows. On this occasion, some of the locations have been grouped into geographical regions to make the searches easier.

- Islands in the Atlantic Ocean: Iceland, North Uist (Outer Hebrides, UK), Azores (west of Portugal)
- Area in the Caribbean and Central America: Caribbean Sea, Sargasso Sea; the islands of Bermuda, Jamaica and Cuba; the countries of Nicaragua, Guatemala, Honduras, El Salvador and Belize; the Yucatan Peninsula in Mexico
- Other countries and regions: India, Saudi Arabia, Siberia (northern Russia)
- Cities: San Francisco (California, USA), Cape Town (South Africa), Perth (Australia), Tokyo (Japan).

4.1 Circulation of the atmosphere

The local winds discussed at the end of Chapter 3 are no more than small eddies within movements of air occurring on a much larger scale. When all this motion is averaged over an extended period of time, then it is possible to see general patterns in the way the atmosphere circulates around the globe. This atmospheric circulation is one of the main ways in which heat is redistributed from hot equatorial regions to cold polar regions (the other involves the large-scale circulation of the oceans). In part, the redistribution takes place through the movement of warm air into cooler latitudes. It also occurs via transport of the latent heat 'locked up' in humid air. As you saw in Chapter 2, this heat is stored in water vapour and released as the water vapour condenses or freezes. In the large-scale patterns of the general circulation, air moves both horizontally and vertically. These movements generate both the distribution of pressure at the Earth's surface and the pattern of prevailing winds, which varies according to latitude.

4.1.1   Circulation cells

The general circulation of the atmosphere is driven by the uneven heating of the Earth, the reasons for which were explored in Chapter 1. In 1735, an English scientist called George Hadley was the first to propose a mechanism for this circulation. His idea is illustrated in Figure 4.1. Warm air rises from the hottest zone near the Equator and flows aloft towards the poles, where it sinks. The air near the surface flows in the opposite direction, towards the Equator. This kind of circulation is called a thermal cell, because the air is visualised as moving in a continuous loop, driven by the temperature difference between the Equator and the poles. Circulation like that shown in Figure 4.1, in which hot air rises and cold air sinks, is called 'direct'. The land and sea breezes you met in Section 2.3.3 are small-scale examples of direct thermal circulation.

Figure 4.1   Cut-away model showing Hadley's mechanism for the circulation of the atmosphere, consisting of two cells, one in each hemisphere. These cells extend to the top of the troposphere, so are deeper at the Equator than at the poles. For clarity, the depth of the troposphere is much exaggerated in relation to the diameter of the Earth. The relative depth of the troposphere at the Equator is also exaggerated compared to its depth at the poles. The Earth's surface features are ignored.

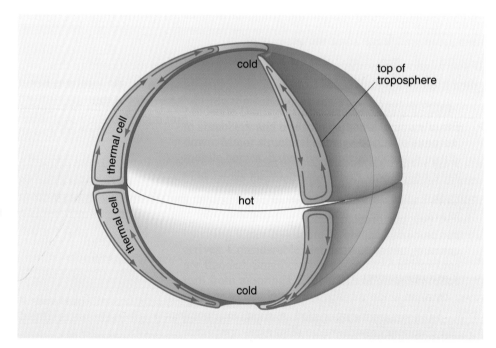

Hadley's model is not actually a very good one for the Earth, because it does not factor in the rotation of the planet. (However, on Venus the atmospheric circulation conforms much better to a simple model like that of Figure 4.1. Although Venus does rotate, it does so only very slowly – so slowly in fact that the day for a single rotation is longer than the year of its orbit round the Sun.)

On the spinning Earth, each of the big cells of Figure 4.1 is broken up, as shown in Figure 4.2. Two cells (one in each hemisphere) operate between the Equator and a latitude of about 30°. These are called Hadley cells, in recognition of Hadley's original concept. Two more cells (again one in each hemisphere) operate between a latitude of about 60° and the poles. These are called the polar cells. In between the Hadley and polar cells, the sinking air around latitude 30° is warmer than the rising air around latitude 60°. Circulation such as this, in which warm air sinks and cold air rises is called 'indirect'. The nineteenth century American meteorologist William Ferrel described the mid-latitude circulation in terms of a single cell in each hemisphere in which air moved Equator-wards aloft and polewards at the surface. It is now understood that mid-latitude circulation is much more complex than this, so on Figure 4.2 the so-called Ferrel cells are shown in a different colour to indicate they are merely a convenient shorthand description of the indirect circulation in the mid-latitudes (corresponding to the net effect of moving weather systems) averaged over time.

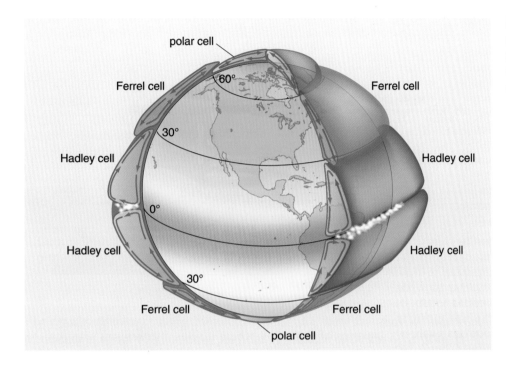

Figure 4.2 A more sophisticated model of the circulation of the atmosphere, with six cells in all (three in each hemisphere).

4.1.2 Global pressure and wind patterns

A closer examination of the model in Figure 4.2 reveals that this six-cell representation explains many of the features of pressure variation, wind direction and precipitation observed at the Earth's surface. Figure 4.3 summarises some of these features. Study it carefully, in conjunction with Figure 4.2 and the following text.

Consider the equatorial regions first. Here the Hadley cells in both hemispheres involve warm and very moist air rising. A zone of relatively low surface pressure can be observed right round the Earth near the Equator. Huge convective clouds produce thunderstorms and tremendous downpours of rain. The latent heat released by the condensation process is converted into other forms of energy that help to drive the circulation within the Hadley cells. The deep convection near the Equator means that the tropopause is raised compared to its height over the poles (as noted in Chapter 2 and in the caption to Figure 4.1). Air rising at the Equator eventually hits the 'lid' of the tropopause and is forced to diverge polewards in both hemispheres. The Coriolis effect results in these flows being deflected to the right in the Northern Hemisphere and to the left in the Southern Hemisphere, so that winds high in the troposphere are westerly in both hemispheres.

A lot of water vapour in the moist air that rises in the equatorial regions condenses into clouds, giving heavy rain near the Equator, and the high-altitude air moving polewards is therefore drier. It continues to move towards the poles

Figure 4.3   Schematic representation of the general circulation of the atmosphere, the major surface winds and the semi-permanent areas of low and high pressure around the Earth. Compare this diagram with Figure 4.2 to appreciate the three-dimensional nature of the circulation cells. The Ferrel cells are indicated by a dotted line for the same reason that in Figure 4.2 they are shown in a different colour to the Hadley and polar cells.

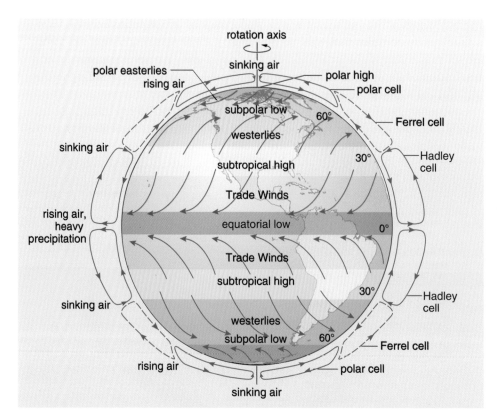

until it approaches latitudes of about 30°, where it sinks. The regions between roughly the Tropic of Cancer and a latitude of about 35° N, and between roughly the Tropic of Capricorn and a latitude of about 35° S are often referred to as the subtropics. Here zones of relatively high pressure can be observed: the so-called subtropical highs are semi-permanent features at these latitudes, moving only a little with the seasons.

◼   How will the temperature of the air change as it sinks in the subtropics? (You might want to check back to Section 2.3.4.)

☐   Sinking air is compressed and warmed.

If the dry air sinks over a subtropical land surface, dry and warm conditions can be expected: as mentioned in Section 2.2, these are the latitudes of some of the planet's largest deserts. Over the subtropical oceans, winds are very light and variable. The zone between 30° and 35° is called the 'horse latitudes'. A possible reason for the name is discussed in Box 4.1. From these zones of high pressure, air near the surface flows back towards the low latitudes, completing the Hadley circulation cell. The Coriolis effect again comes into play, so the flow of air is observed as generally northeasterly winds in the Northern Hemisphere and generally southeasterly winds in the Southern Hemisphere. These are known as the Trade Winds, which are also discussed in Box 4.1. The Trade Winds arise from circulation cells that involve air rising near the Equator and surface air flowing towards the Equator, a situation that applies to the model of Figure 4.1 as well as to that of Figure 4.2. Indeed, one of the great successes of Hadley's original model was that it explained the phenomenon of the Trade Winds.

Box 4.1 Naming the winds

The names of the major surface winds often derive from the days of the large sailing ships.

Sailors were well aware of the problems of trying to make progress in equatorial waters. The region between 5° N and 5° S became known as the 'doldrums' and was a depressing zone for sailors to be. Here the air is rising, rather than blowing horizontally at the surface, so there was no wind to fill their sails. Samuel Taylor Coleridge's *Rime of the Ancient Mariner* described the plight of a ship's company in the doldrums:

> Day after day, day after day,
>
> We stuck, nor breath nor motion;
>
> As idle as a painted ship
>
> Upon a painted ocean.

The term is retained in the expression 'in the doldrums', in its meaning of being gloomy.

Sailors crossing the Atlantic between Europe and North America would also try to avoid the zone between 30° N and 35° N, where they could often get becalmed. It is said that if Spanish vessels carrying horses to the Caribbean islands reached these latitudes and made no progress for a while, then horses would be thrown overboard. This had the dual effect of lightening the cargo so that the ship could move more easily in whatever wind there was, and of conserving drinking water and fodder for the remaining livestock. This zone was therefore referred to as the 'horse latitudes'.

A more positive experience of ocean crossings was obtained if ships took routes at latitudes between the horse latitudes and the doldrums. Here, steady winds of about 12 knots could be expected, blowing from the northeast in the Northern Hemisphere and from the southeast in the Southern Hemisphere. Trading ships could take advantage of these predictable winds, which therefore became known as the Trade Winds.

Not all the air sinking to the Earth's surface near latitudes 30° N and 30° S flows towards the Equator though. Some moves off polewards and this flow, deflected by the Coriolis effect, results in winds that are on average more or less westerly through the mid-latitudes in both hemispheres. The relatively mild surface air travelling towards the poles from the mid-latitudes meets much colder air, an encounter that can occur anywhere between latitudes 70° and 45°.

■ Is the warm air more or less dense than the cold air?

☐ Warm air is less dense.

■ What will happen to the warmer air when it meets the colder air?

☐ It will be forced upwards.

In regions between latitudes of about 50° and 70°, the surface pressure is typically lower than the global average value. These so-called subpolar lows are marked on Figure 4.3. It is in these zones where warm air meets cold air that storms are likely to develop. Some of the rising air moves towards the poles, where it sinks and then flows back towards lower latitudes, completing the circulation of the polar cell. This flow of surface air towards the Equator is deflected by the Coriolis effect to give an airflow that is on average east to west. Surface winds at the higher latitudes are therefore predominantly easterly.

Along the subpolar zone of low surface pressure between the mild westerly airflow of the mid-latitudes and the cold easterlies of high latitudes lies a region called the polar front. The way in which the polar front can move over quite a wide latitudinal range is very important in determining the weather of the mid-latitudes. This will be discussed in more detail in Section 4.3.4.

The picture of general circulation represented by Figure 4.3 is a simplified and averaged one. The surface topography of the Earth, with its oceans, continents and mountains, breaks up this simple model. Figure 4.4 shows the principal features of the time-averaged mean sea-level pressures and wind directions in January and July. This is clearly more complicated than Figure 4.3 suggests. For one thing, the wind directions are more varied than on the simple model of Figure 4.3. The westerly airflow at the surface in the mid-latitudes represents the average situation in both hemispheres, but this is more obvious in the Southern Hemisphere, where ocean covers most of the mid-latitudes, so the flow is not much broken up by surface topography. Locally, anywhere on the Earth, the wind can blow from any direction, although in some places it tends to come more often from a particular direction or to be within a range of directions. If winds come from a particular direction for 50% or more of the time, then this direction defines what is called the 'prevailing wind'. In some locations, the prevailing wind direction is the same throughout the year, although in others (especially those subject to monsoon weather, which will be discussed in Chapter 8) there are clear seasonal differences in the direction of the prevailing wind.

Another obvious set of features in Figure 4.4 are areas of high and low pressure that are present in both summer and winter. As already noted in connection with Figure 4.3, these are called semi-permanent because they persist all year, although they do move slightly with the seasons. The semi-permanent subtropical highs in the Southern Hemisphere which are marked on Figure 4.4 are particularly obvious examples. Other semi-permanent highs and lows show greater seasonal variation: for instance, the Icelandic low is much less extensive in the Northern Hemisphere summer.

Figure 4.4   Regions of high and low mean sea-level pressure (shown red and blue, respectively) and the prevailing winds at the Earth's surface in (a) July and (b) January. Notice in particular: the low near Iceland (visible on both the January and July maps); the high in Siberia (which appears only on the January map); the Azores high (which is far more significant on the July map); and the clear differences in the size and distribution of highs and lows between the Northern and Southern Hemispheres. The continuous dark blue line shows the mean position of the Inter-Tropical Convergence Zone (ITCZ), where the Trade Wind systems of the Northern and Southern Hemispheres meet. (The symbol ≥ means 'equal to or greater than'.)

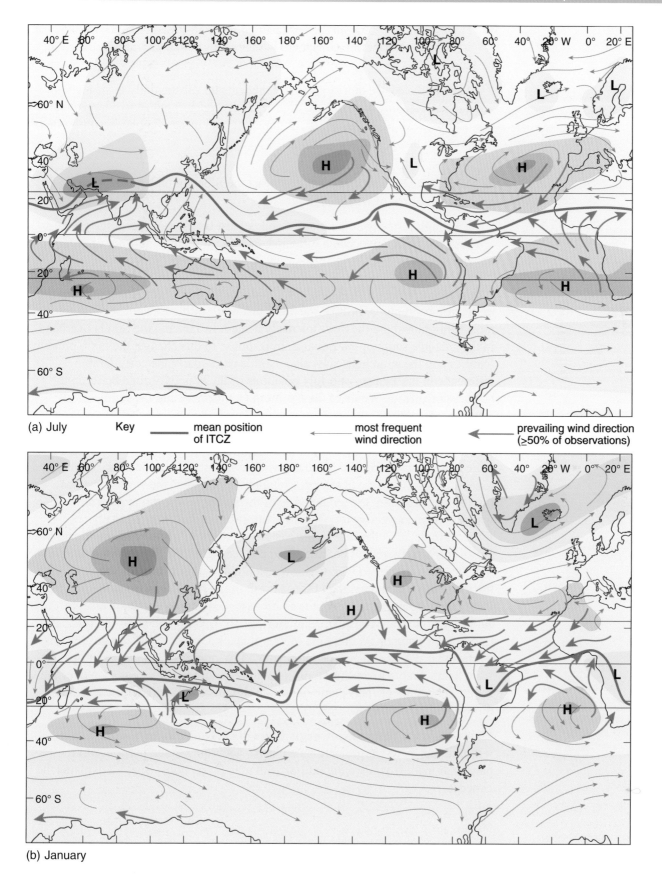

(a) July   Key   ——— mean position of ITCZ   ←— most frequent wind direction   ⇐ prevailing wind direction (≥50% of observations)

(b) January

■ How would you account for the fact that the high-pressure area over the USA in the Northern Hemisphere winter changes to a low-pressure area in summer?

☐ Land at the centre of a large continent heats up substantially in spring and summer, leading to rising air, high-level divergence and so to a large area of low pressure. In winter, the continental land mass is cooler, resulting in a pressure increase at the surface.

■ Suggest an explanation for the fact that the Siberian high is the most extensive area of winter high pressure.

☐ This high forms over the biggest and coldest land mass (it is at the greatest distance from any oceanic influence that might produce warmer or moister air).

If you compare Figures 4.4a and 4.4b, you will see some significant differences in the tropical regions. In July, the areas just north of the Equator receive the most sunlight and are the most intensely heated. In January, the Sun is overhead in the area just south of the Equator. In response to this change, the main pressure features and the wind belts shift also. Notice particularly the considerable difference in the January and July positions of the boundary zone between the northeasterly Trade Winds of the Northern Hemisphere and the southeasterly Trade Winds of the Southern Hemisphere. This boundary is called Inter-Tropical Convergence Zone (ITCZ). Its average position is marked with a dark blue line on the figure. The convergence of air along this boundary results in the ascent of large amounts of warm and generally very moist air to great heights, producing towering clouds and the heavy precipitation that sustains the world's tropical rainforests. However, the temperature of the surface is crucial in determining whether deep convective clouds will form. If the surface is untypically cool for its latitude, as is the case in the eastern equatorial Pacific because of cold ocean currents, there will be little or no convective cloud. Figure 4.4 shows that the position of the ITCZ varies considerably with the time of year and the longitude. In January, the ITCZ is north of the Equator in the eastern Pacific and eastern Atlantic, but is south of the Equator everywhere else. In July (the Northern Hemisphere summer), on the other hand, all of the ITCZ is north of the Equator. At this time of year it takes a major excursion northwards over southern Asia and is associated with a low-pressure area that extends from Saudi Arabia to northeastern India and the summertime monsoon over the Indian subcontinent. This combination of circumstances will be discussed in more detail in Chapter 8.

Figure 4.4 is the first of many maps you will encounter in the course. You will find that different projections are used, according to the purpose of a particular map. If you are unfamiliar with map projections, Box 4.2 explains the concept.

Box 4.2 Map projections

The only way that the Earth's surface can be represented with a uniform scale in all directions is on a globe. Put another way, the Earth must be modelled as a sphere in order for the ratio between a distance portrayed on the model and the equivalent distance on the Earth's surface to be exactly the same in all directions and over all distances. Map projections are methods of showing ('projecting') the Earth's three-dimensional surface in a two-dimensional flat illustration.

Any flat map necessarily distorts some parts of the surface being represented, because the curved surface of a sphere cannot be flattened out without distortion. Some map projections distort all parts of the Earth's surface although only to a moderate extent. Others minimise distortions of some aspects, often at the expense of maximising others. In this course maps are drawn using a variety of projections and scales. Do not be concerned about this. The only requirement is that you should be able to identify the locations and features that are referred to in the text.

Question 4.1

On the basis of the information in Figure 4.4, what would you expect to be the most common wind direction in each of the following cities in January? Are these prevailing winds?

(a) San Francisco (California); (b) Cape Town (South Africa); (c) Perth (southwestern Australia); (d) Tokyo (Japan).

Activity 4.1   'Global circulation and precipitation'

The estimated time for this activity is 30 minutes.

In this activity you will watch an animation that traces out wind patterns round the globe, as shown by the movement of clouds. A whole year of cloud and precipitation activity is represented on this animation.

You will find the detailed instructions for the activity in the Activities section of the course website.

Study comment

In Chapter 2, you tried out various techniques for making notes from the material you study, and you should have continued to use your preferred method for keeping notes as you worked through Chapter 3. You may have found that your notes contained all sorts of different things, perhaps including reminders about important ideas, comments about items you wanted to return to or to discuss with a Study Adviser, and answers to questions. As you work through this chapter, you should try to practise turning some of your notes into short summaries in your own words. This is an excellent way of demonstrating to yourself that you really do understand the material.

Because Section 4.1.3 is fairly short, it is a good section on which to start practising. As you read, note down about half a dozen key words or phrases. Use a separate piece of paper on this occasion, even if you normally make notes in the margin of the book. You may also want to make a few notes on the DVD material that you access at the end of the section.

4.1.3   Jet streams

As well as the prevailing surface winds shown in Figure 4.4, high-level winds have an essential role to play in the general circulation of the atmosphere. In general, wind speed increases with increasing altitude through the troposphere. In certain regions, a strong local flow of air occurs in a narrow band at the tropopause. This is called a jet stream. In some ways, jet streams are similar to fast-flowing rivers, though on a much bigger scale. They are narrow bands of very fast-moving air only a few kilometres deep and a few hundred kilometres wide, which circle the Earth. Like the currents in a river, the winds within a jet stream do not always blow in a straight line, nor do they blow at constant speed. There are lots of eddies, with changes in the direction and speed of the flow. The lower wind-speed limit that defines a jet stream is usually taken to be roughly 90 110 kilometres per hour (50–60 knots), but speeds in the core of the stream are often in excess of 200 kilometres per hour.

The number and exact positions of jet streams vary with time. However, Figure 4.5 illustrates typical positions of two important jet streams in the Northern Hemisphere. The more northerly one occurs at an altitude of about 10 000 m (33 000 ft) and the more southerly at about 13 000 m (43 000 ft). This reflects the increasing height of the tropopause with decreasing latitude. The position of the more northerly jet stream marks the location of the greatest contrast in surface temperature between cold air to the north and warmer air to the south. This is also the region of the polar front, so the northerly jet stream is called the polar jet stream (or sometimes simply 'the polar jet'). The temperature difference across the polar front is at its greatest in the winter, when the air to the north is at its coldest, and that is when the jet stream is at its strongest. Above South Uist in the Outer Hebrides, an astonishing polar jet speed of 656 kilometres per hour was recorded on 11 December 1967.

The more southerly stream shown in Figure 4.5 is associated with the subtropical high and is therefore known as the subtropical jet stream. The polar and subtropical jet streams have their counterparts in the Southern Hemisphere and there are other seasonal jet streams that form over large land masses.

Jet streams wander right round the globe and therefore have a major role to play in the global transport of heat (and atmospheric pollutants). Their general direction is west to east, due to the rotation of the Earth. Commercial aircraft make use of this, since if they can 'hitch a ride' on a jet stream it saves both fuel and time. It is noticeable that flight times from the UK to the USA are longer than they are in the opposite direction. However, the direction of jet streams is not exclusively westerly. As shown in Figure 4.5, they take a meandering course and, while the path of the subtropical jet stream is geographically fairly fixed, the polar jet stream is particularly prone to taking loops northwards or southwards. You will see in Chapter 7 why the position of these loops can have a profound effect on the weather in northern Europe and the USA. However, one such effect can be understood directly from Figure 4.4a. If the polar jet stream passes well

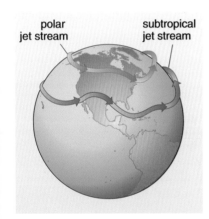

polar
jet stream

subtropical
jet stream

Figure 4.5   Typical positions of the polar and subtropical jet streams in the Northern Hemisphere as they meander in a wavy pattern from west to east. The polar jet stream marks the greatest temperature difference at the surface between cold air to the north and milder air to the south.

to the north of the UK in the summer, then this means that there is warm air covering the country. In that situation, the Azores high may extend northwards and eastwards, bringing settled weather to western Europe.

Now look at the first three video clips in the Jet Stream section of the DVD. You may want to make a few notes as you watch.

Study comment

Now *close the book* and using your notes on this section try to write a paragraph of four or five sentences that encapsulates the main ideas. Title your paragraph 'summary of section on jet streams' and keep it carefully until you have worked through the rest of the chapter. Continue to keep notes as you study the chapter, as you will be asked to write further summaries later.

4.2   Air mass weather

Mid-latitude weather is characterised above all by its variability. The mid-latitudes are areas where cold air from the high latitudes meets warm air from the tropics and where dry air meets moist air. The areas in which these encounters take place are called fronts, or frontal systems, and they can produce many different kinds of weather, often in quick succession. Frontal weather is the subject of Section 4.3, but in order to understand how it arises it is essential first to appreciate what large-scale lateral movements of air occur. This section therefore examines weather regimes in which the dominant feature is the arrival over a region of a large and fairly uniform body of air.

4.2.1   Air masses

What meteorologists call an air mass is formed when a body of air remains stationary over a fairly uniform part of the Earth's surface for long enough to acquire fairly uniform properties of temperature and humidity from that surface. An air mass is distinguished from the 'air parcels' you met in Chapter 2 by its sheer size: air masses may cover thousands, or even millions, of square kilometres and they extend vertically up through the entire troposphere. Within an air mass, the temperature and humidity at a given altitude are largely unchanged for hundreds of kilometres in any horizontal direction, although there will be slight variations depending on the air mass's internal structure of clouds and precipitation. The lateral movements of these huge bodies of air and, especially, of the boundaries between them are responsible for the distinctive weather patterns of the mid-latitudes.

The surface area of the Earth from which an air mass obtains its properties is called its source region. Since air masses have fairly uniform characteristics, they are necessarily formed over areas that are similarly uniform: source regions are typically fairly flat, uniformly composed of either ocean or land, and have only light winds at the surface. For an air mass to obtain its temperature and humidity from the Earth's surface requires prolonged contact, because the processes involving the transfer of heat and moisture to such a large amount of air take place relatively slowly. It might, for example, require several days or even weeks for an air mass to warm up not just near the surface but right the way up through the troposphere. The main source regions are therefore areas that are so placed in the general circulation of the atmosphere that they are covered by more or less stationary high-pressure systems (lows rarely remain in one place for long). The air may circulate around the high, but remains temporarily trapped by it rather than moving on with global-scale circulation.

■ On this basis, where are the ideal source regions for air masses? (Look back at Figure 4.3 and 4.4 for some clues.)

☐ The main high-pressure areas are the subtropics, the polar regions, and the fairly high-latitude continental areas in the Northern Hemisphere where large high-pressure areas develop in winter.

The mid-latitudes are areas into which air masses from both polar and subtropical regions can move. It is the interaction of very different types of air masses moving in from different directions that produces the typically variable weather of the mid-latitudes.

The properties that an air mass obtains from its source region can be deduced from the characteristics of the surface over which it is formed. The air mass can be dry or moist, warm or cold, stable or unstable.

■ Which source regions will produce dry air masses?

☐ Air masses with source regions over land will be relatively dry.

Conversely, air masses that have formed over an ocean always have high humidity, especially in their lower layers.

■ Which source regions will give rise to warm air masses?

☐ Air masses originating from tropical source regions will be warm.

Air masses from source regions in the high latitudes, on the other hand, will be cold.

■ Remembering what you learned in Chapter 2 about the stability of the atmospheric environment, will an air mass with a base that is colder than its surroundings be stable or unstable?

☐ An air mass that is colder at its base than the surrounding air will be stable.

The large-scale circulation of the atmosphere, and the smaller-scale air movements within it, mean that, although air masses are initially fairly stationary, they do not remain so for very long. Eventually they move, usually in response to high-level winds. Once an air mass leaves its source region, it can move over long distances and it can be modified by the nature of the surface over which it passes. Several types of process can bring about this modification, as summarised in Figure 4.6.

■ In the scenario of Figure 4.6c, what effect will the modification of the temperature of the air mass have on its stability?

☐ The air mass is being warmed from below and its lower layers therefore become more unstable.

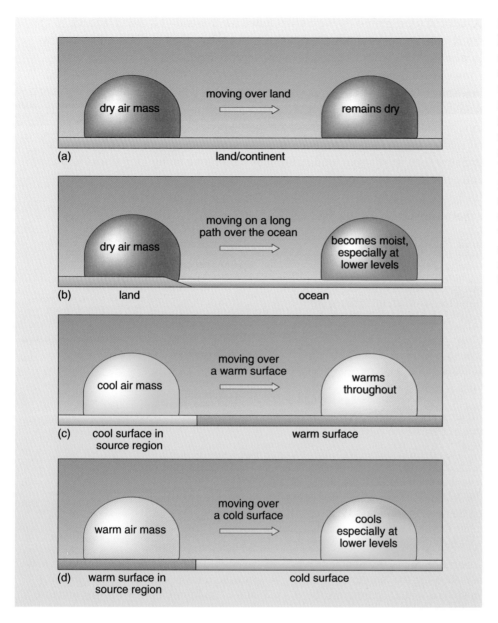

Figure 4.6   The changes in humidity and temperature of an air mass as it moves over different types of surface. (a) An initially dry air mass moving across a continent will remain dry. (b) A dry or slightly moist air mass moving across an ocean will pick up moisture at lower levels due to evaporation from the water surface. (c) A cool air mass moving over a warm surface will be warmed from below. (d) A warm air mass moving over a cold surface will be cooled from below.

As the air warmed by contact with the surface rises, the heating effect is spread up through the atmosphere by convection to a considerable height. If the air is moist, this can result in the formation of deep convective clouds, with the possibility of showers of rain or snow. In the scenario of Figure 4.6d, on the other hand, the cooling from below means that there is little or no convection and the cooling effect takes place only in the lowest layers. If the air is moist, very low cloud or fog may form.

As an air mass moves away from the conditions of its source region and is modified by changing surface conditions, it gradually loses its uniform identity. Finally, its features and characteristic weather phenomena are dissipated and it merges with surrounding air.

Air masses are classified into types on the basis of two aspects of their source region. First they are defined in terms of their latitude of origin and given a capital letter to indicate this. From low to high latitudes the categories are equatorial (designated by the capital letter E), tropical (T), polar (P) and arctic/antarctic (A and AA respectively). Secondly, they are classed according to whether their source region is over ocean or land, and this is indicated by a lower-case letter. Air masses with a source region over the ocean are called maritime (designated by the lower-case letter m), while those originating over land are termed continental (c). All equatorial air masses are maritime. There are thus seven basic types of air mass, as shown in Table 4.1 and Figure 4.7. Some air masses retain their classification for as long as they endure, but others can undergo such substantial modification as they move along long tracks that they end up being reclassified.

Table 4.1 Classification and major characteristics of air masses.

Air mass	Source region	Temperature and humidity
Equatorial maritime (Em)	Equatorial oceans	Very warm and very moist
Tropical maritime (Tm)	Subtropical oceans: Atlantic, Pacific and Indian Oceans to about latitude 40° N and 40° S	Warm and moist
Tropical continental (Tc)	Subtropical hot land masses. Permanent sources are North Africa, Arabia and central Australia. Summer-only sources include a wide belt of Eurasia eastwards from the Mediterranean, Mexico and a small area over Argentina. A winter-only source is a small area over southeast Africa	Warm and relatively dry in winter. Hot and dry in summer
Polar maritime (Pm)	A permanent zone in the Southern Hemisphere between 40° S and 60° S. In the Northern Hemisphere, arises most often by modification of a Pc air mass that has moved in a long sea track across the Atlantic or Pacific	Mild to cold, and moist
Polar continental (Pc)	No source region in the Southern Hemisphere. In the Northern Hemisphere, winter sources are the Canadian and Siberian highs (these are much weaker in summer)	Very cold and generally dry. If the air mass moves over open water the temperature and humidity of its lower layers increase and it becomes Pm
Arctic/antarctic maritime (Am/AAm)	Arctic Ocean in summer. In the Southern Hemisphere all the oceans below 60° S	Cold (colder than Pm) and fairly moist (less moist than Pm)
Arctic/antarctic continental (Ac/AAc)	Frozen Arctic in winter (does not exist in the Northern Hemisphere in the summer). Antarctic ice cap	Very cold and very dry

At first sight it may seem surprising that polar air masses are *less* cold than arctic ones. The reason becomes clear if you look carefully at the source regions shown in Figure 4.7. In the Northern Hemisphere, for example, the source regions for polar air masses are at latitudes around or below the Arctic Circle (66° N), whereas arctic air masses originate directly over the pack-ice areas of the Arctic Ocean (75–90° N). It is a quirk of the nomenclature that the air masses with source regions nearest the poles have been called arctic/antarctic, rather than polar!

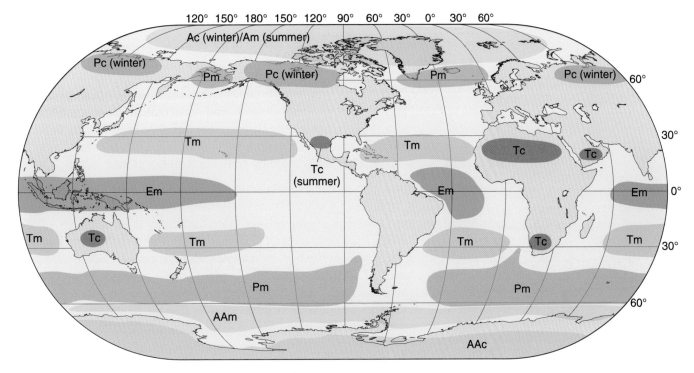

Figure 4.7 Map of the main source regions of global air masses.

Study comment

Practise the same technique as before to write a summary paragraph about air masses. Again four or five sentences should be sufficient to summarise Section 4.2.1. Give your summary a title and keep it safe.

4.2.2 How do air masses affect the weather?

In seeking to understand the weather systems of a particular area in the mid-latitudes, the first step is to discover what air masses affect it in different seasons of the year. In this section you will explore the influence of air masses on the weather of two very different areas in the Northern Hemisphere: the British Isles and the USA.

Situated at the Atlantic edge of Northern Europe, the British Isles experience five different types of air mass, and each brings different weather scenarios. The directions from which these air masses approach are shown in Figure 4.8.

A **tropical maritime** (Tm) air mass reaching the British Isles will have its source region in the warm Sargasso Sea area of the mid-Atlantic between Bermuda and the Azores (as shown in Figure 4.7) and therefore comes on a southwesterly airstream. Like all tropical maritime air, it is warm, moist and conditionally unstable, but as it moves northeastwards towards northern Europe it passes over slightly cooler parts of the ocean.

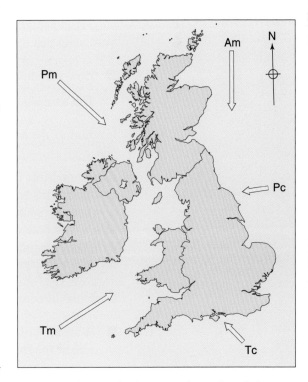

Figure 4.8 Typical approach tracks of air masses that can affect the British Isles.

■ What effect will this have on the temperature and stability of the air mass?

☐ The temperature will be decreased a little in the lower layers, making the air more stable.

The air mass may pick up even more moisture as it moves across the ocean, and this, coupled with the slight lowering of temperature may mean that it becomes saturated. A tropical maritime air mass reaching the British Isles therefore brings warm or mild and very moist air to windward coasts, with low cloud or fog. Drizzle or rain will affect west-facing areas as the air is lifted by coasts and higher ground inland.

Tropical continental (Tc) air comes to Atlantic Europe from North Africa and the Sahara on mainly southeasterly winds. It may affect the British Isles at any time between March and October, though it arrives more commonly in the summer months. Tropical continental air can result in unseasonably warm spells in spring and heat waves in the summer. The highest summer temperatures, including the record-breaking levels of 2003 mentioned in Chapter 1, occur under the influence of tropical continental air masses. Tropical continental air often picks up dust and sand in North Africa and various pollutants as it travels over Europe, so its arrival brings a reduction in air quality and sometimes also in visibility.

The arrival of **polar continental** (Pc) air in the British Isles is solely a winter phenomenon. With a source region over the winter snow cover in Russia and eastern Europe, polar continental air comes in on predominantly easterly winds. Close to the source region, the air is very cold, very dry and stable. The lowest winter temperatures occur under the influence of polar continental air masses that have reached the British Isles more or less unmodified. When this happens, the weather is clear, with very cold nights giving rise to severe frosts. However, if a polar continental air mass follows a longer sea track (down the North Sea), it passes over water that is warmer than the original air.

■ How will this affect its stability?

☐ The air mass will be warmed from below, making it less stable.

In addition, the air will pick up moisture, so it becomes likely to produce snow or rain.

Polar maritime (Pm) air arrives in the British Isles most directly on a northwesterly airstream. This type of air mass initially has continental characteristics (cold and dry) because source regions lie over Greenland and northern Canada, but it covers such a long path over the North Atlantic that by the time it reaches western Europe it is classed as maritime in nature. There is a considerable difference in temperature between the original air mass and the ocean, so once the air is over the Atlantic it warms very quickly and becomes unstable to a considerable height, with the formation of convective clouds.

■ What kind of summer weather will a polar maritime air mass bring to the western side of the British Isles?

☐ Unstable moist air with deep convective clouds will result in heavy rain showers.

Polar maritime air sometimes follows an initially more southerly track over the Atlantic before returning northwards. (In some classification schemes this type of air mass is given a separate category of 'returning polar maritime'.) During its passage south it becomes warmer, moister and very unstable, but once it turns northwards it passes over cooler water. The bottom-most layers are therefore cooled from below, making it more stable at lower levels, though it remains warmer and unstable aloft. This temperature inversion acts like a 'lid' to the tops of clouds, so the weather is usually fairly dry, with only occasional showers, though there may be quite extensive stratocumulus cloud. This type of air mass brings the British Isles their most gentle weather.

Arctic maritime (Am) air does not usually reach the British Isles in the summer, although if it does it will bring abnormally cold weather. Arctic maritime air comes in on a northerly wind and is similar to polar maritime air though it is both colder and less moist because it has covered a much shorter distance over the sea. Like polar maritime air arriving in the winter, it may initially have had continental characteristics, having a source region over frozen pack ice, but develops maritime qualities as it crosses the ocean. Between autumn and spring, arctic maritime air is cold enough and moist enough to produce hail and snow over north-facing coasts and much of mainland Scotland.

Figure 4.9 shows the source regions and initial direction of movement of the main air masses that affect North America. Question 4.2 invites you to try to predict what kinds of weather these air masses might bring to different parts of the USA.

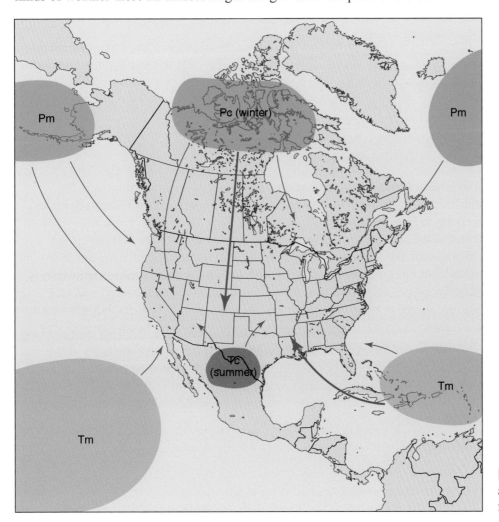

Figure 4.9   Source regions and typical paths of the main air masses affecting North America.

Question 4.2

Figure 4.9 shows that the source region for polar continental air is over the ice- and snow-covered regions of northern Canada. Suppose a polar continental air mass follows the path marked with a bold blue arrow, over the central plains of the USA.

(a) Describe this polar continental air in terms of its temperature, humidity and stability, briefly explaining your answer.

(b) As this air mass invades the centre of the USA, will high or low pressure become established over the area and why?

(c) If this air mass follows this southward path in winter, what kind of weather will it bring to these central areas and why?

(d) What differences might be expected if the air mass followed a similar track in the summer?

Question 4.3

Explain briefly why a tropical maritime air mass following the path marked with a bold red arrow in Figure 4.9 during the summer months would bring muggy conditions with afternoon rain.

Although knowledge of the source region and subsequent track of an air mass is an important part of weather forecasting, it gives only a general indication of the likely weather conditions. The boundary zones between air masses are where the real weather action takes place. These zones, called 'fronts', are the subject of Section 4.3.

4.3   Frontal weather

A huge leap forward in scientists' understanding of weather patterns in the mid-latitudes was made by a group of meteorologists, led by Vilhelm Bjerknes, working in Bergen during and just after the First World War. From their research emerged the idea that most unsettled weather arises in the regions where air masses meet. By analogy with First World War terminology for the line between opposing armies, Bjerknes called the zone of conflict between two air masses a 'front'.

Since air masses are defined by their temperature and humidity, a front is necessarily a transition zone between air masses that have different temperatures, or different humidities, or both. This implies that air on opposite sides of the front will also have different densities. Along the frontal zone (which extends vertically as well as horizontally), warm, less dense air will rise above colder, more dense air. There are several types of front, and each type brings different weather conditions.

4.3.1   Cold fronts

A cold front occurs when cold air is moving in to replace warm air at the surface. This situation is represented in Figure 4.10. As the dense cold air advances, it undercuts the warmer air mass, so the less dense warm air is pushed upwards.

This is rather similar to the process of lifting by convergence that you met in Chapter 2. If the warm air is moist and unstable, condensation occurs as it rises, producing cumulonimbus clouds. A fairly narrow band of heavy showers (about 50 km wide in the example illustrated in Figure 4.10) forms just behind the cold front. If there are strong winds aloft, the icy tops of the cumulonimbus may be pushed ahead of the front, forming cirrostratus and cirrus clouds. If the cold air is drier behind the front, there are usually no more than a few fair-weather cumulus.

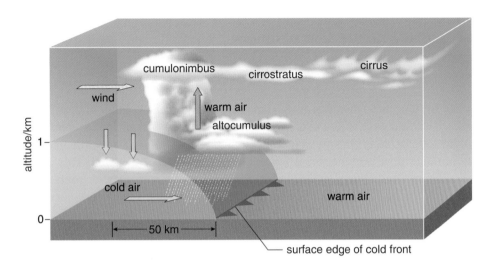

Figure 4.10 Cloud formation at a typical cold front. Note that the horizontal and vertical scales on this diagram are not the same. The vertical scale has been greatly exaggerated by comparison with the horizontal scale in order to show the shape of the front while still fitting the diagram on the page.

The situation depicted in Figure 4.10 is typical of a fairly fast-moving cold front, advancing at about 40 kilometres per hour. A distance of 50 km back from its surface edge (i.e. its boundary on the Earth's surface), the front is about 1 km high. This is succinctly described by saying that the slope of the front is '1 in 50', which would usually be written as 1 : 50. (In fact the slope is steeper than this at the surface edge of the front, since the front itself is curved, but 1 : 50 describes it adequately over the distance that it takes to flatten out.) A slope of between 1 : 50 and 1 : 75 is usual for cold fronts.

■ In Figure 4.10, how far ahead of the surface edge of the front is the furthest extent of the cirrus cloud?

☐ About 100 km.

■ If the front continues to advance at the same speed, how long after the appearance of cirrus cloud above a location will the main rain band arrive at that location?

☐ The time taken to cover 100 km at 40 kilometres per hour is $\dfrac{100}{40}$ hours, so the front will take about two and a half hours to arrive.

Figure 4.10 illustrates a fairly 'typical' cold front, but in practice no two fronts are identical.

If the winds aloft are not strong, virtually no high cloud will be blown ahead of the front. Instead, low cloud will appear not long before the surface edge of the front arrives, with rain starting almost immediately. If the warm air mass ahead of the front is moist but stable, then deep convective clouds do not form. Instead, the warm air pushed upwards along the edge of the front produces low-level stratus clouds and a large area behind the front is affected by persistent drizzle or even fog. If, on the other hand, the warm air is very dry, few if any clouds form and the most obvious sign that a cold front has passed through will be a drop in the temperature. Another difference between cold fronts is that they move at different speeds. Indeed some move so slowly (at less than 5 kilometres per hour) that they are described as stationary. A cold front that advances very slowly into moist unstable warm air often results in a considerable build-up of cumulonimbus cloud, with heavy and persistent rain or snow.

4.3.2 Warm fronts

A warm front occurs when warm air is moving in to replace cold air at the surface. This situation is illustrated in Figure 4.11. The warm air is less dense than the cold air, so it rides up over the cold air. This overriding of warm air above cold air results in the formation of clouds far ahead of the front. This 'frontal lifting' (which as you saw in Section 4.3.1 also occurs at cold fronts) is the fourth method by which air can be lifted to form clouds.

Figure 4.11 Cloud formation at a warm front. As in Figure 4.10, the horizontal and vertical scales on this diagram are not the same. Notice also that both the horizontal and vertical distances represented here are longer than in Figure 4.10.

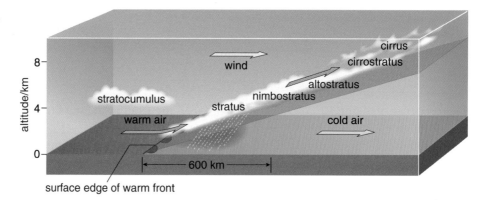

■ Three other methods of lifting were highlighted in Section 3.1.3. What were they?

☐ Surface heating leading to convection, convergence of air at the surface, and orographic lifting.

Now look at the horizontal and vertical distances represented in Figure 4.11. You have seen that the slope of a cold front is typically between 1 : 50 and 1 : 75.

■ Using the same notation, what is the slope of the warm front shown in Figure 4.11?

☐ The front is about 3 km high at locations 600 km forward of its surface edge Therefore it is 1 km high about 200 km forward of its surface edge. So the slope is roughly 1 : 200.

This is fairly typical. The slopes of warm fronts are usually in the range between 1 : 100 and 1 : 200, with an average of 1 : 150.

■ How does this compare with the typical slope of a cold front?

□ It is about a third to half as steep. {For a cold front a vertical height of 1 km would correspond to about 50–75 km along the ground. For a warm front a vertical height of 1 km would correspond to 150 km along the ground on average, which is two to three times the distance.}

Because the warm air is lifted along a very long horizontal distance, clouds are formed well ahead of the surface edge of a warm front, and precipitation occurs over a much larger area than is the case for a cold front. In Figure 4.11, high-level cloud occurs about 1200 km ahead of the surface edge. The lifting is more gradual along a warm front than a cold one, so the clouds are not as deep. Compared to the heavy showers associated with the cumulonimbus of a cold front, precipitation along a warm front is typically less heavy, but more continuous and longer lasting. In the situation shown in Figure 4.11, as the front gets closer the clouds become both thicker and lower. Rain starts a few hundred kilometres ahead of the front's surface edge. Precipitation is light or moderate, being heaviest close to the surface edge of the front, and stops almost as soon as the surface edge passes, although some light rain or drizzle may still occur in patches.

The typical speed of an advancing warm front is considerably less than that of a cold front.

■ If the front in Figure 4.11 is travelling at a steady 20 kilometres per hour, how long after the first appearance of high cloud will the surface edge arrive?

□ High cloud first appears about 1200 km ahead of the surface edge, so if the front is moving at 20 kilometres per hour, it will arrive after:

$$\frac{1200 \text{ kilometres}}{20 \text{ kilometres per hour}} = 60 \text{ hours (about two and a half days).}$$

In fact, warm fronts are less likely than cold fronts to move at a constant speed. Night-time cooling of the surface layers of the warmer air mass can increase the air density and this reduces both the lifting and the horizontal movement of the frontal edge. Over a period of several days and nights, warm fronts therefore often move forward rather jerkily.

As is the case for cold fronts, warm fronts are not all alike. If the warm air mass is very dry, little cloud will form and there will be no precipitation, so the front is hardly worthy of the name. Thus the classical pattern of a warm front is not seen in Australia, because the continental warm air mass is so dry that it simply does not produce cloud and rain.

4.3.3 Occluded fronts

Occluded fronts (more usually called simply occlusions) occur because, as you have seen, cold fronts move horizontally at a greater speed than warm fronts and eventually catch them up. There are then three air masses involved: the original cold and warm ones either side of the warm front, and the additional cold one that has overtaken them. Different types of occlusion occur, depending on whether the newest air mass is colder or less cold than the air that was originally ahead of the warm front. Figure 4.12a illustrates the situation in which the fast-moving cold front brings the coldest air. This is termed a cold occlusion.

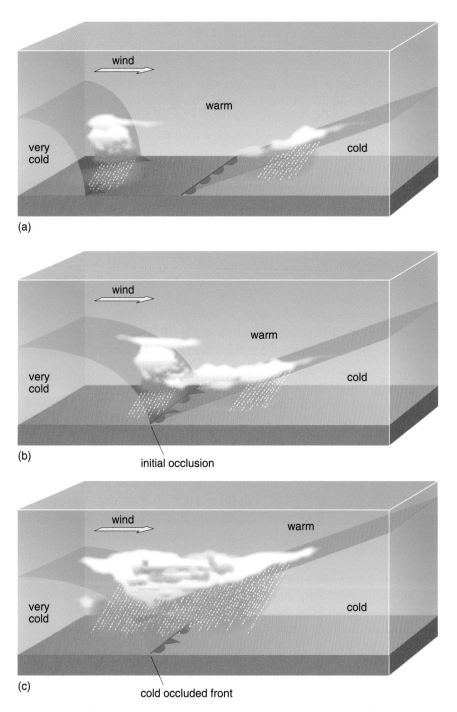

(a)

(b)

initial occlusion

(c)

cold occluded front

Figure 4.12   The formation of a cold occlusion (i.e. a cold occluded front). See text for explanation.

Being the coldest of the three air masses, and hence the most dense, this incoming cold air undercuts both the warm air and the cool air, with the result that the warm air is pushed upwards high above the ground (Figure 4.12c). The weather sequence in advance of the occlusion is essentially that associated with the warm front, so precipitation occurs ahead of the surface edge of the front. Once the occlusion arrives, however, it brings weather more typical of a cold front, with heavy showers. The most extreme weather usually occurs just at the point of the occlusion (Figure 4.12b), because that is where the temperature difference between the cold and the warm air is at a maximum and therefore where the warm air is lifted most rapidly.

If, on the other hand, the air behind the overtaking cold front is *less* cold than that ahead of the warm front, then what is called a warm occlusion is formed. This situation is illustrated in Figure 4.13. Here, the incoming cool air (Figure 4.13a) is less dense than the original cold air mass, so cannot undercut it. The cool air undergoes frontal lifting above the cold air, and pushes the warm air ahead of it, as shown in Figure 4.13b. The weather associated with a warm occlusion is therefore very similar to that resulting from a warm front.

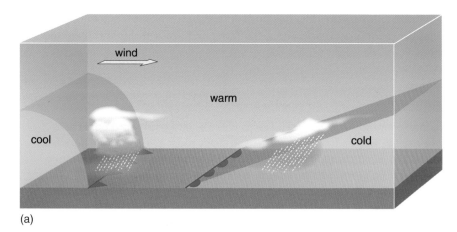

(a)

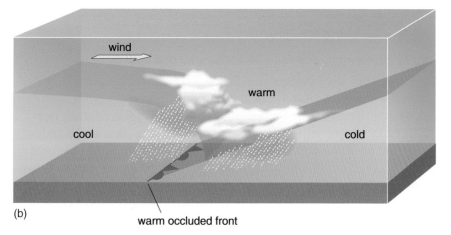

(b)
                    warm occluded front

Figure 4.13   The formation of a warm occlusion (i.e. a warm occluded front). See text for explanation.

93

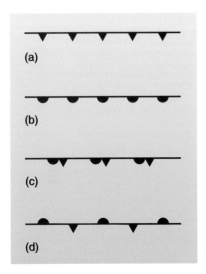

Figure 4.14 Symbols for various types of front. (For use with Question 4.4.)

In each of the Figures 4.10–4.13, you may have noticed that the demarcation line between the air masses at ground level (in other words the surface edge of the front) has been indicated by a line with triangles or semicircles or both. These frontal symbols may already be familiar to you from the surface pressure charts that accompany many weather forecasts. If so, you will be aware that fronts do not usually have straight surface edges along their whole length. Each of the Figures 4.10–4.13 shows only a very small section of a front, for which the surface edge is almost a straight line. In reality a frontal edge may stretch for tens or hundreds of kilometres in a curve or a wavy line. Note that the triangles and semicircles are on the side of the line *towards which* the front is moving. Fronts thus move in a direction that is perpendicular to their surface edge. These symbols were devised in 1924 by Tor Bergeron, another meteorologist in the Bergen group, whose name you have already encountered in relation to precipitation processes.

Question 4.4

Figure 4.14 shows four sets of symbols used to denote fronts. Write next to each one the type of front it represents. (Hint: The type shown in (d), which has symbols on both sides of the line, has not appeared on any previous diagrams. Recall what the symbols tell you about the movement of a front, and then deduce what kind of front (d) might represent.)

Study comment

Now try a more ambitious summary. Try to write a paragraph entitled 'Fronts'. You should explain what a front is, how a cold front most significantly differs from a warm front, and what causes the formation of occluded fronts. This is a more difficult task than the previous summaries, because you are trying to cover a longer section of text. Don't be tempted to write a long essay! Try to condense the really key points into between six and ten sentences. Keep this summary along with the others.

Activity 4.2 'Reading the sky'

The estimated time for this activity is 30 minutes to one hour.

In Activity 3.1 you practised recognising clouds and classifying them according to their genus. As Figures 4.10 and 4.11 show, when a front approaches and then passes over, different types of cloud will succeed, and often overlap, one another. In this activity you will see pictures of 'cloudscapes' in which clouds of several genera are present together, and will further develop your skill in cloud identification. You will put this skill to use shortly, when you carry out your own observations.

You will find the detailed instructions for the activity in the Activities section of the course website.

4.3.4   Frontal depressions

A type of low-pressure region that is characteristic of the mid-latitudes is the 'depression', where the area of low surface pressure is roughly circular or oval and the winds spiral in towards the centre. (This kind of low was illustrated in Figure 3.16a.) Most mid-latitude depressions have a diameter of between 1500 and 3000 km, and a lifespan of between 4 and 7 days. One of the major achievements of the meteorologists of the Bergen group was the first explanation of the life cycle of mid-latitude depressions.

Figure 4.15 shows the various stages of a depression. The first signs of its development begin in (a) at a stationary front, with cold air on one side of the front and warm air on the other, both blowing parallel to the front but in opposite directions. Then a bulge forms on the front (b). The front can develop several such bulges and because of their shape is then called a frontal wave. The winds develop into a continuous anticlockwise circulation (c) and distinct cold and warm fronts form. (Note that Figure 4.15 refers to the Northern Hemisphere. In the Southern Hemisphere the circulation would be clockwise.) The whole system moves (typically northeastwards). As you have seen, the cold front will move more quickly than the warm one, gradually catching it up, so an occlusion begins to form (d). The depression is usually deepest (i.e. has the lowest pressure at its centre) in the period of 12–24 hours following the initial occlusion. Thereafter the depression gradually dissipates as the region between the cold and warm front shrinks (e), until there is cold air on both sides of the occlusion. The 'triangular' region covered by the warm air is called the 'warm sector'. In stages (c)–(e) this gradually moves further and further away from the centre of the low.

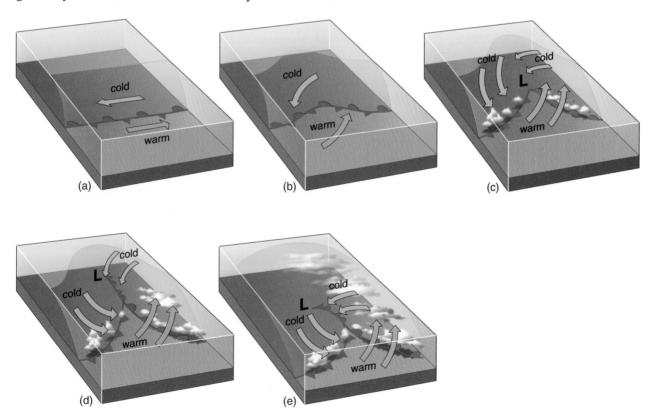

Figure 4.15   Stages in the development of a mid-latitude depression in the Northern Hemisphere. The arrows show wind directions as seen from above, and the various stages (a)–(e) are described in the text.

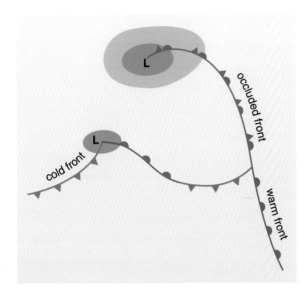

Figure 4.16 Plan view of a distortion on the trailing cold front behind an occluding depression, which will develop into a secondary depression.

Where there is one depression, another is often waiting in the wings. The cold front can stretch back a long way from a depression. So-called 'secondary' depressions frequently form on such a trailing cold front behind a depression that is already occluding. Figure 4.16 shows the process. A secondary depression is usually smaller in extent than its parent, but often deeper (i.e. more vigorous) and faster moving. In fact, depressions frequently occur in families of three or four along a long trailing frontal wave.

The Bergen meteorologists first associated this kind of serial development of depressions with the Atlantic polar front.

■ How was the polar front described in Sections 4.1.2 and 4.1.3?

☐ The region of the polar front was defined as a zone of low surface pressure between the predominantly westerly winds of the mid-latitudes and the easterlies of the high latitudes, i.e. it marks the edge of the polar circulation cell. It is also a boundary zone where there is a marked temperature difference (particularly in winter) between cold air masses to the north and warmer air masses to the south.

The region of the polar front is also associated with the polar jet stream. The abnormally high rainfall in parts of England during the summer of 2007, which was highlighted in Chapters 1 and 3, was attributed to the polar jet looping further south than usual across the North Atlantic, 'steering' a succession of depressions across the UK. You will meet this scenario again in Activity 7.1.

The polar front does not have a monopoly on depressions though. There are many other major zones in which frontal waves and depressions develop, as shown for the Northern Hemisphere in Figure 4.17. For obvious reasons these are often referred to as frontal zones.

Not all depressions have their origin in frontal waves and non-frontal depressions can develop in a number of ways in the mid- and high latitudes. However, the most dramatic type of non-frontal depression – the hurricane – occurs in the tropics. This is the main subject of Section 4.4

Activity 4.3   Observing the weather

The estimated time for this activity is three hours, distributed over one or two days.

In this activity you will make notes about your observations of the sky as a weather system approaches and passes your location. To give yourself the best possible chance of having an interesting weather system to observe, you should access the guidelines for this activity in the Activities section of the course website as soon you have completed Section 4.3.

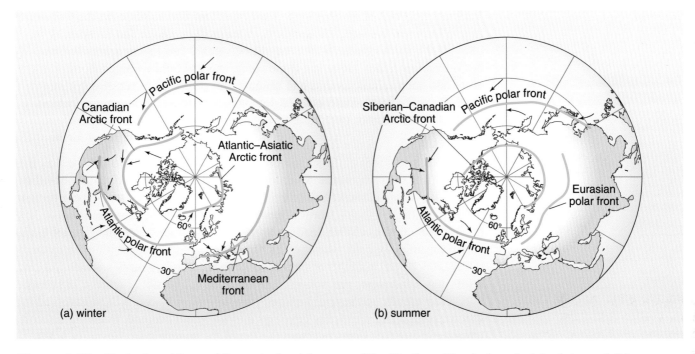

Figure 4.17   Typical positions of the main frontal zones of the Northern Hemisphere in (a) winter and (b) summer.

4.4   Convective weather

In the tropical regions between 23.4° N and 23.4° S of the Equator, climate and weather are very different from those of the mid-latitudes. As discussed in Chapter 1, day length varies much less over the course of a year in the tropics, the Sun is always high in the sky at noon, and there is relatively little seasonal change in temperature. Along coasts, the daily heating of the land can result in sea and land breezes being a regular feature. Tropical areas generally have high humidity, because high temperatures lead to a lot of evaporation. The strong daily heating and the humidity frequently lead to the formation of convective clouds, although precipitation often occurs in distinct 'rainy seasons' associated with the migration of the ITCZ that was illustrated in Figure 4.4. In general, tropical weather systems are less well understood than mid-latitude frontal systems, but because of their awesome destructive power major storm systems in the tropics have been much studied.

4.4.1   Tropical cyclones

Storm systems born in the tropics are the most costly weather-related disasters for coastal areas in and near the tropics. These storms go by different names in different parts of the world: typhoons in Southeast Asia and Japan, tropical cyclones in Australia, and hurricanes in Central America, the Caribbean and the USA. The international agreement among meteorologists is that all such systems originating over tropical oceans are called tropical cyclones, so that is the term generally used in this course. However, the local terms are retained for describing individual storms, such as 'Hurricane Katrina'.

Various categories of weather system may be identified as stages in the formation of a full tropical cyclone. The smallest, in terms of both size and lifespan, is the individual cumulus cloud, which may be between 1 and 10 km across and may last only a few hours. However, if the conditions are right cumulus clouds can grow into deep cumulonimbus and become grouped into clusters. Such cloud clusters may be many hundreds of kilometres in diameter. Some cloud clusters persist for just a day or two, but a few develop into an organised system.

The keys to the growth of a cluster into a full-scale tropical cyclone are convergence of winds at the surface, the outflow of air at altitude and the way the system spins about its centre. A vertical cross-section of the air circulation within a tropical cyclone is shown in Figure 4.18, which shows the organised convection that is essential for such a storm to develop. This allows the rapid build-up of huge cumulonimbus clouds, leading to heavy rain or thunderstorms. The air aloft, which was initially cold, warms quickly because condensation within the clouds releases enormous amounts of latent heat. The surrounding air is warmed, making it less dense and hence promoting more vigorous convection. Figure 4.18 shows only a few clouds, but several hundred cumulonimbus towers will be involved in a storm system that ultimately develops into a tropical cyclone. Once the air aloft warms and more air flows out from the top of the system than converges at the surface, the surface pressure at the centre of the system is reduced. The lowest surface pressure is always at this centre, the region known as the eye.

Figure 4.18 Schematic profile of the clouds and air circulation in a tropical cyclone. The clouds are very deep, so at the top they contain mostly ice crystals. The total amount of air rising in the cloud adjacent to the eye greatly exceeds the amount sinking in the centre of the eye. The surface pressure is low across the whole system, and lowest in the eye.

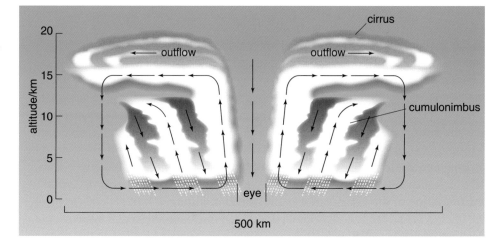

■ When a surface low-pressure area forms, how do the surface winds behave?

□ The winds circulate round the low (anticlockwise in the Northern Hemisphere and clockwise in the Southern Hemisphere) and blow slightly inwards towards the centre of the low.

As surface air moves towards the area of low pressure from all directions, the convergence forces the air to rise. The rising air has already picked up moisture from the ocean and so more and more deep clouds form. These produce more heavy rain. The process of condensation that forms the raindrops releases more latent heat. The warmer the air, the faster it rises, and the lower the pressure at the centre of the system becomes, so the whole system continually reinforces itself. As the central low pressure develops, the winds intensify. Several development stages are distinguished. Once a core of low surface pressure has formed and winds are circulating around it, though with sustained wind speeds of less than Beaufort Force 7 (i.e. less than about 60 kilometres per hour), the system is termed a tropical depression. Most tropical depressions do not intensify further, but some develop sufficiently to become tropical storms. On the Beaufort scale shown in Table 3.2, these may be classed as a gale (Force 8–9) or a storm (Force 10–11). Only if conditions are favourable will a tropical storm evolve into a full-scale tropical cyclone with winds in excess of Force 12 (117 kilometres per hour).

Figure 4.19 shows a cut-away view of the structure of a tropical cyclone. The bands of deep cumulonimbus clouds spiral in towards a central eye, which may have some broken cloud or be completely cloud-free. Surrounding the eye is the eye wall, where the most vigorous cumulonimbus form. The eye-wall zone produces the strongest winds and the most intense rainfall: 25 cm per hour is typical. (To put that in perspective, you might like to reflect that the average *annual* precipitation in London is 60 cm!) The outflow from the tops of the cumulonimbus clouds at altitudes of about 15 km spreads out over the weather system as a dense shield of cirrus cloud. The diameters of tropical cyclones vary greatly. They are typically 500–800 km across but a few are many times that size: Hurricane Gilbert in 1998 had a diameter of 3500 km. The eye is often only 25–50 km across, a tiny fraction of the spread of the whole system. Figure 4.20 is a photograph of a tropical cyclone taken from above, in which the eye can be clearly seen. The surface pressure at the centre of the eye is frequently 950 hPa or less. At the time of writing (early 2008), the record low pressure of 870 hPa is held by the Typhoon Tip, a North Pacific tropical cyclone of 1979; mercifully Tip did not make landfall in its intense phase.

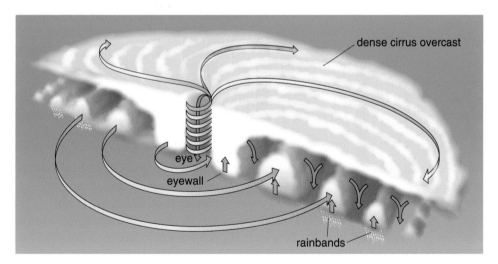

Figure 4.19   Schematic diagram of the structure of a tropical cyclone. The direction in which the winds circulate (anticlockwise as seen from above), show this model to be for the Northern Hemisphere.

Figure 4.20 Photograph taken by a weather satellite of Hurricane Mitch approaching Central America on 26 October 1998. Landmass outlines have been added to show the location. The mountainous terrain contributed to the devastating effect of the torrential rain, as water and mud slides rushed down hillsides, sweeping away everything in their path. Almost the whole infrastructure of Honduras was destroyed and parts of Nicaragua, Guatemala, Belize, and El Salvador were devastated. Mitch was estimated to have been deadlier than any Atlantic hurricane in the previous 200 years. The overall toll of human lives in Central America and southern Mexico was officially estimated at 19 000 dead or missing, and 2.7 million people were left homeless.

A number of conditions must be fulfilled for a tropical cyclone to develop. The first is an extensive ocean surface with a temperature in excess of 27 °C in its uppermost layers.

■   Why is a high sea-surface temperature essential?

☐   The evaporation rate is higher over a warm ocean surface than over a cooler one. The evaporation feeds water vapour into the developing storm system. Condensation of this water vapour provides the heat that allows the system to grow.

Additionally, the atmosphere at middle levels of the troposphere (i.e. at altitudes of between 3 and 6 km) must be fairly moist, so that the growth of convective clouds is not cut off by dry air. The instability of the atmospheric environment must be such as to allow the development of cumulonimbus through the whole depth of the troposphere. Then the conditions also have to favour the organisation of individual cumulonimbus towers into a large-scale system. This requires relatively light winds at the surface, and winds that do not greatly increase with altitude, as strong winds would simply blow the system apart. However, there does have to be a vigorous outflow of air at the top of the developing storm system. As you saw in Figure 2.17, it is the fact of more air flowing out at the top than is being drawn in at the bottom that causes the pressure to fall at the centre. Finally, since the spiral motion of the accelerating winds round the eye are a consequence of the Coriolis effect, the system must be far enough away from the Equator for this effect to be operational. In general, tropical cyclones are born within latitude bands between 5° N and 10° N or between 5° S and 10° S, as shown in Figure 4.21.

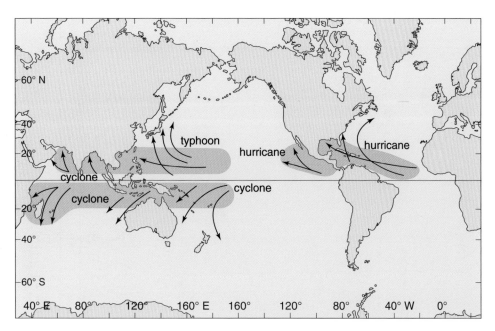

Figure 4.21   Regions where tropical cyclones originate and directions in which they typically move.

4.4.2   Monitoring tropical cyclones

Tropical cyclones generally move both westwards and slightly polewards away from the Equator at speeds of about 18 kilometres per hour. If they reach the mid-latitudes, however, their speed usually increases considerably, sometimes to more than 92 kilometres per hour. If they move far enough polewards they come under the influence of the prevailing westerlies and may take a sudden change in direction. The exact path of an individual tropical storm or cyclone is difficult to predict: some follow almost smooth tracks, while others take erratic paths with sudden changes in direction. Figure 4.22 shows the tracks of North Atlantic tropical depressions, storms and cyclones for one particular season.

You will know from following news coverage of particularly severe tropical cyclones that they are assigned names. The 2005 names for the North Atlantic hurricanes are shown in Figure 4.22. Before naming became standard practice, tropical cyclones were identified by their latitude and longitude, but when lots of tracks have to be plotted this system soon becomes confusing. In 1953 a method was therefore instituted of using female names in alphabetical order, starting with A for the first storm of each season. In the late seventies this was modified to alternate male names with female ones. Named status is accorded to a weather system only once it reaches tropical storm intensity. As you can see from Figure 4.22, there were 27 tropical storms in the North Atlantic in 2005, 15 of which developed into full hurricanes. The letters of the alphabet were exhausted in naming them (especially as Q, U, X, Y and Z were not used), and for the first time letters of the Greek alphabet were used to name the late-season storms.

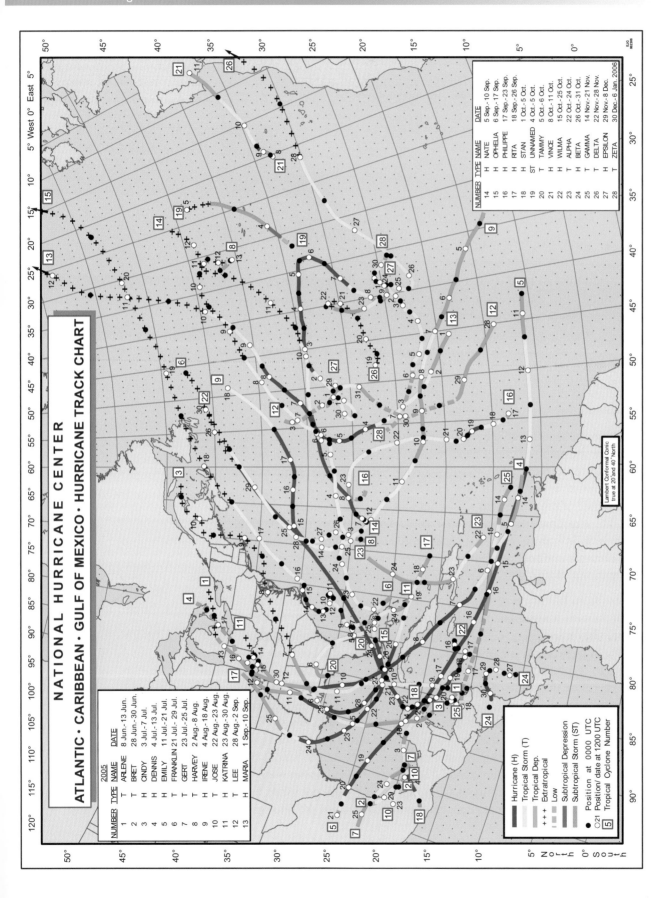

NATIONAL HURRICANE CENTER
ATLANTIC · CARIBBEAN · GULF OF MEXICO · HURRICANE TRACK CHART

NUMBER	TYPE	NAME	DATE
		2005	
1	T	ARLENE	8 Jun.–13 Jun.
2	T	BRET	28 Jun.–30 Jun.
3	H	CINDY	3 Jul.–7 Jul.
4	H	DENNIS	4 Jul.–13 Jul.
5	H	EMILY	11 Jul.–21 Jul.
6	T	FRANKLIN	21 Jul.–29 Jul.
7	T	GERT	23 Jul.–25 Jul.
8	T	HARVEY	2 Aug.–8 Aug.
9	H	IRENE	4 Aug.–18 Aug.
10	T	JOSE	22 Aug.–23 Aug.
11	H	KATRINA	23 Aug.–30 Aug.
12	T	LEE	28 Aug.–2 Sep.
13	H	MARIA	1 Sep.–10 Sep.

NUMBER	TYPE	NAME	DATE
14	H	NATE	5 Sep.–10 Sep.
15	H	OPHELIA	6 Sep.–17 Sep.
16	H	PHILIPPE	17 Sep.–23 Sep.
17	H	RITA	18 Sep.–26 Sep.
18	H	STAN	1 Oct.–5 Oct.
19	ST	UNNAMED	4 Oct.–5 Oct.
20	T	TAMMY	5 Oct.–6 Oct.
21	H	VINCE	8 Oct.–11 Oct.
22	H	WILMA	15 Oct.–25 Oct.
23	T	ALPHA	22 Oct.–24 Oct.
24	T	BETA	26 Oct.–31 Oct.
25	T	GAMMA	14 Nov.–21 Nov.
26	T	DELTA	22 Nov.–28 Nov.
27	H	EPSILON	29 Nov.–8 Dec.
28	T	ZETA	30 Dec.–6 Jan. 2006

Lambert Conformal Conic
true at 20 and 40 °North

Hurricane (H)
Tropical Storm (T)
Tropical Dep.
Extratropical
Low
Subtropical Depression
Subtropical Storm (ST)

● 21   Position at 0000 UTC
○ 21   Position/date at 1200 UTC
⬚5   Tropical Cyclone Number

Figure 4.22 Tracks of tropical depressions, storms and cyclones in the North Atlantic for the 2005 season. Hurricane Katrina, which devastated New Orleans, was the most infamous tropical cyclone of that season. The term 'extratropical' (see the tracks marked by crosses) is used to describe a tropical cyclone that has lost its 'tropical' characteristics. In part this implies that the system has moved polewards, but, as you can see from the examples in this figure, does not necessarily apply as soon as it crosses one of the Tropics (Cancer in this case). For the system to be termed extratropical its primary driver must change from the release of latent heat of condensation to processes dependent on the temperature contrast between warm and cold air masses. A cyclone can become extratropical and yet still retain 'hurricane force' winds. The term UTC can be taken to refer to Greenwich Mean Time (this will be discussed in more detail in Chapter 5).

As well as a name, tropical cyclones are also assigned a category number from 1 to 5 on the so-called Saffir–Simpson scale. This scale is shown in Table 4.2. As the cyclone weakens or intensifies, the category number is changed accordingly. The Saffir–Simpson scale is an attempt not only to describe the meteorological characteristics of a tropical cyclone, but also to predict the damage it might inflict were it to make landfall. As you will see from the right-hand column of the table, in addition to damage caused by high winds, the effect of flooding can be devastating. Flooding may arise partly from the torrential rain, but the main damage is usually done by the way in which the sea surface responds to the low-pressure system. You can get an idea of how a cyclone affects the surface of the ocean by thinking about what happens when you suck air out of a drinking straw placed in a glass of water: the water rises up the straw in response to the reduction in air pressure. A similar effect occurs on the ocean surface in the low-pressure area at the centre of a cyclone: the sea surface develops a 'dome'. The sea level rises by about 1 cm for every 1 hPa fall in the pressure. This effect is compounded by winds pushing the water ahead of the storm and piling it up on low-lying coasts in what is known as a 'storm surge'. There is an even greater potential for disaster if the surge is driven into a confined area such as an estuary. In 1991, a tropical cyclone with a storm surge of 7 metres devastated the coastal estuary and flood plain of Bangladesh, claiming a reported 140 000 lives. Chapter 9 discusses the impact on the same area of a more recent tropical cyclone.

Question 4.5

Explain briefly why a hurricane making landfall on the mainland of the USA rapidly reduces in intensity as it moves inland.

Question 4.6

The 'hurricane season' in the North Atlantic and the Gulf of Mexico is between June and November. Explain briefly why tropical cyclones have seasons.

Table 4.2 The Saffir–Simpson scale for the intensity of tropical cyclones. This scale was developed in the USA to describe the potential damage that could result when a hurricane made landfall. The comments in the right-hand column are therefore appropriate to a country with well-built homes, good infrastructure, organised systems for damage limitation and evacuation plans. In less-developed countries the impacts of a tropical cyclone can be far more severe. You may also find that the quoted ranges for maximum mean wind speeds and storm surges vary from country to country. The mean wind speed is usually calculated as the average over 10 minutes (i.e. a sustained speed), but in the USA a one minute average is used. Storm surge values are very dependent on the geography of the affected coastline. (The symbols > and < mean 'greater than' and 'less than' respectively.)

Tropical cyclone category	Central pressure/ hPa	Maximum mean wind speed/kilometres per hour	Typical storm surge/ metres	Comments
Category 1 (weak)	>980	104–133	1	Minimal Damage: Damage is primarily to shrubbery, trees, foliage, and unanchored mobile homes. No real damage occurs in building structures. Some damage is done to poorly constructed signs. Low-lying coastal roads are inundated, minor pier damage occurs, some small craft in exposed anchorages torn from moorings.
Category 2 (moderate)	979–965	134–154	2	Moderate Damage: Considerable damage is done to shrubbery and tree foliage, some trees are blown down. Major structural damage occurs to exposed mobile homes. Extensive damage occurs to poorly constructed signs. Some damage is done to roofing materials, windows and doors; no major damage occurs to the building integrity of structures. Coastal roads and low-lying escape routes inland may be cut by rising water 2–4 hours *before* the hurricane centre arrives. Considerable pier damage occurs, marinas are flooded. Small craft in unprotected anchorages torn from moorings. Evacuation of some shoreline residences and low-lying island areas is required.
Category 3 (strong)	964–945	155–182	3–4	Extensive Damage: Foliage torn from trees and shrubbery; large trees blown down. Practically all poorly constructed signs are blown down. Some damage to roofing materials of buildings occurs, with some window and door damage. Some structural damage occurs to small buildings, residences and utility buildings. Mobile homes are destroyed. There is a minor amount of failure of curtain walls (in framed buildings). Serious flooding occurs at the coast with many smaller structures near the coast destroyed. Larger structures near the coast are damaged by battering waves and floating debris. Low-lying escape routes inland may be cut by rising water 3–5 hours *before* the hurricane centre arrives. Flat terrain 5 ft (1.5 m) or less above sea level flooded 8 miles (12.9 km) or more inland. Evacuation of low-lying residences within several blocks of shoreline may be required.

Tropical cyclone category	Central pressure/ hPa	Maximum mean wind speed/kilometres per hour	Typical storm surge/ metres	Comments
Category 4 (very strong)	944–920	183–217	4–5	Extreme Damage: Shrubs and trees are blown down; all signs are down. Extensive roofing material and window and door damage occurs. Complete failure of roofs on many small residences occurs, and there is complete destruction of mobile homes. Some curtain walls experience failure. Flat terrain 10 ft (3 m) or less above sea level flooded inland as far as 6 miles (9.7 km). Major damage to lower floors of structures near the shore due to flooding and battering by waves and floating debris. Low-lying escape routes inland may be cut by rising water 3–5 hours *before* the hurricane centre arrives. Major erosion of beaches occurs. Massive evacuation of *all* residences within 500 yards (457 m) of the shoreline may be required, and of single-storey residences on low ground within 2 miles (3.2 km) of the shoreline.
Category 5 (devastating)	<920	>217	>5.5	Catastrophic Damage: Shrubs and trees are blown down; all signs are down. Considerable damage to roofs of buildings. Very severe and extensive window and door damage occurs. Complete failure of roof structures occurs on many residences and industrial buildings, and extensive shattering of glass in windows and doors occurs. Some complete buildings fail. Small buildings are overturned or blown away. Complete destruction of mobile homes occurs. Major damage occurs to lower floors of all structures located less than 15 ft (4.6 m) above sea level and within 500 yards (457 m) of the shoreline. Low-lying escape routes inland are cut by rising water 3–5 hours *before* the hurricane centre arrives. Major erosion of beaches occurs. Massive evacuation of residential areas on low ground within 5–10 *miles* (8–16 km) of the shoreline may be required!

Study comment

Chapters 2 and 3 covered some important concepts that are used often in later chapters. To help you identify these concepts key points were listed at the end of each main section, rather than giving a broader summary at the conclusion of the chapter. However, this chapter and all subsequent ones return to the format of Chapter 1, with an overall summary section at the end.

Retrieve the three summaries you made while you were studying this chapter. Now read the summary of the whole chapter in Section 4.5. You should have no difficulty identifying the paragraphs corresponding to your own summaries. Compare the two versions. Did you cover the same points? If not, you should reflect on why this is. For example, did you miss something important? Did you manage to convey the main ideas within the suggested length? Concise expression is a skill that may require considerable practice, but it is certainly worth aiming for.

4.5   Summary of Chapter 4

The circulation of the atmosphere may be described in terms of two direct thermal circulation cells (the Hadley cells and the polar cells) and indirect circulation in the middle latitudes that may be represented as two Ferrel cells.

Prevailing surface winds between the Equator and the Tropics are generally northeasterly in the Northern Hemisphere and generally southeasterly in the Southern Hemisphere. These are the Trade Winds, which blow from the semi-permanent areas of high pressure situated near latitudes 30° N and 30° S. The Inter-Tropical Convergence Zone (ITCZ) is the boundary zone where the Trade Winds of the two hemispheres converge. The seasonal migration of the ITCZ varies with longitude and has a strong influence on the precipitation patterns of some tropical regions.

In the mid-latitudes the prevailing surface winds are westerly in both hemispheres. In the high polar latitudes they are easterly in both hemispheres. The subpolar boundary where these opposite wind regimes meet is called the polar front. In this region there is the greatest surface temperature difference between cold air to the north and warm air to the south. It corresponds to a zone of low pressure in which depressions often form.

High-speed, upper-level airflows called jet streams occur where strong winds are concentrated into narrow bands at the tropopause. In the Northern Hemisphere the polar jet stream is associated with the polar front, and the subtropical jet stream with the subtropical high. These jet streams flow right round the Earth from west to east, though the polar jet in particular also meanders north and south. There are corresponding jet streams in the Southern Hemisphere.

Air masses are very large bodies of air with relatively uniform properties, which have their source regions in areas covered by more or less stationary highs. Air masses are classified on the basis of their latitude of origin and of their formation over either land or sea. The properties of an air mass may be modified by the nature of the surface over which it moves.

Fronts are boundaries between air masses with different densities. Along a cold front, cold air is replacing warm air by undercutting it. Along a warm front, warm air is advancing over colder air. Cold fronts have steeper slopes and move more quickly than warm fronts. When a cold front catches up with a warm front, an occlusion (or occluded front) is formed. This has features of both warm and cold fronts.

The frontal depression is a type of low-pressure region that is characteristic of the mid-latitudes. Serial development of depressions often takes place along a trailing cold front.

Tropical cyclones (hurricanes) are storm systems that are born over tropical waters in both hemispheres. Their development requires a warm ocean, light surface winds and atmospheric instability that favour the formation of deep cumulonimbus clouds. If these clouds become organised into clusters such that a circulation system is set up with more air flowing outwards near the top of the troposphere than converges at the surface, the low pressure at the centre of the system will intensify. A full-scale tropical cyclone has winds of more than 118 kilometres per hour circulating round the central eye. Damage from tropical cyclones arises from the combination of high winds, torrential precipitation, and storm surges.

Chapter 5
Weather measurements

Measurements of the weather are essential for a variety of reasons: to accumulate an accurate record of what has happened in the past by compiling a day-by-day record and a statistical summary that is known as 'climatology'; to provide an up-to-date picture of what is happening now in the atmosphere; and to give a starting point for predicting what will happen in the future, in other words a weather forecast. The processes of weather forecasting will be described in Chapter 6, but for now it is enough to acknowledge that it is only possible to make a rational prediction of what will happen in the future on the basis of an accurate description of what is happening in the present, or of what has happened in the recent past. A network of meteorological instruments is needed to build up this description.

This chapter describes typical meteorological observations from three different perspectives: observations and measurements on the surface, observations and measurements from space and finally local measurements from within the body of the atmosphere.

If you would like to check up in advance where the places mentioned in this chapter are located, the list follows. (Some of these places have already been mentioned in previous chapters.)

* Countries and land areas: China, India, Tibet, Afghanistan, Saudi Arabia and the Arabian Peninsula, Iraq, Iran, Norway, Finland, Denmark, Sweden, Estonia, the Sahara Desert (north Africa)

* Oceans/seas: Indian Ocean, Persian Gulf, Southern Ocean

* Mountains: the Himalayan range

* Cities: Kolkata (previously Calcutta, India), Edmonton (Canada), Greenwich (now part of greater London, UK).

5.1   Recording the weather: from the surface

For well over a century, formal observations of the prevailing meteorological conditions have been recorded at official weather stations around the globe. In the early days the information was chiefly gathered by the military, ever mindful of the risk that even the most carefully devised strategy is at the mercy of short-term changes in the weather. It is hard to imagine that forecasting success rates were high for more than a few hours ahead, so military discipline and scientific curiosity may have been essential for keeping the observation networks going in the early days. In addition to supplying data for forecasting, records of past weather are an important input into climatology.

5.1.1   What is worth recording?

From an archival point of view it could be argued that it is worth recording anything that changes and that can be reliably measured. If it is not known exactly how to use the data now, a good scientific record might be valuable at a later date. From a practical point of view the important measurements are those that have a known bearing on events.

■ Suggest at least six meteorological quantities that are locally measurable and that might form the basis for a scientific weather forecast.

□ Here is a possible list: atmospheric surface pressure; air temperature; wind speed and direction; humidity; amount of rainfall or other precipitation; cloud amount, height of cloud base and cloud type; visibility.

The quantities just listed are commonly included in reporting of data for meteorological forecasts and/or for climatological archives. You will have already identified such reports for your locality in Activity 1.2. Many meteorological reports list extreme values (such as daily minimum and maximum temperatures), temperature averages, and net accumulations of precipitation over defined periods of time. Daily maximum and minimum temperatures are often taken over a 24-hour period starting at 9 a.m. local time each day rather than midnight. This is to avoid dividing each night in half; one very cold night might then contribute minimum temperatures (one at just before and one after midnight) which would appear in the record as minima for two successive days. As discussed in the caption to Figure 3.13, a vessel designed to catch precipitation can be emptied at set intervals; the accumulation over a period is simply the depth of water collected over the time interval until the instrument is next checked. (This kind of instrument is called a 'rain' gauge even if it catches hail or snow rather than rain.) Note that similar accumulations might result if there was a single rain storm for a short period during an otherwise dry day, or a continuous drizzle. Figure 5.1 shows one example extract of an hourly record from which it is easy to see not only the current weather conditions, but just as importantly, how they are changing. Notice that alongside the pressure reading is an indication that the pressure is falling. You should recognise that, though it may take a few more hourly reports to confirm it, this suggestion of decreasing pressure could be early warning of the approach of a low-pressure weather system.

Somewhere between the observations like those recorded in Figure 5.1 and a weather forecast is a team of professional meteorologists. No doubt among them will be those whose tasks include a consideration of the observers' reports of cloud type, which is a rich source of immediate weather information. It is interesting that few reports available to the general public include the raw information on cloud classification or a realistic measure of cloud extent, although a simple pictogram is often used to describe the cloud cover.

5.1.2   Weather observations

There is a lot more to taking useful meteorological data than simply reading a handy thermometer. For a start the measurement instruments must be 'calibrated' and they should be used in specified ways. Calibration is performed to try to ensure that each meteorological variable is measured in a consistent way at

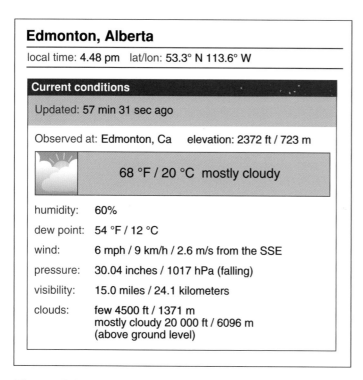

Figure 5.1 An example extract from a meteorological report for Edmonton, Canada.

every surface site; this is required because weather observations at many sites are needed to feed into a forecast model and to build up a weather chart, as you will see in Chapters 6 and 7 respectively. These observations are all made using different instruments, which were built at different times and possibly originate from different manufacturers. If one instrument consistently measures a higher or lower reading than others, then false features will be introduced into the record. A similar concern applies when instruments at the same site are replaced. The new instrument should be calibrated against the old, or at least any differences in calibration should be well understood and documented, for the historical weather record to be reliable. Good scientific practice is essential.

As you can probably imagine, there are manuals and handbooks that set out procedures that must be followed as part of a quality assurance approach to gathering meteorological data. This is to eliminate differences in the way that instruments are sited or are read by observers in different regions. For example, thermometers and other instruments should be sited in a ventilated, white box, placed 1.25 m above the ground with a north-facing door in the Northern Hemisphere. This is known as a 'Stevenson Screen' (named after the civil engineer Thomas Stevenson, father of the famous author Robert Louis Stevenson). Recordings should be made at the same time each day and preferably synchronised with other readings around the world.

For the purpose of synchronising events around the globe, some line of longitude has to be defined as a reference for time zones. For historical reasons this was established as a line of longitude passing through a marker fixed to the ground at Greenwich in London. This line is specified as longitude zero degrees and is sometimes called the Greenwich (or Prime) Meridian. By international agreement, time on the Earth was then set relative to a 'noon' or 'midday' as seen from the Greenwich Meridian. This defined 1200 hours 'Greenwich Mean Time' (GMT). From places lying to the east of Greenwich the Sun will be seen to pass its highest point earlier than 1200 hours GMT, which is why progressively earlier time zones are encountered when travelling eastwards. Conversely, places to the west of Greenwich experience the Sun at its highest at progressively later times with increasing longitude. Coordinated Universal Time (abbreviated as UTC from the French 'Temps Universel Coordonné) is a timescale that is nowadays defined by the use of highly precise atomic clocks, but is equivalent to GMT for most practical purposes. UTC is the scale used by meteorologists.

The main internationally accepted times for weather observations are 0000 UTC (i.e. midnight) and at six-hourly intervals thereafter, but data are often also taken at several intermediate times, and hourly at many stations.

5.1.3 Automated weather observation

The collection of most routine meteorological data is something that can be easily automated using electronic instrumentation. Making electronic measurements of temperature is easy – the electrical properties of some materials are very temperature sensitive, as are the tiny, but easily measurable, electrical voltages generated when two different metals are brought into contact. In fact, there are a large number of other 'thermo-electric' effects and experimental scientists will tell you that when the first prototypes for most electronic measuring instruments are built in the laboratory they often respond to changes in temperature more markedly than to changes in the quantity that they were designed to measure. There is an almost equally rich variety of 'piezoelectric' effects (i.e. effects in which changes in pressure generate changes in electric properties) that can be engineered into electronic barometers. Humidity too can nowadays be monitored in the changing properties of simple electronic components. In fact, all of the above instrumentation can be comfortably fitted into a modern digital wristwatch.

An automated weather monitoring station is essentially a set of electronic sensors linked to a telecommunications channel that need be little more than a mobile phone or a wireless radio link. You may well have seen roadside weather monitoring stations similar to that shown in Figure 5.2. Routine reports from roadside and, at airports, runwayside, automatic weather stations are important for issuing travel safety alerts.

■ Several basic weather observations are difficult to automate, though not impossible. However, the smarter the electronic instrument, the more expensive it is likely to be. Suggest two kinds of observation that a person can do with relative ease compared with an electronic system.

☐ You may have thought of things like visibility, cloud cover and, in particular, cloud type. These can all be recorded by trained observers without any instrumentation beyond the human eye, so the electronic world starts at a disadvantage. (A simple, well-placed, live, video camera, though useful, still needs an observer and places higher demands on data transmission.)

Figure 5.2 A roadside weather monitoring station. Note the anemometer at the top for measuring wind speed, and the characteristic photovoltaic panel, which recharges the station battery to power the instruments.

5.1.4   The global perspective

Local observations are a key ingredient in short-term, local weather forecasting but the data from the global network of ground-based observations are also important in setting initial conditions in larger-scale models for longer-term forecasts, to be described in Chapter 6. Worldwide cooperation on weather can be traced back to 1873. Nowadays, as discussed in Section 2.1.2, the World Meteorological Organisation (WMO) coordinates the international exchange of meteorological data. In 2007 the WMO was collecting and freely distributing meteorological data from more than 100 moored buoys, 1000 drifting buoys, 7300 ships and around 10 000 land-based weather stations. These surface data traditionally form the basis of weather forecasts, risk assessments and weather warnings around the globe. Figure 5.3 shows the extent to which there is now global coverage by international weather stations on the surface.

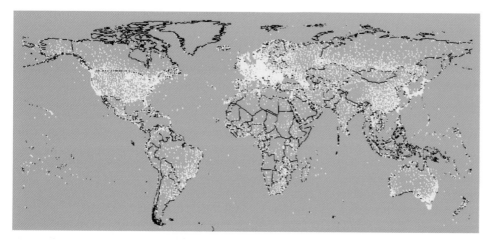

Figure 5.3   The global network of weather stations that make daily reports. The network includes land-based weather stations, both staffed and automatic, and weather stations located on ships and buoys at sea.

■ Examine Figure 5.3 carefully. How does the distribution of surface observation sites on land compare with that of sites at sea?

☐ The distribution of surface observation sites across the globe is not uniform primarily because the oceans are more sparsely covered by observing stations than the land.

■ Suggest some reasons for the land coverage not being uniform.

☐ The land coverage to some extent reflects a combination of population density and economic factors, with richer and/or more densely populated areas being better represented. Population density also reflects geography; deserts and high mountains are usually sparsely inhabited.

■ Why is there a relative imbalance in coverage between the Northern and Southern Hemispheres?

☐ The Southern Hemisphere is under-represented in terms of coverage, because compared with the Northern Hemisphere there is relatively little land area – the surface is predominantly ocean.

Activity 5.1   Meteorological instruments (Part 1)

The estimated time for this activity is 90 minutes, split into three parts.

In this activity you will study images of many different instruments that are used to gather meteorological data and see examples of some of the information that they provide.

The activity is divided into three parts, one for each major section of this chapter. The first part deals with surface-based instruments. You can either study this part now or wait until you have studied the text of the whole chapter and then work through all three parts in one session.

You will find the detailed instructions for this activity in the Activities section of the course website.

Study comment

Chapter 4 gave some suggestions for turning your notes or highlighted phrases into short text summaries. Two of the questions in this chapter give you the opportunity to use a different layout for summarising ideas. As you have already seen, tables can provide a concise way of displaying information, whether quantitative (as for example in Table 3.3), or mostly qualitative (as in Tables 3.1 and 3.2). In the case of qualitative information, tables are particularly useful when comparisons are required, as similarities and differences can be picked out more easily from a table than from paragraphs of text.

Like Activity 5.1, Question 5.1 is in three parts and allows you to compile your own table of ideas related to the huge variety of instruments that can be used to make meteorological measurements. A phrase often used in this context is 'measurement platform'; this denotes anything (such as a surface station, a satellite or an aircraft) that can carry a number of instruments. The overall task is to compare the relative strengths and weaknesses of different components within the meteorological network as you read through this chapter and complete the activities.

Question 5.1

Put a few words into the first row of Table 5.1 to describe what you see as the obvious advantages and disadvantages of surface stations for making meteorological measurements and observations. If you have chosen to defer your study of Activity 5.1 until later, you will need to revisit this part of the table when you have completed the activity. You will also probably find you want to revise or add to your answer once you have read the following sections and have made the comparison with other platforms, so you may prefer to make your initial entries in pencil. Try to resist the temptation to check the suggested answer in the back of the book until you have read the rest of the chapter and completed the other rows of the table.

Table 5.1 Some advantages and disadvantages of various meteorological observing systems. (For use with Question 5.1.)

Measurement platform	Advantages	Disadvantages
Surface stations		
Satellites		
Radiosondes and aircraft		

5.2   Recording the weather: from the top down

The ability to launch artificial satellites has revolutionised the way in which the weather has been recorded over the last 50 years. For the first time, meteorologists have been able routinely to get a view of the whole atmosphere and of the weather systems that it contains.

5.2.1   The view from space

Since the early days of space exploration, 'top-down' weather information has been gathered in increasingly sophisticated ways. Figure 5.4 gives an impression of the kind of view that can be had on arrival at or departure from the International Space Station (ISS) some 320 km above the Earth. The ISS is just one of a vast number of artificial satellites that have been placed in orbit around the Earth. Box 5.1 gives some information about the orbits of Earth satellites.

Figure 5.4   The International Space Station viewed from the Space Shuttle *Discovery*, against the background of the Earth and various types of cloud.

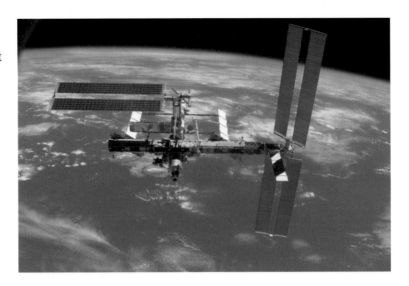

Box 5.1   Satellite orbits

An object that is in orbit about the Earth (or any other planet) is usually referred to as a satellite. Because a satellite is so far above the atmosphere, there is nothing to impede its motion so it is not necessary to keep the engines running. The duration of a single orbit is called the 'orbital period'. The further away a satellite is from the surface of the planet, the longer it takes to make one complete orbit. Figure 5.5 shows the orbital periods, measured in days, for orbits at various distances from the centre of the Earth. The horizontal axis is marked in units of the radius of the satellite's orbit divided by the radius of the Earth (which is about 6400 km). A value of 1.0 on this scale indicates ground level. Values smaller than 1.0 do not represent a real situation, since the satellite would be underground!

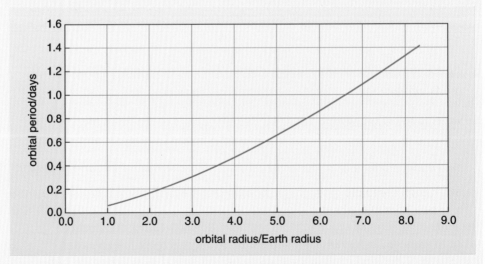

Figure 5.5   Graph showing the duration of a single orbit (the orbital period) for satellites located at various distances from the centre of the Earth. The horizontal scale shows this distance in terms of its relationship to the radius of the Earth.

■ How high above the surface of the Earth is a satellite for which the value of orbital radius/Earth radius = 3.0?

☐ The satellite is placed at 3.0 Earth radii from the centre of the Earth, i.e. 2.0 Earth radii, or about 12 800 km, above the Earth's surface.

■ What is the orbital period in days of a satellite placed at 3.0 Earth radii from the centre of the Earth? (Hint: you will probably need to draw vertical and horizontal lines directly on to Figure 5.5, using the grid lines of the graph to help you.)

☐ This satellite would have an orbital period of about 0.3 days.

If you had difficulty reading this answer from the graph, you should have another look at Box 2.2.

■ What is this orbital period (0.3 days) in hours?

☐ 0.3 days = (0.3 × 24) hours = 7.2 hours = 7 hours 12 minutes

Detailed information about weather systems can be recorded by satellites and transmitted back to ground stations whenever a convenient receiver can 'see' the satellite. A particularly attractive option is to set a satellite into what is called a polar orbit. The satellite passes over the North and South Poles at a height of 700–800 km (about 0.12 times the radius of the Earth) above the surface. You can see from Figure 5.5 that the orbital period of such a satellite is more than 0.05 days and less than 0.1 days. In fact it is 0.07 days (or 100 minutes). From this height, cameras can easily see features as small as 1 km across. At the Equator, with a field of view about 2800 km wide, the tracks below successive orbits just overlap. This is because the Earth rotates below the satellite, so that every time the satellite crosses the Equator in one direction it is over a point 2800 km further west than it was at the previous crossing.

■ The circumference of the Earth at the Equator is about 40 000 km. How many orbits will be required to cover the globe completely?

☐ The number of orbits required is $\dfrac{40\,000\ \text{km}}{2800\ \text{km}} = 14.3$.

■ How many hours will it take for the satellite to go through this number of orbits?

☐ Since each complete orbit takes 100 minutes, the time taken to cover 14.3 orbits will be 14.3 × 100 minutes.

This corresponds to $\dfrac{14.3 \times 100\ \text{minutes}}{60\ \text{minutes per hour}} = 23.8\ \text{hours}$.

Thus a satellite in polar orbit can photograph the whole globe in one day.

The USA's National Oceanic and Atmospheric Administration (NOAA) operates a pair of polar orbiting satellites like this and even has three 'old series spares' dating from before the turn of the century. The European polar orbiter called 'MetOp' went into service in May 2007 and has a similar weather reconnaissance role.

A more immediate picture of global weather can be had from satellites that sit out among the telecommunication platforms. These are in what is termed a 'geostationary' orbit at 6.7 Earth radii from the centre of the Earth.

■ According to Figure 5.5, what is the orbital period if a satellite is placed at 6.7 Earth radii from the centre of the Earth? (Hint: you may need to draw horizontal and vertical lines on the figure to answer this question.) As seen from a satellite in this orbit over the Equator, how would the Earth appear to move underneath the satellite?

☐ The orbit lasts one day. Provided the satellite lies exactly over the Equator, the disc of the Earth will appear fixed.

A satellite that is geostationary sits over the Equator and over a single fixed longitude. Looking back at the Earth from a geostationary platform, the disc of the Earth appears very much as a standard football would to you from a distance of 75 cm. You do not need a powerful telescope to get a good view at this range – all you need is a good camera. Figure 5.6 shows the view from three

Figure 5.6   Visible images on 20 June 2007 at 1200 (noon) UTC from geostationary satellites: (a) GOES East (aligned with the US east coast, longitude 75° W); (b) Meteosat-8 (over the Greenwich Meridian, longitude 0°); (c) Meteosat-7 (aligned with the Indian Ocean, longitude 63° E). The outlines of countries are overlaid and there is also a grid of reference marks (+). These images are illuminated by sunlight and the brightness indicates the amount of light that has been scattered back to the satellite; clouds appear white and the oceans (where cloud-free) appear darker than the land. It is night-time over the Pacific, with dawn breaking over the west coast of South America and evening falling over China and approaching India. It is Northern Hemisphere summer; the North Pole is illuminated in all three frames, whereas the South Pole is in darkness.

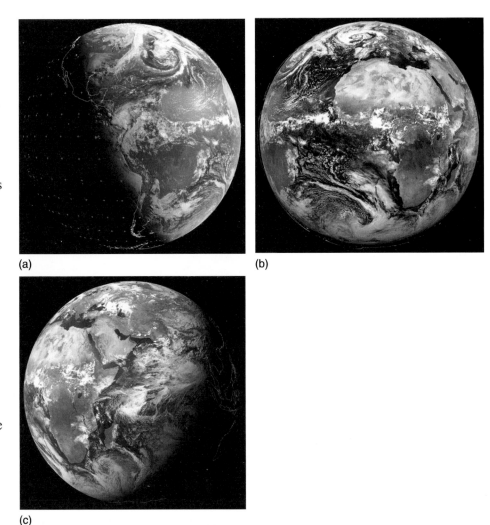

(a)

(b)

(c)

geostationary meteorological monitoring satellites; images like this are sent back to Earth every hour. Note that most satellite images from meteorological satellites are presented as 'grey-scale', i.e. like black and white photographs. Take some time to study the images and the caption of Figure 5.6 carefully.

5.2.2 Observing the Earth in the visible and infrared

Satellites can do much more than just showing us what we would see if we were to be on board. They can also show us things that human eyes could not see. At its best, the human eye sees only what we call light, i.e. visible radiation. As discussed in Chapter 1, the Sun and other warm bodies also emit non-visible radiation, and you will be familiar with other types of radiation such as X-rays. The collective term for all these types of radiation is 'electromagnetic'. Box 5.2 explains what distinguishes the various kinds of electromagnetic radiation.

Box 5.2 The electromagnetic spectrum

Sunlight is in fact a veritable rainbow or 'spectrum' of different colours that we describe as red, orange, yellow, green, blue and violet. Vegetation appears green because the chemicals within it mostly absorb the other colours, scattering the green light back to our eyes; a cloudless sky appears blue because of all the colours blue light is scattered the most (i.e. its direction of travel is most altered) on encountering very small particles high in the atmosphere; these have much less effect on yellow and red light. If there were no scattering, the daytime sky seen from the Earth's surface would mostly appear dark, as it does at night. From the surface of the Moon, which has no atmosphere, the sky always appears dark apart from the bright illumination from the direction of the Sun.

You may like to try a simple demonstration of light scattering yourself. You will need a torch and a large, straight-sided clear glass. Fill the glass about two-thirds full of water and then add about half a teaspoon of milk (you may need to experiment to get the correct proportions of milk to water). In a darkened room, shine the torch down onto the top of the water. The liquid should appear distinctly blue-ish if viewed from the sides, as blue light is scattered through a large angle by particles in the milk more effectively than the other colours, which travel from top to bottom. The sky appears blue (except when you look towards the Sun or at clouds) due to a similar scattering effect from tiny particles and molecules in the air. Then shine

the torch upwards from below the glass and look down from above. You should see a red hue to the light which penetrates directly through the liquid, because the red light is least scattered by the small particles in the milk.

Although the human eye can't see it, the Sun's radiation is spread across a wider spectrum than the visible range (red to violet). There are 'colours' beyond each end of the visible spectrum: beyond the violet end there is ultraviolet (UV) radiation and beyond the red end there is infrared (IR) radiation. The human eye cannot detect UV radiation but bees' eyes apparently can. Most people are aware of UV in the context of sunscreen, because human skin tissue is damaged by UV resulting in sunburn. The human eye cannot detect IR radiation either, but it has been found that snakes' eyes have sensors that do, and the heat that we feel, for example from a glowing fire, is detected by infrared sensors in our skin.

You need to know a little more about radiation emitted by the Sun, by the atmosphere and from the surface of the Earth to appreciate the enormous insight into the weather that can be gained from satellite images. This radiation is described as being 'electromagnetic' because it can be understood in terms of the physics of electricity and magnetism. The physics of electromagnetism describes how electromagnetic radiation transports energy. It can also account for how electromagnetic radiation crosses the empty space from the Sun and stars to the Earth and beyond.

On encountering matter, radiation is transmitted, absorbed and scattered to varying degrees, depending on the chemical and physical nature of the matter. For example, the visible radiation in sunlight is certainly transmitted through panes of window glass, but some is also reflected (or scattered) by the glass, especially when it strikes the pane of glass at oblique angles. Scientifically the process is usually referred to as 'absorption' or 'excitation' if the radiation is converted into heat within the matter, and as 'scattering' if the path of the radiation is changed, but it is not absorbed. So on a sunny day the Earth's surface is heated by absorbing radiation from the Sun, whereas on a cloudy day much of this radiation is scattered back into space before it reaches the ground.

Our physiological experience of colour is just a means of expressing the response of the light-sensitive detector cells of the eye's retina to stimulation by different frequencies of electrical excitation. Red light stimulates these detectors electrically at around four hundred million, million times a second, whereas violet light stimulates them at almost twice that frequency. The way that the visible colours map into the wider electromagnetic spectrum over a broad range of frequencies is shown in Figure 5.7. The unit of frequency is the hertz (abbreviated as Hz).

Figure 5.7   The huge range of frequencies associated with electromagnetic radiation: sunlight corresponds to the small range marked visible, to which our eyes have been adapted, and a little way beyond to higher and to lower frequencies. Visible light is only a tiny proportion of the whole. Frequency is measured in hertz (Hz).

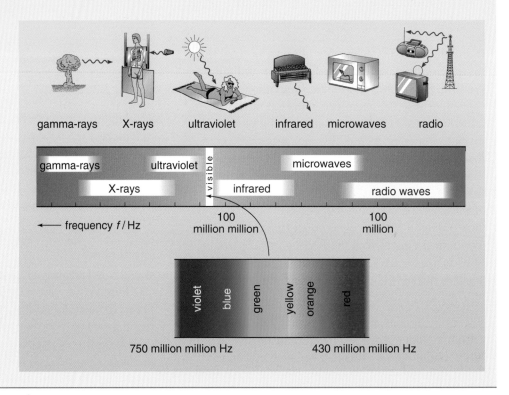

The Earth is bathed in electromagnetic radiation from the Sun at a variety of frequencies though visible light is in the frequency range that reaches the Earth's surface most readily. Much of the incoming UV radiation is absorbed by a form of oxygen known as ozone which is most common high in the atmosphere (in fact in the stratosphere; Figure 2.7 shows how far away from the surface this is). Some of the incoming visible radiation is reflected from clouds and land masses, but clouds are especially effective at blocking incoming IR radiation, which is also absorbed by atmospheric gases, including water vapour. The absorbed radiation warms the atmosphere, which itself emits IR radiation.

As discussed in Chapter 1, all warm objects emit IR radiation, in amounts roughly in proportion to how warm they are. Thus, in complete darkness, the bodies of warm-blooded animals, including humans, can be imaged by IR-sensitive 'night vision' cameras (and by snakes), contrasted against a cooler, inanimate background. Making a camera that 'sees' IR radiation is not difficult in the digital age. Even the cameras built into many consumer electronic devices (such as some mobile phones and laptop computers) do so, though they are not specifically designed for this purpose. An IR image is shown in Figure 5.8.

Both the Earth and its atmosphere emit IR radiation, a significant fraction of which escapes out into space, especially when skies are clear. As a result, IR cameras, mounted on satellites and looking back at the Earth, are extremely useful for weather observation on a global scale. Figure 5.9 shows IR and visible images from Meteosat-7, above the Indian Ocean. Unlike the artificial colour representation of Figure 5.8, the IR image of Figure 5.9 is presented as a grey-scale picture. This is normally the case for IR as well as visible images from meteorological satellites (compare with Figure 5.6). On the day shown in Figure 5.9, the Sun set at 6.19 p.m. local time in Kolkata, which is 5.5 hours ahead of UTC, so the Indian night was around half-way through at the time the image was taken. The visible image, Figure 5.9b, confirms that at the time most of the view was in darkness. The IR image of Figure 5.9a, on the other hand, shows lots of detail.

Figure 5.8   Infrared image of sailing boats. The colours are false and show the variation in intensity of IR radiation, which is related to the temperature of the surface emitting the radiation. (This is quite different to a standard colour photograph taken in visible light, where the colours correspond to the variation in the frequency of the radiation.) Many IR images are monochrome (i.e. shades of a single colour, such as green) and show temperature information simply as a variation in brightness, but the colour here helps to accentuate small differences. The scale runs from white (warmest) through red, yellow, green and blue to purple (coldest). The image was taken during daytime and the buildings, sailing boats and the surface of the land can be seen to have been warmed by the Sun to higher temperatures than the surface of the water, which still appears green and blue. Differences in IR radiation from the sky can also be seen. Warmer colours (yellow-green) indicate the presence of low clouds over the coastline, while colder colours (blue-purple) indicate areas where IR radiation is emitted from thinner, high clouds or a clear sky.

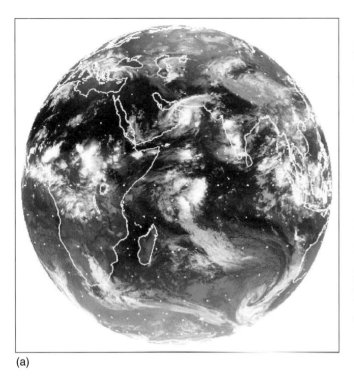
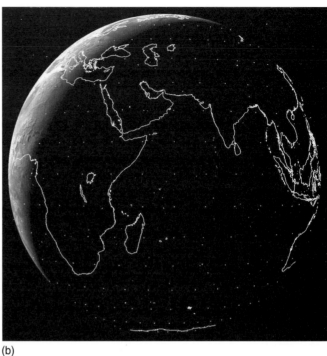

(a)   (b)

Figure 5.9   One of the six-hourly archive infrared (a) and visible (b) images from Meteosat-7, a geostationary satellite above the Indian Ocean at 1800 UTC, on 5 June 2007. Landmass outlines are added for clarity.

■ In a conventional black and white photographic print, what is represented by the light to dark contrast?

☐ The lighter parts of a black and white picture come from the brighter surfaces of the scene being photographed – highlights and reflections are lightest; shadows and shade are darkest.

The conventional arrangement for 'black and white' photographic prints uses a positive image that looks recognisably similar to the real full-colour scene, whereas negative images reverse the contrast. Meteorological IR photographs are presented as a negative image: the darker regions correspond with the IR-emitting (i.e. warmer) surfaces and lighter tones tell of much reduced IR emission, i.e. relative coldness.

■ What colour does the view of space outside the disc of the Earth appear in the two images in Figure 5.9?

☐ Space appears black in the visible, but white in the IR image.

Space is the coldest part of the image, being around 290 Celsius degrees colder than the average temperature of the surface of the Earth (which is around 15 °C).

■ What is the coldest thing visible within the Earth's disc in Figure 5.9a?

☐ The cloud tops, which appear very light grey or white.

■ What is the warmest thing visible within the Earth's disc in Figure 5.9a?

☐ The very dark-coloured land visible in the Sahara region of North Africa and in the Arabian Peninsula.

Land and sea surfaces are heated during the day and cool down at night but their temperature stays above 0 °C at low latitudes and they remain significant emitters of IR throughout the night-time. Clouds form in cold air and, in general, the higher the clouds are, the colder must be the tiny droplets and ice particles of which they are made; cloud tops are much colder than 0 °C and are not strong IR emitters. The whitest clouds in the IR image in Figure 5.9a are therefore also the highest. Lower-level clouds, which are more prevalent in mid-latitudes in this image, are a mid-grey tone. Figure 5.10 shows the relative amounts of IR radiation emitted by the Earth's surface and clouds.

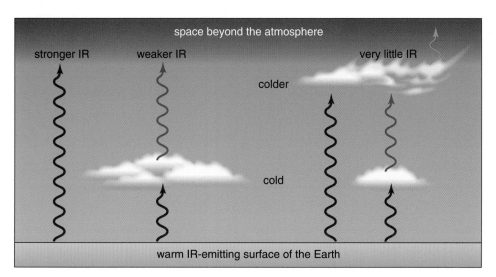

Figure 5.10 IR radiated from the surface of the Earth gets out into space under clear skies but it does not penetrate dense clouds. The highest, coldest clouds radiate very little IR, whereas lower, less cold clouds radiate weakly.

In Figure 5.9a you should now try to identify the following features.

1 The cold, high cloud over most of India, where the image is very light. The IR emission from the land is absorbed by the cold, high cloud and all the camera registers is the small amount of emission from the top of the cold clouds.

2 A band of clearer skies that extends over North Africa, Saudi Arabia, Iraq, Iran, Afghanistan and Tibet, where the darkness of the image shows strong IR emission from warm land masses.

3 The very sharply defined northern edge to the cloud-free region just to the north of India that corresponds with the Himalayan range.

4 A region of cold, high cloud near the bottom of the Persian Gulf. This is partially veiling lower cloud spiralling anticlockwise in a (Northern Hemisphere) low-pressure system.

5 A (Southern Hemisphere) low-pressure weather system in the Southern Ocean, at the bottom right of the image, with the cloud spiralling in a clockwise direction.

In general a rich variety of weather patterns can be read from an infrared global image, traced in layers of cloud even, as you have seen in Figure 5.9, when the picture is taken at night. A yet more vivid impression of developing weather can be seen in a sequence of successive images. Meteorologists can make use of sequences of cloud images to measure the wind speed and direction in the atmosphere at levels where clouds are present. Video clips of this nature make fascinating viewing.

Study comment

The following question gives you another opportunity to use a table layout to summarise and compare qualitative information.

Question 5.2

The top two rows of Table 5.2 show how various types of area visible in satellite images interact (or don't) with sunlight, and whether they emit IR radiation. These rows have been partly completed. Fill in the empty boxes. (You may find Figure 5.10 is helpful.) The bottom two rows of the table categorise the grey-scale visible and IR images captured by satellites. These rows have also been partially completed. By referring to your entries in the top two rows and to Figures 5.6 and 5.9, fill in the remaining empty boxes.

Table 5.2 For use with Question 5.2.

	Ocean	Land	Low-level clouds	Very deep clouds	Space
Interaction with sunlight			scatter sunlight back into space		no scattering or absorption of sunlight
Emission of IR radiation	radiate IR strongly upwards into space				no radiation of IR along satellite line of sight
Visible image (positive) in daytime		various shades of grey	pale grey		
IR image (negative)					

The water vapour in the air, as well as the droplets from which clouds are formed, absorbs radiation particularly effectively over a range of frequencies that lie within the infrared part of the electromagnetic spectrum. By looking at the detail of the IR spectrum passing through the atmosphere to a satellite, and by comparing absorption at individual frequencies, it is possible to make a good estimate of the total amount of water and water vapour along any line between a point on the surface of the Earth and the satellite. Most of the water is in the lowest 10 km or so of the atmosphere. Figure 5.11 shows a 'water vapour image' for the same time as Figure 5.9, with increasing brightness corresponding to higher water vapour content and darkness indicating dryness.

Figure 5.11
5 June 2007: a
'Water vapour' image
from Meteosat-7
in geostationary
orbit over the
Indian Ocean. High
brightness implies
moist air; darkness
implies dry air.
Landmass outlines
are added for clarity.

■ What is shown in the water vapour image of Figure 5.11 at locations where the IR image of Figure 5.9a shows thick cloud cover? (Hint: look particularly at central and southern Africa.)

☐ Figure 5.11 shows large quantities of water vapour over the regions where cloud cover can also be deduced from the IR image.

■ What is shown in the water vapour image, Figure 5.11, where the IR image, Figure 5.9a, shows little or no cloud cover? (Hint: look at the central Indian Ocean.)

☐ The water vapour image also detects diffuse regions of moist air between the bright, thick cloud regions of the IR image.

As a result of absorption and emission of radiation at other IR frequencies, often by carbon dioxide gas, it is also possible for scientists to measure temperatures within the atmosphere, not just at the cloud tops. This is done by a careful calculation of the amount of IR radiation expected to be seen at a whole series of frequencies for a particular distribution of temperatures all the way along the line of sight. That distribution of temperatures is then adjusted until the IR spectrum predicted from it matches the one observed by the satellite, to within a reasonable tolerance. This laborious calculation is repeated for every point where the satellite makes an observation. Measuring a quantity of real interest (e.g. temperature) using a remote measurement of another quantity (e.g. IR radiation at various frequencies) can be challenging, but is vital across a range of scientific disciplines ranging from studies of the Earth's core via earthquakes to medical scanning of the human body.

Activity 5.1 (continued) Meteorological instruments (Part 2)

In the second part of the activity you will follow sequences of images from geostationary satellites to see how these show the development, movement and decay of various weather systems. You can study this part now, or wait until you have studied the text of the whole chapter, and then work through all three parts in one session.

You will find the detailed instructions for the activity in the Activities section of the course website.

5.2.3 Comparing with the view from the ground

So, how does the view from space correlate with the charts of the weather that meteorologists can construct from surface observations? The answer is 'remarkably well'. A geostationary satellite sees higher latitudes increasingly foreshortened owing to the curvature of the Earth's surface. However, image processing experts can tilt and distort the image so that it appears to be taken from overhead. Figure 5.12 shows both the full globe in the IR, as seen from the MTSAT geostationary satellite, and a reprojection of the same image in the region of Australia and New Zealand, suitable for weather reports in that region. This image was taken at 0630 UTC on 19 February 2008, just over six hours after the time for which the weather map in Figure 2.15 was valid.

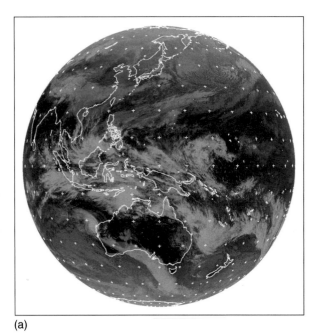

(a)

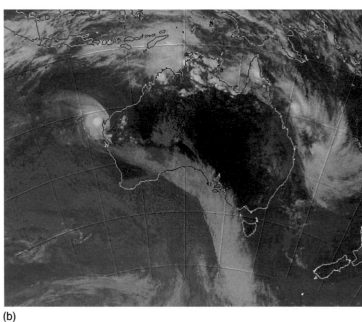

(b)

Figure 5.12 MTSAT geostationary satellite infrared images taken at 0630 UTC on 19 February 2008 showing (a) the whole globe, centred on longitude 140° E, and (b) a reprojection of (a) for the area around Australia and New Zealand.

■ There is a bright white, circular region of cloud lying just off the northwestern coast of Australia in Figure 5.12b, in the centre of a spiral pattern. Why does this cloud appear whiter in the image than the band of cloud over the ocean to the south of Australia? (You may find it useful to refer to Figure 2.15.)

☐ This cloud surrounds the centre of tropical cyclone Nicholas, a region of strong upward motion. The cloud tops are high, and consequently cold, and so the clouds emit little IR radiation and appear white in the IR image. The clouds over the Southern Ocean are associated with a front. The cloud tops here are lower in the atmosphere, warmer and so appear greyer in the image.

The more complex features are not always easy to interpret. However, you should be able to imagine the potential of a sequence of images like this to inform meteorologists of likely developments.

Satellite measurements are described as 'remote', since the instrument is not placed within the atmosphere that it is observing, but instead it measures an electromagnetic spectrum at a distance from its target. From this spectrum, scientists are able to infer the most likely temperatures or water amounts which fit the observed radiation, but they are not directly measuring the physical quantities in which they are interested. Remote measurements are thus different in nature from the type of surface station measurements already discussed in Section 5.1, and a check against 'ground truth' is always of particular importance for satellite measurement. For example, a check might be made by comparing a surface temperature inferred from a satellite measurement with a direct measurement made using a thermometer on the surface at the same location and time. Satellite instruments must also be monitored in case they degrade with time.

5.2.4 Observing at other frequencies

All of the satellite images you have seen so far, and most that you will find on the DVD and on websites to which you may be directed, are made using either visible or IR radiation. However, these are not the only frequencies that can be used for meteorological measurements.

Higher frequencies from the blue end of visible light to UV are used to measure and to map gases that absorb in that region of the spectrum, notably ozone. Lower frequencies, including microwaves, also have observational uses. You have already seen that neither visible nor IR radiation penetrates through thick clouds, a fact that can be used to good effect to image cloud tops in the IR. Radiation at lower frequencies is much less strongly scattered by small particles; you would not expect a radio signal to be blocked by clouds or fog. In the microwave region of the spectrum, all clouds, except the thickest cumulonimbus, also appear transparent. A sensor that operates at microwave frequencies can therefore 'see through' clouds and fill in parts of the atmosphere and surface that are invisible to a satellite observing in the IR.

5.2.5   Where to see satellite images

Satellite images are a common part of TV and internet weather forecasts, especially the time sequences of hourly satellite images issued by national weather agencies. They provide a unique synopsis of the situation within the last few hours and in combination with other weather data they provide the starting point for the forecast. Rapid dissemination of this 'current/latest' information is vital, so that meteorologists can make a swift visual assessment of the next few hours covering a wide region.

The data from satellites are transmitted by radio signals to various ground stations from where they are fed to the WMO for sharing around the globe. Archives of images extending back several years can be accessed via the internet.

Question 5.1 (continued)

Revisit Table 5.1 and put a few words in the second row to describe some advantages and disadvantages of satellites for meteorological observations. If you have chosen to defer your study of the second part of Activity 5.1 until later, you will need to come back to this row again when you have completed the activity. Don't check the answer in the back of the book yet; wait until you have completed the whole table.

Question 5.3

Explain briefly why:

(a) polar orbiting satellites are not as convenient as those in geostationary orbit for providing sequences of weather images at frequent intervals;

(b) the highest latitudes are poorly served by geostationary satellites (for instance, look at what Figures 5.9, 5.11 and 5.12 can tell you about weather in Antarctica).

5.3   Recording the weather: filling in the middle

There is a sophisticated network of surface observation stations that can catalogue what occurs at ground level, at least over land, and an array of geostationary satellites that look in from above. Between them, these systems furnish a valuable range of data on the current state of the weather and the way it is changing, but quite a lot is missing.

Winds above ground level and the nature of air masses are key to the development of local weather. Ground-based and satellite observations of clouds can be used to infer the wind directions and nature of the air masses – interpreting sequences of images in this way is an essential skill for a meteorologist. However, even for the skilled, there are blind spots: little can be inferred about winds where there are no clouds tracing out the airflow; there are few surface observations made over the oceans, where weather systems may be developing; and geostationary satellite data are not useful for monitoring weather at high latitudes (although satellites in polar orbit are more useful in these regions).

There are two more ways to gather data from the bulk of the atmosphere. The first is to get a set of instruments up there and make measurements; the second is to probe it from the ground.

5.3.1   Radiosondes

Hot-air balloonists care a great deal about how the wind changes with height. It offers them their only means of steering. The launch is a particularly critical phase in ballooning as there is precious little room for manoeuvre, so just before committing to a launch the pilot usually arranges for a brightly coloured, helium-filled balloon to be released. As it rises it traces the local air movement giving a vivid impression of how the wind speed and wind direction vary with height.

'Hot air rises' is a general maxim, although Chapter 2 demonstrated that things are a little more complicated than that. In fact, air will rise as long as it remains warmer than its surroundings, but the rising air will itself be expanding and cooling, as discussed in relation to Figures 2.19–2.22.

■   Why is it possible to have a stable atmospheric environment in the troposphere, where the air temperature is observed to fall by about 5 °C per kilometre as height increases, in apparent contradiction of the 'hot air rises' maxim?

☐   Air from lower in the troposphere, although warm when at its original level, would cool to a lower temperature and so become denser than its surroundings if it were raised.

Chapter 2 showed that this situation is indeed stable, unless the temperature falls by more than about 10 °C per kilometre for unsaturated air. Only if the temperature falls with height even more rapidly than 10 °C per kilometre, would any rising air still be warmer than its surroundings, even after cooling, and continue to rise. In that case, convection would cause the warmer, lower air to rise until the overall change of temperature with height is such that the atmospheric environment is stable.

A balloon filled with air tends to sink because of the weight of the skin of the balloon and because of the weight of the extra air blown into it in order to inflate it. A soap bubble appears a great deal more buoyant as its skin is relatively light and very little extra air is used in its inflation, but unless caught on an upward-moving air current a soap bubble also sinks. Balloons filled with helium or hot air on the other hand tend to float upwards. The reason is that they are inflated with gases that are less dense than the surrounding air. If the total weight of skin and gas is less than the weight of surrounding air that would otherwise occupy the same space, then it inevitably follows that the balloon will float upwards.

From the start of systematic weather observations in the mid-nineteenth century it was recognised that data from above the ground would be useful in predicting how the weather might develop. Putting a thermometer and a barometer on a kite was easily done, though reading them was more of a challenge. By stacking many kites, or using a hot-air balloon, it was possible to generate enough lift to get a person aloft in a basket complete with instruments and record book. But, as you might imagine, this was not the basis for routine observation.

Figure 5.13   A radiosonde being launched.

The practical solution to probing the atmosphere with airborne instruments is to carry them on a helium-filled balloon large enough also to carry a radio transmitter and its power source. This arrangement is called a radiosonde ('sonde' is a French/international word meaning probe). The weight and value of the instrumentation posed serious challenges before the advent of microelectronics in the latter half of the twentieth century, but today the radiosonde is virtually a disposable automatic observation system, with the investment in the recovery of instruments being driven as much by tidiness as by economy. A modern radiosonde is shown in Figure 5.13. Radiosonde balloons will normally reach an altitude of about 25–30 km (i.e. into the stratosphere), at which point the balloon expands so much that it bursts. A small parachute then slows the descent of the instrument payload to prevent impact damage on landing. During its flight a radiosonde transmits data on temperature, pressure and humidity for 90 minutes or so. The balloon itself can also be tracked to map wind speed and direction; nowadays this is often done by an onboard Global Positioning System (GPS).

There are more than 800 sites around the world that launch radiosondes daily at 0000 and 1200 UTC and, as with other meteorological observations, radiosonde data are shared through the WMO.

5.3.2   Precipitation radar

As described in Chapter 3, the water droplets from which clouds are formed are typically in the range of a thousandth of a millimetre to a tenth of a millimetre in diameter and are widely dispersed. Raindrops on the other hand are much larger, typically 1–2 mm across. Regions of the atmosphere through which rain is falling contain markedly more water than an equivalent volume of cloud. As a consequence, a region of falling rain presents a more significant obstacle than a cloud to anything passing through it.

The word radar is an acronym for RAdio Detection And Ranging. Radar works by sending out a pulse of electromagnetic radiation and timing how long it takes for a portion of the signal to return as a result of reflections from objects encountered along the path. The delay time between the main pulse and its echo determines the distance between the target object and the radar station. The delay time is three-millionths of a second per kilometre and, although that sounds like a short time, it is easily possible to determine the distance between the emitting source and the reflecting object to within one metre.

The strength of a radar echo depends on two factors – how far away the target is and what it is made of. Strong radar echoes are created by dense, nearby objects whereas echoes from very small remote objects are easily 'lost in the noise'. If you were spotting distant aircraft by radar, you might try turning up the receiver only to be frustrated by finding that faint signals from distant objects get lost in what is known technically as 'clutter'. This is the radar equivalent of the hiss you hear on audio systems. Among the various contributions to clutter is rainfall.

Most developed countries operate radar networks to detect precipitation. By comparing the strength of an echo with the delay time (which effectively gives the distance) precipitation radar will provide estimates of the rates of rainfall;

the larger the raindrops detected, the stronger the return signal. This is especially valuable in warning of imminent flooding as the radar images give a clear indication of the intensity of the rain.

A single radar station can be expected to detect the presence of rain within a radius of 100 km or so. The network is planned to give appropriate coverage with overlapping areas. A complete scan of the skies around each station takes a few minutes, so typically data are updated every 10–30 minutes. The precipitation radar coverage of the stations operated over part of the USA is shown in Figure 5.14.

The curvature of the Earth over the range of precipitation radar is significant: because a radar beam is straight, the beam effectively climbs away from the Earth's surface with increasing distance from the radar station. The geometry is illustrated in Figure 5.15. At a distance of 50 km the radar simply cannot 'see' lower than about 0.5 km and by 200 km from the radar station the minimum height for detection by radar is almost 5 km. At 200 km range, a great deal of rain will therefore go undetected below the beam.

Determining the lateral speed of movement of a patch of rain can be done in two ways. The simplest is to track the rainfall and to compare its position at successive times, a few minutes apart. An even more immediate measure can be obtained from technology that works like the radar speed traps designed to identify speeding motorists. In this kind of device, the exact time difference between the reflections of successive radar pulses is measured electronically, and from this the speed of the reflecting object can be calculated. Thus rainfall radar gives a means of assessing wind speed at the cloud base, from the ground, without the use of radiosondes. Better still, thanks to the ingenuity of the instrument engineers, meteorologists can pick out radar reflections from patches of turbulence and dust in the air, so air movements can be 'read' from the ground even when it isn't raining! For this reason, radar is especially valuable for detecting tornadoes (the formation of which will be described in Chapter 8).

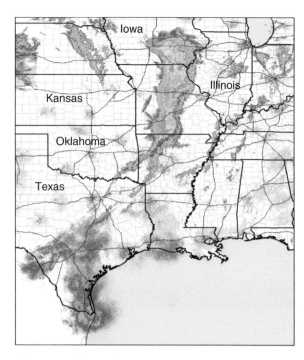

Figure 5.14 The composite radar reflection image from a large network of weather radar stations across some of the central states of the USA at 1148 UTC on 2 May 2008. The colours show the intensity of the reflected radar echo, with red indicating a much stronger reflected signal than blue, and white showing regions of no reflection. The reflected intensities are related to the density of water drops in each cubic metre of air; when this density is large the reflected intensity is also large. Typically, the bright green colour corresponds to regions of light rain. The red band of extremely heavy rainfall is prominent and occurs along the line of a cold front, with yellow areas indicating more moderate rain further north and west (i.e. behind the surface edge of the front). The front reaches the southern tip of Texas, where it is much weaker and there is only light rain.

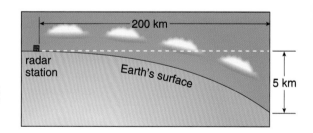

Figure 5.15 Owing to the curvature of the Earth, radar cannot detect low-level precipitation at long distances. The curvature of the Earth is greatly exaggerated for clarity.

5.3.3   Aircraft

Just as the oceans are relatively poorly sampled by surface stations, except for some buoys and weather stations mounted on ships, the air above them is even more difficult to access for direct measurements. Radiosonde ascents are normally made from land-based sites and radar techniques have a range of only about 100 km away from the coasts. The advent of satellites has made a huge impact on observations for ocean regions, where weather systems may develop otherwise almost unobserved until they reach land. Not everything, however, can be observed remotely and local, direct measurements are still needed, particularly of winds and other features too small to be sensed easily from orbit.

One valuable source of information derives from commercial air-traffic. Most large aircraft carry some meteorological instruments and report data back to meteorological centres. In fact, it is very much in their interests to do so. There are clear safety issues connected with visibility, pollutants, clouds and precipitation, turbulence and wind gusts. Airlines also have a particular interest in the position and strength of winds in the middle and upper troposphere; they can save enormous amounts of fuel by tailoring long-distance routes to make best use of tail winds and to minimise head winds in the meandering jet streams.

Aircraft reports are naturally concentrated in the main air-traffic lanes, but there are a handful of specialist meteorological research flights around the world. These do not participate in routine weather reports, but can instead be targeted on individual phenomena, such as clouds of a particular type or large storm systems, and used to make detailed observations.

Activity 5.1 (continued)   Meteorological instruments (Part 3)

The third part of this activity gives you the opportunity to learn a little more about some of the instruments that are used to gather meteorological data at various levels in the troposphere.

If you have already studied the first two parts of the activity, then now is the time to work through the third part. If you have chosen to leave the whole activity until this stage then start the activity from the beginning.

You will find the detailed instructions for the whole of this activity in the Activities section of the course website.

Question 5.1 (continued)

Revisit Table 5.1 and put a few words in the third row to describe some advantages and disadvantages of radiosondes and aircraft for meteorological observations. Now you have read the whole chapter and completed Activity 5.1, you may also see some more comparative advantages and disadvantages of surface stations and satellites. If so, add these to the table. You will find some suggested answers at the back of the book.

5.4   Summary of Chapter 5

There is a large international network of surface observation stations that record, among other things, air temperature, humidity, pressure, wind speed, wind direction, cloud type, cloud cover, and precipitation.

Satellites provide global, or at least hemispheric, coverage, from either polar or geostationary orbits, using remote instruments which operate at various frequencies in the electromagnetic spectrum.

To complement surface data and observations from space, data from within the atmosphere itself can be gathered by radiosondes, aircraft and by radar.

The collation and distribution of atmospheric data is coordinated by the World Meteorological Organisation.

Chapter 6
Weather forecasts

This chapter describes how an understanding of the physical processes that govern atmospheric behaviour, together with a range of observations of what the atmosphere is doing now, can be used to predict how the atmosphere might evolve in future and hence to make a weather forecast. The combination of an ability to predict the behaviour of the atmosphere and a knowledge of its present state is vital to any attempt to forecast the weather.

The idea of looking ahead to how the weather might develop is a theme throughout this chapter. Predictions can be made informally, based on local 'weather lore' and simple visual observations, or can be derived from previous experience and weather records. To make global forecasts and to predict the weather in detail more than a few hours ahead requires supercomputers and highly complex mathematical models of the atmosphere, combined with data from a variety of satellites, aeroplanes, radiosondes and ground stations.

If you would like to check up in advance where the places mentioned in this chapter are located, the list follows. (Some of these places have already been mentioned in previous chapters.)

- Cities: Edmonton (Canada), New Delhi (India), Canberra (southeastern Australia)
- Countries: Ireland, New Zealand, Singapore, Japan
- UK locations: London, Boscastle (Cornwall).

6.1   Seaweed, statistics or science?

Weather forecasts are of interest for a wide range of personal, commercial and leisure activities. Among the important users of weather forecasts are the energy utilities, especially in developed areas with excessively cold winters or excessively hot summers. The energy supply sector needs not only a detailed analysis of the current weather but also a forecast of how it will develop in the future on various timescales – hours, days, weeks and months – together with some estimate of how reliable meteorologists think the forecast may be.

■ From the following list, identify those that are likely to seek accurate, local weather forecasts for one to five days ahead to help in the planning of their activities: organisers of outdoor sports or leisure activities; airport operators; road and rail network operators; the construction industry; farmers.

□ All of them.

The impacts of weather on these and other types of activity will be discussed further in Chapter 9. It is difficult to imagine anyone who would completely ignore information in weather forecasts; even submariners have specialised forecasts prepared for them and although astronauts may be immune from the effects of weather for long periods, their launch into space and return home will be guided by advice from meteorologists.

Study comment

In this chapter you will look at different types of forecast, how they are made, and how reliable they are likely to be. There are a number of different strands to the story that you will want to keep track of. Before starting to study the material, this would be a good point at which to think about the various techniques you have practised while studying previous chapters (skim reading ahead of careful study, making notes, highlighting, compiling information into tables and writing a summary of the main points of particular sections). Decide which techniques have worked best for you, and try to make these a regular part of your study routine for this and subsequent chapters.

There are various ways of gaining knowledge about future weather conditions, other than gazing into crystal balls or simply waiting for events to happen. For example, you might just guess or invoke folklore, you might appeal to statistics or else you might try to work out, by applying scientific principles, what is most likely to happen next. This section will contrast these approaches in a little more detail.

A handful of seaweed or a pine cone or indeed many other water-absorbing materials from wool to wood will respond to local changes in humidity – fine fibres will respond more rapidly than bulky vegetable matter. Seaweed becomes progressively more brittle in a dry atmosphere, but suppleness returns with increased humidity. A pine cone opens in dry air and closes when moisture levels increase. But these are relatively slow responses to recent weather rather than predictions of the future and are not relevant to real weather forecasting.

It's interesting to examine instead the extent to which a weather forecast might simply be based on place and time; it could after all be argued that weather is to a considerable extent determined by where on the Earth you are and by where the Earth is in relation to its annual orbit around the Sun. For example, Figure 6.1 shows the monthly mean temperatures for March and December between 2000 and 2007 for Edmonton in central Canada (latitude 53° N) and for Singapore (which is close to the Equator, latitude 1° N).

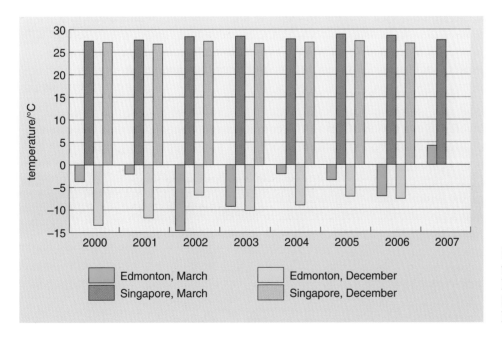

Figure 6.1   Monthly mean temperatures during March and December in Edmonton and Singapore between 2000 and March 2007.

■ Assuming that temperatures are measured once per hour, how might daily mean temperature be calculated? (You may like to refer back to Section 2.1.2 for a similar, but not identical, example.)

☐ The 24 temperature values taken on each day are added together and divided by 24 to obtain the daily mean temperature for that day.

■ How is monthly mean temperature found from the daily mean temperatures for March and December?

☐ The 31 daily means for each day of the month are added together and divided by 31.

■ How could the monthly mean temperature be found directly from hourly measurements?

☐ Adding all the hourly temperatures taken during a month and dividing the total by $(31 \times 24) = 744$ in a single step will give the same result as taking the monthly mean of the daily mean temperatures.

■ How does the monthly mean temperature in Edmonton and Singapore vary from year to year for each of the two months shown in Figure 6.1?

☐ In Singapore the monthly mean temperature in both March and December is very similar from year to year over the period from 2000 to 2007. In Edmonton the monthly mean temperature in these months appears to vary more erratically between years.

The erratic pattern shown for Edmonton in Figure 6.1 means that it cannot be used to predict monthly mean temperatures for March and December with a useful level of accuracy. The companies supplying power for heating in Edmonton need a better assessment of the future likely winter and spring demand than these data can provide. Other commercial and domestic sectors will be equally concerned about what to expect from other variable aspects of the weather such as rain, low visibility or high humidity, and so on.

Can historical data be used more satisfactorily? Although there may be rapid, local changes within a particular weather pattern, weather systems, in general, develop over a period of days. As a consequence, on any given day, in a given location, it might be suggested that tomorrow's weather is likely to be 'much the same as today', and that at least offers what is called a 'persistence forecast' for the following day. A persistence forecast simply uses the present as the best guess for the future. Figure 6.2 illustrates the extent to which this simplistic approach would have earned forecasters credit in four different locations during March in 2000, 2001, 2002 and 2005, again with reference only to temperature.

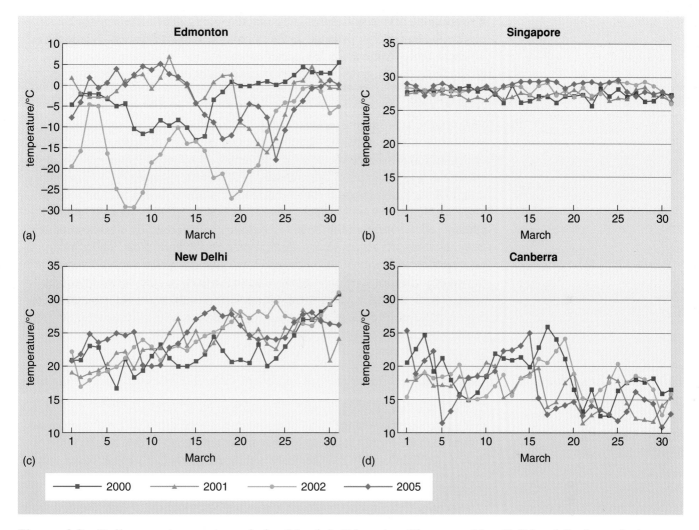

Figure 6.2   Daily mean temperatures during March in Edmonton, Singapore, New Delhi and Canberra during 2000, 2001, 2002 and 2005.

■ By examining the plots for Edmonton in Figure 6.2a, suggest how reliable a simple, next-day persistence forecast of temperature would be for March in the four years shown.

☐ Around this time of year the mean daily temperature in Edmonton can be rather variable and persistence is not generally a good guide, since there are large temperature changes between successive days on many occasions.

■ How does temperature variability compare at the three other locations?

☐ Canberra, New Delhi and Singapore experience progressively less variable temperatures from day to day.

■ At which location would persistence forecasting be most successful?

☐ Singapore.

The accuracy of this 'much the same as today', persistence forecast can be readily quantified. For instance, in Edmonton the data of Figure 6.2 show that the mean daily temperature in March was less than 1 °C different from that of the previous day on no more than five occasions in any of the years covered. By contrast, in New Delhi in 2005 just over half of the days in March had a mean daily temperature less than 1 °C different from that of the previous day. Singapore's daily mean temperature is even more reproducible, with about 80% of days being within 1 °C of the previous day's mean temperature. This is typical of the differences between a mid-latitude location (Edmonton) and an equatorial one (Singapore). New Delhi (29° N) and Canberra (35° S) provide intermediate examples from each hemisphere. As described in Section 4.1, the atmospheric circulation in equatorial regions is dominated by an overturning Hadley cell, whereas mid-latitude regions are characterised by a succession of low- and high-pressure systems which form near the polar front. The growth, propagation and decay of the highs and lows give rise to the variability and day-to-day changes seen in latitudes outside the tropics. Mid-latitude weather forecasting is a significant challenge for a few days ahead. In the equatorial region, weather forecasting is a very different proposition, although no less challenging in other respects, largely as a result of the multitude of smaller convective systems.

Question 6.1

You are told that the daily mean temperature in New Delhi was 20 °C on 1 March in a particular year. On the basis of a persistence forecast, what prediction could you have made for the most likely daily mean temperature for 6 March that year in New Delhi? Roughly how accurate is this prediction likely to be, based only on the information in Figure 6.2?

The effectiveness of a persistence forecast could be improved by combining the historical, seasonal statistics for any given area with the present conditions. This would be effective in incorporating longer-term trends such as the fall of temperature across March each year in Canberra, though this trend is not steady and there are particular times when the temperature increases from one day to the next. But this *statistical* approach is not likely to be able to forecast local weather very far ahead with the degree of certainty that is expected in the twenty-first century. For that you have to look to ways of using *scientific* understanding of the weather to guide the prediction of future conditions from current measurements and analyses of key physical quantities such as temperature, pressure, humidity, wind speed and wind direction. Thus, instead of simply 'it will probably be warm tomorrow because it is warm today,' or 'because it was warm this time last year', a skilful forecaster should be able to assert that 'over the next few days it will remain warm and dry as warm air continues to be fed overland from the south by a slowly moving high-pressure system ...'. The scientific approach to weather forecasting requires more than the past record of observations needed by the statistical approaches; it also requires an understanding of how weather systems develop and an appreciation of the fundamental physical laws that govern the behaviour of the atmosphere.

6.2 Weather models

Weather forecasting based on un-instrumented, ground-based observations alone is something we can all try every time we look up at the sky. Just identifying the cloud types can give an idea of what will happen in the next few hours. The speed and direction of clouds provide further clues about the near future. However, reading the sky for signs of the weather a day or more ahead is a serious challenge, and not one to be lightly undertaken without the benefit of instruments and considerable training. This section aims to show why.

As you saw in Chapter 5, satellite images, ground-based radar and other surface stations can produce a snapshot picture of the atmosphere, as close to the present moment as is practical. The weather at the present moment can be used to produce a short-term forecast of up to six hours ahead, referred to as a 'nowcast'. A nowcast is very useful for a wide variety of purposes where the weather across a region at the present time and in the next few hours is of critical importance. To predict the weather a few hours ahead, an experienced forecaster can visualise how the weather will evolve; you should now have begun to develop the ability to do the same and will find that your skill improves with further practice, as a result of looking at sequences of satellite images (which you did in Chapter 5) and weather charts (which you will work on in Chapter 7). The further ahead in time a weather forecast is required, the larger the area the picture must cover. This is clearly revealed by sequences of satellite images on the course DVD, which show weather systems crossing entire continents and oceans in a few days. Eventually the complexity and size of the problem defeats any human attempt to forecast the details of what will happen.

In order for scientists to predict the future behaviour of a system they require a 'model' of that system. The term 'model' has a special significance in science. It does not necessarily mean a physical model, although that is certainly possible; it may instead be a set of mathematical equations or a computer program. More generally, models are simplified versions of real systems. A model of some sort is essential to predict the future evolution of a system, or to explore what would happen under a different set of circumstances. Whether that model is correct or not is tested by making predictions and then comparing those predictions with observations of the real system; a weather forecast is a good example of precisely this process in a very complex situation.

Models range from simple concepts through mathematical equations solved with pencil and paper to computer calculations used for scientific research. At the most complex end of the range lie numerical simulation models. Here almost everything that is thought to be important is included to the highest level of detail that is practical with available computing resources and every effort is made to simulate reality. Complex numerical simulation models, based on physical laws and processes, are used to help make weather predictions.

6.2.1 Forecasts based on local trends and weather lore

Many simple weather models are, in fact, applied subconsciously. You may well have taken a quick look out of the window to decide whether to wear a coat or to carry an umbrella when you were about to go out for the day. This is performing a weather forecast. You have clearly taken an observation by looking out of the window, but you are also applying a simple model based on your experience of the weather in order to predict, for instance, that the weather for the next few hours is likely to remain much the same as it is now. You have made a 'forecast' (i.e. 'cast' your observation forward in time), almost without thinking about it. This is a persistence forecast model, as described in Section 6.1, and is actually a reasonable prediction for short times into the future. You may think that the weather is changeable in your region, but if we lived on a planet where the weather really did change completely every few minutes then you would not have bothered to look before deciding what to wear or carry because you would always have to be prepared for all eventualities. In making forecasts, you need to apply your knowledge of the typical timescales associated with weather systems.

You were also aware of the limited applicability of your persistence model, because you would probably not rely on just a quick look out of the window to pack for a longer trip away from home. In that case you might take into account the time of year to decide that, although it is warm and dry today, for example, it might well get colder and rain later. You have not made a detailed forecast, but you have recognised that there are times beyond that at which your persistence forecast model might be reasonably reliable. You have then fallen back on what you know usually happens at this time of year. This is more formally known as 'climatology' and, in a much extended form, is the basis for complex statistical weather predictions based on detailed records of what has happened in the past. Climatology is generally a very good predictor of typical conditions and their likely range, and is much used in assessing insurance risk, for example. It is limited by the accuracy with which past observations were made and by the length of the historical record at any particular site, which will not include all the possible extreme events. But climatology cannot hope to tell you about the detailed evolution of a particular storm that might be passing in the next few days.

■   Apart from an inability to predict the evolution of specific events, is there any other problem you can think of when relying on climatology to predict the future from the past record?

☐   A forecast based on climatology assumes that the range of weather observed in the past is the same as that likely to be encountered in the future. This may not be true if the past record is incomplete or if there are changes in climate.

A way of improving upon the persistence forecast for the short term is to make a more careful observation of the sky. You have had some opportunity to develop this skill as you study this course, for example during Activity 3.1; it is not a difficult skill to acquire and is practised routinely by sailors and hill-walkers. As a simple example, suppose that you see dark clouds forming on the horizon in the direction from which the wind is blowing. You may then expect that, although the weather is fine now, some rain may arrive in an hour or so. If you can roughly judge the speed of the wind, you may even have a better idea of how soon the rain will arrive. This is a simple 'trend' forecast. You have built upon the persistence forecast by adding a rate of change with time of some aspect of the weather. It may well be that you decide the weather is settled and that there is no obvious trend, so the best prediction of the future turns out to be a persistence forecast; in other words, you judge that the weather will remain the same as it is now.

Some weather folklore has its roots in experience and careful observations of weather trends. It has been estimated that there are more than 3000 weather-related sayings in the English language alone and other languages have equally rich traditions based on years of experience when the weather was of critical importance to most people. Many are largely myths, such as the famous

> St Swithin's Day, if it does rain
>
> Full forty days, it will remain
>
> St Swithin's Day, if it be fair
>
> For forty days, t'will rain no more.

(The rhyme works better in dialects in which 'more' is pronounced as 'mair'.)

St Swithin's Day (15 July) is no more significant than any other day of the year for weather. A persistence forecast over 40 days seems extremely unlikely in mid-latitudes, as you have seen! Similar sayings exist based around other days in other parts of the world, e.g. Groundhog Day (2 February) in the USA; all lack observational evidence.

Some pieces of weather lore, on the other hand, are based on good observations of approaching weather systems.

> Mares' tails and mackerel scales make tall ships take in their sails.

A mackerel sky of cirrocumulus (or altocumulus) clouds (which you saw a picture of in Activity 3.1) generally precedes a warm front.

■ Why might a mackerel sky 'make tall ships take in their sails'?

☐ Ships would 'take in their sails' to adjust, or 'trim', them for a change of direction in the wind and for safety in the event of bad weather. The approaching warm front is likely to bring precipitation and a sudden change in wind direction.

Question 6.2

Imagine that you are standing on the west coast of Ireland and see a mackerel sky, directly overhead. The wind is a fresh westerly breeze, with a steady speed of 30 km per hour. Taking the values given in Section 4.3 of 1 : 75 for the average slope of a cold front and 1 : 150 for the average slope of a warm front, and using the typical value of 5000 m for the cloud base of a mackerel sky:

(a) how far away would you expect the approaching front to be at ground level?

(b) when would you estimate that it will reach you on the ground, assuming that the front moves over the ocean at roughly the same speed as the wind?

A similar example is found when rings are seen around the Moon (these are called lunar halos). Rings around the Moon are taken to be a sign of bad weather to come. A halo is the result of rays of moonlight (actually sunlight reflected from the Moon, of course) being bent and defocused during their passage through small ice crystals high in the atmosphere. This can form a brightish ring around the Moon (cloud halo effects are also mentioned in Table 3.1). The ice crystals are within high altitude, thin cirrostratus clouds that may precede a warm front by one or two days, as illustrated in Figure 4.11. Thus their presence may signify the approach of a low-pressure system and precipitation.

The weather folklore goes on to say that the number of stars that can be seen within the Moon ring will tell you the number of days before the weather arrives. The number of stars visible may indeed have some relation to cloud thickness, but must also depend on other factors such as the phase and position of the Moon or the brightness of street lighting, and in reality would be unlikely to vary much once the clouds appear.

> Red sky at night: shepherds' delight
>
> Red sky in the morning: shepherds' warning.

This rhyme also has a basis in fact, and is of very ancient origin. There are two explanations for a red sky at night. The first is that small dust particles and pollutants in the atmosphere will tend to scatter blue light further away from its original path than red light, leaving a red colour around the Sun at sunset, which corresponds with a reddening of the western sky. A temperature inversion in the lower atmosphere (as described in Section 2.1.4) is often associated with a high-pressure system, which in turn can imply fine weather. The stable layer of the atmosphere associated with the inversion will trap more of the dust particles close to the surface and hence increase the reddening seen in the evening sky.

A second explanation is that the red light is seen at sunset because it is reflected off cloud tops, which corresponds with a reddening of the sky overhead and to the east. When the Sun is setting in the west, the red light is reflected back from clouds to the east of the observer. In mid-latitudes, weather systems normally pass from west to east, because of the prevailing wind direction described in Chapter 4. This means that a red sky at night is a sign of a front that has already passed by to the east, leaving clearer air behind. In contrast, a red sky in the morning is a sign of very high and thin cirrus cloud overhead and to the east, again scattering blue light and leaving red illumination. Just as with the lunar halos, the high, thin cloud is a sign of an approaching warm front and probable bad weather still some distance away to the west.

These phenomena are well worth looking out for when you observe the sky.

Trend-based forecasting ultimately has its limits in the local nature of the observations that are available. To predict the weather on timescales of days and longer really requires observations and models of behaviour over length scales of thousands of kilometres. This is where more sophisticated data-gathering and numerical models begin to be required. Box 6.1 explains length and timescales in more detail.

Box 6.1 Length scales and timescales in meteorology

When describing the typical 'size' of weather phenomena there are various horizontal length or distance scales associated with weather forecasting and each has a corresponding timescale that reflects the extent to which weather systems develop in distance and time. These are summarised in Table 6.1. These scales are not precise, but give a feeling for the sizes and times of evolution of different weather phenomena. In the vertical, the length scale is quite different from that in the horizontal, and the roughly 10 km vertical distance from the surface to the tropopause is important for features at nearly all horizontal scales, except perhaps at the microscale.

Table 6.1 Approximate length scales and timescales relevant in weather forecasting and modelling.

Descriptor	Horizontal length scale	Timescale
Microscale	1 km and smaller	minutes
Mesoscale	1 km to 250 km	hours
Synoptic	250 km to 2000 km	days
Global	2000 km to planet-encircling	weeks to seasons

'Microscale' atmospheric phenomena include convective cumulus clouds, as described in Section 3.1. The 'mesoscale' refers to a broad range of weather on scales larger than the microscale but smaller than typical mid-latitude highs and lows; a good example you have already encountered in an earlier chapter is a sea breeze. The 'synoptic scale' is a term commonly used in meteorology and refers to motion at the scale of typical high- and low-pressure mid-latitude weather systems, i.e. to circulations of several hundred kilometres and more in extent, which evolve over the course of a few days. The word 'synoptic' is derived from the ancient Greek for 'together' and 'seeing' and describes observations that give a broad view of a subject at a particular time. A 'synoptic chart' can show several highs and lows and might cover a large geographic region, such as the North Atlantic and western Europe, or Australia and the surrounding ocean, or perhaps Southeast Asia. Figure 2.15 is an example of a synoptic chart and you will see many more in Chapter 7. On still larger scales, the jet streams and the tropical Hadley circulation, both described in Chapter 4, are examples of global-scale, planet-encircling phenomena.

In general, the larger the length scale at which events happen, the longer the timescale on which they happen, and vice versa. If meteorologists are concerned to predict the weather several days ahead, then they need to be aware of the full synoptic, and possibly global, atmospheric state.

6.2.2 The beginnings of calculated weather

Forecasting further than a few days ahead requires very considerable skill to foresee the development of weather systems from snapshots provided by satellite images and synoptic charts. The experts are expected to predict the evolving weather over a huge range of horizontal length scales and they are sufficiently challenged by this that they generally call on computers to guide them, making great use of the ability of computers to process vast quantities of data. Numerical Weather Prediction (NWP) is therefore the name given to the process of computer-based weather forecasting. The basic idea of calculating what happens next in the atmosphere was discussed in 1904 by a Norwegian physicist, Vilhelm Bjerknes (whose contribution to the theory of fronts was mentioned in Section 4.3). Soon afterwards, a British mathematician, Lewis Fry Richardson, took up the challenge; various other people throughout Europe were simultaneously developing similar ideas. Richardson's distinctive contribution came when he attempted a synoptic-scale forecast based entirely on numerical calculations by hand, starting from a set of measured atmospheric conditions. His aim was to determine what would happen over the next few hours using only the laws of physics to calculate the movement of air and the redistribution of heat. The attempt was a glorious failure as a forecast and anyway took much longer to complete than the time interval covered by the forecast, being finally published in a book in 1922, a decade after the period to which it related! Owing to the failure of its single forecast and the impracticability of employing sufficient human 'computers' to make a timely numerical prediction, Richardson's book made little impact at the time, but his work foreshadows many of the developments of modern NWP.

Richardson realised that the atmosphere could be subdivided into boxes, for each of which he calculated a separate pressure, temperature, humidity, wind speed and wind direction. The distribution of these boxes across Europe is illustrated in Figure 6.3, which is taken from Richardson's book. He divided the atmosphere into five layers of boxes in the vertical. The number of boxes was restricted by the enormous number of calculations that had to be performed by hand. Nowadays it is possible to recreate Richardson's forecast in a few minutes on even a modest home computer, but he spent probably a thousand hours, over more than a year, working with a slide-rule (a mechanical device used primarily for multiplication and division). Remarkably, he did not seem to make any serious errors in the calculations as far as we know. His final forecast was in error for more complicated reasons.

What Richardson lacked was the awareness of how to set up the initial state of his model from the observations and how to 'smooth' the results of his calculations so as to focus on the large-scale, slowly evolving weather and to stop small-scale, erroneous fluctuations from developing. He was also unaware of which were the important factors on which to concentrate the calculations – without the power and speed of an electronic computer there just wasn't enough time to do the sums. The first successful numerical prediction was reported in 1950, after the advent of the electronic computer, by a team composed of an American meteorologist Jule Charney, a Norwegian meteorologist Ragnar Fjörtoft, and an applied mathematician, Hungarian-born American John von Neumann.

Box 6.2 shows how physical relationships can be described in mathematical terms, a procedure that is at the heart of calculating the weather.

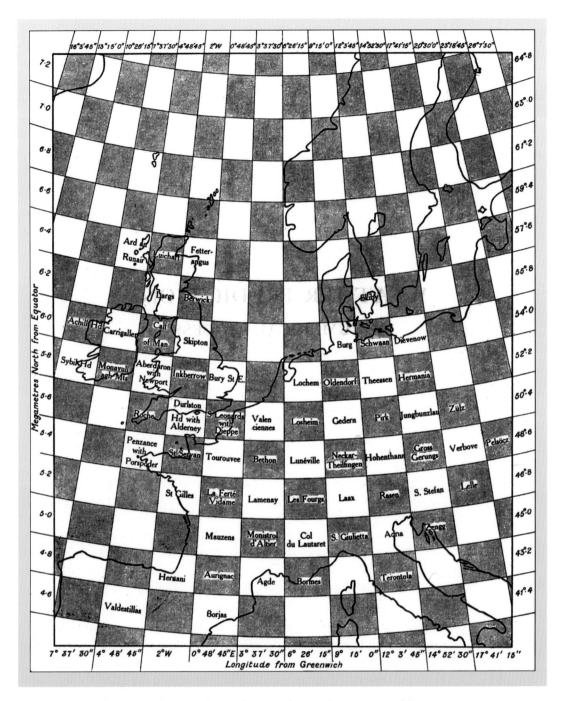

Figure 6.3 The frontispiece of *Weather Prediction by Numerical Process*
(L. F. Richardson, Cambridge University Press, 1922), showing the 'chessboard' of boxes
into which Richardson divided the atmosphere, each covering 200 km in the north–south
direction and 2° 48′ 45″ in longitude. There were five 'strata' or layers of such boxes in
the vertical. (A minute, symbol ′, of longitude or latitude is $\frac{1}{60}$ th of a degree. A second,
symbol ″, of longitude or latitude is $\frac{1}{60}$ th of a minute, i.e. $\frac{1}{360}$ th of a degree. A megametre
is one million metres, i.e. 1000 km.) The longitudinal division of the boxes may seem an odd
choice, but Richardson elected to size his boxes such that it required exactly 128 to go right
round the world.

Box 6.2 How to describe relationships with mathematics

If you want to work out what happens next using mathematics rather than intuition, then you will need to express mathematically what you know about the system you are studying. For weather forecasting, scientists need to be able to describe the properties of the atmosphere in mathematical relationships, i.e. 'equations'. If your calculations involve a single independent quantity, say temperature, then you will need just one equation to tell you what it is. For a given, single location, it may be as simple as

temperature = 15 °C

or it may be a little more complicated, such as

temperature = starting temperature + heating rate (in °C per second)
 × heating time (in seconds)

With two quantities, say temperature and pressure, then you will need two equations to determine them at each location. The simplest and least challenging scenario would then be two equations assigning constant values such as

temperature = 15 °C

and

pressure = 1013 hPa

A little more challenging would be

temperature = 15 °C

and

pressure = [temperature (in °C) + 273 °C] × 3.517 hPa per °C

so, in this example, pressure can be calculated from the known temperature as

pressure = [288 °C] × 3.517 hPa per °C = 1013 hPa

As a general rule, for every quantity that a problem involves you need one equation, but there may be many similar equations if a quantity needs to be known at many locations, as is the case in meteorology.

The equation given above to relate pressure and temperature assumes that the density of the air is constant. In fact, all three of these quantities can vary and are linked by another equation:

pressure = [temperature (in °C) + 273 °C] × [density (in kg per cubic metre)]
 × 2.871 hPa × cubic metre per kg per °C

Do not be concerned about the complexity of the units in this equation. It is included here only to show how more than two quantities may be linked and to give you a more realistic impression of the equations describing the atmosphere. The constant number 2.871 hPa × cubic metre per kg per °C is determined by the mixture of gases that make up the atmosphere. If you enjoy maths, you might like to check that this equation gives a similar result for the pressure as the one above it if the air density is 1.225 kg per cubic metre (which is typical of the atmosphere near the Earth's surface).

This last equation allows any one of three quantities – pressure, temperature or density – to be calculated at any location, but only if the values of the other two are already known at the same location. It does not say anything about how any of these quantities will change with time. In order to forecast the behaviour of the atmosphere, this equation therefore needs to be combined with other equations, which also link these and other quantities with time and place.

When many quantities are interlinked, as they normally are in the atmosphere, it is often convenient to call on the computing experts to complete the calculations. These relationships are not just simply about the quantities that must be determined but also involve the way in which these quantities change with time or from one location to another.

6.2.3   Modelling the atmosphere

NWP is based on mathematical equations that encapsulate the relationships between five key physical quantities in the atmosphere – one quantity that combines the speed of the wind (both horizontal and vertical) and its direction, and others that specify air temperature, pressure, density and humidity – so there will have to be five equations to link them at any point. Each equation links two or more of the quantities. The relevance of each of the five relationships, each of which is provided by physical laws, may be described as follows:

- Equation 1 describes the flow of the air as it is subjected to the effects of the Earth's rotation, gravity, pressure changes and friction.

- Equation 2 makes sure that the amount of air in the atmosphere remains fixed: whenever and wherever parcels of air move about in the wind, the density changes as the parcels expand or are compressed, but air is not created and not destroyed.

- Equation 3 concerns the way that the temperature at a point in the atmosphere can change because cooler or warmer air is carried to that point by the wind, or because locally the air expands or contracts, or because of heating by absorption of radiation, or because of water evaporating or condensing.

- Equation 4 links the pressure of the air to its density and temperature, and takes a form like that of the final equation in Box 6.2. The numerical value 2.871 in this equation depends on the mixture of gases that make up the atmosphere.

- Equation 5 describes the way in which the amount of water vapour in any small parcel of air changes as it is carried along by the wind and as condensation and evaporation occur in response to temperature changes.

Further equations, very like Equation 5 above, can be added for any other atmospheric quantities that the model might be required to keep track of, one additional equation for each quantity. These might include dust, pollen, ozone and atmospheric pollutants, all of which are transported by winds and which enter or leave the atmosphere at the surface or as a result of chemical reactions within the atmosphere.

The equations describing the atmosphere are rather complicated because almost every quantity depends on several other quantities and on the way in which the quantities are changing. Each quantity varies throughout the atmosphere with position and with time. To write equations like these in a form that can be programmed on a computer, it is necessary to divide the atmosphere up into layers like those of an onion. Each layer is subdivided into boxes, with each box having a separate value for its temperature, pressure, etc., often taken to apply at the centre point of each box. These values must be specified initially and are then updated by the computer program as it performs its calculations. The Equations 1–5 above link what is happening within each box to what is happening within all surrounding boxes, within a layer and between the layers. The arrangement of boxes is shown in Figures 6.4 and 6.5. The values of temperature, pressure, etc. are recalculated as time is advanced by using these equations to determine how much each quantity in each box is changed in a given time by its surroundings.

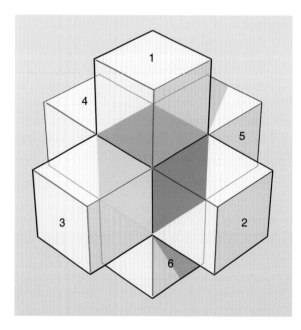

Figure 6.4 A small part of a grid of boxes for NWP. At each step forward in time, values of temperature, pressure, humidity and wind speed and direction in each box are updated based on data values in all surrounding boxes. The central purple box is influenced most strongly by boxes 1–6 around it, while another 20 boxes (not shown) which are a little further away and touch the purple box only at the corners or edges, exert a lesser influence.

In a global model, as the name implies, the entire globe is covered in a grid of boxes, which narrow towards the poles as the lines of longitude converge, as illustrated in Figure 6.5b. This narrowing must be taken into account when formulating Equations 1–5 for each box.

The boxes into which the atmosphere is divided by a numerical model are in some ways analogous to pixels in a digital-camera image, each with their own values of colour and brightness, although the digital camera may form only a two-dimensional image. An atmospheric model is both three-dimensional (longitude, latitude and height) and more like a movie than a still image, since each box in the grid changes with time. As with the frames of a movie, the model is advanced through a series of small 'time-steps', chosen to be a time interval over which the pattern of atmospheric quantities will change by only a small amount. A model might even be thought of as a series of simultaneous three-dimensional movies, one for each quantity under investigation. Each movie is coupled to and affects the others through links in Equations 1–5.

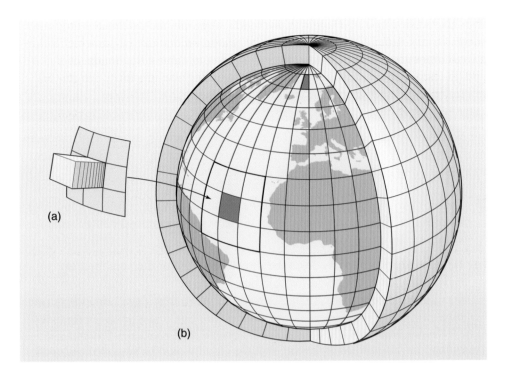

(a)

(b)

Figure 6.5 (a) A single column of boxes within an atmospheric model. Similar columns surround the one shown. Many layers of boxes are used to represent the atmosphere and each layer has an influence on the layers above and below. The boxes are not all the same depth in the vertical direction; thinner layers of boxes are used in regions where more attention needs to be concentrated, in particular near to the surface. The depth of the boxes is exaggerated here for clarity and in reality there are likely to be many more layers. (b) The globe is covered with layers of boxes, which are here drawn as a regular 10° latitude by 10° longitude grid. All the boxes have the same width in the latitudinal direction (about 1100 km), but each narrows in the longitudinal direction as they near the poles. The two purple boxes at the surface illustrate this effect: the box in the tropics would look very nearly square when seen from directly above (i.e. in plan view), whereas the box in the Arctic Ocean is noticeably narrower in the east–west than the north–south direction. However, the boxes do not have to be chosen to be square in plan view at the Equator. For example, boxes that are elongated in the longitudinal direction at the Equator might be deliberately chosen in order to get roughly square boxes in plan view at mid-latitudes. The horizontal size of the boxes in the grid is much exaggerated in this diagram for clarity; typically a finer grid composed of smaller boxes would be used in a global model.

As in a high-specification digital camera with many pixels, it is desirable to have many boxes in the model in order to 'see' the most detail. But this detail comes at a cost in terms of the computer memory and processing power required. There is always a compromise that has to be made between the number of boxes, usually described as the 'resolution' of the model, and the computing resources available to run the model within a certain time, e.g. when required for a forecast. A model with fewer larger boxes (lower resolution) permits more rapid model calculations, but may misrepresent important weather features at smaller scales. There are alternatives to dividing the atmosphere into the regular boxes described so far; these include using offset and irregular grids, boxes of different shapes, boxes that adapt their shape to changes in the model atmosphere, and so on. Ultimately, however, any model has some limit on the resolution that can be achieved within a fixed amount of computer time. Referring back to Table 6.1, a model of a certain resolution can only hope to describe weather phenomena on length (and related timescales) greater than the size of its boxes.

The values of the atmospheric properties within a box can change as air moves, for example as warmer or cooler air is carried by the winds, as taken into account in Equation 3 above. The process in which properties change at a fixed location as a result of air movement is known as 'advection.'

■ Referring to Figure 6.4, why might the cloudiness in the purple box increase as a result of horizontal winds, even if there is no new cloud being formed within the box?

☐ If the wind were blowing from the direction of one of the neighbouring boxes, say box 2, and the air within box 2 were presently cloudier than the air within the purple box, then cloud would move from box 2 into the purple box.

This situation is described by saying that the cloud would be advected. Advection is not confined to the horizontal direction, but can also happen as a result of vertical motion. The cloudiness in the purple box might well increase if additional, humid air were advected upwards from box 6 below. It would be less likely to increase if air were advected downwards from box 1 above, since air higher in the atmosphere is often drier and less cloudy.

■ How will the temperature of any air being advected downwards from box 1 change and what likely impact will this have on cloudiness within the purple box? (You may want to look back at some of the key points in Chapters 2 and 3.)

☐ The air will be warmed as it descends, permitting it to hold more water vapour, and the air in the purple box is therefore likely to become less cloudy.

In addition to all the explicit physical processes described so far, an NWP model also has to represent many processes that occur *within* each box. These are often known as 'parameterisations' or 'sub-models' and represent much of the work involved in designing a model. They also require much of the resources when the model is run on a computer, since most parameterisations must be calculated separately for each box in the model, once for each time-step. Processes that must be represented by parameterisations include: modelling the detailed absorption, scattering and emission of radiation (both sunlight and infrared emission from the Earth); modelling the effect of small-scale convection and mixing within the atmosphere; modelling the formation of clouds and precipitation; modelling the interaction of the atmosphere with a rough or smooth solid surface, or with vegetation or with the oceans; modelling the formation and melting of ice; and many other processes, such as chemical reactions within the atmosphere. These are modelled at different levels of detail for different purposes, but all are potentially important for forecasting the weather. There is normally no attempt to model each individual cloud within a box but a cloud parameterisation scheme is likely to keep track of the overall fraction of a box that is occupied by clouds, i.e.

to use a summary of the cloudiness within that region. A cloud parameterisation scheme may separately keep track of clouds of each of several different types.

The set of relationships, the array of boxes and the method of visiting each box in turn to 'ripple through' the effects of changes to quantities in surrounding boxes, together constitute a model for Numerical Weather Prediction. There are three key features in any numerical forecasting model at a particular scale. Two of these – the initial conditions (i.e. the initial values of the atmospheric quantities in each box) and the equations – have already been described. The third feature relates to what are termed the 'boundaries' and refers to:

- the way in which the atmosphere interacts with the Earth's surface, whether ocean, ice sheet or land at the bottom of the lowest layer of boxes
- the way in which the upper regions of the atmosphere are treated as the atmosphere becomes increasingly tenuous
- for models that do not cover the whole globe, the way in which artificial vertical walls are introduced around the region being modelled.

Boundary conditions are essential to provide a complete system, over which Equations 1–5 apply.

In summary then:

Numerical forecasting models have three key features:

1   the initial conditions

2   the equations

3   the boundary conditions.

If any of these features is handled incorrectly then the whole modelling process is jeopardised.

6.2.4   Global, synoptic and mesoscale models

The biggest models follow large-scale movements in the whole atmosphere – these are called global models, or sometimes General Circulation Models (GCMs, although rather confusingly this acronym also stands for Global Climate Models). The surface area of the Earth is about 500 million square kilometres and the model needs to follow circulations to at least 40 km up into the atmosphere.

To follow the global-scale weather, one might choose boxes with sides of around 50 km on average over the Earth's 500 000 000 square kilometre surface. Each box will cover an area of the Earth's surface of 50 km $\times$ 50 km, i.e. 2500 square kilometres. In each global layer there will therefore be:

$$\frac{500\ 000\ 000\ \text{square kilometres}}{2500\ \text{square kilometres}} = 200\ 000\ \text{boxes.}$$

To get a reasonable approximation to the atmosphere about 50 layers are needed, each of 200 000 boxes. That makes 10 million boxes for which temperature, pressure, etc. need to be determined.

The process of using observations to set up the initial conditions in the boxes within each layer is called 'initialisation'. Since around two-thirds of the Earth's surface is covered by oceans and much land is sparsely populated, this is challenging even at ground level, and initialising higher layers is even more difficult. Chapter 5 gave an overview of the various types of observations that are used for this process.

In practice, most meteorological centres conduct an ongoing process of 'data assimilation' with new observations being continually combined with previous model output. The model output effectively fills in any gaps where new observations are not available. At any point, a weather forecast can be initiated from the most recent result of this assimilation process.

Figure 6.6 is a highly simplified, schematic diagram of this process. One model run, often termed the 'analysis', is conducted. This analysis forms a record of the past and current behaviour of the atmosphere; it is kept in sequence with real time and is not forecast into the future. As new observations become available, they are assimilated into the analysis. The analysis therefore forms a good record of the behaviour of the atmosphere up to the present time. To make a forecast, an NWP model (often, though not necessarily, identical to the model used to conduct the analysis) is initialised with the latest information from the analysis and is then run forward in 'model time' as rapidly as possible in order to issue a forecast. In the example in Figure 6.6, a five-day forecast is initialised once per day, but in practice different lengths of forecast may be initialised at different intervals.

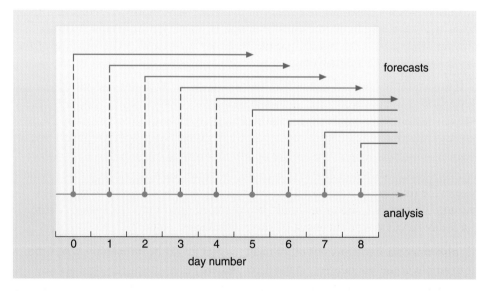

Figure 6.6 A schematic representation of a simple analysis/forecast procedure. The 'analysis' (thin blue line) is a model run that proceeds at the same rate as real time, shown in terms of a day number along the axis. In this case, a five-day forecast (red line) is initialised once a day from the most recent available information in the analysis run (the transfer of information is represented by a red dashed line). The forecast does not run in sequence with real time, but must be completed in less than one day to be useful. One day later, another five-day forecast is run, using an initial state from one day later in the analysis and projecting one day further into the future.

Forecasts made closer to the time at which they are valid benefit from an initial state that comes from the analysis at a later point and includes more recent observations.

■ Looking at Figure 6.6, on the evening of day 4 there will be five forecasts available for day 5; a 1-day forecast made on day 4, a 2-day forecast made on day 3, and so on, up to a 5-day forecast made on day 0. Which would you expect to be most accurate and why?

□ The 1-day forecast made on day 4 should be the most accurate, because it will have been the result of an NWP run initialised from the analysis on day 4, which includes information from all the observations assimilated up to that point.

You may wonder whether there is any value in keeping the longer forecasts from earlier in the record, once they have been superseded by more recent forecasts. They will not be used for public weather broadcasts, but they can later be compared against the analysis and the 'accuracy' of the forecast can be measured by how well they agree. It is important to know how far ahead forecasts can be trusted and, indeed, how they can be improved. Activity 6.1, which is outlined later in this chapter, requires you to follow a forecast cycle for yourself, at least for a short time, by keeping a record of forecasts for your area.

Once the data for the starting condition are established, then at each model step forward in time the data on temperature, pressure, etc. for each of the 10 million boxes are updated, under the influence of all the data in all the surrounding boxes, using the five basic equations outlined in Section 6.2.3. Parameterisation schemes are run for each box before the next step forward in time. It's exhausting just thinking about a single time-step and long runs are only possible at all through the power of electronic computers.

The step forward in time must not be too large. Even a very gentle wind of 10 km per hour would carry air 240 km in one day, advecting atmospheric properties across at least five boxes. Stronger winds would travel further still and the consequence of advancing the model by steps of one day at a time would be a complete failure of the numbers to represent real physical processes. It's essential to keep the time-step short enough to avoid such large-scale movements in any one step. At best, the situation should be advanced only a few minutes at a time, so a 5-day forecast would consist of several thousand individual time-steps.

It is also important to consider other changes that might be happening with time, for example at the boundaries. If the forecasts are being made at global scales, should the effects of ocean surface temperature changes be included somehow? This is probably not necessary for 1- or 2-day forecasts, for which a model with a static ocean might be good enough, but the interaction between ocean and atmosphere is vital for large-scale, long-range forecasts. Ultimately this requires complex ocean-, ice- and land-surface models, built up from boxes in a similar way to the atmosphere model and joined together with the atmospheric global model at the surface to provide a dynamic common boundary.

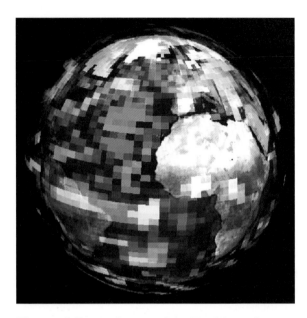

Figure 6.7   An image of the Earth's surface, showing land, ice and oceans, has been projected onto a sphere to give context to this image of cloudiness in the climate*prediction*.net low-resolution climate model. This model is designed to be run on a typical modern home computer. The boxes are large: 2.5° in latitude and 3.75° in longitude. The cloudiness in each grid box is shown by the degree of transparency, ranging from transparent (clear sky) to white (very cloudy).

Figure 6.7 shows an example of the grid of boxes used in a global model of the Earth's climate. Cloudiness is illustrated by shading each box over an image of the Earth's surface. This global model has been designed for the climate*prediction*.net project to run for several hundred years of model time using the spare capacity of modern home computers over a typical period of a few months. At the time of writing (early 2008), there have been a quarter of a million runs, giving a total of 32 million years of model simulations. The model resolution is consequently low compared with a dedicated NWP model, which is only required to run for a few days of model time on a dedicated computer system, but the mechanics of the model are almost identical.

For mesoscale weather forecasts, the horizontal sides of the boxes are refined down to a few kilometres, but the model can no longer span the whole globe if a similar amount of computer resource is available as for the global model. This kind of model is therefore called a Limited Area Model (LAM). An LAM is able to take into account the local effect of hills and mountains and also to make distinct forecasts for land and sea. The finer scale calls, of course, for even more initialisation data to be supplied, either from observations or from a global model. An LAM will have artificial boundaries, since it does not span the whole globe, and these need to be carefully considered. Often data are 'fed' into the edges of an LAM from nearby boxes in a global model, so that atmospheric properties at the boundaries are updated with time. Local, short-range forecasts tend to be conducted using an LAM, and are initialised routinely every 12 hours or so.

As well as the more detailed mesoscale models, it is often useful to run the NWP global models at lower resolution in longitude and latitude, comparable with the climate model in Figure 6.7. This may seem strange, but it permits a model to be run to make a whole series, known as an 'ensemble', of global forecasts covering the same period (typically in the region of 30–100 forecasts, all initialised at the same time but with slightly different initial conditions) and to predict conditions from about 10 days to up to a year ahead. A forecast over more than a month is called a 'seasonal forecast'. Ensembles will be further discussed in Section 6.3.2, but it is worth noting here that a seasonal forecast is not an attempt to predict the weather on a particular day several months ahead of time, which is presently impossible. In such uncertain circumstances, an ensemble is designed to cover a range of reasonable possibilities and the results of the group of models can be analysed to see what the most likely outcomes are and how forecasts diverge with time. Figure 6.8 shows an example of a three-month seasonal forecast of air temperature 2 m above the ground. There is no attempt to show actual temperatures on any day; instead the information presented indicates in general terms what proportion of the members of the ensemble exceeded or fell below the climatological mean temperatures over this period. The predictions indicate that warmer than average temperatures during March, April and May were forecast in most of the models over much of the Northern Hemisphere land (except for parts of North America and southern Asia), whereas the Southern Hemisphere (with the possible exception of New Zealand) was typically forecast to be cooler than usual.

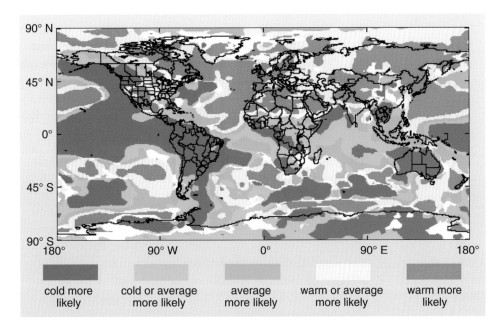

Figure 6.8 A seasonal forecast of air temperature 2 m above the ground, made by the UK Meteorological Office in February 2008 and covering the three months of March to May 2008. Rather than show actual forecast temperatures at any one date, the colours show a forecast of the likely range of temperatures compared with the climatological monthly means, based on a comparison of a large number of model forecasts. White regions correspond to areas in which the predicted temperatures cannot be ascribed to one of the categories given in the key.

The resolution of model grids is constantly improving with increases in computing power. Table 6.2 shows one example of the range of weather models in use at the Japan Meteorological Agency (JMA) as of October 2007. Appreciating the general relationship between models is much more important than focusing on the individual values for model resolution shown here; in any case these are constantly changing as models are updated. Other large national agencies have broadly similar ranges of models. Most also have a flexible range of targeted LAMs which can be focused on various areas in the world; these are used to model tropical cyclones, and also to help with transport planning or to support drought and famine relief efforts.

Table 6.2 Simplified summary of Numerical Weather Prediction models in use at the Japan Meteorological Agency, as of October 2007. The size of the model boxes is given by their width in the north–south direction. This is the same as their length in the east–west direction at the Equator, but the boxes get narrower in this direction towards the poles as lines of longitude converge, as illustrated in Figure 6.5b. The number of boxes is given as number in longitude × number in latitude × number in vertical.

	Seasonal forecasting	One-month ensemble	Global model	Regional/ synoptic model	Mesoscale model
Area covered	global	global	global	east Asia	Japan
Box width, north–south	210 km	125 km	60 km	20 km	5 km
Number of boxes	$192 \times 96 \times 40$	$320 \times 160 \times 40$	$640 \times 320 \times 40$	$325 \times 257 \times 40$	$721 \times 577 \times 50$
Forecast time	6 months	1 month	3–9 days	2 days	15 hours

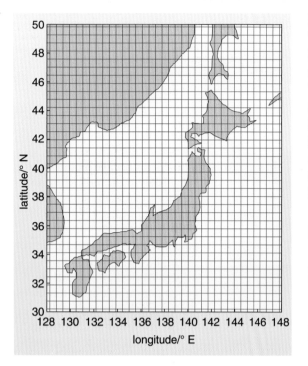

Figure 6.9   A grid of boxes equivalent to the resolution of the JMA global model laid over an outline of the Japanese coastline. This figure just shows a small portion of the entire, global grid.

Despite the impressive number of boxes in the global model in Table 6.2 (8 192 000 boxes), it is worth bearing in mind that each box still covers a large area of land and sea, possibly including mountains, lakes, forests, cities and coastlines all within one box. This is illustrated in Figure 6.9, which shows a portion of a grid of boxes equivalent to the resolution of the JMA global model laid over an outline of the Japanese coastline. In many places the Japanese islands are only two or three boxes across and it is easy to see why the regional and mesoscale model are required so as to 'focus in' on Japan and produce weather forecasts for the islands.

■   Would you employ a mesoscale model or a global model for a 12-hour weather forecast covering Japan and why?

☐   The mesoscale model will give better resolution. (You can see this from Table 6.2.)

■   Why not use a mesoscale model alone for a five-day forecast?

☐   The weather in the region of the model will be strongly affected by systems initially outside the domain of the model, which would move into the model region during a five-day period.

■   How would you overcome this problem?

☐   Use additional information from a global model and/or a regional model.

The resolution of models used for NWP is restricted by the practical constraint that a forecast has to be completed typically within a few hours (or perhaps days for a seasonal forecast) in order to be useful. Computer systems are in constant development to allow higher model resolution. The restriction can be further lifted for research purposes or for the study of particular phenomena, where a timely forecast is not required. One spectacular example is shown in Figure 6.10. The global Earth Simulator runs on a vast cluster of computers and is presently run with better than 10 km horizontal resolution and with 96 levels in the vertical (equivalent to almost one thousand million boxes). In contrast to Figure 6.7, the boxes are smaller than the dots of colour used to print Figure 6.10a and cannot be seen. Figure 6.10b shows more detail in the region of two tropical cyclones and, on the right of the image, many small patches of convective rain. Even this model, however, is unable to resolve most individual clouds.

When you are next at your computer, have a look at the Tropical cyclones section of the DVD, where you will find an animation of precipitation predicted by the Earth Simulator. The situation shown in Figure 6.10b is within the period covered by the animation.

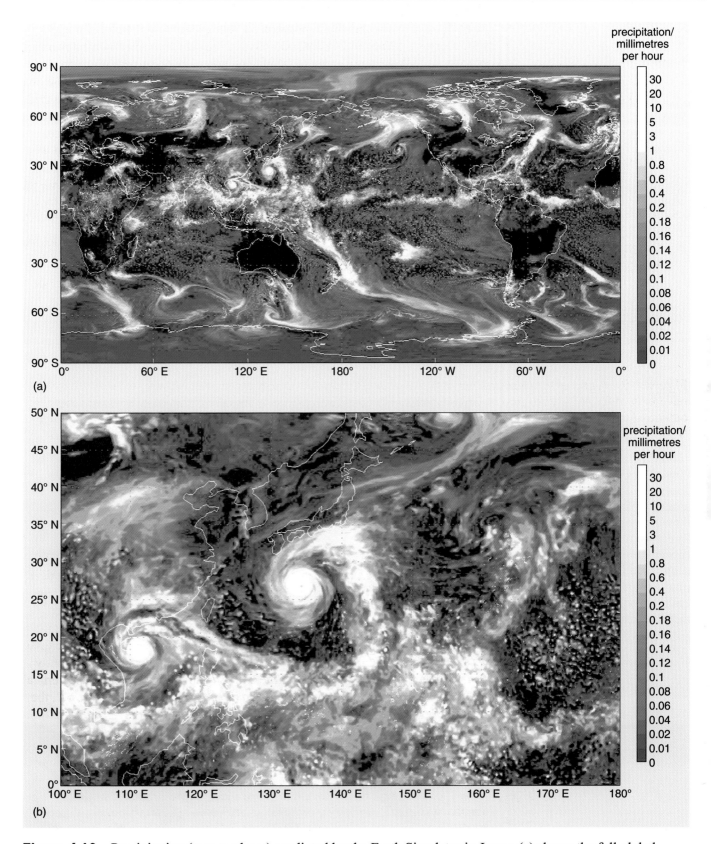

Figure 6.10   Precipitation (mm per hour) predicted by the Earth Simulator in Japan: (a) shows the full global model; (b) is a detail of (a) showing two tropical cyclones near the coast of Southeast Asia.

The effect of higher resolution is further demonstrated by Figure 6.11, which shows a study of the rainfall that led to the 2004 flooding at Boscastle, an event described in Chapter 1. The approximate position of Boscastle and the rain catchment area around it is shown by the circle. Figure 6.11a shows estimates of the accumulated rainfall in a 6-hour period, made by radar measurements as described in Section 5.3.2. Figures 6.11b–d show mesoscale model predictions of that rainfall with an increasingly high resolution, as indicated by the size of the coloured blocks. It is clear that the model with 12 km boxes (6.11b) fails to capture the full intensity of the rainfall and the model with 4 km boxes (6.11c) places the rain incorrectly. The rainfall is best represented by the model with 1 km boxes (6.11d), although even that does not correctly predict the intensity. This is an extreme case, but shows how rainfall can be determined by very small-scale features which are not 'seen' by models with lower resolution. Note that, in this case, these features would have included the shape of the coastline and the hills and valleys in the region.

Question 6.3

How would you expect the heights of the highest mountains and the depths of the deepest valleys, as represented in an NWP model, to vary with model resolution?

Figure 6.11 (a) Radar measurements of total rainfall, in millimetres, accumulated between 1200 UTC and 1800 UTC on 16 August 2004. The circle shows the approximate catchment area around Boscastle. The other three frames each show forecasts of the same quantity (using the same colour scale), each made from a mesoscale model initiated at 0000 UTC. Each has square grid boxes with different resolution: (b) 12 km; (c) 4 km; (d) 1 km.

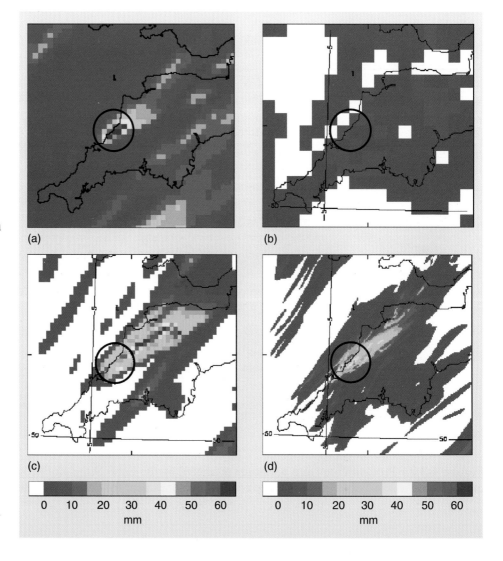

Section 6.2 has introduced you to the idea of models and, more specifically, to ways in which weather can be predicted using a numerical model. As computers become faster, you might expect the weather forecast to become more accurate, but that is far from the whole story, as you will see in Section 6.3.

Activity 6.1   Observational activity: monitoring the weather forecast

The estimated time for this activity is three hours, distributed over a period of a week.

In this activity you will keep a record of five-day forecasts over a period of seven days, updating daily and comparing the predictions with your observations of the actual weather. This ongoing part of the activity will take about 15 minutes per day, spaced over the week. You will need some additional preparation time at the start and further time to review the results at the end. If you have not already started this activity, you should access the instructions in the Activities section of the course website and begin collecting your data as soon as possible.

6.3   Forecast accuracy and reliability

Once a weather forecast has been produced, perhaps the most obvious question to ask is 'How reliable is it?', but this is rarely answered by the information in a typical media broadcast. Most often a single forecast is presented and information about probability and accuracy is regarded as too complex to convey to the general public. Contrary to the commonly held opinion that weather forecasts are largely useless beyond a day or so ahead, they are in fact improving with time at a measurable rate. It is worth noting as a rule of thumb that forecast accuracy measured in a consistent way seems to improve by about a day in the forecast over the course of a decade. In other words, a 3-day forecast made today is about as accurate as a 2-day forecast was ten years ago, and so on. On the face of it, this improvement might seem less spectacular than the advances in computing power in the same time. Improving forecasts is not, however, simply a matter of increasing model resolution with increasing computing power, although that certainly is important. Improvements in forecast accuracy with time can also be traced to major changes in the formulations of the numerical weather prediction models and, perhaps most importantly, to the introduction of new observing systems.

6.3.1   Forecast accuracy

The sophistication of current models is such that numerical forecasts for five or seven days ahead are regarded as having a useful level of accuracy and a target of around 14 days is regarded as a maximum that can be achieved on both theoretical and practical grounds.

There are many measures of forecast accuracy, the details of which are fairly complex, but all of which involve an after-the-event comparison of forecasts either directly with observations, or, more likely, with the analysis model run into which the observations have been assimilated. A statistical match is then sought between the forecast and the analysis and used to measure how well the forecast predicted the subsequent analysis, generally compared against what climatology alone would have achieved.

Figure 6.12 shows one such measure, the statistical correlation of '500 hPa height' between the forecast and analysis, with 100% indicating a perfect match and 0% meaning that the forecast bears no resemblance to the analysis. Many 3-, 5-, 7- and 10-day forecasts have been assessed on this basis at the European Centre for Medium Range Weather Forecasts (ECMWF) since 1981, using their global NWP model, and Figure 6.12 represents the distillation of an enormous amount of work. The term '500 hPa height' refers to the height above sea level at which the pressure in the atmosphere falls to 500 hPa. This may appear to be a very odd choice of quantity to use for comparison and the reasons are largely historical, being connected with forecasting for aviation. However, there is some merit in the choice of 500 hPa as a rough half-way point in the atmosphere: MSL pressure is close to 1000 hPa and so half the molecules in the atmosphere typically lie between the surface and 500 hPa, a pressure that tends to occur at an altitude of around 5.5 km, as noted in Figure 2.14. The height at which

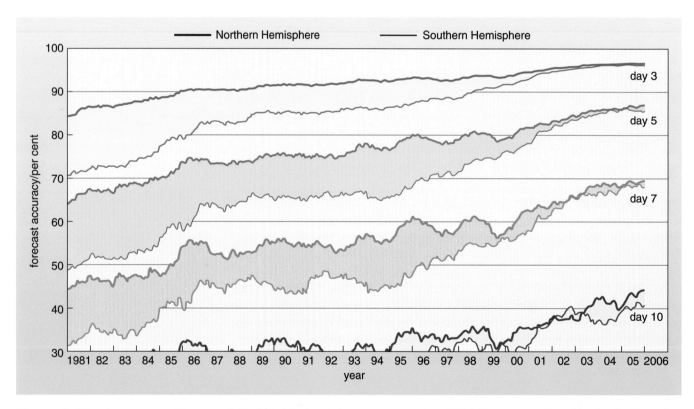

Figure 6.12 A measure of how well the height at which pressure reaches 500 hPa was predicted in 3-, 5-, 7- and 10-day forecasts with a global model based at the European Centre for Medium Range Weather Forecasts (ECMWF) from 1981 to 2005. Separate lines have been drawn for the correlation of the forecast with the later analysis at all points in the Northern and Southern Hemispheres (the coloured shading indicates the range between the two hemispheres for each length of forecast). Forecasts of 500 hPa height in the Northern Hemisphere are normally better than they are in the Southern Hemisphere. On this scale 100% would indicate a perfect forecast at every point and 0% would indicate no accuracy in the forecast; the vertical axis starts at 30% where there is some detectable accuracy.

the pressure reaches 500 hPa is affected both by changes in surface pressure and by the average temperature of the lower atmosphere. If surface pressure increases then a pressure of 500 hPa will tend to be reached at a greater height above the surface. If the atmosphere is warm on average then the gases expand and the 500 hPa point moves higher; conversely if the atmosphere is cool on average then the atmosphere contracts and the 500 hPa point falls. Thus the 500 hPa height for each column of model boxes is determined by quantities of meteorological interest in the lower atmosphere. For the present purpose, the important point is that use of the 500 hPa height enables meteorologists to make a fairly simple comparison of forecast accuracy with time.

There are several features of interest in Figure 6.12. Firstly, it can be seen that the 5-day forecast in 2005 is roughly as good as the 3-day forecast was 20 years earlier. Similarly the 7-day forecast in 2005 is about as good the 5-day forecast was in 1985. Figures of this type substantiate the claim that the accuracy of the weather forecast improves by about one day per decade.

Figure 6.12 also compares the forecasts made for the Northern and Southern Hemispheres.

■ How do the Northern and Southern Hemisphere forecasts compare with each other in 1981 and 2005?

☐ In 1981 the Northern Hemisphere forecast was much better than that for the Southern Hemisphere. In 2005 the gap had narrowed considerably.

The small wiggles on the curves in Figure 6.12 are a consequence of the changing state of the atmosphere, which is easier to predict at some times than others. Larger changes are often related to changes in NWP model formulation, model resolution and to the addition (or loss) of observing systems.

■ Given that the ECMWF model is global, with the same resolution in both hemispheres, explain how the Southern Hemisphere forecast has improved so markedly from 1981 to 2005 to become similar to that for the Northern Hemisphere

☐ This is probably related to the increasing importance of satellite observations. Satellites observe both hemispheres equally, whereas the Northern Hemisphere is much better served by surface observations (as shown in Figure 5.3). As satellite observations are increasingly used, the disparity between the number of surface stations in the two hemispheres becomes less important.

New weather satellites and networks of meteorological stations are often extremely expensive and it is usual for their 'impact' on the forecast to be carefully assessed by trial model experiments during their design. It is important not just to measure more of everything that can be measured easily, but to concentrate effort on those measurements or locations that will have most impact in improving weather forecasts.

The claims of accuracy on the large scale may seem to be at odds with your experience that the forecast often 'gets it wrong' with regard to local rainfall, which is one of the aspects of weather that people are most likely to notice. In fact, both surface pressure and temperature are actually forecast rather better. Reasons for this relate back to the length and timescales of various atmospheric phenomena, as summarised in Table 6.1. Surface pressure reflects the large-scale movement of air masses and evolves relatively slowly. Rainfall, frost or fog may reflect very local phenomena within the bigger picture.

■   If a forecast has told you that there is likely to be thundery rain in your region, yet it has remained dry where you are, does that mean that the forecast was wrong?

☐   Not necessarily; it might have been perfectly accurate. Thundery downpours are very small-scale convective phenomena of a few kilometres across and smaller. There may have been many of them in your region, without one happening to occur over your precise location.

The precise arrival time of fronts is another aspect of forecasts that can lead to very large local errors, despite the synoptic-scale forecast maps appearing reasonable. Fronts are very narrow, in the sense that the change between warmer and cooler air masses is abrupt at any given height. Fronts are therefore not well resolved even by quite high-resolution numerical weather prediction models, which may have a box spacing of 1–10 km, as you saw in Section 6.2. The models will give an indication of where the fronts may form, to within, say, 10 km, but the actual fronts will not be modelled in complete detail and often have to be 'drawn' into the model prediction by experienced forecasters later. It was mentioned in Chapter 4 that fronts can move erratically at varying speeds, over land in particular. It is easy to imagine that a front may be misplaced by tens of kilometres or more at some point in a forecast. If this means that your location is crossed by the front at a different time from that expected, you may experience a rapid change in temperature, humidity, wind and rainfall that was apparently not predicted, or was predicted to happen at a different time.

In science it is common to quote a measurement or prediction with a level of likely uncertainty. Evaluating the uncertainty is as important as the measurement itself. You may suspect that a forecast temperature could easily be 1 °C in error, but what is the chance of it being 2 °C wrong, or 5 °C wrong? How large an uncertainty is acceptable before the forecast becomes useless? For example, you could predict that the temperature tomorrow will be within 75 °C either side of −15 °C. If you check back to the temperature extremes given at the end of Section 2.1.2, you will see that this prediction will almost certainly be fulfilled wherever you are on the Earth and whatever the season. However, it is completely worthless as a forecast! On the other hand, it may be very useful to know that tomorrow's temperature has a 90% chance of lying between 2 °C and 4 °C.

6.3.2   Ensemble forecasting

The relatively modest, though steady, improvement in forecast accuracy in the last 30 years, in contrast to the massive advances in computing power and satellite technology, emphasises the complex nature of the interactions in the atmosphere. Small variations in the initialisation of an NWP model may lead to large variations in the long-term behaviour of the model.

This phenomenon is related to the so-called 'Butterfly Effect,' made famous by the work of the meteorologist Edward Lorenz, who was studying a highly simplified numerical model using an early electronic computer (with only three variable quantities in total, compared to the many millions of boxes, each with its five or more variable quantities, in a modern NWP model). Lorenz found that if he entered the initial value of one variable as 0.506, instead of the full 0.506 127, the computer would calculate a very different result after some time. In 1963, Lorenz noted that 'One meteorologist remarked that if the theory were correct, one flap of a seagull's wings could change the course of weather forever'. Later speeches and papers by Lorenz and others changed 'seagull' to 'butterfly' and the idea entered the popular imagination! The idea of sensitivity to initial conditions had been around in various forms since the late-nineteenth century, at least, and the idea of a butterfly changing the course of history might be traced to the 1952 Ray Bradbury time-travel story *A Sound of Thunder*.

Sensitivity to initial conditions means that a small difference between two model forecasts, or a small error in a model forecast compared to reality, will grow very rapidly. If the error doubles in a certain period of time, then doubles again in the same amount of time, and so on, this is termed 'exponential growth'. Such exponential growth occurs when the differences between the model forecast and reality are relatively small; after a while the errors will become so considerable that the forecast is simply completely wrong.

As an example, consider the surface pressure at one location, and assume that the initial state has a 1 hPa error. Suppose that this error undergoes exponential growth, and, for the sake of this simple illustration, doubles in size every 12 hours. The error will become 2 hPa after 12 hours, 4 hPa after 24 hours, 8 hPa after 36 hours and 16 hPa after 48 hours (2 days); at this point the forecast is probably useless.

■ Suppose that the pressure could be measured more accurately than the previous example so that the initial error was instead only 0.5 hPa. How long would it then take for the error to grow to 16 hPa?

☐ The error will double to 1 hPa after 12 hours. Then it will take a further 2 days, as before, to grow exponentially from 1 hPa to 16 hPa, so the total time for the error to reach this value will be 2½ days.

Halving the error in the initial state does not allow the forecast to see twice as far ahead into the future, it merely extends the point at which errors grow to the same size by one doubling time (12 extra hours in this example). Sensitivity to initial conditions may give one clue as to why weather forecasts have not improved at the same rate as observing and computer technology. This type of error growth from uncertainty in initial conditions would occur even if scientists had a perfect simulation of the atmosphere. There are no perfect simulations, despite highly complex NWP models, and model error just compounds the problem!

Since the atmospheric state will never be known precisely, the weather forecasting problem may seem hopeless, but there are times and places at which differences grow more slowly than at others, often when the weather is in a particular pattern. At these times the atmosphere is said to be more 'predictable' and there is a higher level of confidence in a forecast.

Predictability can be assessed by running a number, or ensemble, of identical forecast models, each initialised with a state that is equally consistent with observations to within suitable uncertainties. (Look back at Section 6.2.4 if you need to remind yourself about ensembles.) If the ensemble predictions rapidly spread apart, then the atmosphere is unpredictable and not much confidence can be placed in the forecast. If, on the other hand, the ensemble predictions remain closely consistent with one another, then much more confidence can be placed in the forecast.

Clearly only a limited number, perhaps up to one hundred, models can be run to produce a forecast in time to be useful, if the model resolution is not to be too far compromised. It is a balancing act to decide whether to put effort into a few very high-resolution models, or whether instead to use a larger number of lower resolution models, which cover a wider range of possibilities but are each potentially less accurate. The design of the ensemble of initial conditions is also a matter of ongoing research.

■ Look at Figure 6.13 for two sets of ensemble forecasts for temperature in London at the end of June in two different years. Roughly how far ahead would you have advised people to trust the forecast in each case?

☐ In 1995, the atmosphere seems to have been in a very predictable state and the forecasts stay together and would have been reliable out to at least four days. In 1994, the ensemble rapidly diverged so a forecast should not have been trusted beyond two days.

Question 6.4

Figure 6.14 shows three ensemble temperature predictions for one location on three different days (a, b, c). Each ensemble consists of 32 forecasts. Describe the simple temperature forecast that you could issue for each case by interpreting the results from the ensembles.

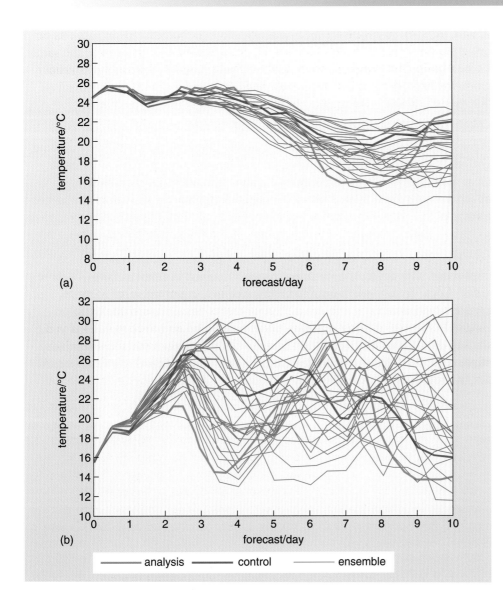

Figure 6.13 Examples of an ensemble of ten-day weather forecasts for periods in June 1994 and June 1995 for London made using the ECMWF ensemble prediction system. In 1995 (a) the atmosphere was relatively predictable and all the members of the model ensemble (red lines) gave similar predictions to the single 'best guess' control forecast (green line). The dark-blue line shows what actually happened. In contrast, in 1994 (b) there was a wide range of predictions within the ensemble showing that the risk of significant departures from mean conditions was high, and indicating a more unpredictable regime.

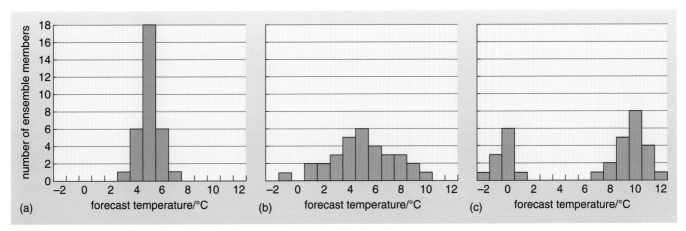

Figure 6.14 Ensemble forecasts of temperature at one location on three different days (a, b, c), for use with Question 6.4. Each ensemble has 32 members and the histograms show the number of members that predict a temperature within each 1 °C temperature interval.

6.4   Summary of Chapter 6

In order to predict the weather beyond a day or so ahead, meteorologists need a model that describes how the atmosphere will behave and a set of observations that give a realistic starting point from which calculations should begin.

Modelling the atmosphere is done using a set of mathematical equations that express the interrelationships between pressure, temperature, humidity and wind. Different models are used depending on the time and length scales of interest: these are the global, synoptic, mesoscale and microscale. Data derived from observations are assimilated into the models to produce initial states for weather forecasts.

Short-term forecasts of one or two days are much more accurate than predictions over longer times. Five-day forecasts have a reasonable success rate and are improving, with attempts now being made to forecast in detail as far as 14 days ahead. Local factors might need to be invoked to account for some of the apparent inaccuracies of a forecast. Longer-term forecasts are made using an ensemble average of many separate model runs based on minor variations in the starting data. Considerable skill is required to improve on a statistical summary of past events for long-term forecasting, but seasonal forecasts of overall trends can be issued several months ahead of time.

Chapter 7
Weather charts

In Chapter 6, you saw how the huge amount of weather data that is gathered every day is fed into NWP models and processed to generate forecasts. When those forecasts are presented to the general public on TV, online or in newspapers a 'weather map' is often included. An example is shown in Figure 7.1; this map indicates the predicted conditions by pictograms. Other maps may use colour coding. Sometimes arrows, numbers or symbols are included to indicate wind speed and direction. Values for maximum and minimum temperatures are often added, or presented on a separate map. You will probably also have seen maps superimposed with a depiction of the cloud coverage. These sorts of weather maps are intended to convey the forecaster's predictions efficiently to a general audience.

However, if you want a better insight into why these predictions have been made, you need to access charts showing the highs and lows of MSL pressure over a wide area. For example, the chart shown in Figure 2.15 covers the whole of Australia and New Zealand and the surrounding ocean. Charts drawn up in connection with weather forecasts for the British Isles often cover the whole of the North Atlantic, most of the Mediterranean and western Europe. Such a chart captures a kind of 'snapshot' of the state of the atmosphere near the surface over a large region. From today's chart you can understand why the current weather conditions are as they are. By following charts over a number of days, you can follow the development of patterns of weather, and see what kind of weather is coming your way in the very near future. If your normal source of weather forecasts does not show pressure charts, a current one is usually available online from official meteorological services.

You have already met the main features depicted on pressure charts: highs, lows and fronts, so in working through this chapter you will not have to get to grips with many new concepts. Rather, you will have opportunities to consolidate your understanding by revisiting a number of ideas that have already been discussed. At the same time you will also be able to practise 'reading' pressure charts and extracting various sorts of information from them. Being able to interpret the message of pressure charts is a very useful skill and is one of the important Learning Outcomes of the course.

There is no need to look up locations in advance of reading this chapter. Any discussion of specific areas is usually accompanied by a map.

Figure 7.1   A forecast map for the UK at 1500 UTC on 24 March 2008, in the style used by the public online services of the UK Met Office to indicate general weather conditions. Other similar maps are also made available to show separate forecasts for temperatures, wind speeds and wind directions.

7.1   Pressure patterns

The pressure charts released to the public typically show patterns of MSL pressure superimposed on an ordinary map. The maps of Figure 4.4 are rather similar, but charts accompanying forecasts show the pressure variations in considerably more detail.

7.1.1   Variations in pressure

A very large number of individual pressure readings are used to draw up these charts, supplied – as described in Chapter 5 – by land-based weather stations and airports, and by ships and drifting buoys at sea. You may recall from Section 2.3.1 that any reading not taken at sea level is converted to its mean sea-level equivalent before being used to draw up an overall picture of the surface pressure across an area.

The highest surface pressure ever recorded was 1083.3 hPa, at the centre of the Siberian high in the winter of 1968.

■   What is the average value of the MSL pressure in hPa? (You will probably need to refer back to Section 2.3.1 to find this.)

☐   It is 1013.25 hPa.

MSL pressures are very rarely lower than 920 hPa; if you refer back to Table 4.2 you will see that pressures lower than this occur at sea level only in the eye of devastating Category 5 tropical cyclones. However, because pressure decreases with altitude (as shown in Figure 2.14), the *measured* pressure in mountainous regions can be very much lower than 900 hPa. At only 1000 m above sea level the average value for atmospheric pressure is 900 hPa; at 3000 m it is 700 hPa. There are a great many places in the world where the altitude is well above 3000 m. That is why all station readings are converted to MSL equivalents before being entered into most models and charts. If pressure charts were plotted on the basis of recorded pressures, the topography of the Earth's surface would dominate parts of the picture and the pressure variations associated with weather features would be completely masked.

Once all the MSL equivalent pressures have been entered in their correct positions on a map, lines are drawn to indicate 'contours' along which the pressure has a particular value. These lines are called isobars (the prefix 'iso' meaning equal). It is the pattern of isobars, rather than the set of individual readings, that is referred to as an MSL pressure chart. If isobars form closed loops within the region covered by the map, they must enclose an area where the pressure is either higher or lower than the pressure outside that area. Closed isobars on a map are therefore demarcation lines for highs and lows.

Figure 7.2 shows various patterns of isobars that might appear on portions of MSL pressure charts. By convention, isobars are drawn at intervals of 4 hPa (4 mb) above and below a base value of 1000 hPa (1000 mb); no isobar in a sequence is ever missed out, though they are not all necessarily marked with their value. Thus the highest possible pressure on Figure 7.2b is 1015 hPa (to the nearest whole number of hectopascals), because the highest marked value on any isobar is 1012 hPa; if there were any data points of 1016 hPa or above, another isobar would appear on the chart.

Study comment

In this chapter you will be presented with a number of MSL pressure charts. It is important to study these carefully, looking both at the overall pattern of the isobars, and at the values marked on the isobars.

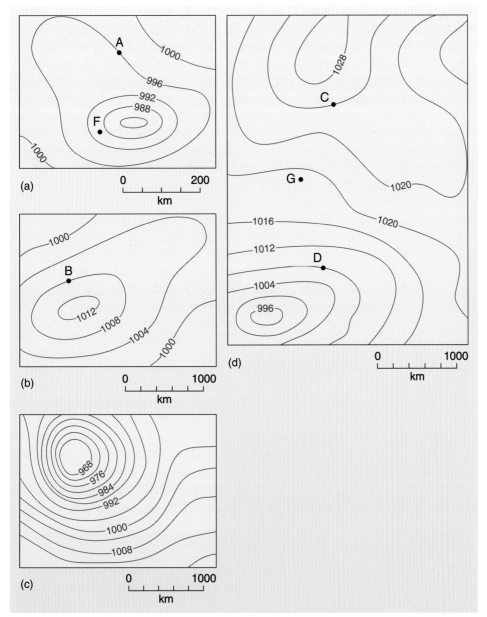

Figure 7.2   Portions of four MSL pressure charts for sea areas in mid-latitude regions. The isobars are drawn at 4 hPa intervals. Note the scales on each chart. (For use with Question 7.1.)

Question 7.1

(a) As you have already seen in Figures 2.15 and 4.4, the centres of highs and lows are usually marked on pressure charts. Write an H or an L or both on each of the charts in Figure 7.2 to indicate centres of high and low pressure, respectively.

(b) What is the MSL pressure at the positions marked A, B, C and D?

(c) Estimate the MSL pressure at the positions marked F and G.

When MSL pressure charts were produced by hand, a lot of time was spent just drawing isobars. This was a skilled job. Even if there were many points marked 1000 hPa, drawing the 1000 hPa isobar involved a lot more than just 'joining the dots'. There might be large portions of the chart where no data point was exactly 1000 hPa, but where there were many locations with MSL pressure values of, say, 999 hPa, 998 hPa, 1002 hPa or 1003 hPa, making it necessary to decide where the isobar should go. There might be apparently 'rogue points', where the pressure value was at odds with neighbouring points, requiring decisions to be made about whether to exclude the suspect data. As discussed in Section 5.1.4, there might also be large regions of the chart where there were no data points at all. Nowadays computers are programmed to draw the isobars, using sophisticated mathematical techniques to analyse the data. You will notice that the isobars in Figure 7.2 are fairly smooth curves, and the extent to which small 'wiggles' in the isobars are to be smoothed out can be specified in the computer program. This smoothing is important because it helps to make large-scale patterns clearer at the expense of relatively insignificant detail. However, this does not mean that there are never any kinks in the isobars; as you will see in Section 7.2, a sharp kink in the isobar pattern can indicate the presence of a front. Programs have also been developed to allow computers to take account of other types of data, such as wind direction, when drawing the isobars. Once the more mundane aspects of the task have been performed by a computer, quality control is handled by a human forecaster. At this stage, data that do not appear to fit the overall pattern will be highlighted and the forecaster will be able to reject, amend or confirm individual data points. The computer can then redraw the isobars within seconds.

The answer to Question 7.1 was based on the assumption that approximate values of MSL pressure for any location could in principle be deduced directly from a chart. However, it is important to remember that because the isobars have been smoothed a chart does not fully represent the many local variations in pressure. (And of course if the location is not at sea level the actual pressure there will always be less than the MSL pressure indicated by a chart.) A smoothed chart showing variation in *any* of the weather elements will only give a broad-brush picture and may not reflect local values. In the case of the smoothed temperature chart shown in Figure 7.3, for example, it is clear that no account has been taken of small variations in topography although these will have a significant effect on local temperature values.

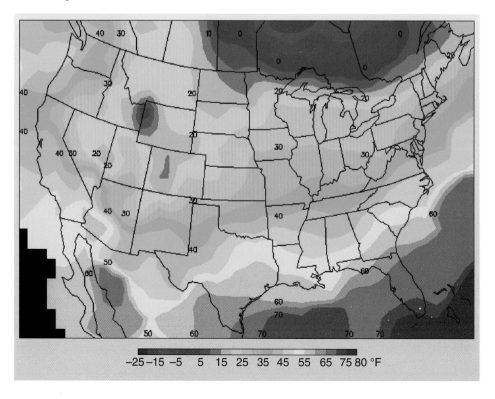

Figure 7.3   Temperature chart for North America at 1400 UTC on 23 March 2003. Here, coloured bands have been used to denote temperature ranges, much as they were used on Figure 2.16 to denote pressure ranges. This chart was produced for an American audience, so the temperatures are given in degrees Fahrenheit.

The spacing of isobars on an MSL pressure chart is extremely variable. In some cases the pressure change of 4 hPa between isobars corresponds to a large distance 'on the ground', and in others to a much smaller distance. You can see examples of this in Figure 7.2. If a low is surrounded by widely spaced isobars, it is described as 'shallow', especially if the pressure at its centre is not very low. If a high is surrounded by widely spaced isobars, it is described as 'weak', especially if the pressure at its centre is not very high (Figure 7.2b shows an example of a weak high). A low with closely spaced isobars is called 'deep' (Figure 7.2c is an example) and a high with closely spaced isobars is termed 'strong'. Large areas of low pressure sometimes contain several different low-pressure centres, as exemplified by the pattern of isobars in Figure 7.4. Such a system is called 'complex'. You will notice that on this chart the lowest MSL pressure value is given within each centre. It is common practice to do this, and similarly to mark the highest pressure value within highs. The position at which this highest or lowest pressure was measured is often marked with a cross.

■ The value in the centre of the middle low is marked as 984 hPa. Why is there no isobar corresponding to this value?

☐ The cross indicates that this is the lowest pressure value measured in the area and that it was measured at a single location. It is therefore not possible to draw an isobar for this value.

The centres of both highs and lows are usually bounded by isobars that are roughly circular or oval. However, isobars that enclose areas of high or low pressure but are further out from the centre often have an asymmetric shape. An elongated area of high pressure at the side of a high is called a ridge, while an elongated area of low pressure extending from a low is called a trough. Figure 7.5 shows an example of an MSL pressure chart with a ridge and a trough marked.

■ Which of the charts in Figure 7.2 show long ridges or troughs?

☐ There is a trough in (a) extending from the centre of the low towards the top left; a ridge in (d) across the middle right portion of the chart; and a ridge in (b) extending from the centre of the high towards the top right.

Incidentally, you will find that nearly all the MSL pressure charts in this chapter cover mid-latitude areas. It is only in these regions that there is sufficient pressure variation at the surface for patterns of isobars to be helpful in explaining the weather. In low latitudes, forecasters instead plot lines of constant wind direction, which are known as 'streamlines'. These are useful in showing areas of convergence and divergence of air.

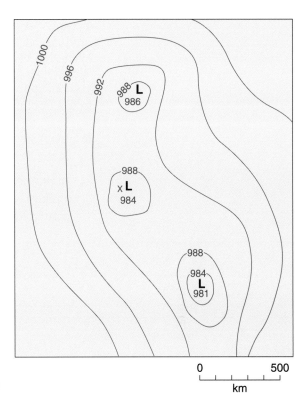

Figure 7.4 A portion of an MSL pressure chart showing an area of complex low pressure over the sea in a mid-latitude region.

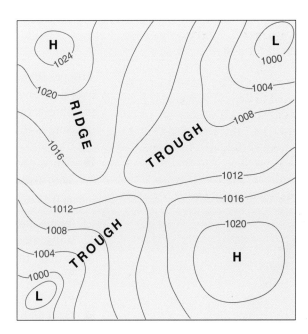

Figure 7.5 A portion of an MSL pressure chart showing a ridge of high pressure and a trough of low pressure.

7.1.2 Reading pressure charts

Once you know where the highs and lows are on an MSL pressure chart, you should then be able to make several kinds of deductions from it. For example, you can apply your knowledge and understanding of the concepts in Section 3.3.3 to work out the average wind direction.

■ In which direction do surface winds blow round mid-latitude highs and lows in the Northern Hemisphere? (You may want to refer back to Figure 3.16.)

☐ In the Northern Hemisphere surface winds blow clockwise around highs and slightly outwards from the centre of high pressure. They blow anticlockwise around lows and slightly inwards towards the centre of low pressure.

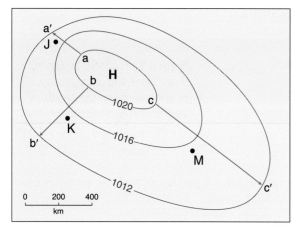

Figure 7.6 Isobars around an area of high pressure. The pressure does not fall uniformly in all directions away from the centre of the high.

An MSL pressure chart therefore gives an indication of the direction of the wind at the surface. It is often said in forecasts for the general public that winds blow parallel to the isobars, but at the surface this is only true in areas well away from centres of high or low pressure. Figure 3.16 showed that higher-level winds, which are not affected by friction with the surface, will also blow nearly parallel to the isobars round highs and lows. Surface winds, on the other hand, blow round lows and highs but also to some extent *across* the isobars, being 'drawn in' towards low-pressure centres and diverging away from high-pressure centres. The net effect is to 'fill in' lows and remove air from highs, making both extremes less pronounced. The angle at which the winds cross the isobars varies considerably. It is typically 15°–20° over the oceans but can be a lot bigger over a land surface; in some circumstances the surface wind may cross the isobars almost at right angles.

You can also make deductions about the likely strength of the wind from the pattern of isobars. Because wind is associated with pressure *differences*, winds close to a deep low will be stronger than those close to a shallow low. However, the change in pressure over a given distance in different directions away from a centre of high or low pressure is rarely uniform. A typical pattern of isobars around an area of high pressure is illustrated in Figure 7.6.

■ Three geographical directions are shown on Figure 7.6 by red lines marked with arrows. In which of these directions does the pressure fall most rapidly across a given distance from the centre of the high?

☐ In the direction a to a′, the pressure falls by (1020 − 1012) hPa = 8 hPa across a distance of about 200 km. This is the biggest fall over this distance. (From b to b′ the same fall in pressure takes place over a distance of about 400 km. From c to c′ it takes place over about 800 km.)

■ At which of the locations J, K or M will the wind be strongest?

☐ The change in pressure over a given distance is greatest at J, and therefore the wind will be stronger there than at K or M.

This example illustrates the important principle that the closer the spacing of the isobars, the stronger the wind. Look back at the chart in Figure 2.15. The very closely packed isobars associated with Tropical Cyclone Nicholas are an indication of extremely strong winds, though the cyclone was weakening and rated Category 2 at the time.

Question 7.2

Figure 7.7 shows an MSL pressure chart for the UK and part of western Europe.

(a) What roughly would the direction of the surface wind be at the sea locations P, Q and R? (Hint: you can orient the chart using the lines of latitude and longitude.)

(b) Would the surface wind have been stronger at location T or at location U?

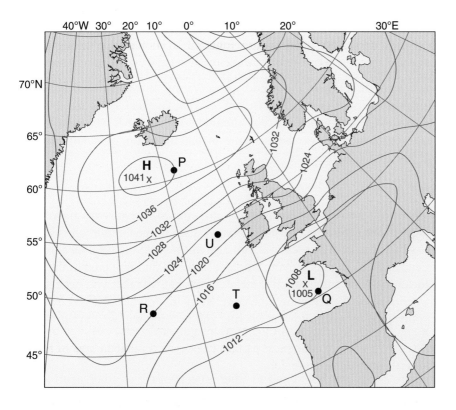

Figure 7.7   MSL pressure chart, showing a large area of high pressure to the south of Iceland and a shallow low in the Bay of Biscay. (For use with Question 7.2.)

Now imagine someone on a ship at point Q in Figure 7.7. You found in Question 7.2 that the wind there would be just roughly southwesterly, so if they had had their back to the wind, the centre of low pressure would have been on their left. You may recall that in Question 3.4 you worked out that if you were in the UK and the wind above the surface was southerly, then the nearest centre of low pressure would be west of you. Both of these examples are specific cases of the general rule that if you have your back to the wind in an open area in the Northern Hemisphere then lower pressure will always be to your left. (In the Southern Hemisphere, lower pressure will be on your right if you have your back to the wind.) This is a useful rule of thumb that you can apply to your own weather observations as well as to the interpretation of pressure charts. However, you need to apply the rule with due regard for local circumstances. Remember that isobars are 'smoothed out' when pressure charts are produced. The wind speed and direction suggested by the isobars are therefore an indication only of the overall flow of the air, and your observations may show that the local wind is rather different. Over the open sea, there are no topographic effects that might change the wind direction, but in coastal areas local effects can be important. You have already seen in Section 2.3.3 that winds may blow onshore during the day and offshore at night (sea and land breezes). Over land surfaces, there are many local features that may affect wind direction. For example, Chapter 8 discusses winds that may blow down mountain slopes at night. Physical obstacles in the path of the wind may deflect it; these obstacles can be as big as a mountain range, or as small as a building. In built-up areas, winds can swirl round city blocks and be funnelled down streets. Careful observation will make you familiar with the way in which such local features may affect the winds in your area. In some cases these kinds of effects can dramatically change the speed of the wind as well as changing its direction from that expected from the smoothed isobars of the MSL pressure charts.

Figure 3.16 illustrates the change in wind direction with altitude. In trying to gauge the overall direction of the wind by observation, it is sometimes better to look at the movement of clouds than to rely on what you feel at ground level. However, if you use this technique, you should be mindful that the overall wind direction at the surface will not be the same as that higher up, especially close to centres of low and high pressure.

Question 7.3

You are observing the weather from a position in the Northern Hemisphere, and you know from the MSL pressure charts that you are in the circulation system of winds round an area of high pressure. You also know from the weather forecast that the centre of this high is moving from west to east and will pass to the south of your location. Draw some rough sketches to explain whether you expect the wind to veer or to back during the time covered by the forecast. (If you need to remind yourself of the definitions of veering and backing winds, you can look back to Section 3.3.1 or refer to the Course Glossary.)

MSL pressure charts also hold clues to other aspects of the weather, apart from the wind. By noting the position of highs and lows on a mid-latitude MSL pressure chart in relation to the locations on the ground, you can make some general comments about the weather in the vicinity of those locations. You have seen that, near a well-developed low (i.e. one with a regular pattern of isobars surrounding the centre) in the mid-latitudes, the surface winds blow across the isobars to a greater or lesser extent and inwards towards the centre of the low. There is therefore convergence of air at the surface and this means that such lows are associated with rising air.

■ As air rises what happens to it and how does that affect its temperature?

☐ Rising air expands and is cooled.

If the air is moist and is cooled below its dew point, then clouds will form. Lows are therefore often associated with cloudy weather.

Close to a well-developed high, on the other hand, cross-isobar winds are taking air away from the centre of the high. This divergence of air at the surface means that overall there is sinking air over the centre of the area. Air that is sinking is compressed and warmed. In warming air, evaporation may take place, with the condensed water droplets within clouds being transformed into water vapour. If this happens, clouds disappear, so highs are often associated with clear weather. However, while upper levels of the atmosphere above a high are indeed normally cloud-free, it is not necessarily the case that ground-based observers see blue sky and sunshine. If the sinking, warming air does not reach the surface, air near the ground will remain colder than air higher up. You may recall from Section 2.1.4 that this situation is called a temperature inversion, because the change of temperature with height is reversed from the usual situation through the troposphere in which temperature decreases steadily with altitude.

■ Will cold air at low levels with warm air above it be stable or unstable?

☐ It will be stable.

The result of an inversion is therefore that very stable air is trapped near the ground, and in this stable layer cloud or fog may form. It is a common experience to find that fog forms overnight in high-pressure conditions during autumn or winter, as the land quickly loses heat and the layer of air near the ground becomes colder than the air aloft. (This type of fog was described in Section 3.1.4.)

7.2 Fronts

Once the pattern of isobars on an MSL pressure chart has been established, the next step is to place the fronts on the chart. You identified in Question 4.4 the symbols used to denote various types of front.

■ Look back at Figure 2.15. What type of front is shown on this chart?

☐ There is a cold front in the lower part of the chart.

Whether the placement of fronts on a chart is done from scratch by hand (nowadays this in effect means by mouse click) or by importing and modifying the fronts from the most recent previous chart, it is a difficult task which relies heavily on the skill of the meteorologist. Weather stations supply temperature readings and these can be entered on the chart to help to identify air masses. An abrupt temperature change across a short distance is one indication of the presence of a front. Another is a sharp kink in the isobars. Satellite imagery of cloud formations can also be particularly useful in identifying fronts. The rapid ascent of air along the leading edge of a front often results in a sharply delineated line of clouds that shows up clearly on satellite images.

The position of a front as marked on an MSL pressure chart is the edge of the front at the surface. In order to deduce the weather conditions from the chart you therefore need to be able to visualise the three-dimensional movement of air masses and clouds (as shown in Figures 4.10–4.13) that correspond to the flat representation of the map. Figure 7.8a illustrates an MSL pressure chart with a several fronts marked on it, and Figure 7.8b shows a number of diagrammatic cross-sections through the atmosphere. (You can think of these as vertical 'slices' through the pictures in Figures 4.10–4.13 and 4.15.) Work carefully through the following questions to match up the cross-sections with the chart. Remember that the semi-circular or triangular markings on the fronts in Figure 7.8a show which way the fronts are moving.

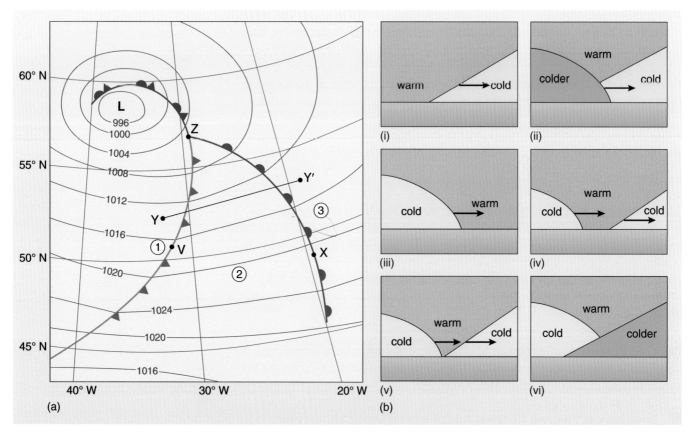

Figure 7.8 (a) An MSL pressure chart for part of the North Atlantic during the early autumn. The symbols on the warm and cold fronts show them to be moving roughly from west to east (i.e. to the right on this diagram.) If you look carefully you will see a slight kink in the 1008 to 1020 hPa isobars at the surface edge of the cold front. Lines of longitude and latitude orient the map. As on previous charts, letters denote particular locations. Additionally, various regions of the map are marked with numbers. (b) Cross-sections of fronts, showing the relative temperatures of the air masses involved. (Note that in these cross-sections the vertical scale is greatly exaggerated.)

■ Which diagram in Figure 7.8b is the correct cross-sectional representation of the air masses around position V in Figure 7.8a?

☐ Diagram (iii) shows the air masses round location V, with cold air from region 1 advancing and undercutting the warm region 2 air.

■ Which diagram in Figure 7.8b is the correct cross-sectional representation of the air masses around position X in Figure 7.8a?

☐ Diagram (i) shows the air masses around location X, with warm air from region 2 advancing and riding up over the cooler region 3 air.

■ Which diagram in Figure 7.8b is the correct cross-sectional representation of the air masses along the line from location Y to location Y′?

☐ Diagram (iv) represents the situation along this line.

■ Which diagram in Figure 7.8b is the correct cross-sectional representation of the air masses at position Z in Figure 7.8a? How would you describe position Z?

☐ Diagram (v) represents the situation at Z. This is the point of occlusion (cf. Figure 4.12b).

■ Explain whether it is possible to identify the occluded front as a warm occlusion or a cold occlusion, given only the information presented on the chart in Figure 7.8a.

☐ It is not possible to say what type of occlusion is occurring, since the chart does not give any information about whether the air mass around point Y is warmer or colder than the air mass around point Y′.

As mentioned in Section 4.3.4, the triangular area between the two fronts in Figure 7.8, which contains the warm air mass, is called a warm sector. The isobars in the warm sector are often straight, and observation shows that the low moves along a line parallel to them. The ways in which lows and highs move are described in more detail in Section 7.3.

Look at the 1012 hPa isobar near where it intersects with the warm front in Figure 7.8a. Just ahead of the surface edge of the warm front (i.e. in region 3) the area where the MSL pressure is about 1012 hPa will experience winds that are roughly southwesterly. Just to the west of the warm front (i.e. in the warm sector of region 2) the area where the MSL pressure is about 1012 hPa will experience winds that are roughly west-southwesterly. So as the warm front moves gradually in a generally eastward direction, observers who are initially to the east of it will notice both a change in the temperature and a change in the wind direction as the front passes over their position. The temperature will increase as the warm air mass behind the front arrives. At the same time, as the leading surface edge of the front passes their location, they will see the direction of the wind shift from southwesterly to west-southwesterly.

■ Is this change in the wind direction described as 'veering' or 'backing'?

☐ The wind would be described as veering (because it would have gone through a clockwise change in direction).

In the Northern Hemisphere, the surface wind always veers (though to a variable extent) when a front passes over.

Having connected the fronts on the weather map representation with their air masses, you can now use Figures 4.10 and 4.11 to describe the cloud that is likely to be associated with various areas of the map shown in Figure 7.9. This illustrates the same frontal system as Figure 7.8, but this time the lines of latitude have been removed to reduce the complexity of the diagram. Remember that this frontal system was said to have occurred over the North Atlantic in the early autumn; you can therefore assume that all the air masses are fairly moist.

Figure 7.9 The frontal system of Figure 7.8a, showing areas of cloud and precipitation. The various areas marked by coloured shading are described in the text.

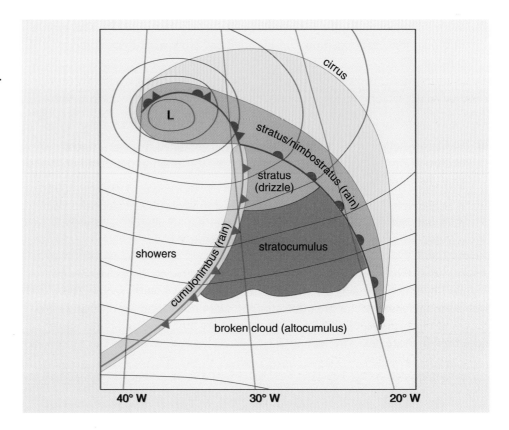

Look first at the right-hand side of Figure 7.9. Hundreds of kilometres ahead of the surface edge of the warm front there is cirrus cloud. Near the leading edge of the warm front, the cloud will be stratus or nimbostratus and it will probably be raining.

■ What kind of clouds will there be in the yellow shaded area of Figure 7.9 between the cirrus and the stratus/nimbostratus, and will these clouds give any rainfall? (You may want to check back with Figure 4.11.)

☐ As the distance from the leading surface edge of the warm front decreases, the height of the cloud base will also decrease, so cirrus will be followed by cirrostratus, then by altostratus (neither of which will produce rain) and finally by stratus/nimbostratus (which are precipitating clouds).

Annotate Figure 7.9 to include this information. In the warm sector, the sky is likely to be overcast and there may be drizzle. Immediately behind (i.e. to the west of) the surface edge of the cold front, a belt of cumulonimbus will give the heaviest of the rain associated with that front. As you saw in Figures 4.10 and 4.11, the slope of a cold front is much steeper than that of a warm front, so the width of the cloud belt is much narrower.

The zones of precipitation marked on Figure 7.9 are typical of 'active' fronts. However, not all fronts exhibit such clear characteristics. If the temperature difference between the air masses either side of a front is very small, the front will be weak: there may be very little or no precipitation associated with it, and an observer will not see any marked changes as the front passes over.

Question 7.4

Briefly explain the sequence of events and describe what you would expect to observe as the leading edge of an active cold front passed over your position.

7.3 Weather patterns

If you look at MSL pressure charts on successive days, you will soon see that the patterns change with time, as the pressure alters at the centre of highs or lows and as weather systems are caught up in the general circulation of the atmosphere. When the pressure at the centre of a low is decreasing, the low is said to be 'deepening'. If on the other hand the central pressure is increasing, the low is said to be 'filling'. When the pressure at the centre of a high is increasing, the high is said to be 'building'. When the central pressure is decreasing, the high is said to be 'weakening'. The most dramatic examples of rapidly deepening and filling lows are provided by tropical cyclones. Figure 7.10a tracks the movement of the 1999 Tropical Cyclone John, as it intensified and was upgraded to its final Category 5 status, before making landfall in northwestern Australia. Figure 7.10b shows a sequence of MSL pressure charts during the approach and landfall of the cyclone.

- Using Figure 7.10a, briefly describe the direction of cyclone John's path and its status on the Saffir–Simpson scale between the 13 and 16 December.

- On 13 December John was a Category 3 cyclone. It followed a path towards the south-southwest and intensified to Category 5 by the evening of 14 December. Its direction of travel then changed markedly between 14 and 15 December, such that it moved due south. Once it made landfall as a Category 5 storm on the morning of 15 December, it rapidly weakened.

On the sequence of MSL pressure charts in Figure 7.10b, you can follow the way in which John developed rapidly between 11 and 12 December, and intensified over the following two days. Its rapid dissipation once it made landfall is also obvious: by 16 December all that is left of it is a relatively weak low. However, by then a new tropical cyclone, named Ilsa, had developed off the same area of the Australian coast.

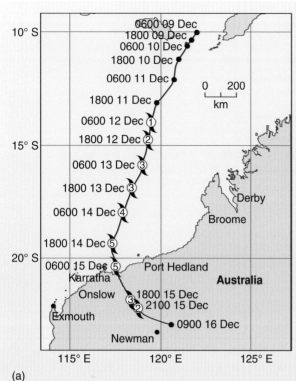

(a)

Figure 7.10 Tropical Cyclone John. (a) Path and development of the storm system. The numbers in the circles indicate the category of the cyclone on the Saffir–Simpson scale. The progress of the cyclone is shown according to local time. (b) Sequence of daily MSL pressure charts from 11 to 16 December 1999, covering the intensification, landfall and dissipation of Tropical Cyclone John. The values in square brackets correspond to the MSL pressure at the centre of the cyclone (the eye). These charts also show the development and movement of other lows and highs.

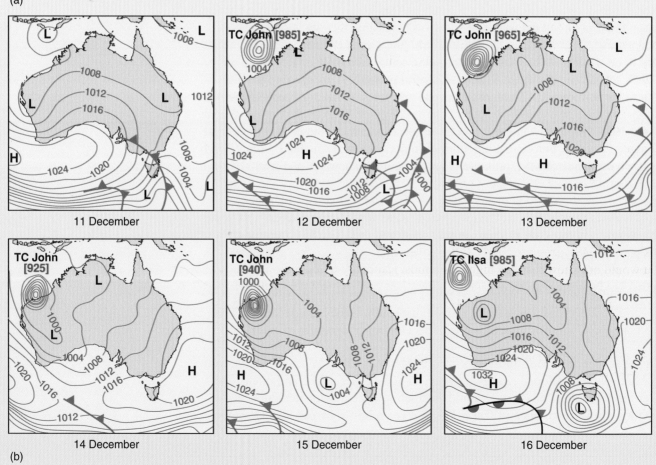

(b)

The first four charts also show that a high-pressure area was moving east along the south coast of the Australian mainland and across the island of Tasmania.

■ On the final two charts in the sequence, a low-pressure area is rapidly deepening over Tasmania. Explain why this is a mid-latitude storm that could not develop into another tropical cyclone.

☐ This is a large low-pressure area that may bring high winds and rain, but it originated over the ocean south of Australia, not over tropical waters, so could not develop the circulation system of a tropical cyclone because the sea-surface temperature is too low.

Figure 7.10b illustrates how useful MSL pressure charts are in showing the development and movement of storm systems. It also shows how much the charts for a particular area can change in the space of less than a week. A single pressure chart gives useful information, but to see the whole picture it is essential to have several charts covering a period of several days.

The movements of mid-latitude weather systems are essentially controlled by the highs, because highs can be either travelling or stationary. Major lows, on the other hand, are nearly always moving. Mid-latitude travelling highs, as their name suggests, move along with the lows in the generally westerly circulation of both hemispheres, and this is the most common pattern of behaviour. Characteristic weather is therefore brought by a succession of lows and travelling highs, although the normal pattern of that succession will of course vary from locality to locality. Stationary highs sit over an area for days or even weeks at a time, bringing unvarying weather, but weather that may be far from typical for that area. If a high becomes slow-moving or stationary in an unusual place (i.e. anywhere that does not correspond to the semi-permanent highs of Figure 4.4), then lows cannot follow their typical paths across the area. A high that bars the routes for lows is therefore called a 'blocking' high. Because the lows have to go round the high, they may bring unseasonably bad weather to areas round the edge of the high. Figure 7.11 shows an example of a blocking high over the Atlantic west of Scotland. Notice that the point at which the highest pressure was measured is marked with a cross. As noted in connection with Figure 7.4, it is common practice to mark extremes of high and low pressure in this way on MSL pressure charts. (Of course, since only one chart is presented you would not know that this high was almost stationary unless you were told.) In this kind of situation, lows cannot follow their more usual tracks between the British Isles and Iceland. Instead they are diverted further north or south, bringing rain to areas that would not necessarily expect it. For instance, if the low shown in Figure 7.11 lying in mid-Atlantic to the west of Portugal were to deepen, it might bring unseasonably wet weather to the Iberian Peninsula and the Mediterranean.

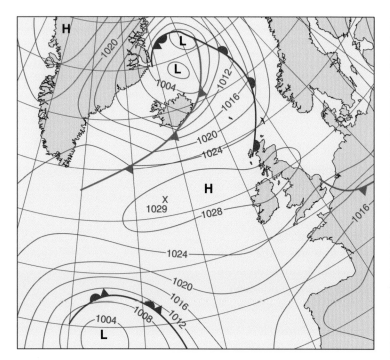

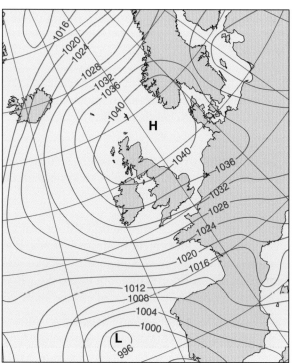

Figure 7.11   MSL pressure chart showing an autumn blocking high established over part of the North Atlantic, Northern Ireland, northern England and southern and central Scotland. Because the high has remained in the same position for many days, lows have been forced to move round the high-pressure area. Look carefully at the warm sector to the east of Iceland, and notice the pronounced kink in the isobars at both the cold and warm fronts (cf. Figure 7.8a).

Figure 7.12   A winter blocking high in northwest Europe, 17 January 1963.

Blocking highs can of themselves bring abnormal weather to the area they sit over because of the winds circulating round them. Figure 7.12 shows the MSL pressure chart for the British Isles and part of continental Europe on 17 January 1963. A persistent high had developed, centred on the North Sea between Scotland and Norway.

■   What would the wind direction have been on that day over most of the UK?

☐   Easterly (because in the Northern Hemisphere the winds flow clockwise round a high).

Because that particular high remained nearly stationary for a long time, the easterly airstream became established across Britain, bringing very cold air from the snow-covered areas of eastern Europe. That January was the coldest of the last century in the UK, with heavy snowfall, especially on the eastern side of the country, and unbroken frost by day as well as by night, for a period of several weeks. In fact, in England and Wales the winter of 1962/3 was the coldest since 1740.

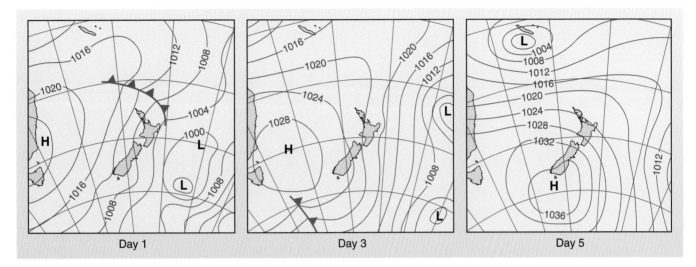

| Day 1 | Day 3 | Day 5 |

Figure 7.13   MSL pressure charts showing a slow-moving winter high building near New Zealand.

Figure 7.13 shows a rather similar situation that can arise when a slow-moving high develops over New Zealand in the Southern Hemisphere winter.

■   What would the wind direction be on the eastern side of this high?

☐   Southerly (because in the Southern Hemisphere the winds flow anticlockwise round a high).

If a high moves quickly across this area the air in its circulation comes from the ocean just south of New Zealand. However, because the high shown in Figure 7.13 is pretty slow-moving, the persistent southerly wind has time to bring moist and very cold air from the Antarctic, a journey that takes 48–72 hours. This kind of situation can therefore result in heavy rain or snow on the southern and eastern sides of New Zealand.

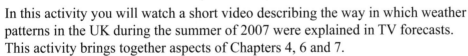

Activity 7.1   Forecasting weather patterns

The estimated time for this activity is 20 minutes.

In this activity you will watch a short video describing the way in which weather patterns in the UK during the summer of 2007 were explained in TV forecasts. This activity brings together aspects of Chapters 4, 6 and 7.

The detailed instructions for this activity are in the Activities section of the course website.

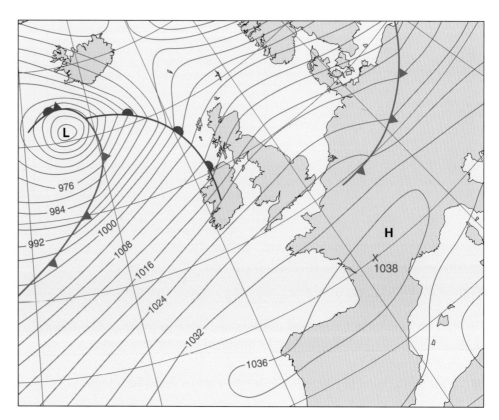

Figure 7.14   MSL chart showing a slow-moving high in southern Atlantic Europe in February.

Question 7.5

A contrasting pattern of UK winter weather to that of Figure 7.12 is shown in Figure 7.14. On this occasion, a slow-moving high is centred on the south of France and northern Spain. Describe the airstream that will affect the British Isles and countries bordering the North Sea in this situation. Do you expect the weather to be colder or milder than average for the time of year?

7.4   Summary of Chapter 7

The pattern of isobars on an MSL pressure chart shows the location of highs and lows.

Temperature data, wind directions, satellite imagery and the skill of experienced meteorologists are used in placing the surface edge of fronts on these charts. Active fronts will bring veering winds in the Northern Hemisphere, clouds and precipitation.

Blocking or slow-moving highs can bring unusual weather to the area over which they remain stationary. They can also cause lows to diverge from their usual paths.

Chapter 8
Weather situations

This chapter covers a number of different meteorological situations that illustrate interactions between the Earth's surface and the various factors that drive the weather. The weather phenomena are arranged in order of increasing scales of distance and time. The first section discusses thunderstorms, which in the course of less than an hour or so may produce not only localised thunder, but also lightning, heavy rain and sometimes even tornadoes. The next examples concern fog, rain and wind in the vicinity of coasts and mountains; here conditions are often set up for days at a stretch, though mountain weather can change treacherously fast. The Asian monsoons that form the third main topic are quite literally seasonal events on a continental scale. The final scenarios extend to global-scale interactions between the atmosphere and the oceans that can set the general weather patterns for a year or more.

The disposition of oceans, landmasses, mountains, hills and valleys is important in discussions of real weather situations because such physical geography can have a strong bearing on the meteorology. In this chapter there is a particularly large number of references to specific regions and geographic features. If you would like to check up in advance where these are located, the list follows. (Some of these places have already been mentioned in previous chapters.)

- Cities: San Francisco (California, USA); Edinburgh (UK); Ushuaia (Argentina); Ahmedabad, Bangalore and Mumbai (previously Bombay, India)
- Countries: Central African Republic, South Africa; Colombia, Venezuela, Ecuador, Peru, Argentina, Paraguay (South America); France; Spain; India; Pakistan; Bangladesh; Indonesia; Malaysia; Australia; New Zealand
- Land areas: Siberia (Russia); Antarctica; Nevada and Utah (USA); Canterbury Plains (New Zealand); Horn of Africa (mostly in Somalia); Tibetan Plateau
- Oceans/seas: Adriatic; Arabian Sea; Bay of Bengal; Gulf of Mexico; Mediterranean; Golfe du Lion
- Mountain ranges: Southern Alps (New Zealand); Alps (European); Massif Central (France); Rockies (North America); coastal ranges, Sierra Nevada, San Bernadino and San Gabriel Mountains (California, USA); Sierra Madre (Mexico); Western Ghats (southern India); Himalaya
- Rivers: Rhône (France).

Study comment

This is a long chapter, but you will find much in it that is familiar. Many of the concepts and terms you met in earlier chapters are used again in this one, so you will have the opportunity to apply these ideas in different situations (which is one of the Learning Outcomes of the course) and in so doing to consolidate your understanding. The only new meteorological concepts in this chapter relate to the electrification of clouds, large-scale currents in the oceans, and some details of the interactions of the bulk of the troposphere with the oceans below and the subtropical jet stream above.

8.1 Thunderstorms

At any one time there are about 2000 thunderstorms occurring in the Earth's atmosphere. These storms involve electrical activity in the troposphere that is revealed by giant sparks of lightning and peals of thunder, so thunderstorms are also known as electrical storms. Flashes of lightning can occur anywhere round the globe, though, as Figure 8.1 shows, the storms with which they are associated are not evenly distributed, occurring predominantly over the larger land areas in the tropics and mid-latitudes. The high humidity that can arise in these regions is a key factor in the development of thunderstorms, with convection leading readily to the formation of cumulonimbus clouds. Thunderstorms may therefore also be referred to as convective storms.

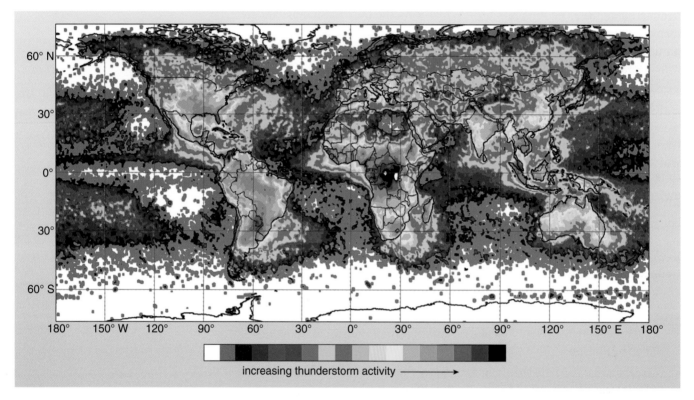

Figure 8.1 Average annual thunderstorm activity based on satellite observations of lightning. The colour code shows areas of zero activity as white and those of very low activity as grey. The colour spectrum from violet, through blue, green and yellow, to red reflects increasing activity. Areas with the most intense activity are depicted in black and this level of activity corresponds to over 100 lightning flashes per square kilometre per year.

Statistics show that lightning over land tends to occur most often in the mid-afternoon between 1500 and 1800 local time, especially in periods of warm weather.

■ What might underlie this sensitivity to the time of day? (You might like to look back at your answer to Question 2.2.)

☐ In periods of warm weather, both daytime temperature and humidity tend to build up during the day, peaking in the afternoon.

■ According to Figure 8.1, in which places would you have the best chance of seeing lightning?

☐ Looking at the map from east to west, the best places appear to be Malaysia, the extreme northern areas of India or Pakistan, central equatorial Africa, Venezuela, Colombia and perhaps northern Argentina/Paraguay.

8.1.1 The evolution of convective storms

Thunderstorms arise when growing cumulus, and eventually cumulonimbus, clouds are able to extend rapidly upwards, driven primarily by the process of convection. The conditions that prevail when convective storms form are therefore those in which moist, initially warm, air rises almost vertically through cooler drier air. You saw in Figure 3.2 how a big cloud forms under such conditions. You also saw in Chapter 4 how tropical cyclones form by cumulonimbus clouds over warm oceans clustering on a lateral scale of hundreds of kilometres and growing into an organised storm system. The horizontal scale of an individual thunderstorm is much smaller: typically such storms are a few kilometres across.

In contrast to tropical cyclones, it is apparent from Figure 8.1 that thunderstorms occur mostly over land: the pattern of colours corresponding to thunderstorm activity crudely maps out the continental land masses of the equatorial and mid-latitude zones, although in a few places significant thunderstorm activity does occur over the ocean.

The life cycle of a thunderstorm can be described in terms of three main stages: the initiation phase during which a cumulus cloud forms, the mature phase during which a cumulonimbus cloud is formed and produces heavy rain, and the dissipation phase during which the activity gradually dies down.

Initiation

■ What are the four processes that can cause the uplift of moist air and so initiate the formation of clouds?

☐ Convection, which causes air in contact with hot ground to rise; convergence of air streams at the surface; orographic lifting in which air is forced to rise as it passes over rising land; and frontal lifting as warm air rides up over a colder air mass.

All of these processes can contribute to the formation of thunderstorms, but convection is by far the most important. The initiation phase of a thunderstorm involves moist air carried into the atmosphere by convection. As you know from Chapter 3, when the temperature of the rising air reaches its dew point, water vapour condenses on condensation nuclei such as particles of salt, sand and dust. Even insects caught up in the airflow can act as nuclei for condensation. A cumulus cloud forms and grows taller as the updraught continues to move air upwards.

■ What process sustains the updraughts in convective clouds?

☐ Latent heat is released when condensation occurs, so the rising air remains warmer than the surrounding air and rises still further.

The initiating scenario is illustrated in Figure 8.2 as stage (i); the lateral extent of the region involved is a few km.

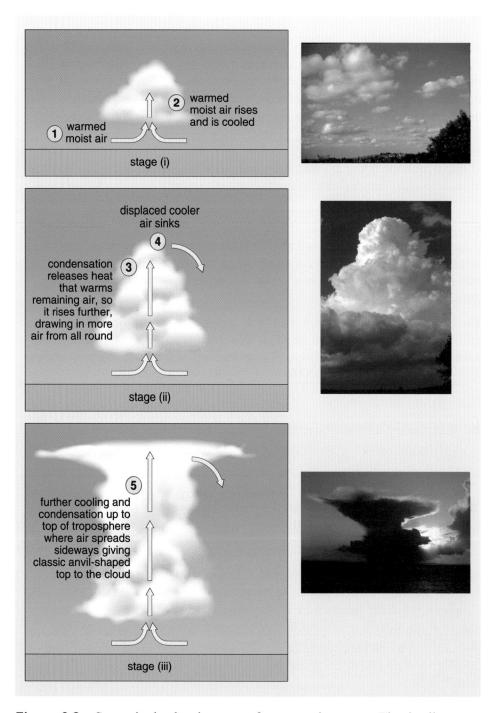

Figure 8.2   Stages in the development of a convective storm. The details are discussed in the text.

Maturation

The cloud continues to grow as long as the air feeding the process is sufficiently warm and sufficiently moisture-laden, as shown in stage (ii) in Figure 8.2. This is a situation of conditional instability. You might want to look back at Figure 2.22 to remind yourself about this. Eventually, the cloud develops into a deep (i.e. tall) cumulonimbus. Thunderstorms are associated with cumulonimbus clouds that extend right to the top of the troposphere.

The speed of the updraughts within a developing thundercloud varies from a few metres per second to tens of metres per second.

■ How long would it take air rising at a steady 10 metres per second to reach a height of 6 km?

☐ To travel 6000 metres at 10 metres per second takes

$$\frac{6000 \text{ metres}}{10 \text{ metres per second}} = 600 \text{ seconds} = 10 \text{ minutes}.$$

It typically takes around 20 minutes or so for the billowing tower of cumulonimbus to develop into stage (iii) where the top reaches right up to the top of the troposphere.

The situation changes when the top of the growing cloud reaches the tropopause, because from then on upwards colder air underlies warmer air.

■ Does this correspond to a stable or an unstable situation? Will moist air continue to rise? (Look back at your answer to Question 2.3 for a clue.)

☐ This situation is stable, so the air will stop rising.

The tropopause therefore puts a 'lid' on the vertical growth of the cloud. Moist rising air diverges horizontally, giving the thundercloud its typical anvil-shaped top. Stage (iii) in Figure 8.2 shows a cumulonimbus cloud with an anvil top. This is a so-called cold cloud, because much of it is in a part of the troposphere where the temperature is well below 0 °C.

■ In what forms does water exist inside such a cloud? (You might want to check back with Figure 3.10.)

☐ Deep cold clouds contain water vapour, water drops with temperatures above 0 °C (near the bottom of the cloud), drops of supercooled water and ice crystals.

During stages (ii) and (iii) in Figure 8.2 the latent heat being released by the condensation of moisture is continuing to sustain the updraught. Figure 3.2c showed how air sinks around a building cloud. The growing cloud is part of a vast convection process and by this stage is sufficiently stocked with moisture to be called a 'convective storm cell'. By the time stage (iii) is reached, water drops and ice crystals have become too heavy to be held up by the updraft and are falling through the cloud, dragging air with them. This produces some downdraughts. Colder air is drawn into the upper part of the cloud. This air is denser than the air within the cloud, so it too sinks, resulting in more vigorous downdraughts. This situation was illustrated in Figure 3.2d. The appearance of downdraughts signals that the thundercloud is fully mature.

Because of their small lateral extent and their speed of formation, the exact locations of thunderstorms are not easy to forecast.

■ How does the scale of a single convective storm cell compare with the horizontal spatial resolution of mesoscale NWP models? (Look back at Table 6.2 if necessary.)

☐ A single convective storm cell is a few kilometres across, generally comparable with the typical 5 km box size of mesoscale NWP models.

Numerical weather prediction therefore does not generally resolve individual storms because the lateral extent of a storm cell is smaller than, or at best comparable with, the size of the boxes that the models use. The models show when conditions are right for storm formation, but do not pinpoint individual storms. The best that you can hope for is an estimation of the percentage chance of being in the path of any convective storm cells that actually form. Higher resolution is possible, as was illustrated by the study of the Boscastle event shown in Figure 6.11, but still may not correctly predict the storm conditions.

Dissipation

The effect of ice crystals and water drops falling through the cloud, combined with sinking cold air, effectively halts the updraughts, although circulations within the cloud may continue for some time longer. Eventually the bulk of the water in the warm moist air has condensed and the cloud disperses.

Replication

The lateral extent of the patch of cumulonimbus that marks out any one convective storm cell is a few kilometres. Although the active life of an individual cell may only be a few tens of minutes, the conditions that favour the development of convection cells are likely to prevail over a wider area and it is therefore quite common for a succession of cells to develop as components of a more widespread 'multi-cell' storm.

Supercells

The most severe storms arise when the thermal updraught in a convective storm cell is also rotating. This condition occurs particularly when the wind feeding into a storm varies with height. The variation of wind strength or direction with height is technically referred to as wind shear. (The word 'shear' implies a tendency for layers to slip sideways past each other, rather like an untidy stack of papers on a desk.) Frontal systems are likely places to find a significant amount of wind shear as the warmer air masses ride up over the cooler ones. Where storms develop in the presence of wind shear, the effect is to feed air into the core of the storm from beyond the normal margins of the downdraught. This allows a single storm cell to continue to grow beyond its usual limit, with the potential to develop into a so-called supercell, extending laterally over several tens of kilometres. Conditions around a supercell are similar to those in the early stages of a tropical cyclone.

■ How does the lateral extent of a supercell thunderstorm differ from that of a fully developed tropical cyclone? (You may want to look back at Chapter 4 to remind yourself of the diameter of a typical tropical cyclone.)

□ Supercells are much smaller. Tropical cyclones typically have diameters of 500–800 km, though some are very much larger than that.

The more extreme thunderstorms, tropical cyclones and the occurrence of tornadoes (which will be described in Section 8.1.4) are associated with supercell conditions. Why doesn't every supercell develop into a tropical cyclone? The answer is that for a supercell to grow into the massive size of a tropical cyclone the development of deep cumulonimbus clouds needs to take place over a wide area and in the presence of enough moisture to fuel convection over several days; these conditions are restricted to particular geographic areas, being most likely to occur over warm tropical oceans.

8.1.2   Precipitation, electrification and lightning

The Bergeron process by which precipitation is produced in cold clouds, which was described in detail in Section 3.2.2, is central to the processes that result in lightning.

■ What initiates the precipitation processes in cold clouds?

□ These processes are initiated by falling ice crystals.

■ In the part of the cloud that contains both water droplets and ice crystals, which grow more readily?

□ The ice crystals grow more readily, at the expense of the droplets.

As discussed in Sections 3.2.2 and 8.1.1, droplets and ice crystals will fall out of, or even down through, the main updraught if they become heavy enough. Falling droplets and ice crystals push air ahead of them and so create downdraughts within the cloud itself.

■ What will happen to water droplets and ice crystals caught up in the airflow of a convection cell?

□ The water droplets and ice crystals will be carried around in the convection flow through regions of different temperature, changing in size as they do so.

■ What may happen to ice crystals if they collide with each other or with water droplets (this is part of the Bergeron process described in Chapter 3)?

□ On collision with other crystals they may break up and re-cluster as snow flakes; smaller fragments may then get caught up again in the updraught; on collision with droplets, the droplets may freeze, so the ice crystals grow.

2 cm

Figure 8.3   Evidence of the formation of hailstones in convection cells. The larger hailstones in particular show a thick onion-skin structure that tells of several distinct cycles of growth. There are layers of clear ice (glaze) and of opaque ice (rime). There may also be dirty looking layers if the growing hailstone has gone through a region where a lot of dust has been carried into the cloud by the updraught. Note that the various layers do not correspond to the number of times the hail has travelled through nearly the full depth of the cloud (which probably only happens a couple of times). Rather they indicate the number of different areas containing supercooled water droplets that the growing hailstone has visited.

Evidence for repeated cycles of ice-particle growth can easily be seen in larger hailstones, which reveal a cored structure, as shown in Figure 8.3. Precipitation can accompany any of the three stages of development of a convective storm, though it is likely to be at its most intense during the maturation phase. The form of precipitation that finally reaches the ground depends on the conditions at the base of the cloud and below; this was illustrated in Figure 3.11b. The way in which a convection cell carries water round in the form of droplets and ice particles is summarised in Figure 8.4.

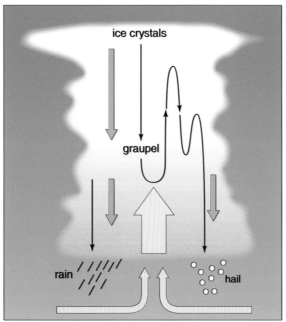

Figure 8.4   A growing cumulonimbus cloud, showing the updraught (broad yellow arrow), and the downdraughts (blue arrows) driven by rain or ice crystals falling through the cloud. Compare this diagram with Figure 3.11b, for a reminder of the precipitation processes involved.

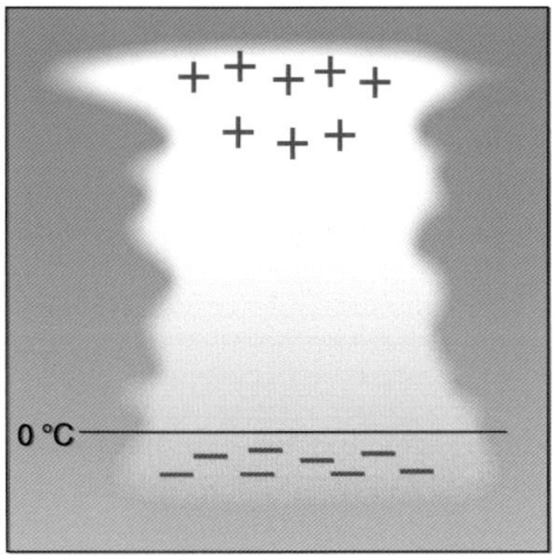

Figure 8.5   The distribution of electrical charge in a deep cumulonimbus cloud. Positive charge accumulates near the top of the cloud and negative charge near its base.

Ice crystals and droplets caught up in an airflow will rub past one another; they will also rub past others that have grown too heavy to be supported and are now falling. In the process, droplets and ice crystals become charged with static electricity as readily as a nylon comb or brush does when it is dragged through dry hair. The process of electrical charging by rubbing is called tribo-electrification. If you are unfamiliar with the science of electricity, Box 8.1 provides some general background. The detailed chain of events in thunderclouds is still being debated but measurements show that the consequence is a build-up of electrical charge in two major regions. Positive charge accumulates near the top of the cloud where ice crystals predominate, while an equal amount of negative charge is clumped much lower down, just below the level at which the air temperature is 0 °C. This is illustrated schematically in Figure 8.5.

In the deep cumulonimbus clouds of convective storms the positive and negative electrical charges are held apart by the action of the updraught, and continue to accumulate so long as the cell remains active.

Box 8.1 Electricity

Electricity is a vital commodity for industrial societies, though it is as natural a phenomenon as rainfall and sunshine. The scientific study of atmospheric electricity was well under way in the eighteenth century, most notably by the efforts of Benjamin Franklin, who in 1752 was inspired to try to drain electricity from a developing storm cloud, using a kite. It seems he was wise enough to avoid experimenting with a fully developed thunderstorm. In 1753 Georg Wilhelm Richmann was less prudent and perished in St Petersburg, electrocuted by lightning that directly struck a metal rod, several metres long, that he had deliberately pointed upwards towards a storm cloud.

Voltage, current and charge

In your everyday use of electricity from the domestic mains and from batteries you may be familiar with the terms voltage and current. One other concept, that of electric charge, is also required to understand electric storms and lightning.

One of the distinctive and important markings on an electrical battery is the number of volts that it provides. For example, the common type of electrical battery designated AA is marked '1.5 volts' or, using the standard symbol V for volts, '1.5 V'. This quantity measures the amount of 'electrical push' that the battery provides between its terminals, analogous to the pressure that water at the end of a sealed pipe is given when

the pipe is connected to a reservoir or tank filled to a particular depth. Double the depth and you double the pressure. In a similar manner, stack one AA battery on top of another and there will then be an electrical push of 1.5 V + 1.5 V = 3 V. The analogy between the water tank and the battery is shown pictorially in Figure 8.6. A few tens of volts are sufficient to deliver an electric shock; in hospitals, the defibrillators that are used to restart a stopped heart do so by providing a controlled electric shock of a few hundred volts on the surface of the chest, close to the heart.

In the case of the reservoir and pipe, what is being 'pushed' is the water. In the case of a battery it is electric charge that is pushed by an electrical voltage. Charge is a fundamental property of matter. You saw in Chapter 2 that the smallest particles of most of the atmospheric gases are called molecules. However, those molecules have even smaller components: atoms. For example, a nitrogen molecule is made up of two nitrogen atoms, an oxygen molecule of two oxygen atoms and a carbon dioxide molecule of one carbon atom and two oxygen atoms. In their turn, atoms themselves have even smaller components: protons, which are designated as positively charged (+); electrons, which are designated as negatively charged (−); and neutrons, which are uncharged. An important property of electric charge is that positive charge and negative charge are attracted to each other, whereas positive charge repels positive charge and negative repels negative. Electrical attraction between these constituent charges is what holds matter together at the atomic scale.

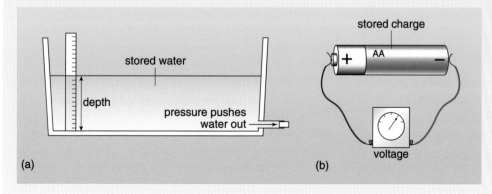

Figure 8.6   (a) The pressure at the outlet of a water reservoir or tank increases with the depth of water. (b) The analogous electrical 'push' is measured in volts.

The amount of charge associated with a proton is equal and opposite to that of an electron. Simplified pictures, such as that in Figure 8.7, can be drawn to represent individual atoms, but it should be remembered that atoms are too small to see under a microscope so sketches like this are distinctly 'unrealistic'. However, they serve to encapsulate the concept of atoms and their component parts. Figure 8.7 shows that an atom has a core, called a nucleus, made up of protons and neutrons. The presence of the neutrons is important as they provide some extra cohesion (or 'stickiness') that overcomes the tendency for the positively charged protons to push apart.

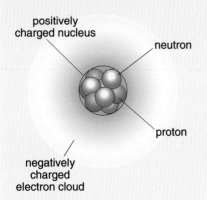

positively charged nucleus

neutron

proton

negatively charged electron cloud

Figure 8.7
A simplified representation of an atom of oxygen. The nucleus contains eight protons and eight neutrons. (Note that this diagram is not drawn to scale.)

The nucleus accounts for almost the entire weight of an atom, and because the protons are positively charged while the neutrons are neutral, the nucleus is always positively charged. Electrons have relatively little weight and swirl around in a 'cloud' outside the nucleus. The number of electrons in an atom is always equal to the number of protons. So the net charge of any atom is zero: atoms are neutral, even though they are composed of charged particles.

■ An atom of oxygen contains eight protons. How many electrons must it also contain to ensure that it is neutral?

☐ In a neutral atom, each positive charge of a proton must be matched by the equal and opposite (that is negative) charge of an electron, therefore an oxygen atom must contain eight electrons.

Charge in effect is the glue that holds atoms together and to one another when they form molecules. However, there are mechanisms by which a certain amount of negative electrical charge (i.e. some electrons) can be broken free from a parent atom leaving the remaining part of the atom with an equal amount of positive charge. Reactions between specially selected chemical compounds are one way to liberate charge from atoms. Batteries use chemical reactions to extract some of the charge from the substances from which they are made. Physical processes such as those in the sparks of lightning provide another route to freeing electrical charges from matter. Whenever positive and negative charges are separated, the further they are drawn apart the larger is the voltage difference between the clumps of opposite charge.

The unit of measurement that quantifies electric charge is the coulomb. During its life, a single (non-rechargeable) AA battery can deliver a few thousand coulombs of electric charge, pushed by a voltage of 1.5 volts. The exact quantity of charge depends only on the amount of specific chemicals built into the battery.

The third important concept in electricity is that of electric current. This is a measure of the rate at which electric charge flows from one place to another, expressed as the flow of a quantity of charge per second. In the analogy with the reservoir, as illustrated in Figure 8.6, the rate at which the water flows through the outlet pipe when the bung is removed might be measured in litres per second. Electric current is usually measured in amps (short for amperes) for which the standard symbol is 'A'; a current of one amp is equivalent to the flow of one coulomb of charge per second. Domestic appliances such as electric irons and microwave ovens are designed to operate with currents of a few amps; industrial machinery might use tens to hundreds of amps. The more electrical push (voltage) that is given to electrical charge, the faster the flow of electrical charge, i.e. the greater the current. For an electric lamp, for instance, increasing the applied voltage necessarily increases the current, and in turn there is an associated increase in brightness.

Electric current needs some material to transport the charge from one place to another. However, not all materials support the passage of current. Those that do (for example metals, graphite, water and damp ground) are called electrical conductors. Those that do not (such as plastics, glass, ceramics, dry ground, oils and gases) are called electrical insulators. In practice there is no sharp divide between conductors and insulators. Silver is an excellent conductor and diamond is an excellent insulator; almost everything else lies somewhere between them.

One of the important things to remember about electric current is that when it flows through all except the most excellent conductors it generates heat; the poorer the conductor the greater the heating. If the heating is sufficient, light is also produced.

In summary, the three basic electrical quantities that are needed in a discussion of atmospheric electricity and thunderstorms are voltage, charge and current. Whenever charge is extracted from matter, whether by chemical reaction or by the physical processes that create electrical sparks, there is always an accompanying electrical voltage. The greater the total charge separated, and the further the positive and negatives charges are held apart, the larger the voltage.

Tribo-electrification

Matter, being made up of neutral atoms, is normally electrically neutral because it generally contains equal numbers of positively and negatively charged components. Remarkably, simply rubbing two dissimilar materials together readily displaces a tiny but nevertheless significant fraction of electrical charge from one to the other, often with one sign of charge accumulating preferentially on one material of any pair. A large voltage (typically many hundreds of volts) accompanies this charge separation. Tribo-electrification is a Greek-based term that describes the science behind the process: 'tribo' implies rubbing. The effect is most noticeable in dry weather when, for instance, synthetic carpet that is rubbed by your shoes can leave you 'charged up'

to a large enough voltage for you to get an electrical jolt when you touch a metal door handle. Similarly a nylon brush dragged through dry hair transfers a small quantity of charge from the molecules of the hair onto the molecules of the brush, as illustrated in Figure 8.8. It is a fundamental property of separated charges that there is a natural tendency for them to reunite, so the hair is attracted to the brush. How is it that tribo-electrification by carpets and brushes is not fatal? The answer is that the total amount of charge involved in these cases is fortunately too small to do any damage to the heart. Medical defibrillation and accidental electrocution involve much larger quantities of charge.

Figure 8.8   Charge transferred onto a brush by passing it through someone's hair leaves an equal amount of opposite charge on the hair. The separated charges are attracted to each other so that strands of hair are drawn up towards the brush.

Since positive and negative electrical charges attract each other, tribo-electricity is short lived unless at least one of the materials involved is a good electrical insulator or someone or something has worked hard to keep the charges far apart. However, where adequate isolation is achieved charges can remain separated indefinitely. The expression 'static electricity' is used to distinguish tribo-electrification from the many uses of electricity in which the continuing movement of electric charges (i.e. electrical current) is central to the story.

Look back at Figure 8.5 and the associated text, to remind yourself about how a deep cumulonimbus cloud becomes charged by tribo-electrification. Air is not normally a conductor of electricity, so the difference in voltage that exists between the charged regions of a storm cloud signals that charge has been separated and is being held apart by continued convective activity. However, building up regions of separated positive and negative charges is a bit like stretching an elastic band – in the case of an elastic band the more it is stretched (or 'stressed') the greater is its tendency to resist further stretching, until in the end the material can bear it no more and it breaks. What happens in the case of air that has been 'electrically stressed' beyond its limit is called electrical breakdown and it is manifested by a big spark.

To understand how electrical breakdown occurs in the air, it is necessary to examine how regions of separated charge affect the atoms and molecules in the air. Figure 8.9 illustrates schematically how a neutral atom is distorted by the presence of external opposite electrical charges. Eventually some of the negative charge can actually be pulled off the atom. A similar process can occur with molecules.

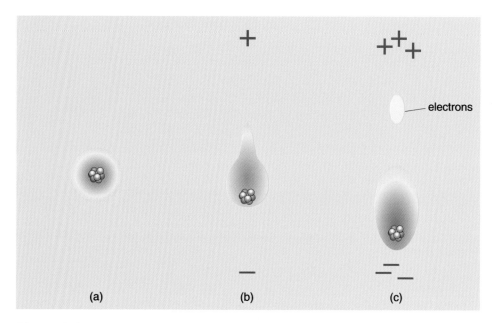

Figure 8.9   The distortion and eventual pulling apart of an atom under the influence of nearby opposite electrical charges. (a) The neutral atom. (b) An external positive charge attracts some of the negative electrons in the atom and the external negative charge attracts the positively charged nucleus. (c) If the external charges are strong enough, some of the electrons can be stripped from the atom. The remaining fragment of the atom is positively charged because it contains fewer electrons than the neutral atom but the number of protons is unchanged.

Now imagine what happens when a few air molecules are each separated into two charged fragments (one negative and one positive) in a thundercloud like that illustrated in Figure 8.5, where there are large regions of positive and negative charge. The negative fragments are drawn towards the positive external charge and the positive fragments towards the negatively charged region. The attractions are very strong and the charged fragments move rapidly, so that they collide violently with the neutral atoms and molecules of the air. The force of these impacts can result in electrons (i.e. negative charge) being 'knocked off' the atoms and molecules, thus creating more charged fragments. These new charged fragments are then also drawn towards regions of charge, causing in turn more charge separation through collisions. This 'chain reaction' continues and the amount of separated charge grows rapidly so that, within a millionth of a second, the normally non-conducting air is able to form a conducting path between the charge reservoirs in the cloud. This conducting path is actually a narrow, ragged channel, just a few millimetres wide, along which an electric current can flow: this current corresponds to the movement of the charged fragments of atoms. Electrical breakdown has occurred. As soon as this happens, a huge current suddenly starts to flow.

■   What will happen to the temperature of the air along the conducting path?

☐   The temperature will increase, because the passage of electric current generates heat.

In fact, because the current is so large the heating is very rapid and the air in the channel becomes hot enough to glow. A bright spark is produced – this is what we call lightning.

It is interesting to compare the sizes of the voltages, currents and charges involved in a lightning strike with those in domestic situations. Laboratory measurements show that electrical breakdown in clean dry air occurs when the reservoirs of charge give rise to around 3000 volts per millimetre of separation between the reservoirs (equivalent to three million volts per metre). In moist air the situation is more complicated and it turns out that breakdown occurs with substantially fewer volts per millimetre. Experiments in storm clouds have measured many millions of volts between the upper and lower clumps of charge, separated by only a few kilometres. The current that flows during a lightning flash allows positive and negative charges to come together and recombine. The current can be tens of thousands of amps but it typically flows for only a few millionths of a second. Because the flash is so brief, the amount of charge that is recombined is not large: a lightning flash associated with a current of 10 000 A that flows for ten millionths of a second recombines just one tenth of a coulomb of charge. It does take several flashes, often in quick succession over a second or so, to discharge the static electricity built up in a storm cloud, but the total charge amounts to only about one coulomb. The amount of charge in a thundercloud is thus a thousand times smaller than that delivered by a single AA battery over its working life. What makes lightning so much more potent is that the charge is pushed by an electrical voltage millions of times that of a single AA battery.

The severity of a thunderstorm depends on the amount of charge that is built up within a cloud. The stronger and more persistent the updraughts, the more the cloud will charge up.

Figure 8.10 illustrates two types of lightning flash. The first, called 'intracloud', takes place entirely within the cloud and simply reunites charge separated in the tribo-electrification process. This is shown in Figure 8.10a. When the bright channel of the lightning is seen through thick cloud it has the appearance of a diffuse sheet of brightness and is then often called 'sheet lightning'. The second type of lightning, which is shown in Figure 8.10b, is called 'cloud-to-ground'. This is a flash between the lower charge clump in the cloud and the ground where there is secondary charge separation. The secondary charge separation arises in response to the relatively low-lying negative charge in the cloud base and the positive charge high up in the cloud top: positive charges in the ground are attracted to the base of the cloud, leaving an equal and opposite charge on the ground around the edge of the region. The charge accumulated on the ground cannot normally reach the cloud as the air does not usually conduct electricity. However, once there is a build-up of enough electrical charge to take the electrical stresses beyond breakdown, a conducting channel is formed between the cloud and the ground.

Figure 8.10 Electrically charged clouds: (a) intracloud and (b) cloud-to-ground lightning. Charge separation in the cloud is the result of tribo-electrification driven by convection. Charge separation on the ground is the result of the closeness to the ground of the charge at the base of the cloud.

(a)

(b)

The closer you are to a lightning flash, the more it sounds like the crisp crack of a whip. The sound comes from the rapid expansion of air in the lightning channel, heated by the sudden flow of a huge electric current. The expansion is initially so fast that it sends out a shock wave – that is what makes the whip-crack of sound. Thus thunder cannot occur unless lightning has occurred first. When you hear thunder 'rumbling' it is because different parts of the lightning channel are at different distances from you, so the sound does not reach you all at once. This effect is accentuated by the sound bouncing off obstructions such as mountains and buildings.

Sound travels through the air at a speed of 1 km in three seconds whereas light travels a million times faster. So you can see a flash of lightning almost instantaneously but you may have to wait a few seconds for the peal of thunder. It's fairly easy to estimate the distance between you and the nearest part of the lightning channel on the basis of 1 km for every three seconds between the flash and the first sound.

■   Suppose you see a flash of cloud-to-ground lightning and count 12 seconds before you hear any thunder. How far away did the lightning strike?

☐   Sound travels 1 km in three seconds so in 12 seconds it travels 4 km. The lightning strike will have hit the ground 4 km away from you.

A cloud-to-ground strike neutralises the positive charge on the ground immediately below the cloud. This effectively stretches the overall charge separation from the top of the cloud (which is positively charged) down onto the negatively charged ground that surrounds the area directly under the storm. The final recombination of positive and negative charge usually occurs over the next few hours and even days without further lightning, by means of charges drifting down through the air on raindrops and solid particles.

Question 8.1

(a)   How does the voltage associated with charge clumps in a thunder cloud compare with that of an AA battery?

(b)   How does the current in a lightning strike compare with that drawn by a vehicle starter motor (which is about 30 A)?

(c)   How does the duration of a single lightning strike compare with that of a camera flash (which might be about a five-hundredth of a second)?

8.1.3   The global pattern of thunderstorms

There are clear geographic patterns of lightning activity evident in the satellite record of Figure 8.1. The peak activity over equatorial landmasses reflects the abundance of warm moist air in the tropical latitudes and the ease with which the warming and initial lift can be triggered over land. As you worked out when you first studied Figure 8.1, Venezuela and Colombia on the northwestern edge of South America, the aptly named Central African Republic and Malaysia experience the highest numbers of tropical thunderstorms.

The larger inland areas of the mid-latitude continental regions also provide the right conditions for thunderstorms: look back at Figure 8.1 and examine the mid-latitude regions of North America, southern Europe, Asia, Australia, South Africa and South America. You can see that lightning activity is particularly intense in the Himalaya, the Mexican Sierra Madre, and if you look carefully, the Alps. The strongest mid-latitude activity is associated with regions where major orographic lift is able to work in conjunction with the large areas over which the uptake of moisture and subsequent warming occurs. Regions of high activity must in some way be associated with an optimum combination of moisture, warming and uplift. In southern Asia, for example, thunderstorms are associated with summer monsoons. Moisture-laden air blown off the Indian Ocean is warmed as it passes over the Indian subcontinent, and is then forced to rise over the Himalaya.

In the mid-latitudes, the frequency of thunderstorms depends on how often large quantities of pre-warmed moist, tropical air arrives in regions where there can be further heating to drive convection, possibly with additional lift triggered either orographically or by frontal systems. Maximum thunderstorm activity in the mid-latitudes is therefore seasonal: most Northern Hemisphere thunderstorms occur between May and September; most in the Southern Hemisphere are between November and March.

■ There is no shortage of moisture over the sea, but Figure 8.1 shows that in large areas over the major oceans thunderstorm activity is very low. Why is this?

☐ Out over the ocean only frontal systems can initiate the lifting of air. Only rarely is this sufficient on its own to produce thunderstorms.

However, there are some regions where thunderstorms do occur relatively frequently over the ocean. In Figure 8.1 this is especially obvious in the northern Gulf of Mexico and in the Atlantic Ocean close to the southern states of the USA.

■ Why might these particular sea areas experience high numbers of thunderstorms? (You might like to look back at Figure 4.4 for a clue.)

☐ Florida and the Caribbean islands have high thunderstorm activity in the summer. The wind patterns in the July map of Figure 4.4 suggest that the storms may have been formed over the land, but then drifted out to sea.

Thunderstorms over the oceans can usually be traced back to their continental origin. In the mid-latitudes there is a general eastward drift of activity across eastern coasts. In tropical regions, the drift is westward, under the influence of the northeasterly and southeasterly Trade Winds.

■ In latitudes higher than about 65° N and 50° S, thunderstorms are extremely rare. Why is this?

☐ In these latitudes, air near the surface is cold and therefore there is little convective activity.

There are also relatively few thunderstorms in regions that are dominated by semi-permanent high-pressure centres, such as the northwestern USA in summer and Siberia in winter. When these highs are well developed, they are associated with sinking, warming air which inhibits the formation of convective storm cells.

Question 8.2

A great deal of thunderstorm activity occurs over *inland regions* in *tropical latitudes,* in the *late afternoon.* Write one or two sentences about each of the italicised phrases to explain why these particular conditions are favourable to the production of convective storms.

Figure 8.1 shows that thunderstorms are particularly common over Florida. These happen mainly in the summer. Explain briefly why summer thunderstorms are more common here than in neighbouring parts of the USA. (Hint: look back at Figure 3.4b for a clue.)

8.1.4 Tornadoes

Thunderstorms bring heavy precipitation and danger from lightning strikes. But they can also spawn far more destructive storms in the form of tornadoes. A tornado is a violently rotating column of air – literally a whirlwind – that extends from the base of a severe thunderstorm, a tropical storm or a tropical cyclone, right down to the ground. Figure 8.11 shows a classic tornado, with the characteristic tight vortex of spinning air.

Figure 8.11 A classic tornado. Notice how narrow the tornado is in relation to its height.

The essential requirements for a tornado to form are a cumulonimbus cloud and wind shear (i.e. strong horizontal winds, the strength and direction of which are rapidly changing with height). Under these circumstances, the side-wind can get drawn into the rising thermals at the heart of the cumulonimbus system, and the whole updraught then starts to spin. For reasons that are not fully understood, this spinning column of air sometimes then rotates faster and faster, while simultaneously narrowing and extending below the base of the cloud. At this stage the most obvious sign that a tornado is forming is that dust and debris on the ground get picked up and whirled into the air. As the rotating column descends further below the cloud, it becomes more obvious, because cloud droplets are contained within it. At this stage it is called a funnel cloud, due to its shape. Finally, the funnel cloud touches the ground and officially becomes a tornado. Most tornadoes are formed in a matter of minutes but shortly after reaching peak strength they are just as quickly dissipated. The one per cent or so that are particularly destructive are associated with supercells and may last tens of minutes.

Although tornadoes commonly originate within thunderstorms, the necessary conditions of strong thermally driven updraughts and high wind shear may arise under other conditions. For example, when a tropical cyclone makes landfall it is not uncommon for a series of tornadoes to be triggered. The sudden slowing of ground-level winds, caused by the frictional drag on air passing over the land, creates the necessary wind shear.

A tornado is usually soon spent but during its brief existence it unleashes a swathe of violent weather. Almost everything about tornadoes is highly variable. While their track is typically tens of metres wide over a distance of a few kilometres, an infamous tornado travelled 352 km (219 miles) through three states of the USA on 18 March 1925, leaving in its wake 695 people dead and over 2000 injured. The average forward speed of tornados is 45 km per hour (30 miles per hour) but may vary from nearly stationary to 100 km per hour. The typical Northern Hemisphere tornado moves from southwest to northeast, but tornadoes have been known to move in any direction. They can also rotate in either direction, although most tornadoes in the Northern Hemisphere spin anticlockwise, and most in the Southern Hemisphere spin clockwise.

Although tornadoes occur in many parts of the world, they are noticed most frequently in the USA, where the largest total number per year is reported, and in southeast England, where the largest number per square kilometre per year is reported. The frequency of reports clearly depends not only on the number of tornadoes that actually occur, but also on the number of observers. The high population density in the UK means that few go unnoticed there. In an average year, the USA records around 1200 tornadoes, mostly from the eastern half of the central area of the country, which is known as Tornado Alley, but also around the Gulf of Mexico, where tornadoes form within hurricanes. The UK annual average is a mere 33, which is comparable with the annual numbers reported from South Africa and Argentina; around 20 are reported annually in Australia and New Zealand alike, though many more may go unobserved in those countries.

As with tropical cyclones, the strengths of tornadoes are most easily described in terms of their destructive effects. In fact, the degree of damage is the only way that wind speeds can be reliably inferred, as conventional instruments do not survive the passage of the more severe grades of tornado. There are two general tornado scales – the Fujita and the Torro, giving F and T ratings, respectively. They are more or less similar, although the Torro scale, which is shown in Table 8.1, has twice as many divisions as the Fujita scale.

Table 8.1 The Torro scale of tornado severity.

Grade	Description	Wind speed/ km per hour	Description of damage
T0	Light	60–90	Loose, light litter raised from ground level in spirals. Tents, marquees seriously disturbed; most exposed tiles, slates on roofs dislodged. Twigs snapped; trail visible through crops.
T1	Mild	90–115	Deck-chairs, small plants, heavy litter becomes airborne; minor damage to sheds. More serious dislodging of tiles, slates, chimney pots. Wooden fences flattened. Slight damage to hedges and trees.
T2	Moderate	115–150	Heavy mobile homes displaced, light caravans blown over, garden sheds destroyed, garage roofs torn away, much damage to tiled roofs and chimney stacks. General damage to trees, some big branches twisted or snapped off, small trees uprooted.
T3	Strong	150–185	Mobile homes overturned/badly damaged; light caravans destroyed; garages and weak outbuildings destroyed; house roof timbers considerably exposed. Some of the bigger trees snapped or uprooted.
T4	Severe	185–220	Motor cars levitated. Mobile homes airborne/destroyed; sheds airborne for considerable distances; entire roofs removed from some houses; roof timbers of stronger brick or stone houses completely exposed; gable ends torn away. Numerous trees uprooted or snapped.
T5	Intense	220–260	Heavy motor vehicles levitated; more serious building damage than for T4, yet house walls usually remaining; the oldest, weakest buildings may collapse completely.
T6	Moderately devastating	260–300	Strongly built houses lose entire roofs and perhaps also a wall; windows broken on skyscrapers, more of the less-strong buildings collapse.
T7	Strongly devastating	300–345	Wooden-frame houses wholly demolished; some walls of stone or brick houses beaten down or collapse; skyscrapers twisted; steel-framed warehouse-type constructions may buckle slightly. Locomotives thrown over. Noticeable de-barking of trees by flying debris.
T8	Severely devastating	345–390	Motor cars hurled great distances. Wooden-framed houses and their contents dispersed over long distances; stone or brick houses irreparably damaged; skyscrapers badly twisted; shallowly anchored highrises may be toppled; steel-framed buildings buckled.
T9	Intensely devastating	390–435	Many steel-framed buildings badly damaged; skyscrapers toppled; locomotives or trains hurled some distances. Complete debarking of any standing tree-trunks.
T10	Super	435–480	Entire frame houses and similar buildings lifted bodily from foundations and carried some distances. Steel-reinforced concrete buildings may be severely damaged.

Question 8.4

Coincidentally, a T3 'strong' tornado and a Category 3 'strong' tropical cyclone have comparable strength winds. The corresponding damage according to the Torro and Saffir–Simpson scales might therefore be expected to be similar. Compare the damage statements for a T3 tornado in Table 8.1 with that for a Category 3 tropical cyclone in Table 4.2 and comment on the chief differences between these events.

8.2   Coasts and mountains

The Maori name for what is generally known as New Zealand, 'Ao-tea-roa', combines ideas of 'long' and 'white' and 'cloud', and the Isle of Skye off the coast of the UK mainland is named after a Norse combination of words for 'cloud' and 'island'. In fact, for early long-haul navigators clumps of low-lying cumulus on a distant horizon were a sign that they were approaching land; the 'long' part of the Maori description may also relate to the duration of a journey as much as to the extent of the cloud. An example of coastal cloud was shown in Figure 3.5b.

Land-marking clouds occur because the local combination of land and ocean has a major influence on the movement of air and water vapour. By now you should be familiar with the ways in which clouds can form along a coastline. For example, evaporation from a mid-latitude ocean loads moisture into the air passing over it.

■   Why do clouds form when this moist airflow encounters rising land along a coast?

☐   The moist air is forced to rise (orographic lifting). Rising air expands and is cooled. If it cools below its dew point, moisture condenses from it and clouds form.

As you saw in Section 2.3.3, there may be daytime sea breezes which blow onshore and enhance this effect over the land. At night, on the other hand, a land breeze may push the cloud offshore. However, sea and land breezes may sometimes be masked by stronger weather systems.

8.2.1   San Francisco fogs

You saw in Section 3.1.4 how fog is often associated with moist air being cooled below its dew point by contact with cold ground at the end of a long cold night with cloudless skies.

■   What is the physical process by which the ground becomes cold overnight?

☐   The ground loses heat because it is emitting IR radiation while there is no incoming solar radiation to warm it.

Because of the key role of radiation in cooling the ground, this kind of fog is often called 'radiation fog'. There are, however, other situations that can result in fog. For example, fog can be formed over a cold ocean surface and then carried inland on a very gentle breeze. The ocean surface may be cold because of large areas of ice floating on it or because cold water has been brought by a cold current or has somehow been stirred up from deep down. Radiation has not played a significant role in cooling the surface layer of water, so the fog is not radiation fog. In Section 6.2.3 you met the term 'advection', which captures the idea of the conditions at a given location changing because of an airflow moving into the area. Fog that is brought in on a gentle breeze is therefore called 'advection fog'.

On the west coast of the USA mild, wet winters and dry summers are the norm, owing to the mainly westerly winds and the summer warmth of the mid-latitudes. Somewhat against this trend, San Francisco, which is on this western seaboard, has its own characteristic weather pattern in the summer months, and may be affected by banks of cool advection fog for days at a time.

To understand the San Francisco fog you need to appreciate the close interaction there can be between wind and ocean. The surface of water can easily be pushed around simply by blowing across it. Try this for yourself with a large bowl of water (or maybe a wide-brimmed cup), blowing as near horizontally across the surface as you can. You should find that you can easily stack the water up by a few millimetres against the far side of the container. It is friction between the moving air and the stationary liquid that distorts the surface, literally dragging it in the direction of airflow. The same thing happens at a much larger scale as winds blow across the oceans. In fact, ripples and waves on the surface increase the friction between airflow and the ocean and hence enhance the efficiency with which the winds drive surface currents. Ocean–air interactions on the global scale will be discussed further in Section 8.4.

In general, local meteorology is strongly influenced by features of the landscape. Figure 8.12a is a map of part of California, with an inset showing the geography around San Francisco in more detail. You can see that there is a coastal mountain range bordering the Pacific Ocean for most of the length of California. The only complete breach in the range is in line with the entrance to San Francisco Bay. At the mouth of the Bay this gap is known as the Golden Gate. As a result, the Bay region provides a natural meeting place for continental and maritime air masses. Through the funnel of the Golden Gate and San Francisco Bay, moist air blows off the ocean into the large mass of warmer, drier air that is naturally trapped by the coastal range and subjected to day-long solar heating. As you know from your study of Chapter 4, different air masses do not easily mix and the front between the moist ocean air and the warm, dry continental air washes forwards and backwards through the city and surroundings of San Francisco.

Throughout the late spring, the Central Valley of California, a 500-mile-long basin surrounded by mountains, is a source of thermals. Air that rises in thermals has to be replaced by surrounding air being drawn in at the surface. This surface air tends to funnel through the Golden Gate. From the ocean side, air that has sunk in the semi-permanent high of the North Pacific pours shoreward to replace air that is rising over the warm land. (You may like to look back at Figure 4.4 to locate this high.) The Coriolis effect deflects the flow to the right, so that as it crosses the coast the air is coming from the northwest, as marked by the arrows in Figure 8.12a. This airflow drags on the surface of the ocean and creates a steady surface current running southward parallel to the shoreline.

Figure 8.12 (a) The geography of California. Notice the long low-lying area bounded by the coastal ranges to the west and the Sierra Nevada mountains to the east. The inset shows a more detailed map of the Golden Gate. Surface airflow in the summer is indicated by the arrows. (b) The bridge across the Golden Gate shrouded in advection fog.

■ The rising current of air caused by thermals draws in air from the surroundings to replace it. What happens in the analogous situation in the ocean when a surface current is driven by the wind?

☐ Seawater flows away in the surface current, and must be replaced by water drawn in from the surroundings.

In the case of the ocean, water is not only drawn in from the surrounding surface, but also pulled up from below the surface. Steady wind-blown currents on the ocean surface tend to draw water up from several tens of metres below the surface. This process is known as upwelling. The water originating from depth will be several degrees colder than the surface would otherwise be, so the sea surface is cooled by upwelling. Moist air over the now cold ocean surface may cool below the dew point and will then form a great bank of offshore fog. When this happens around San Francisco, the action of inland thermals drawing the air in through the Golden Gate pulls the fog bank into the Bay and further onshore. Figure 8.12b illustrates the effect.

The factors that need to coincide to make the San Francisco fog are moist ocean air, the semi-permanent Pacific high, the Coriolis effect, upwelling of cold ocean water, thermals over the Central Valley, and the Golden Gate itself. In the winter months (November to April) the cooler air takes up less moisture over the northern Pacific and this reduces the chance of fogs forming.

■   What else may change in the winter months that also tends to leave San Francisco relatively fog-free?

☐   The solar heating of the Central Valley will be reduced and consequently the thermals there will be weaker.

The weaker thermal activity in the Central Valley during winter means that air is no longer drawn onshore through the Golden Gate and the wind-blown surface currents are no longer there to cause upwelling and cooling of the ocean surface. In short, the whole mechanism for the San Francisco advection fog is out of action in winter.

Question 8.5

During the winter months in the Central Valley of California, dense fogs are often formed overnight under clear skies, particularly after a period of heavy rain. Contrast this winter fog with the San Francisco summer fog: what type of fog is it in each case; what is the characteristic weather that initiates it; and where does the moisture to form the fog droplets come from?

8.2.2   Rain shadows

The windward slopes of mountains generally receive increased rainfall whenever they lie in the path of moisture-laden air.

■   Why?

☐   Orographic uplift promotes the formation of clouds from moisture-laden airflow; with sufficient uplift the clouds become rain-bearing.

There are even examples where quite modest elevations combined with very moist air can stimulate rain. The western coasts of Ireland, Scotland, Wales and England, for example, are all noted for their relatively wet weather, as a result of very moist westerly airstreams off the Atlantic.

It follows that on the leeward side of a range of mountains, and further downstream in the airflow, we can expect to encounter relatively drier conditions. For one thing, much of the moisture is spent as rain on the windward side and over the top. But there is a second effect that reduces the prevalence of rain-bearing cloud on the leeward slopes of mountains. Air that has risen over high land has been cooled on the way up and it may continue to lose more heat if it is still warmer than the surface. As the down slope is reached on the leeward side the airflow slows as it follows the land profile. The reason for this change in flow is explored in Box 8.2.

Box 8.2   Constrained flow

You have probably seen slow-moving rivers change to faster flows when the river becomes narrower or shallower, or both. Whenever a flow of water is constricted by a narrow channel (or a narrow pipe) it has to speed up to ensure that the rate at which it is passing through the constriction is equal to rate at which it is flowing in from, and out into, a broader flow pattern.

The same phenomenon occurs in the flow of air in the atmosphere though the scale of events is much larger. Here the major physical constraint acting on the flow of air is caused by mountains. Surface wind speeds tend to increase where the flow has no option but to pass over the top of a mountain. It is also the case that winds speed up wherever surface air is channelled through gaps between mountain peaks or into valleys. Equally, as a surface wind moves clear of any topographic constrictions it tends to slow, though winds passing through sudden changes of contour can emerge into calmer air as a jet of high-speed wind that persists for many kilometres 'downstream'. (Note that any narrow band of air moving at high speed can be described as a jet, but this is not to be confused with 'jet streams' which only occur near the tropopause.)

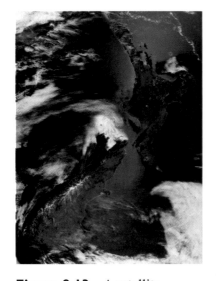

Figure 8.13   A satellite photograph of New Zealand. The snow-capped spine of mountains on the South Island is known as the Southern Alps. With the general directions of the winds being westerly, there is verdant land on the coastal strip to the west of these mountains, which shows up as dark green in the photograph. To the east of the mountain range the land is in the rain shadow and is markedly less lush, appearing brownish in the photograph.

■   Why do clouds tend to disperse on the leeward slopes of mountains (where air flows down the mountain)?

☐   Descending air is compressed and as a result it becomes warmer. Evaporation of cloud droplets increases, so clouds disperse.

A leeward slope is thus a region of reduced rainfall, which is often called a 'rain shadow'. The rainfall is suppressed throughout the downstream region until there is another opportunity for uplift. The Southern Alps in New Zealand provide a clear illustration of the consequence of orographically stimulated rain on one side of a mountain range and a rain shadow on the other. Figure 8.13 shows a satellite image of New Zealand, in which the lushness of the western slopes of the snow-clad Southern Alps can be seen, starkly contrasting with the bare eastern slopes in the rain shadow.

8.2.3   Characteristic winds

As discussed in Chapter 4, the global-scale circulation of air in the atmosphere causes strong surface winds, the most noticeable of which are the northeasterly and southeasterly Trade Winds. Smaller-scale winds are associated with more localised meteorology. For instance, there are the simple sea (onshore) and land (offshore) breezes that have already been discussed in Section 8.2.1 and in earlier chapters.

Many regions have characteristic winds, which are usually given local names – often more than one. Figure 8.14, for example, shows some of the characteristic winds of the Mediterranean. There are winds that are cold and dry, winds that are warm and dry, and winds that are heavily loaded with sand. These winds are the result of a combination of factors, including synoptic-scale weather systems, local geography and the daily cycle of solar heating.

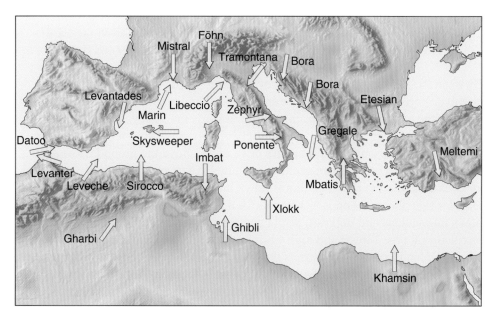

Figure 8.14   Some of the characteristic winds of the Mediterranean region. This map shows the approximate locations and typical directions of these winds, but their path on any particular day will depend on local conditions.

Mountain slopes without large-scale airflow: microscale to mesoscale winds

In still, summer conditions, winds arise in valleys where an adjacent mountain slope is bathed in day-long sunshine, simply because air on the slope is warmed and becomes unstable relative to the air in the rest of the valley. To replace the air that rises in thermals from the warm upper slopes, a gentle up-slope wind or 'valley breeze' develops. This wind will persist as long as the sunshine is strong enough to sustain the situation. To complete the circulation loop, there is a return flow down over the valley. This is illustrated schematically in Figure 8.15a. The meteorological term for this phenomenon of a localised up-slope wind is an 'anabatic' wind.

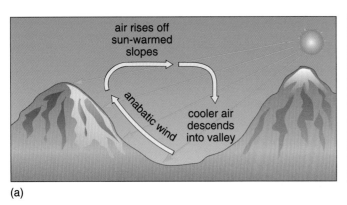
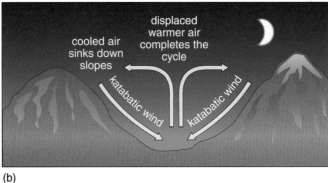

(a)   (b)

Figure 8.15   The pattern of (a) anabatic and (b) katabatic winds on mountain slopes.

◼ What will happen to the temperature of the air on upper slopes after nightfall, especially on clear nights?

☐ The slopes will cool because IR radiation is being emitted from the Earth's surface, and in turn the air in contact with these slopes is cooled from below.

By night the situation will therefore reverse from the daytime conditions, with mountain-top air cooling and becoming denser than that trapped in the valley. As a result, the air along the slope sinks down towards the valley, as illustrated in Figure 8.15b. When such a wind is a purely night-time phenomenon, it is quite shallow, involving only the first metre or so of air above the ground. However, local down-slope breezes can occur at any time of day, requiring only dense cool air over upland areas that then drains down into valleys. The meteorological term for this phenomenon is a 'katabatic' wind. A katabatic wind drains cold air down into valleys and hollows, displacing warmer air upwards to complete the circulation. Large forests and high walls are often enough to hold up the flow, but where the landform only constricts the flow the wind speed may be increased. The most extreme example of a katabatic wind is found in Antarctica where cold air tumbles off the intensely cold, high plateaus where the mean temperature is around −50 °C. Here, funnelled through ice-clad valleys towards the coast, katabatic wind speeds in excess of 300 km per hour have been recorded!

◼ How does that compare with the wind speeds in hurricanes and tornadoes?

☐ It is faster than a Category 5 hurricane and comparable with a T7 tornado.

Mountain slopes and large-scale air movement: mesoscale winds

When winds cross mountain ranges and then make a rapid and unimpeded descent, the topography and airflow combine to create a warm, dry blast of down-slope wind spilling onto the plains below.

◼ When unsaturated air sinks through a height of 1000 m, what will be the change in its temperature? (You may want to check back to Figure 2.19.)

☐ Unsaturated air warms by about 10 °C for every 1000 m of descent.

When such winds plunge down mountains with peaks at 2000–3000 m and head out across the plains they can therefore raise the temperature by 20–30 °C in a just a few hours, even in winter. In the Mediterranean area, shown in Figure 8.14, the classic example is the Föhn wind (often anglicised as 'Foehn'), in which air is warmed as it descends the slopes of the Alps. Although the term Föhn was originally applied to alpine winds, it is now used for all winds that arise in a similar way. Because Föhn-type winds have travelled down a mountain slope they can also be described as warm, katabatic winds.

There are often westerly Föhn-type winds on the rain-shadowed, lee side of the Scandinavian mountain ranges that intercept Atlantic air. In New Zealand there is a Nor'Wester which drops its moisture on the west coast, and crosses the Southern Alps from where it descends almost 3000 m, warming considerably before crossing the Canterbury Plains as a characteristically hot, dry wind. In North America a Föhn-type phenomenon occurs in the Rockies (which rise to 3000–4000 m above sea level), also driven by air moving from west to east – here it is called a Chinook wind.

Deserts and mountain ranges with low- and high-pressure systems: synoptic-scale winds

Many of the characteristic winds of the Mediterranean fall into this category. Look back at Figure 8.14 to remind yourself of some of the wind patterns in this region. A number of the named Mediterranean winds are simply synoptic-scale winds circulating around regions of low pressure. You have met this kind of circulation many times already, particularly in Chapters 3 and 7. (Look back at Figure 3.16 and Section 7.1.2 if you need a reminder.)

- For a low-pressure system (a depression) in the Mediterranean region, in which direction do winds a few kilometres aloft blow relative to the isobars?

☐ Winds aloft blow round the centre of a low-pressure system, almost parallel to the isobars, in this case anticlockwise since the Mediterranean is in the Northern Hemisphere.

- For a low-pressure system (a depression) in the Mediterranean region, in which direction do the surface winds blow relative to the isobars?

☐ Winds at the surface blow anticlockwise round the low but across the isobars to some extent, inwards towards the centre of the depression.

The Leveche (a Spanish word), Sirocco (an Italian word) and Ghibli (an Arabic word) marked in Figure 8.14 are all essentially the same phenomenon shifted along the North African coast. They arise from air circulation around low-pressure systems passing from west to east along the Mediterranean or the North African coast. Ahead of the centre of such a drifting depression these winds carry sand-laden air off the desert causing dusty, dry conditions along the northern coast of Africa. They cross the Mediterranean gathering moisture and this adds considerable rain (and often dust) to the storms that the low-pressure system carries over southern Spain and France, storms that often last for several days. Figure 8.16 shows the MSL pressure chart for a situation that gave rise to a Ghibli and a satellite view of the wind-flow traced out in a distinct band of airborne sand. Dusty rain is not very surprising close to the Mediterranean, but from time to time a belt of rain like this gets through to northern Europe leaving windows and other external shiny surfaces dulled by a film of dust.

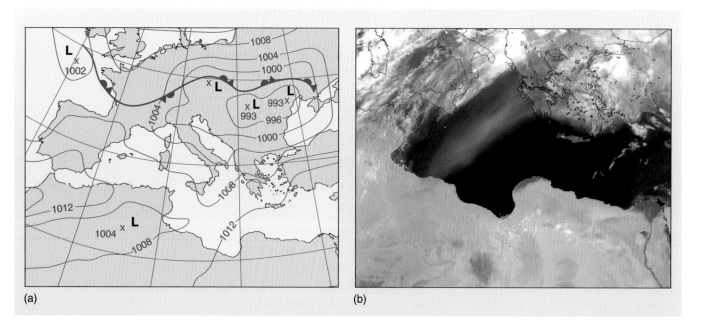

(a)   (b)

Figure 8.16   (a) The MSL pressure chart for midnight on 26 March 2001, indicating a long trough of low pressure over northern Africa; (b) a satellite view of a Ghibli some 12 hours later, sharply delineated by airborne sand over the Mediterranean.

Many people attribute health problems to the Leveche, Sirocco and Ghibli. On the African side this is because of the heat and dust that it carries onto the populated coastal strip. Across the other side of the Mediterranean it is the cool dampness of the winds as they reach southern Europe that is said to cause illness. The winds can blow at speeds of up to 100 km per hour and are most common during the autumn and the spring. The wind-driven dust within them causes severe wear if it gets into mechanical apparatus and it provides a natural sand-blasting effect, which is usually unwanted.

A different synoptic-scale pattern comes from a combination of high- and low-pressure regions. The Mistral ('magisterial' or 'masterly') is a phenomenon that occurs mostly in the winter and spring over southern France and out into the Golfe du Lion. As it crosses the coast into the Mediterranean it is felt as a strong, cold, northerly wind. The Mistral is caused by air being cooled as it is driven south, over the mountains of central France (Massif Central) and the western edge of the Alps, by the combination of an Atlantic high sitting out to the west of France and a low-pressure area located well to the east of the country. Anticlockwise circulation of air round the low and clockwise circulation round the high results in a strong northerly airstream moving down the middle of France towards the Massif Central. The Mistral often reaches gale force, especially in winter when it can also bring freezing temperatures to the south of France. Figure 8.17 shows the particular case of a low-pressure area that often remains close to the west coast or the northern half of Italy for days on end (and is termed a Genoa Low); this is effective in keeping the Mistral going. After crossing the Massif Central, the north wind is naturally channelled southwards by the Rhône valley. Funnelling into the valleys speeds the flow, as discussed in Box 8.2. By the time it reaches the Mediterranean coast the Mistral extends from the ground to high levels and can be recognised in satellite images that reveal the airflow traced out by the wisps of high clouds. On the ground, no such clues are needed, because the wind makes itself felt, day and night, sweeping the skies clear of heavy cloud and leading to bright and dry, but cold, weather.

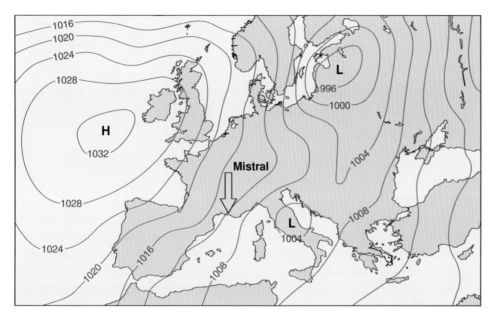

Figure 8.17   MSL pressure chart showing low pressure over Italy and high pressure over the Atlantic, a configuration that can set off a Mistral.

The Bora and Tramontana winds are similar examples of cold mountain air being driven and channelled over land towards the coast. The Bora is a north to northeasterly wind that usually occurs in winter. The Tramontana develops in the winter season when a low-pressure area is sited over the Adriatic and an area of high pressure lies further west.

You might wonder why some airflows down cold mountain slopes lead to cold winds, as is the case for the Mistral, Bora and Tramontana winds, whereas in the case of Föhn-type winds there is considerable warming accompanying compression as the wind moves down the mountain slope. The answer is that in the Mistral, Bora and Tramontana the initial down-slope flow is broad and unrushed, and the mountain slopes themselves are cold enough that the air in contact with them is also kept cold. It is not until the wind reaches the valleys that it is funnelled and accelerated.

As a rather different example of a synoptic-scale wind, it is interesting to look at an airflow that passes over deserts and mountains of the western USA. In the Los Angeles (LA) Basin in southern California, which is virtually at sea level, a characteristic katabatic flow of air gives rise to a warm, dry wind known simply as a Santa Ana. You may like to refer back to Figure 8.12 to understand the geography. This phenomenon is associated with air sinking out of a high-pressure system over the high (2000 m) desert plateau of Nevada and Utah and occurs particularly in the autumn and spring. At these times of year the deserts are relatively cool. Surface winds spiral clockwise round and outwards from the high-pressure area so that a cool, dry, north or northeasterly wind blows towards southern California. This wind funnels through the San Gabriel and San Bernadino mountains and finally reaches the LA Basin. The funnelling increases its speed and it blows particularly fiercely through the Santa Ana canyon from which it gets its name.

■ Why is the Santa Ana both very dry and very warm?

☐ The airflow originates over a high desert, and does not cross any areas from which it could pick up moisture. The air is heated by its overall descent of about 2000 m to the LA Basin.

In Chapter 9 this warm and dry wind will be linked to the spread of wildfires.

Question 8.6

The name Chinook comes from a Native American word meaning 'snow-eater'. It got that name because winter snow on the Great Plains (1000 m above sea level) that lie on the eastern side of the Rockies (3000–4000 m above sea level) is rapidly thawed when subjected to a few hours of a Chinook that brings down mountain air which can be as warm as 20 °C when it reaches the plains, even in midwinter when there are air frosts (i.e. air temperatures of below 0 °C) in the Rockies. How does the Chinook get so hot?

8.3   Monsoons

People living in the mid- and high latitudes are accustomed to four distinct weather seasons that are coupled to the changing day length and the associated extent of solar heating. Summer and winter are separated by intervals of transition, namely autumn (or fall) and spring. In the tropics the annual variation of weather is more readily matched with just two seasons – one wetter, the other drier, with barely any transition phase. These types of seasons have become known in various regions as summer and winter monsoons, based on the Arabic word for season ('mausin'). The changeover from one to the other is quite marked. For example, in India and nearby parts of southern Asia there is a sudden reversal of the prevailing wind from northeasterly to southwesterly as the season switches between winter and summer. The northeast wind that is characteristic of the winter monsoon persists between September/October and May/June. This season is relatively dry, because to the north and east of India there is the vast land mass of central Asia. By contrast, the southwesterly wind of the summer monsoon bears moisture-laden air from the Arabian Sea and the Bay of Bengal. Similar monsoon scenarios also occur in tropical regions of America, Africa and Australia.

8.3.1 The Indian monsoons

At any particular location the rapid changeover from winter to summer monsoon can be seen almost from one day to the next. Figure 8.18 shows observations of the monsoon season in India, as recorded in Mumbai during 2006. The arrival of the summer monsoon is evident in the daily rainfall pattern, though the daily mean temperature doesn't show a strong seasonal pattern: the temperature only peaks slightly at the start and finish of the rainy period that defines the summer monsoon. Mumbai is situated on the coast. In summer cooling winds blow in off the sea to keep temperatures there a little lower than further inland.

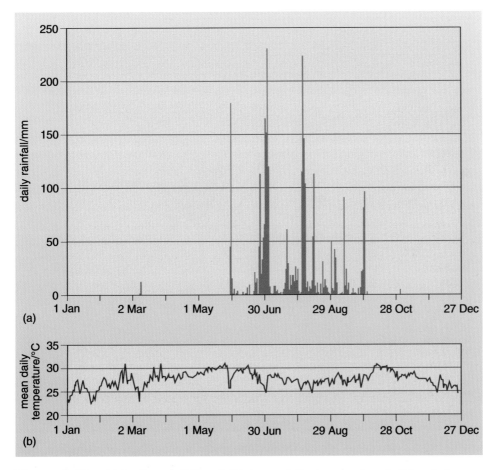

Figure 8.18 (a) Daily rainfall and (b) mean daily temperature in Mumbai during 2006. The rainy period between late May and early October defines the summer monsoon season. There is no marked seasonal pattern in the mean daily temperature; indeed the temperature variations through the whole year are quite small. The mean daily temperature is at its highest near the start and finish of the rainy period.

The Indian monsoons spread across the subcontinent gradually, so that for example the onset of the summer monsoon starts in southern India in late May but does not reach northern India until the end of June, or even the beginning of July. Observations show that the summer monsoon sweeps in along a path directed from southeast to northwest. The pattern of progress is broadly similar each year with increasing rainfall heralding the arrival of the summer monsoon at more or less the same time each year, though no single year necessarily matches the overall average. Figure 8.19 shows the advance of the summer monsoon across India in 2007. The monsoon is taken to have 'arrived' when rainfall increases by more than 6 mm per day for a few days in succession. The end-of-season reversal is measured in a similar way: when the daily rainfall has declined to less than 6 mm per day, then the summer monsoon is over. The withdrawal of the rainy conditions retraces the pattern of their onset, with drier weather tracking southeastwards between mid-September and mid-October.

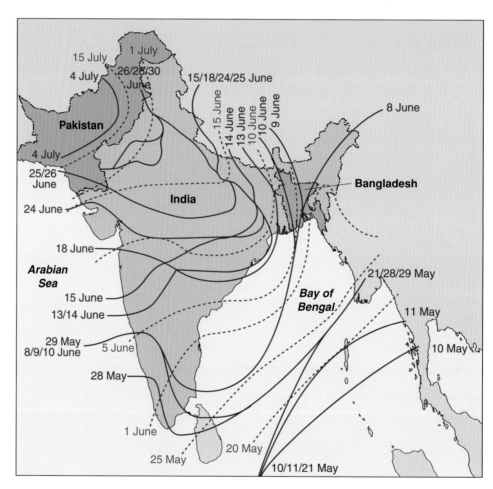

Figure 8.19   Progress across India of the onset of the summer monsoon in 2007. The continuous purple lines show the dates at which the monsoon is deemed to have arrived that year in particular regions. The broken red lines show the pattern of the onset of the summer monsoon in a 'normal' year.

■ According to Figure 8.19 how many weeks does it normally take for the summer monsoon in India to become established over the whole of the country?

☐ About six or seven weeks: in a normal year the summer monsoon starts at the southern end of the country around the end of May and reaches the northwest border with Pakistan in mid-July.

The arrival of the summer monsoon in India is a greatly anticipated event as the persistent rain initiates the crop-growing cycle; however, it also poses the risk of catastrophic flooding on occasions when the rain is extremely heavy. Severe drought impedes germination of seeds or survival of plants and severe flooding destroys crops, livestock and buildings. There is a delicate balance between prosperity and disaster at the hands of nature.

Activity 8.1   Watching a monsoon

The estimated time for this activity is 30 minutes.

In this activity you will return to the cloud and precipitation animation you studied in Activity 4.1, and observe the arrival and withdrawal of the Indian monsoon.

The detailed instructions for this activity are in the Activities section of the course website.

8.3.2   A simple explanation of the Indian monsoons

As you discovered in Activity 8.1, you can get a good overall view of tropical monsoons from the NWP models described in Chapter 6. The model you studied included enough detail to see the Indian monsoon quite clearly. However, watching a complex numerical model of the atmosphere will not enable you to pick out exactly which meteorological processes are involved. To do this scientists tend to start with the simplest possible explanation, introducing complexity only as a last resort. In scientific terms, an 'explanation' amounts to a description of a model system that behaves in the same way as the real thing.

One of the earliest recorded explanations of two-season monsoons can be traced back to the writings of Edmund Halley in 1688. His explanation linked together a number of ideas that should by now be very familiar to you from earlier chapters. Halley's simple model does not consider all the features of real monsoons, but it is a good starting point. The discussion will be taken to a more sophisticated level in Section 8.3.3.

Here are the steps of the simple monsoon model for the Northern Hemisphere:

1   Between the March equinox and the June solstice the path of the Sun appears to migrate day by day from the Equator northwards towards the Tropic of Cancer. The resulting increase in solar warming builds up the temperature of tropical land masses north of the Equator. This starts the summer monsoon in the Northern Hemisphere.

2   Over the adjacent ocean the sea-surface temperature responds more slowly because of the high specific heat capacity of water and the ease with which heat is transported away from the water surface. (Look back at Section 2.1.2 or check the Course Glossary if you need a reminder about specific heat capacity.)

Figure 8.20 shows evidence for these first two steps. The surface temperature in the Arabian Sea during 2004 increased slowly during the period between May and September, whereas the mean monthly air temperature recorded at Ahmedabad in northern India, some 150 km from the nearest (Arabian Sea) coastline, rose significantly between March and May.

3   The warmed continental air is unstable and readily contributes to thermal convection currents that carry air upwards, drawing in replacement air from where the surface is cooler, i.e. from over the ocean. This is in effect an onshore breeze of the sort outlined in Chapter 2.

4   The thermal cell is completed by higher-level flow directed offshore which then cools and descends over the ocean to replace air drawn inland.

Figure 8.21a illustrates the processes of steps 3 and 4 schematically.

5   The onshore wind brings moisture-laden air over the land where orographic uplift initiates rainfall.

6   The end of the summer phase comes as the Sun's daily track appears to move back over the Equator. The daily heating cycle of the land mass weakens enough to allow the now warmed ocean to drive convection day after day, drawing air off the land as it does so. This winter phase moves low-level dry air across the continent, from the northeast, and out over the ocean. The rains stop for several months until the cycle repeats from the first step.

You can see in Figure 8.20 that from October to February the sea-surface temperature of the Arabian Sea exceeds the mean daily temperature over the landmass. Figure 8.21b is a schematic illustration of the thermal cell associated with the winter monsoon.

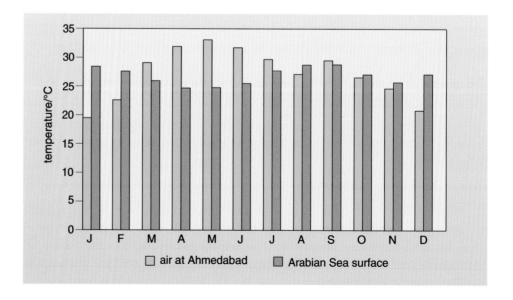

Figure 8.20 Data for 2004 comparing the mean monthly temperatures of the surface of the Arabian Sea with the mean monthly air temperature at Ahmedabad, northern India.

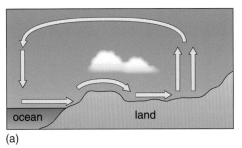
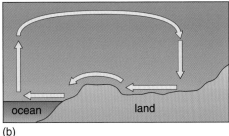

(a)   (b)

Figure 8.21   The direct thermal cell of Halley's monsoon model: (a) summer; (b) winter. Note that the vertical scale is greatly exaggerated for clarity. The height of the thermal cells is in fact less than 10 km.

The problems with this simple explanation of the monsoon processes can be seen with reference to the behaviour of the Indian monsoon outlined in Section 8.3.1.

■   Look back at the description in Section 8.3.1 and at Figure 8.19 if necessary, and identify one characteristic pattern of the Indian monsoon that is not included in the simple model set out here.

☐   The pattern that is missing is the way in which the onset of the summer monsoon sweeps over the country on a northwestward track (and retraces this path as the winter phase takes over).

The simple description has nothing in it to explain why the passage of the Indian monsoon is not along a simple north–south path, following the midday Sun. It also suggests that the summer monsoon in India should begin in late March shortly after the equinox, whereas the summer monsoon does not normally start to move in until two months later. In addition, the simple model doesn't help us to understand why monsoons are only observed in the tropics. Section 8.3.3 introduces factors that address these shortcomings, though what results is still by no means a complete model of the monsoon. If it were it would be of enormous value in predicting the arrival of the life-giving (or life-threatening) rain. Building accurate monsoon-prediction models continues to be a research challenge for meteorologists.

8.3.3   A better model for the Indian monsoons

The general occurrence of the Indian summer monsoon certainly coincides with a large-scale 'breeze' that reflects the changed balance of air temperature over land and sea. The direct thermal cell associated with this giant sea breeze was illustrated in Figure 8.21a. However, the overall picture is more complicated than that because, at the same time, there is the larger-scale circulation of the Hadley cells. One manifestation of this global circulation is the Inter-Tropical Convergence Zone (ITCZ), the January and July positions of which are marked on Figure 4.4.

The ITCZ is where the northeasterly Trade Winds of the Northern Hemisphere converge with the southeasterly Trade Winds from the Southern Hemisphere. This convergence occurs in a band around the globe and feeds air into the strong, rising air current which is driven by strong solar heating. At the equinoxes the band lies along the Equator, but as the latitude at which the noonday Sun is overhead shifts up towards the Tropic of Cancer and back south towards the Tropic of Capricorn the ITCZ tends to follow it. If the Earth's surface were entirely covered by smooth land the ITCZ would make a simple excursion north and south, following lines of latitude. But the Earth's surface is part ocean and part rough land. This complicates the behaviour, not least because the land and the sea respond on different timescales to changes in solar heating. The net effect is that the band of the ITCZ has large-scale wiggles that are particularly emphasised over the continental land masses.

The ITCZ is also mapped out as a trough of low surface pressure, associated with the rising air current. This feature is a major driver of monsoon conditions and the rising air links the upper troposphere to monsoon events at ground level. The subtropical jet stream at the tropopause thus has a bearing on monsoon weather.

Figure 8.22 is a magnified section of Figure 4.4, centred on India. Notice the large displacement that occurs in the position of the ITCZ between July and January.

Figure 8.22   Detail from Figure 4.4 showing the extreme locations of the ITCZ and prevailing wind directions in the vicinity of India during (a) July and (b) January.

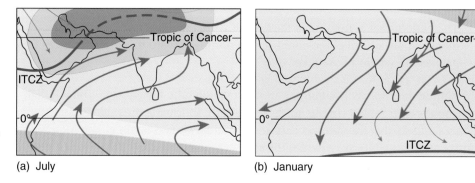

(a) July   (b) January

■   In July, what is the direction of the prevailing wind over the Arabian Sea?

☐   The prevailing wind is from the southwest.

July is when the ITCZ is at its most northerly position and the summer monsoon has crossed into all of India and beyond into Pakistan and Bangladesh.

In the preceding six months the ITCZ over the Indian Ocean (between longitudes 60° E and 100° E) has moved northward from its January turning point about 10° south of the Equator. By late May it is approaching India. The presence of the continental land mass of Asia creates a wiggle in the ITCZ, bending the line of the low-pressure trough that accompanies it, so that over India the ITCZ stretches sideways from south-southwest to east-northeast. This distortion of the ITCZ is a consequence of the temperature differential that builds between land and ocean, which the Halley model treated as the cause of a giant sea breeze. The giant breeze is certainly present, but the Halley model does not take account of the fact that it also locks onto and modifies the passage of the ITCZ. Thus the summer monsoon takes a roughly northwestward track through June and early July, as illustrated in Figure 8.19. It retreats along a southeastward track as drier winds switch in and the progress of the monsoon follows the ITCZ.

The Indian summer monsoon blows moisture-laden air off the Arabian Sea onto the west coast of India. Here the air is forced to rise over the mountain range known as the Western Ghats. This orographic lifting occurs on top of the strong convection associated with the low-pressure trough of the ITCZ. The monsoon rain results from the combination of these two forms of uplift. Evidence for the important role of the orographic effect can be seen in satellite photographs: Figure 8.23 shows a greener strip, bounded by the west coast of India and the Western Ghats mountain range, that bears witness to the high precipitation associated with the windward side of the range.

■ On the evidence of Figure 8.23, where is the rain shadow of the Western Ghats?

☐ The rain shadow marked by less lush vegetation appears to extend to the east of the Western Ghats and a long way right across the southern half of India.

The rainfall statistics support the proposition that the rain shadow extends at least as far as Bangalore in central southern India. Figure 8.24 shows the total monthly rainfall during 2006 in Bangalore and in Mumbai, which lies further north on the western seaboard. Although these rainfall data relate to a single year, the pattern is fairly typical. The average onset time for the summer monsoon in Bangalore is right at the start of June and a little over a week later it reaches Mumbai. The rainfall in Bangalore during March, April and May is due to convective storms drifting in from the Bay of Bengal on the tail of the winter monsoon, ahead of the advancing ITCZ. Notice that the rain shadow does not totally eliminate the monsoon rains carried onshore by the southwesterly wind; it merely accounts for the relatively lower rainfall east of the Western Ghats.

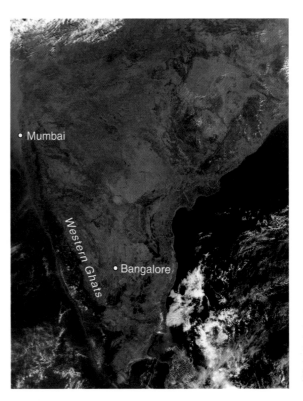

Figure 8.23 A satellite photograph of part of India, showing changes in the amount of vegetation either side of the Western Ghats.

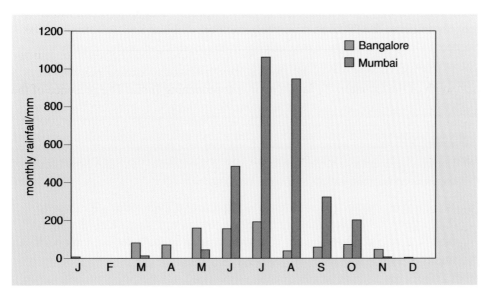

Figure 8.24 Total monthly rainfall in Mumbai and Bangalore during 2006.

Not all of the summer monsoon weather crosses onshore over the west coast of India. Southwesterly winds also pass the southern tip of India and blow into the Bay of Bengal. After a prolonged passage over the ocean, wet conditions reach the northeastern provinces of India from out of the top of the Bay, blowing in from the south. Where this airflow reaches the edge of the Himalayan range there is the greatest rainfall of all of the Indian monsoon.

There is one further factor that is linked to the movement and severity of the Indian monsoon and that is the behaviour of high-level winds over the ITCZ. The fast-moving high-level current of air that is the Northern Hemisphere subtropical jet stream plays an important role in the summer monsoon. You may want to look back at Figure 4.5 to remind yourself of the path of this westerly (i.e. west to east) jet. As the northern subtropical jet stream carries air eastwards, it also drags air at its edges into the subsiding flow at the northerly edge of the Hadley cell. During Asia's summer monsoon, over the Himalaya and beyond, over the Tibetan plateau, the rising air currents get caught up with the subtropical jet. As the southwesterly monsoon takes over in the Himalaya, the subtropical jet is strongly disrupted. During this phase, an eddy forms alongside the jet stream that draws upper-level wind back round in a clockwise direction into an easterly (i.e. east to west) flow over India. This reinforces the thermal updraft, sucking air more strongly inland from the Arabian Sea and strengthening the summer monsoon. It is a complicated story and it is not surprising that predicting monsoon behaviour remains a major challenge for meteorologists.

The situation is by no means static and the subtropical jet in particular is far from stable, wandering north and south from day to day. As a result, there can be sudden breaks to the strength of the fully formed summer monsoon, during which rainfall patterns change for a few days at a time.

The weakening and subsequent withdrawal of the summer monsoon over India is driven by the strengthening of the Siberian High, which, as Figure 4.4 showed, is primarily a winter feature. Subsidence of upper air into this region, and air circulating clockwise round it and flowing out from it, provides relatively fair and stable weather for southern and eastern Asia. The surface-level winds switch from southwesterly to northeasterly as the winter season spreads down India, roughly tracking the ITCZ as it moves generally southeast and onwards into the Southern Hemisphere. There is relatively little rain in most of the country until the summer monsoon returns.

Question 8.7

Figure 8.25 shows the pattern of rainfall over Australia between October 2006 and September 2007.

(a) Looking particularly at the northern part of the country, explain how these data are consistent with a monsoon pattern.

(b) Write a short paragraph outlining the sequence of events that gives rise to this pattern of weather, making reference to times of year, solar heating and the ITCZ. (To see how the ITCZ moves in relation to Australia, look back at Figure 4.4.)

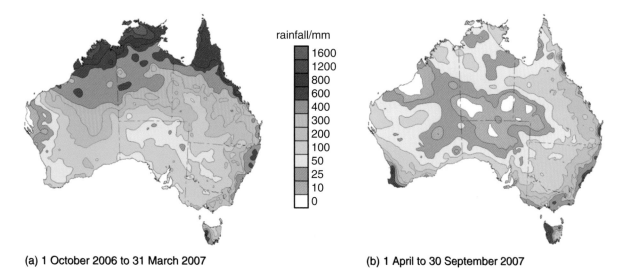

rainfall/mm

	1600
	1200
	800
	600
	400
	300
	200
	100
	50
	25
	10
	0

(a) 1 October 2006 to 31 March 2007   (b) 1 April to 30 September 2007

Figure 8.25 Rainfall over Australia for two half-year periods in 2006/7.

8.3.4 Everest weather windows

Climbers whose expeditions have taken them to the Himalaya and Mount Everest (8872 m) are familiar with the patterns of the Asian monsoon. That is because the monsoon cycle dictates when it is best to climb to the top. Up on the slopes of Everest there is a fierce wind almost all the year round, contributing significantly to the hazards of climbing at high altitude on ice and rock. The last 1000 metres are high enough to intercept some of the seasonal jet-stream winds. It was mentioned in Chapter 4 that the lower wind-speed limit that defines a jet stream is roughly 90–110 km per hour.

Between November and February the average summit wind speed on Everest exceeds 120 km per hour (compare that with Saffir–Simpson hurricane speeds in Table 4.2 and the tornado speeds in Table 8.1). During the summer the average is lower but hurricane-strength wind occurs for a day or so at a time during most weeks. Expedition meteorologists would tell you that the main weather window for summit attempts must await the approach of the time of the changeover from northeasterly to southwesterly monsoons, when the ITCZ has reached its most northerly excursion. This window occurs around the second half of May, slightly ahead of the lower-level advance of the rain-bearing southwesterly monsoon over northern India. In this brief phase, summit winds are light, there is little precipitation and climbing conditions are favourable, though not guaranteed to last particularly long.

So much for the theory. What do the summit climbers make of it in practice? Figure 8.26 presents a histogram of the entire catalogue of successful ascents of Everest up to the end of 2006.

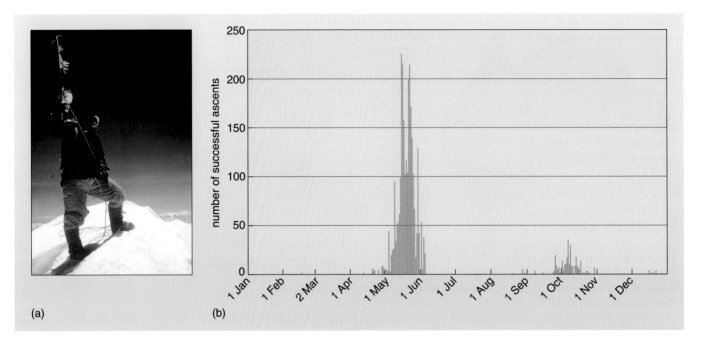

(a)

(b)

Figure 8.26   Climbing Mount Everest. (a) The first successful ascent on 29 May 1953 by Sir Edmund Hillary and Tenzing Norgay: this picture of Tenzing Norgay close to the summit was taken by Hillary. (b) The number of successful climbs to the summit up to and including 2006, analysed by the day of achievement.

■ The main window in May is apparent in Figure 8.26b, but so too is a later window in October. What could be the reason for the second window?

□ The second window corresponds with the changeover between southwesterly and northeasterly monsoons. It is likely that once again there is a brief interlude in the strong winds when climbers can go for the summit.

Meteorological records reveal that the October weather window is less stable, which accounts for its relatively low popularity. Two other factors also favour the May window over that in October. The first is that the initial climbing and logistical support period for the May window can take place in the fair weather of the winter monsoon, whereas the build-up for an October attempt takes place during the tail-end of rainy season. The second reason is that the southwesterly monsoon leaves the mountain slopes covered in fresh snow, so climbing in the latter window will be more challenging. Remarkably, and in spite of the kind of reasoning presented here, summit attempts are made occasionally at other times of the year and some are successful.

8.4   The global influence of the oceans

The daily input of solar heating to the Earth is redistributed and continuously re-radiated into space, maintaining an overall balance. The oceans play an important part in the redistribution process, but they do so with a more sluggish response than is characteristic of the atmosphere. In spite of the different speeds of reaction, the oceans and the atmosphere are strongly linked. You saw in Chapter 6 that the more sophisticated NWP models incorporate this linkage. Because of the different speeds of reaction, the coupling is not rigid and atmosphere and ocean interactions end up oscillating around some average situation rather than being perfectly steady. In this section there are two examples of global-scale weather scenarios that result from ocean currents: one in the North Atlantic and the other in the South Pacific.

8.4.1 Ocean circulation

The influence of the oceans on global weather becomes clearer when the changing temperature of the sea surface can be seen, together with flows within and between the oceans.

■ Which of the following would you expect to be useful in monitoring sea-surface temperatures and ocean flows: radiosonde flights; geostationary satellites; polar-orbiting satellites; tethered buoys; drifting buoys?

☐ All of them, except perhaps the radiosonde.

Radiosonde flights are clearly better matched to atmospheric monitoring. Satellites *are* used for measuring ocean properties, but are not always ideal for this purpose. Geostationary satellites are rather a long way above the Earth and don't cover high latitudes very well. Polar-orbiting satellites are well placed to scan the ocean and to map its characteristics, but 'seeing' its slow drift from satellite images is not easy. Tethered and drifting buoys with on-board communications and a Global Positioning System (GPS) are in the right place to experience local sea temperature and flows.

In fact, a huge number of 'smart' drifting buoys are now in use. These are automatically able to dive and resurface daily, mapping the ocean temperature and currents as effectively as radiosondes probe the atmosphere. Added to the data from buoys are secondary measurements such as those made from satellite images and from sea-level surveys of plankton. The strangest method of all is based on charting the progress of cargoes lost overboard in heavy seas: running shoes, hockey gloves and bath-tub ducks have all been accidental tracers of global ocean currents.

Winds over the ocean tend to stir up the top few metres of water, through long-travelling 'swell', short-travelling 'mixed sea' waves and smaller surface ripples. Observations show that a steady wind blowing over deep water will drag the near-surface water along at about one per cent or so of the wind speed. In the North Atlantic, for instance, the wind-driven drift amounts to a surface ocean current of about 1 km per hour. As discussed in Section 8.2.1, in relation to San Francisco fog, the displacement of the sea surface drags the underlying water towards the surface, though the effect weakens with depth so that the influence of the surface wind penetrates no more than a few tens of metres.

Just as with the wind itself, the rotation of the Earth affects ocean currents through the Coriolis effect, deflecting them from their original path.

■ Will the deflection tend to be greater at higher latitudes or at lower latitudes?

☐ The Coriolis effect is zero exactly on the Equator and increases towards the poles, so the deflection will be greater at higher latitudes.

The deflection also increases with flow speed.

■ In what direction would a sea-surface current be deflected in the Southern Hemisphere?

☐ The deflection is to the left of the direction of flow.

In the Northern Hemisphere the deflection is to the right. Figure 8.27 shows surface currents across the globe. Notice how there are circulating cells in the North and South Atlantic, the North and South Pacific and in the Indian Ocean. If you compare Figure 8.27 with Figure 4.4, you will see that in these regions the ocean surface circulation is similar to the general pattern of air circulation.

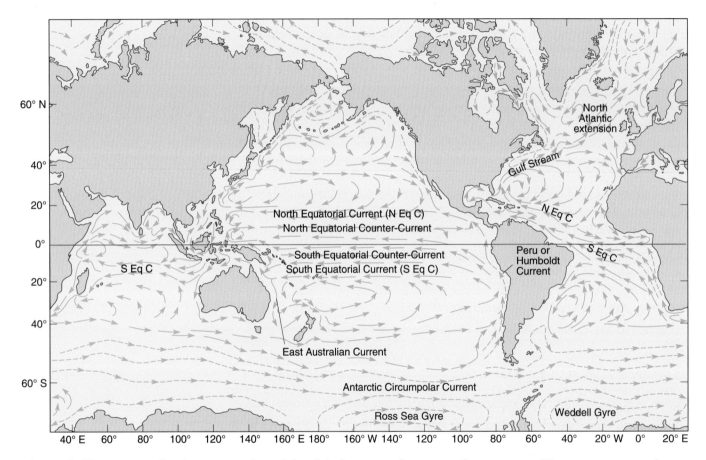

Figure 8.27   A generalised representation of the global system of ocean surface currents. Warm currents are shown by solid arrows and cool currents by dashed arrows. The currents shown correspond to average conditions in July. A January map would show local differences, especially in regions with monsoon patterns of weather. (The term 'gyre' describes a flow pattern that is more or less circular.)

In addition to the effect of winds and the Earth's rotation, there is another large-scale effect that also moves seawater around. It is called thermohaline circulation to reflect the contributions of both temperature (thermo) and salinity (the salt in seawater is mainly the compound sodium chloride, which is a member of a family of compounds known generally as halides). Thermohaline circulation is caused by the rising and sinking of deep ocean water in response to changes in its density. Seawater that is cold and rich in dissolved salt (high salinity) is denser than that which is warmer and/or less salty.

■   How can a surface current of seawater become saltier (and hence denser)?

☐   When water evaporates, the salt will be left behind, increasing the salinity of the water that remains.

■   How can a surface current of seawater become colder (and hence denser)?

☐   If the current takes seawater into a region where the air is cold the surface water will lose heat to the air above it.

A surface current of warm water dragged along by winds from the mid-latitudes to higher latitudes thus becomes denser through wind-aided evaporation and the presence of cold air at higher latitudes. At some stage the surface current may become denser than the underlying body of ocean water; the current will then start to sink, becoming part of a thermohaline circulation. Wind-driven and thermohaline currents can provide a strong coupling between the oceans and the weather, taking heat from one side of an ocean to another and beyond.

8.4.2   Basking in the North Atlantic Drift

The Gulf Stream is a wind-driven flow of ocean surface water out of the Gulf of Mexico, where it has been warmed by the Sun. As Figure 8.27 shows, this flow then continues as the North Atlantic extension, driven on by the general thermohaline circulation and carrying with it some of the heat picked up in the Gulf of Mexico. As a result of this 'North Atlantic Drift' the climate in coastal northern Europe, and the British Isles in particular, is kept warmer than coastal land masses elsewhere but at a comparable latitude. In Section 2.1.2 you saw how average temperatures in Edinburgh (UK) and Ushuaia (Argentina) illustrated the effect of the North Atlantic Drift.

The coupling between the oceans and the atmosphere is an important factor in determining weather and the calculations underlying long-range weather forecasts need to include its effects. The large-scale air circulation that stimulates the Gulf Stream is intimately linked to the North Atlantic westerly airflow that initiates and carries the frontal weather systems across northern Europe. It turns out that a prolonged period of weakened Atlantic air circulation may disrupt the whole balance, weakening the heat flow into the North Atlantic; then, for tens of years at a stretch, the pattern shifts and northern Europe experiences cooler weather with frontal weather systems being pushed further south. Such conditions notably prevailed between 1930 and 1960.

8.4.3   ENSO: El Niño and La Niña

ENSO is an acronym that stands for 'El Niño Southern Oscillation'. The ENSO phenomenon is often simply called 'El Niño' and it relates to a cycle of conditions in the Pacific Ocean between Southeast Asia and South America. Measurements show that the long-term average sea-surface temperature on the Asian side is several degrees warmer than on the American, but every few years that imbalance breaks down and swings the other way for a year or so, before reversing once more, often by way of an overshoot corresponding to an even colder season than usual on the American side. The consequences of these oscillating conditions are felt around the globe through the interaction of the central Pacific Ocean with equatorial maritime air masses.

The global circulation of air usually leads to strong surface winds from east to west along the Equator in the Pacific. (You may like to look back at Figure 4.3 to remind yourself about this.) Look carefully at the direction of the ocean surface current across the Pacific very close to the Equator, as shown in Figure 8.27; you will be able to see the imprint of this easterly wind on the current. This ocean surface current carries warm surface water into the western part of the central Pacific. One consequence of this is that the average level of the sea surface around Indonesia is about half a metre higher than it would be if the wind were absent. Another consequence is that the surface water around Indonesia is normally warm. In the eastern part of the central Pacific, off the coast of Ecuador, the situation is different. Here the surface water is flowing westwards and cooler water from deep below the surface is drawn up to replace it. This is the same upwelling process that you met in Section 8.2.1. As a result, the surface water in this region is usually comparatively cool. Figure 8.28 shows satellite observations of ocean-surface temperature in January 2008. Comparisons with data recorded over many decades suggest that Figure 8.28 displays the 'normal' situation in the central Pacific.

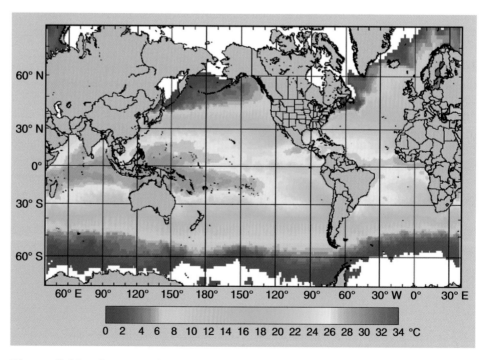

Figure 8.28   Ocean-surface temperature as recorded by a satellite on 10 January 2008. The oceans areas are colour coded according to the surface temperature of the water. (White areas correspond to regions for which there are no data or where there is sea ice.) At the time this image was recorded, the conditions were 'normal'.

■ According to the data shown in Figure 8.28, what are the temperatures of the ocean surface along the Equator in the western Pacific (Asian side) and in the eastern Pacific (South American side)?

☐ The surface temperature of the water at the Equator in the western Pacific is around 30 °C, whereas that in the eastern Pacific is around 22 °C.

This is typical of the 'normal' situation: the ocean-surface temperature is roughly 8 °C warmer on the western side of the Pacific than on the eastern side. Cool offshore conditions maintain a climate in coastal Ecuador and neighbouring Peru that is less warm than might be expected for an equatorial location. The upwelling cold water carries with it nutrients that sustain fish stocks and commercial fishing thrives as a result. In addition, the coastal waters on the western side of South America (i.e. the eastern Pacific) are also cooled by a cold surface current, called the Humboldt current, that runs right up to the northern border of Peru. You can see the path of this current on Figure 8.27.

Now consider what is happening in the atmosphere immediately above the Equator line across the Pacific when these 'normal' conditions prevail. You already know that at sea level there is an airflow from east to west. There is also a considerable temperature difference between the eastern and western sides of the Pacific.

■ On which side will air rise more easily and why?

☐ Air will tend to rise more easily on the western side, because the convective lift will be stronger where the sea is warmer and because surface air is flowing into that area.

To balance the easterly surface wind and the rising air in the western central Pacific, air flows from west to east at higher levels and sinks over the eastern central Pacific. In other words, a thermal circulation cell operates roughly *along* the Equator (i.e. along the line of latitude 0°). This should not be confused with the Hadley cell of Figure 4.2, in which air is envisaged as circulating between the Equator and latitudes of about 30°. In practice both circulations coexist as part of the overall global-scale circulation.

■ On which side of the central Pacific will there be the heavier precipitation and why?

☐ The western (Asian) side, where air is rising over a warm ocean, has the conditions that lead to the formation of large cumulonimbus clouds and torrential tropical rain. On the eastern side, where air is sinking, cloud formation will be inhibited and drier conditions are more likely,

Figure 8.29a summarises the story so far by illustrating schematically the sea-surface conditions and the atmospheric thermal cell along the Equator under 'normal' conditions. Study this figure and its caption carefully before reading on.

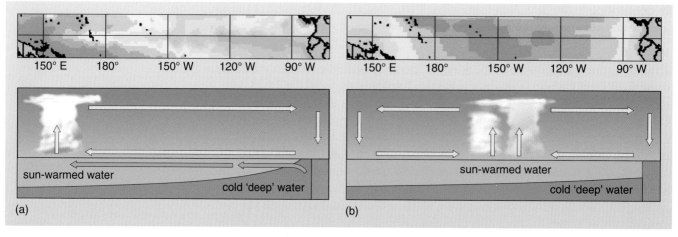

Figure 8.29   Coupling of ocean and atmosphere in the Pacific Ocean under (a) normal and (b) El Niño conditions. As usual, the vertical scale is greatly exaggerated. The upper (plan) views show the sea-surface temperature in a strip across the equatorial Pacific region, using the same colour key as Figure 8.28. The lower (cross-sectional) views show what is happening below the sea surface and in the atmosphere along the same strip. Under normal conditions the warmest sea surface is in the western Pacific where it maintains a direct convection cell that sustains easterly winds at sea level; this reinforces the situation because cold water is dragged up from below on the eastern side. During El Niño conditions the warmest sea surface is in the central Pacific where a direct convection cell draws in air on both westerly and easterly winds; there is insufficient drag on the ocean surface for upwelling of cold deep water to occur, and the South American side in particular enjoys warmer, moister conditions than 'normal'.

Every few years a prolonged period of weakened air circulation arises in December or January. The easterly winds along the Equator over the Pacific are less strong and the ocean surface current that is directed away from the South American coast is therefore less strong as well. As a result, not quite as much cold water gets pulled up from below by upwelling. These changes tend to make the water in the eastern Pacific, and the weather that forms over it, warmer than it otherwise would be. The warmer ocean then starts to interact with the equatorial maritime air mass and over a period of days to weeks a long-term shift in weather pattern is built up, which can last for several months.

For centuries this late-December onset of a prolonged warm spell near the South American coast was heralded as a gift associated with the celebration of the arrival of 'the baby boy' (in Spanish, El Niño), after whom Christmas and this weather scenario are both named. Anomalously warm sea temperatures in the eastern equatorial Pacific are the hallmarks of El Niño years. Figure 8.29b illustrates how the atmosphere and ocean interact during El Niño conditions. As you study this figure, compare it carefully with the 'normal' scenario of Figure 8.29a.

■   What differences do you notice in precipitation patterns across the central Pacific between 'normal' and El Niño conditions and why does a shift occur?

☐   In 'normal' years, the heaviest rain occurs over the western Pacific, because that is where the air is rising within the thermal circulation cell, and the eastern side of the Pacific is dry. In El Niño conditions, the warmest ocean surface water is further east and the heaviest precipitation is therefore also further east.

In exceptionally strong El Niño conditions, heavy rainfall and flooding can occur in Ecuador and Peru.

When El Niño gets going in the eastern half of the Pacific, there is a very slow, swelling wave that drifts slowly westwards towards the Asian side at a speed of roughly 3.5 km per hour. This slow ocean wave brings slight cooling to the Asian side, which is enough to switch off the normal convective weather. When El Niño is strong, not only is there less tropical rain in the western Pacific but also there are droughts right across Australasia.

So what brings El Niño conditions to an end and resets the global circulation back to 'normal'? After several months of travelling to the Southeast Asian coast the slow ocean wave is reflected and returns eastward. It turns out that the changes in the ocean temperature associated with El Niño are cancelled out on the return of this wave, allowing the equatorial easterlies to return to their normal strength, so that upwelling again drags up cold water in the eastern equatorial Pacific. However, the oscillation does not necessarily stop there because the system easily 'overshoots'. When this happens, water that is even colder than usual joins the circulation, bringing in a period of colder than average offshore conditions. The period of overshoot is called La Niña (the baby girl) as the counterpart of El Niño. You can think of La Niña scenarios as the opposite of El Niño situations, i.e. as more extreme versions of 'normal' conditions.

■ Will a La Niña episode bring wet conditions or dry conditions to Australia?

□ A strong El Niño is often associated with droughts in Australasia, so La Niña is likely to bring wetter than normal conditions into this region.

8.4.4 Worldwide weather and ocean–atmosphere interactions

Although El Niño events arise from changes in conditions in the region of the equatorial Pacific, the effects are felt over a much wider area. In fact, the atmosphere as a whole responds to these changes with changed patterns on a global scale. This is because the disturbance caused by El Niño shifts the pattern of air circulation and tropical rainfall, which in turn affects high-level winds, connecting the disturbance to other parts of the globe. As a result, ENSO events have a strong influence on the seasonal migration of the ITCZ, on monsoon winds in general and on patterns of rainfall in widely dispersed areas. The effects, however, vary a lot from season to season and region to region. For example, El Niño conditions are often associated with above-normal rainfall over the equatorial parts of eastern Africa from October to December (e.g. during the 'short rains' in Kenya) and below-normal rainfall further south. (As you might expect, La Niña events often have the opposite effects.) Figure 8.30 shows some of the most marked changes that accompany the onset of an El Niño event.

Figure 8.30 Map showing the effect of El Niño events on both temperature and precipitation in areas that tend to be particularly affected. This map corresponds to December – January conditions (Southern Hemisphere summer). During the Southern Hemisphere winter, the 'drier than usual' conditions in the western Pacific area move even further southwards, affecting the whole eastern half of Australia.

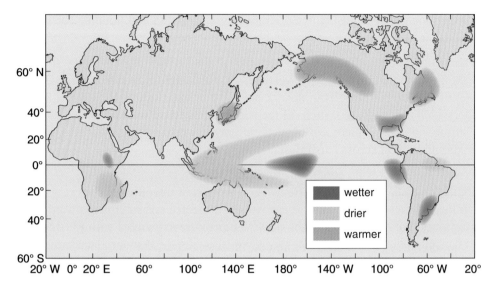

There is also a significant statistical relationship between El Niño events and tropical cyclones. The number of hurricanes in the Atlantic tends to fall to about half the normal number during El Niño years, while the number of typhoons tends to increase in the eastern Pacific. La Niña conditions are also linked to drought in the western USA. The ENSO influence spreads as far as Antarctica where mean sea-level pressure in a particular region shows a strong correlation with El Niño years.

Question 8.8

Figures 8.31a and b each show a map on which are recorded the *differences* in sea-surface temperatures from 'normal conditions'. These differences from normal are called 'anomalies' because they correspond to behaviour that is anomalous (i.e. different from usual). Decide which corresponds with El Niño conditions and which with La Niña conditions. Then write a few sentences about each to explain how the temperature anomalies have arisen.

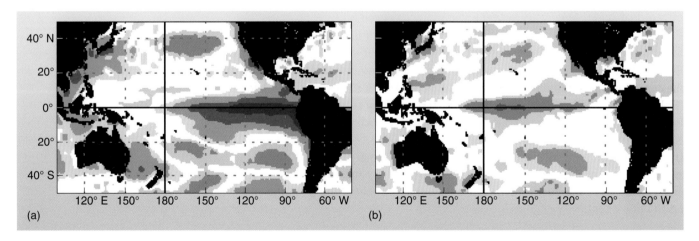

Figure 8.31 Maps of the sea-surface temperature anomalies between (a) January and March 1998 and (b) January and March 1989. Yellow, orange and red colorations indicate temperatures that are respectively 0.5 °C, 1 °C and 2 °C *above* 'normal'; pale blue and dark blue colorations represent temperatures that are respectively 0.5 °C and 1 °C *below* 'normal'.

Before reading the summary of this chapter, you may like to reflect on the way in which the selection of weather situations you have studied were presented in order of increasing scales of distance and time, beginning with local storms and then moving on to the effects of larger and larger geographic features such as mountain ranges, continents and oceans. You should be able to see where other weather phenomena you have studied elsewhere in this course, such as the frontal weather systems and hurricanes of Chapter 4, fit on the scale. The final chapter revisits a number of these situations from the point of view of their impact on us and on the way we live.

8.5 Summary of Chapter 8

Thunderstorms arise when warm moist air rises rapidly, forming towering clouds of cumulonimbus in a matter of minutes. In these clouds, the movement of ice crystals can result in the build-up of static electricity, corresponding to millions of volts. When the electric charge builds up to a sufficient level, sparks of lightning occur. The sparks make shock waves as the air in them is rapidly heated and expands, giving rise to peals of thunder.

Severe thunderstorms provide conditions that can cause the thermal updraught to rotate and so initiate tornadoes. A strong change of wind speed with height, so-called wind shear, is required to initiate the rotation.

The weather in coastal regions interacts locally with the adjoining oceans. Moisture-laden air is often carried in by onshore breezes to form coastal fogs or to bring rain to windward mountain slopes inshore. The leeward slopes of mountains under these circumstances receive relatively little precipitation and are said to be in a rain shadow. There are types of wind that are characteristic of mountain slopes.

Around the tropics there is a complicated interaction between high-level winds, the Inter-Tropical Convergence Zone (ITCZ), and seasonal heating of land and ocean. The combination can give rise to monsoons. The characteristic of a monsoon region is a seasonal reversal of the prevailing wind with accompanying dramatic changes in general weather. In the case of the Indian monsoon, the summer monsoon advances northwestward across the subcontinent, bringing heavy rain, whereas the winter monsoon season is relatively dry.

El Niño and La Niña events are the extremes within a cycle of conditions in the central equatorial Pacific that is known as the El Niño Southern Oscillation (ENSO). Under 'normal' conditions, an easterly airflow keeps the western Pacific area warm and wet, and the eastern side cooler and drier. During an El Niño event, the easterly winds are less strong, the area of convective rainfall shifts eastwards, and the eastern (South American) side of the central Pacific experiences warmer conditions than normal. A La Niña event represents an overshoot in the change from El Niño towards a restoration of normal conditions. ENSO is such a large-scale phenomenon that it affects weather in many parts of the globe.

Chapter 9
Weather impacts

Severe drought leads to famine. Wildfires destroy vegetation and dwellings. Intense rain leads to flash floods. Tropical cyclones may cause high levels of death and devastate property. There is no shortage of news stories concerning the effects of weather on the daily lives of people around the world. Internet searches for 'extreme weather' will turn up links to catalogues of the most extreme weather events, accounts of weather-related disasters, pictures and videos and also some of the basic facts about various kinds of weather phenomena. It seems that we have an insatiable appetite for weather stories. This chapter contains a few examples of contemporary media reports that capture some of the immediate sense of discomfort, tragedy or disaster. By this stage in your study of the course you will probably consider that coverage by the popular media often remains superficial in meteorological terms. This is at least in part because the audience is not expected to have the necessary fundamental knowledge and understanding of the processes involved in the weather. That should no longer apply to you! Therefore, the discussion of recent severe weather events later in this chapter does include the meteorological context, enabling you to appreciate the background of these events in the light of your scientific understanding.

If you would like to check up in advance where the places mentioned in this chapter are located, the list follows. (Some of these places have already been mentioned in previous chapters.)

- Cities and towns: Cardiff, Glastonbury, Edinburgh, London (UK); Dublin (Ireland); Paris (France); Prague (Czech Republic); Bratislava (Slovakia); Dresden, Hamburg (Germany); Moscow (Russia), Kemerovo (Siberia, Russia); Abu Dhabi (United Arab Emirates); Beijing (China); Canberra (Australia); New York (USA), Los Angeles, Santa Barbara and San Diego (California, USA); Montreal (Canada)

- Countries: France, Portugal, Germany, Austria, Czech Republic, Slovakia, Romania, Russia, China, Somalia, Ethiopia, Kenya, Canada, India, Bangladesh

- Land areas: Azores; Siberia; Florida and California (USA); East Africa; Horn of Africa; Ganges–Brahmaputra Delta

- Oceans/seas: Arabian Sea, Bay of Bengal, Gulf of Mexico, Persian Gulf.

9.1   Inconvenience and disaster

Negative impacts of weather can be usefully discussed in terms of the adverse effects they have on things that are commonly regarded as essential for life in a civilised society. For example, food and water are indisputable essentials and the effects of severe weather on their supply can lead to terrible consequences.

■ Identify two more weather-dependent essential requirements of twenty-first century societies from the following list: shelter, clothing, energy, transport, sport/leisure activities, communication, holidays, trade.

☐ You could have suggested any two, though many would question whether sport/leisure activities and holidays are essential in the way that the other requirements are.

The various essential requirements of modern civilisation are susceptible in different ways to different aspects of the weather. For instance, water supplies often depend on there being a minimum quantity of rain (but not too much), whereas shelters are usually designed to withstand specified ranges of wind, precipitation and temperature. The statistical averages that define a region's climate are the basis for these designs, but it is not enough to work only with averages if all likely scenarios are to be considered.

■   What further information from the weather records should be taken into account?

☐   The normal variations and extremes should also be considered.

Normal variations of the weather may on occasions cause us some inconvenience – for instance, weather-related disruptions sometimes frustrate our travel arrangements. When extreme weather events occur, such that lives and environments are at risk, and there are huge economic consequences, then inconvenience gives way to disaster.

9.1.1   Variation and extremes

In the mid-latitudes the normal variation of the weather means that we cannot always rely on it adopting a particular pattern at any particular time more than a few days ahead. So, for example, there is an English idiom that advocates an opportunistic activity by saying: 'Make hay while the sun shines'. It is not just haymaking that cannot be planned far ahead with 100% certainty. The harvesting of many crops can be severely disrupted by periods of wet or cold weather. For example, root crops are difficult to gather when the ground is frozen, cold slows the final stages of the ripening processes of fruit and grain, and rain may make agricultural land inaccessible.

Expectations of what is normal variation are not always built on firm foundations. For example, many people in the UK and in central Europe are surprised to find that climate statistics generally show July and August to be among the wettest months of the year in the region. Figure 9.1 compares the 1971–2000 rainfall statistics in various cities throughout the region; Cardiff is the only city that does not, on average, experience a peak in rainfall in July or August, even though July and August are normally wetter in Cardiff than in any of the other seven places.

■   Why might it be that July and August are the wettest months in central Europe?

☐   The westerly winds, which are the most common winds in the mid-latitudes, are likely to bring the moistest air of the year from over the Atlantic during July and August when the air is warmest.

9.1.2   Insuring against the risk

The economics of insurance favour it as a means of offsetting the expensive consequences of relatively low-probability adverse events. The more likely is the occurrence of an undesirable event, the higher will be the insurance premium.

Figure 9.1   Mean monthly rainfall for the 30-year period 1971–2000 in various European cities, showing the tendency for July and August to be the wettest months in central Europe.

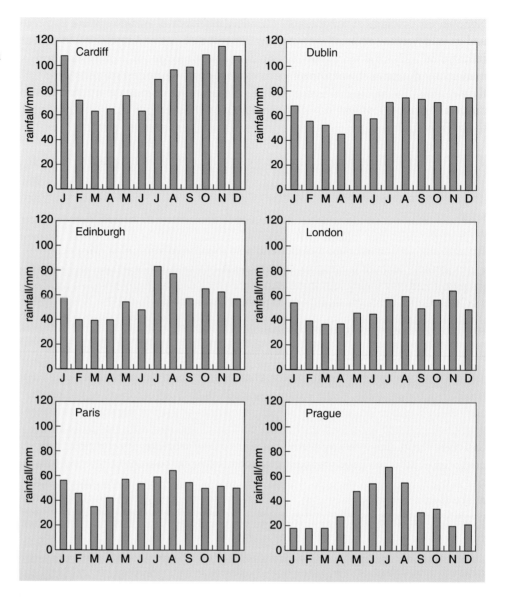

Figure 9.2   24 June 2005, Glastonbury, southwest England. The international music festival, attended by many tens of thousands of people, suffered major flooding.

■ Think about the consequences of a major, long-planned, outdoor activity, such as an international sports fixture or a music festival being rained off or severely disrupted by rain. Suggest three groups of associated businesses that may wish to insure against the loss of income that might then occur.

☐ Any of the following would be wise to take out insurance: the main event promoters; the caterers and those who supply them; the providers of transport and related services; the sellers of related merchandise and branded goods. You may have thought of others.

It is to be hoped that all parties involved in organising the 2005 Glastonbury festival (Figure 9.2) were suitably insured!

National meteorological services provide data and forecasts to enable safe air, sea and ground transportation, and to facilitate the maintenance of national energy-supply infrastructure, food production, trade and commerce in general. But the insurance markets need specialist weather forecasts that are quantitative and statistical, and a thriving private sector has emerged to fulfil this need. Insurance cover can in principle be taken out to cope with the impact of weather on most aspects of life, but may be difficult to obtain and/or prohibitively expensive if the risk of severe consequences is high.

9.1.3   Damage limitation through planning

The impact of some of the 'not wholly unexpected' weather events (such as high temperatures and high humidity in the tropics, intense cold in Siberian winters) is better planned for than insured against. This in effect means understanding the climate, i.e. the average weather and also its normal variations. Montreal, for example, has built a complex subterranean city centre that makes high-street shopping and city living less traumatic throughout the intensely cold winter. The city's McGill University website told prospective students in 2007:

> In winter, as some strap on their skates or cross-country skis and head for the mountain, others seek their exercise below street level, in the 'underground city', a subterranean network of over 30 km of office and apartment towers, major stores, hotels, restaurants, railway stations, parking garages, movie theatres, concert halls and much more, all connected by Montreal's clean, fast, and convenient metro trains.

Another illustration of a planned approach to uncertain weather is provided in the design of sports stadiums. The monthly rainfall charts for Cardiff, Dublin, Edinburgh and London were included in Figure 9.1. Since 1995 these cities have refurbished major sporting stadiums. It is perhaps not surprising that the Millennium Stadium in Cardiff is the only one that has invested in a roof that can be closed completely.

Question 9.1

Which of the following might be expected to be insured against and which might be expected to be accommodated through planning? Outline your reasoning in one sentence for each case.

(a) Being drenched in a downpour while walking across town.

(b) Suffering skin damage through regular, day-long, strong sunshine in the mountains.

(c) A televised football match being cancelled owing to fog.

(d) Buildings in the USA sustaining wind damage.

(e) Buildings in Bangladesh being flattened by a tropical cyclone.

9.1.4   Major weather events

The remainder of this chapter consists of short studies of particular weather events and their impacts. To set these events in context, the following activity gives you the opportunity of watching a compilation of news clips covering some of the extreme weather described in this and other chapters.

Activity 9.1   Weather events

The estimated time for this activity is one hour.

In this activity, you will watch some news reports of adverse weather round the world. There is no particular task associated with the activity, although you may be asked to revisit one or more of the clips as part of the course assessment.

The detailed instructions for finding the compilation of news reports is in the Activities section of the course website.

Study comment

In Chapter 5, you saw how a table could be a useful way of summarising information, especially when comparisons between categories are required. In subsequent sections, the impacts of various weather-related events will be compared and contrasted. Table 9.1 sets out a general framework that you can fill in as you consider these events and the ways in which they affected the societies that experienced them. You will be referred to it by numbered questions as you work through the chapter.

Table 9.1 The impacts of certain weather events. Essential requirements for a twenty-first century society are listed across the top of the table. Six weather events discussed in this chapter are listed on the left. For each of these events you can fill in the appropriate row of the table to show which particular aspect(s) of the weather adversely affected the various societal requirements, using the following code: H = heat; C = cold; F = fog; L = lightning/fire; W = wind; D = drought; R = rain (or other form of precipitation)/flood.

Weather event	Food/ water	Shelter	Energy	Transport/ trade	Communications	Health (illness, injury or death)
Europe, Jan 2007						
London, 1952						
Canberra, 2003						
East Africa, 2005–7						
Central Europe, 2002						
Bangladesh, 2007						

9.2   Extremes of temperature

Both exceptionally hot and exceptionally cold weather can cause problems in places that are not geared up to cope, and both may affect people's health.

9.2.1   Heat

In the first half of August 2003 a heat wave swept across western Europe. In Activity 1.1, you saw some of the effects of the record high temperatures in the UK. Further south it was even hotter, and daytime temperatures in Paris approached 40 °C for several days, with little respite overnight. There was an almost immediate increase in mortality, with 14 000 more deaths than normal across France for the whole month. Victims were chiefly among the elderly.

■ According to the criteria established in Table 2.1b, what would you suggest was the most likely cause of the extra deaths in France during August 2003?

□ Heat exhaustion arising from high body temperature and dehydration would have been most likely, though heatstroke would also have been a high risk for anyone unable to keep cool.

Although August is normally the hottest month in Paris, 40 °C is a long way above the norm. The situation had been building for many weeks. During May the high pressure normally located in summer over the Azores and the position of the ITCZ over western Africa were both further north than usual. As a result, the sea-surface temperature west-southwest of Portugal was higher than normal and much of Europe had prolonged periods of warm sunshine and less rain than normal. Persistent clear skies through May, June and July caused a significant loss of moisture from the land surface of much of Europe. By August the land had dried out so much that the lack of soil moisture meant that evaporative cooling of the land was almost non-existent. The only effective way that the heat built up each day could be balanced was by an equivalent amount of cooling through the radiation of heat into the night sky. Because of the short period of darkness in summer, this process often did not bring sufficient cooling, and temperatures tended to rise day by day. A blocking high over northern Europe helped to maintain these conditions into August.

9.2.2   Cold

When polar or arctic air is channelled into the mid-latitudes cold weather ensues. Weather that is significantly colder than normal challenges systems that have been designed for more benign conditions. For example, because water expands when it freezes, burst water pipes are a regular side effect of anomalously cold weather.

When raindrops freeze on contact with cold surfaces, glaze can build up on many structures. The collapse of ice-clad power lines and the towers that support them is the main reason for power failures during this so-called 'freezing rain'. Telephone wires, trees, lamp-posts and roofs are similarly susceptible to excessive loads. In places where copious amounts of freezing rain occur, these conditions are known as ice storms. A strong El Niño that started in 1997 has been linked to the severity of ice storms that affected Canada in January 1998, during which freezing rain fell for four days without break – much longer than usual. The weather situation involved warm moist air, driven up from the Gulf of Mexico by a high-pressure system over the mid-Atlantic, meeting a large arctic air mass, associated with a higher pressure centre over northeast Canada. Along the front that developed, weak low-pressure systems were formed, initiating rain from the warm air riding up over the extremely cold arctic air. As the raindrops fell through the cold layer they were supercooled to well below 0 °C. At ground level the raindrops transformed into ice on contact with every exposed surface, building up layers that were several millimetres thick. Figure 9.3 shows the crippling effect on some of the power distribution network.

Figure 9.3   Electric power distribution pylons near St Bruno, south of Montreal, Canada on 10 January 1998, that collapsed after a severe ice storm hit southwest Quebec. The storm left more than a million households without electricity for several days.

Icy winds blowing across Siberia from the Arctic in mid-January 2006 led to record low temperatures in Moscow. The cold weather was carried on northerly winds circulating around a large high over northern Russia. After a mild day on 16 January with a daytime maximum of −0.5 °C, temperatures plummeted overnight to −23 °C, reaching −33 °C two nights later. Energy supplies struggled to cope with demand. Prolonged cold has serious consequences for warm-blooded creatures, particularly people. Remarkably, only around 30 people in the Moscow area are believed to have died as a direct result of this particular cold spell. Further to the east, in the Siberian city of Kemerovo, the temperature fell to −40 °C.

In January 2007 there was widespread disruption to transport across western Europe that was a consequence of a severe dose of normal, but relatively uncommon winter weather. By comparison with the Siberian conditions described above, there was little to complain about, though the temperature did fall unusually low in parts of France. A contemporary Reuters news agency report is reproduced as Extract 9.1. Notice how little is said about the reason for the particular meteorological conditions; the temperature is given in Fahrenheit.

■   The report mentions a temperature of −14 °F. What is the equivalent in Celsius? (You can use Figure 2.2 to make the conversion.)

☐   −14 °F can be seen to be equivalent to about −26 °C.

Extract 9.1   Europe finally gets snow, and travel chaos

At least 3 deaths, thousands of cars stranded and power outages.

Three people were killed as snow and ice caused travel chaos across Europe on Wednesday, halting trains and planes and cutting off electricity to thousands of homes.

In Germany, icy roads caused multiple accidents, killing three people and injuring dozens, police said. In the southern city of Stuttgart, about a thousand airline passengers were stranded overnight as 70 flights were cancelled due to heavy snowfall, the airport said.

In Britain, the first snow of winter disrupted road and rail travel across the southeast. Commuters faced severe delays on many routes into London. Southeastern, a train company serving the region, said it expected delays to continue into the afternoon and said its website crashed from a flood of passenger queries. Britain's Met office said heavier snowfalls were expected in parts of the southeast on Thursday and Friday.

Temperatures dipped to minus 14 °Fahrenheit in parts of France. About 5000 vehicles were stranded when the A6 motorway that runs through eastern France was cut off by snow and 200 police and firefighters were sent to help stranded motorists. Power was cut off to about 85 000 homes in central France and train travel was disrupted.

In Austria's Carinthia province 12 000 homes lost electricity when heavy snow toppled trees onto power lines and officials issued an avalanche warning for nearby Alpine mountains. A blizzard deposited more than three feet of snow within hours, stranding hundreds of vehicles on roads.

But the weather was good news for Europe's ski resorts which have been struggling due to a lack of snow. The cold weather is expected to continue for the rest of the week.

24 January 2007 Reuters

Question 9.2

Use Table 9.1 to record the impact of Europe's cold spell in January 2007. Put one or more of the code letters given in the table caption into the appropriate boxes. (For example, if you thought that people's houses were significantly damaged by the cold you would put a C in the 'shelter' column.) You will complete other rows as you work through this chapter. You may like to look at the suggested answer in the back of the book after you have completed each separate row, or wait until you have read the rest of the chapter and completed the whole table.

9.3   Fog

The primary impact of fog is reduced visibility but when it occurs in conjunction with high levels of pollution there are also health consequences. On 4 December 1952, thick radiation fog formed overnight in London. Such fogs were not then uncommon, though this particular one persisted longer than normal. Visibility at Heathrow Airport was as low as 10 metres throughout 6 and 7 December. High pressure trapped cold air at the surface and ensured that there was no ground-level wind to disperse the fog. The fog was especially thick because of the heavy pollution caused by coal being burnt throughout the city as the major source of domestic heating. Smoke particles are effective condensation nuclei, so fog forms more readily when there is smoke in the air; fog that has formed in smoky conditions is often called 'smog'. The smog of December 1952 lasted for

Figure 9.4   Smog in Beijing, April 2007.

four days and was responsible for 4000 more deaths than would have normally been expected; these deaths were attributed to respiratory problems exacerbated by the air pollution. In 1956 the UK Government took steps to control the domestic burning of coal in towns and cities. Figure 9.4 shows that China has now encountered the connection between coal burning and smog due to its recent industrialisation.

Fog closes airports all around the world, often with particular seasons suffering worse disruption than others. This is not just a problem for cold damp countries; Abu Dhabi International Airport and others on the Persian Gulf regularly have closures through fog. In September and October Abu Dhabi International Airport has on average five days per month when overnight fog persists through the morning. The airport was only opened in 1982, so this is not the normal 30-year average statistic, but is based on data reported up to the end of 2007.

■ What sort of fog is typical of high pressure and still air on cold, clear nights?

☐ Radiation fog.

■ Under what circumstances does advection fog form?

☐ Advection fog forms in moist air that is slowly moving over cold land or sea surfaces, where it is cooled to below its dew point.

Fog in the Persian Gulf forms by a mixture of advection and radiation processes. It occurs when air is carried gently off the warm waters of the Gulf by onshore breezes in the late afternoon, taking moist air over the desert. Radiation cooling of the desert surface then chills the air below the dew point and moisture in the air condenses to form fog. In very light winds the fog is pushed around but not dispersed until winds rise to a few kilometres per hour or prolonged sunshine 'burns it off' (i.e. the warmth causes the fog droplets to evaporate). Light, late afternoon breezes carrying moist air are most likely in the autumn, and this is why September and October see the highest incidence of fog.

Question 9.2 (continued)

Use Table 9.1 to record the impact of London's 1952 smog. Put one or more of the code letters given in the table caption into the appropriate boxes.

Figure 9.5 A lightning strike to the Empire State Building, New York. Lightning strikes to tall structures are not unusual: the operators of the Empire State Building report that it is struck by lightning about 100 times per year.

9.4 Lightning and wildfires

Lightning has a major impact on anything that gets in its path. Buildings, trees, aircraft, motor vehicles, people and the ground itself are all vulnerable to immediate damage. There is also a delayed impact arising from lightning following a strike to ground, in the form of fires that take hold in vegetation, often burning out of control for days on end.

9.4.1 Direct effects of lightning strikes

Excess electrical charge tends to concentrate on the sharply pointed parts of an object. For this reason, high-rise buildings, pylons and radio masts under a thunder cloud are particularly susceptible to lightning, as Figure 9.5 shows. Damage to tall structures is avoided by placing a sharp metal lightning rod right at the top, presenting an easy path for the lightning current into a thick copper strip that takes the current directly into a large plate buried in the ground at the bottom.

The channel of a lightning discharge where it passes through the air glows very brightly for a very short time (usually less than one-thousandth of a second), temporarily bleaching an image on the retina of those who observe it directly with no intervening cloud. The gas in the discharge channel reaches an extremely high temperature (typically 30 000 °C) because it carries a huge electric current. About one in five strikes to ground is longer though less intense, and result in a current of several hundred amps passing through anything in its path. The current also causes significant heating where the strike hits the ground. A lightning strike into sandy ground melts the sand particles to form small beads of glass (known as fulgarites); to have melted sand, the temperatures must have been in excess of 1600 °C.

■ Lightning sometimes strikes tall trees since their core of watery sap presents an easy path for the current to flow. What is likely to happen to the water within the tree when heated by the current of a lightning strike?

☐ The water will instantly evaporate.

The generation of extremely hot steam within the wood is the reason that lightning strikes destroy trees. The steam explodes within the tiny cells from which wood fibres are made, often causing the entire trunk to be burst open. Not surprisingly, lightning that strikes ground covered in dry vegetation is a common cause of wildfires.

It's not just trees that can be burst apart by lightning; concrete ruptures in a similar way, with steam being generated from water locked up within the solid. That is why lightning protection of a building includes a copper strip to prevent the lightning current from having to pass through the main fabric of the structure.

The metallic skins of aircraft and other vehicles fare better than trees when subjected to the large currents of lightning. This is because metals are relatively good conductors of electricity and as such, for any given level of current, they pass the current with less heat generation than poor conductors. Also, metals are effective in dispersing any localised heating because they are equally good conductors of heat. So, what is the likely impact on aeroplanes if they end up flying through thunderstorms? In fact, aircraft generally avoid thunderstorms because of the severe turbulence within storm cells, flying round them wherever possible. Planes are therefore at their most susceptible to lightning when passing inadvertently below a mature storm shortly after take-off or during landing, and in fact such strikes are not uncommon. However, the skins of the aircraft are able to survive a direct hit, sometimes passing the current along the entire length of the fuselage, or from one wing to the other, with little more than a burn mark at the contact points. The main risk is damage to electronic flight systems by electrical interference.

Immediate death from being struck by lightning is the result of cardiac arrest or complications arising from it, but the chances of escaping with severe burns and shock are surprisingly high. In Britain about 50 people are struck by lightning each year, with only 10% receiving fatal injuries. This compares with almost ten times as many incidents in the USA, and nearly 20 times as many fatalities. The proportion of fatalities in any given region depends on factors such as the typical severity of thunderstorms and patterns of human behaviour locally. In the USA, Florida is the state with far and away the highest annual number of deaths by lightning – more than twice that of any other state.

■ Why does Florida, only the ninth most densely populated state in the USA, have many more deaths from lightning than any other state? (Look back at Figure 8.1 for the answer.)

☐ On an annual basis, Florida has more lightning activity than any other state.

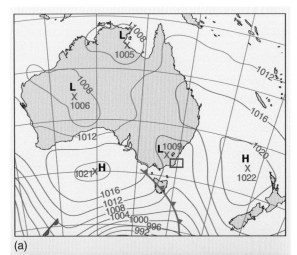

(a)

(b)

(c)

Figure 9.6 (a) MSL pressure chart for Australia at 0000 UTC on 18 January 2003. (b) An enhanced satellite image of southeastern Australia in mid- to late January 2003, showing smoke driven by west-northwesterly winds. The region covered by this image is indicated by the red box on the MSL pressure chart. (c) Bushfires threatening the city of Canberra.

As you noted in answering Question 8.3, convergence of surface air over the Florida peninsula provides a particularly effective trigger for thunderstorms.

Being inside a car in a thunderstorm is generally considerably safer than being outside it. Just as with the aircraft, the electrical current passes along the skin of the vehicle without causing marked damage, except at the contact points. If you are outside, statistics show that you are most at risk in open country. In this case, the best position to adopt is curled up on the ground and as far away as possible from isolated trees.

9.4.2 Wildfires

Lightning, volcanoes, human negligence or deliberate nefarious activity can all trigger fires in vegetation that has been dried by prolonged drought. Such fires easily run wild as the heat they generate causes thermal updraughts that draw in air which in turn fans the flames, intensifying the blaze. Wildfires become extremely difficult to get under control, especially when natural winds add to the thermal updraught. Many regions around the world experience a wildfire (or bushfire) season.

In southeastern Australia the bushfire season is in late summer. January 2003 was no exception: a series of thunderstorms occurred on 8 January across the highlands of southeast Australia, but there was no accompanying precipitation at ground level. There were, however, many lightning strikes and some of them initiated forest fires in the region. Then, on 17/18 January, a low-pressure system brought steady west-northwesterly winds across the region, gusting at over 50 km per hour.

■ Figure 9.6a shows the MSL pressure chart for Saturday, 18 January. Check the wind direction in the region of Canberra, shown by the red box. Is this consistent with the west-northwesterly smoke plume in Figure 9.6b?

☐ Yes. Air circulates clockwise around a region of low pressure in the Southern Hemisphere. It is difficult to be precise about the wind direction, since the region marked by the box is in a trough of low pressure, but the wind will certainly be between westerly and northerly as it crosses the coast.

Strengthening winds and high temperatures brought the fires into the urban area of the capital, Canberra (Figure 9.6c). The fires caused the death of at least four people, destruction of buildings (including 500 homes and an astronomical observatory) and energy infrastructure worth about a quarter of a billion Australian dollars, and the scorching of over 70% of the surrounding land.

Use Table 9.1 to record the impact of the bushfires around Canberra in 2003. Put one or more of the code letters given in the table caption into the appropriate boxes.

In California, wildfires are often driven by the seasonal Santa Ana winds that were described in Section 8.2.3. Santa Anas tend to blow in autumn and spring. They are associated with high pressure over Nevada that pushes air from the high desert plateau towards the south and west of California, over and through the passes and canyons of the San Gabriel, San Bernadino and Santa Ana Mountains. By September or October the vegetation in southern California has often been left rather dried by the late summer heat, so this is a time of heightened risk for wildfires.

In late October 2007 more than 500 000 people living in coastal southern California, from Santa Barbara down to San Diego, were ordered to leave their homes to escape wildfires. This was the biggest US evacuation since Hurricane Katrina at the end of August 2005. Fierce Santa Ana winds fanned the flames as the fire spread rapidly, leaving three dead and many more injured. The wind speed averaged about 60 km per hour (35–40 miles per hour), locally reaching about twice that speed. Figure 9.7 shows the rapid development of a smoke plume north of Los Angeles originating in the area of Castaic Lake. You can deduce a rough value for the mean wind speed from this figure: using the scale bar, the plume in the right-hand image can be seen to have extended about 175 km in less than 3 hours 15 minutes. Some 120 000 hectares

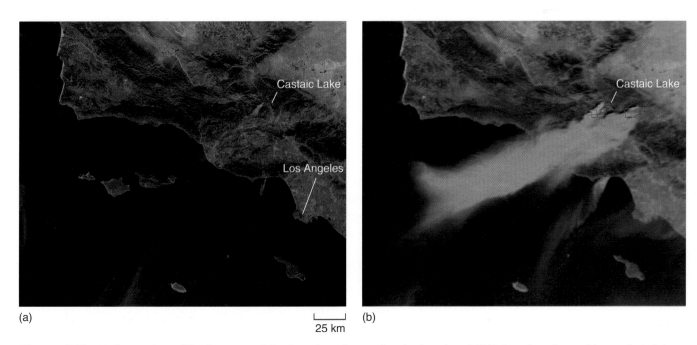

(a)   25 km   (b)

Figure 9.7   Enhanced satellite images of the Los Angeles region in October 2007 showing the sudden, wind-driven onset of the wildfires as indicated by the fast-developing smoke plume. The interval between images (a) and (b) is 3 hours 15 minutes.

(300 000 acres) of land were scorched and thousands of homes and businesses were destroyed. A month later, Santa Ana conditions returned and with them, more wildfires.

Question 9.3

When Santa Ana winds are forecast for the Los Angeles region in September and October, fire risk is usually graded at the level of 'extreme danger'. Explain briefly why this is the case. (You may want to look back to the end of Section 8.2.3 for a clue.)

9.5   Drought

A prolonged abnormally dry period during which there is insufficient water for normal needs is classed as a drought. A drought can occur because it has not rained at all for some time, or because rain has not been intense enough and/or has not lasted long enough. Because the rainfall requirements for the natural environment, for crops, and for domestic and industrial water supply vary widely round the world, there is no universal definition of drought in terms of the length of the dry period or the fraction of normal rainfall that has occurred. The meaning of 'drought' must therefore always be understood in a local context.

Serious, though not necessarily continuous, drought has plagued parts of East Africa for decades. Why should this be so? Consider the simple observation that water may be scarce when there is insufficient moisture in the atmosphere to interact with the local geography in a way that leads to rain. That prompts a series of questions.

■ First, how does moisture get into the atmosphere?

☐ Most of the moisture originates from open water, such as oceans and large lakes, and enters the atmosphere via the process of evaporation. Some comes from transpiration of plants.

■ Second, what factors affect the amount of moisture taken up by airflow over open water?

☐ The degree of evaporation is affected by the surface temperature of the water, the temperature and humidity of the air passing over it and to some extent the speed of the airflow.

In seeking to explain East African droughts, the third question is the most important one: what is the pattern of surface airflow around the region? In this area, winds exhibit a monsoon character (i.e. they are seasonal, with changes roughly every six months). Figure 9.8 shows the directions of the surface winds that characterise and define East Africa's northeasterly and southeasterly monsoons. They are clearly strongly linked with the Indian monsoons discussed in Section 8.3. However, in the northeast sector known as the 'Horn of Africa', which mostly corresponds to Somalia, the monsoon exhibits a distinctive pattern, with two very brief rainy periods separating two very long dry periods. Rain is associated with neither the season of northeasterly winds nor the season of southeasterly winds, but only with the brief intervals of the changeovers of the prevailing wind direction. This is quite different from the Indian pattern of a wet monsoon brought by winds from the southwest and a dry monsoon associated with winds from the northeast. Further south in Kenya the two changeover intervals last much longer, giving so-called long (April to June) and short (October to December) rainy seasons. To the west, in Ethiopia, there is just one rainy season, from April to September.

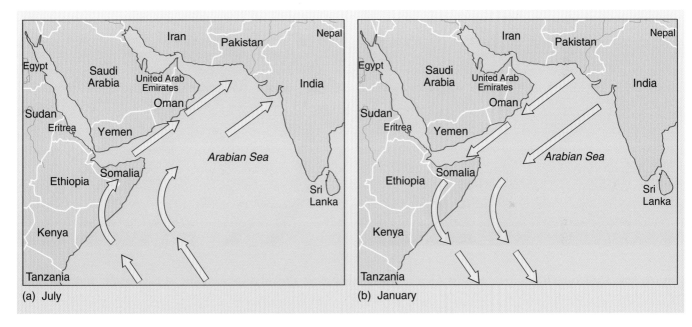

Figure 9.8   Prevailing surface wind flow in the Horn of Africa and Arabian Sea in (a) July and (b) January. These wind flows show that the monsoon phenomenon in East Africa is linked to the Indian monsoon.

The reasons for the pattern of the East African monsoons are complicated and involve details of the airflow and the land profile. However, the consequences of the pattern are obvious: with such brief intervals in which rains might fall in the Horn of Africa, the region is a prime candidate for drought. If something disrupts the occurrence of rain in the changeover window, it is almost six months before favourable conditions for rain reappear.

Reduced sea-surface temperature off the East African coast will lead to a major decrease in the amount of atmospheric moisture being carried onto the continental land mass, either as water vapour or in the form of clouds. It has been proposed that the trigger for prolonged drought is just a single rainy season with reduced rainfall, prompted by reduced sea temperature. This leads to a decrease in the amount of vegetation. Scientific models like those used in long-range weather forecasting suggest that the reduction in vegetation then disturbs the balance of atmospheric moisture and the tendency to form clouds, so that the amount of rain that falls in the *next* rainy season is greatly decreased. This further reduces vegetation and within a couple of cycles an enduring drought is almost inevitable. Figure 9.9 captures a snapshot of the start of a drought phase that extended from early 2005 to late 2007.

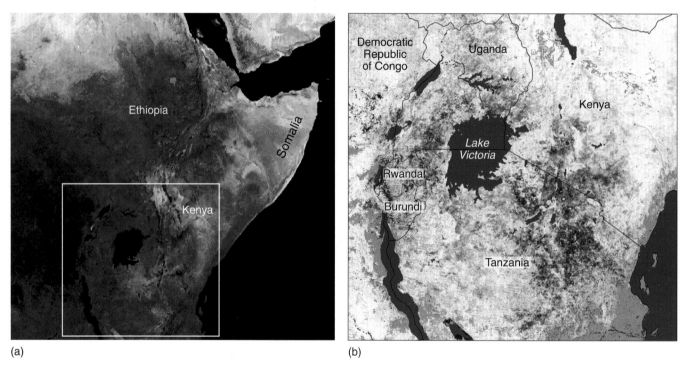

(a) (b)

Figure 9.9 (a) A satellite image of East Africa. The colours show the relative amounts of vegetation, reflecting the different patterns of monsoon rainfall. The white box marks the region featured in the right-hand photograph. (b) An enhanced satellite image of part of East Africa showing areas that in March 2005 were drier than they were in the period 2000–2004: brown indicates reduced vegetation, green increased vegetation.

Question 9.2 (continued)

Use Table 9.1 to record the impact of the East African drought. Put one or more of the code letters given in the table caption into the appropriate boxes.

9.6   Rain and flood

One scenario for high-impact flooding arises when the natural capacity of rivers is unable to drain water away from regions of intense precipitation. Another is associated with storm-driven surges of seawater onto coastal areas, which can be especially destructive when a surge arises in combination with a swollen river. The former case is discussed in this section, and the latter is featured in Section 9.7 as part of the impact of a tropical cyclone.

In 2002 a 'once in a hundred years' combination of factors resulted in severe weather in central Europe. Areas of Germany, Austria, the Czech Republic and Slovakia were subjected to flash flooding following abnormally high rainfall on 12 and 13 August. Figure 9.10 shows an example of the scenes that ensued. As the rainwater drained into rivers, there were major inundations, notably in Prague and Dresden where flood levels were unprecedented. Flooding is not unknown in this region in summer, but the 2002 event was remarkable for its severity. In all, there were over 100 fatalities, with damage to property and transport infrastructure estimated at 15 billion euros.

It seems that there were four interrelated factors involved in this example of extreme weather. First, during the build-up, particularly humid air was being fed in from the Mediterranean on upper-level winds. Second, central Europe is a mountainous region so there are plenty of opportunities for orographic uplift. Third, several frontal systems over the Mediterranean and central Europe were stalling, allowing pockets of unstable air to rise. Figure 9.11 shows the MSL pressure charts for 10, 11 and 12 August. Finally, several low-pressure systems merged, forming a large slow-moving trough of low pressure which contained the above mixture of moist, unstable air, and the resulting rain was concentrated in a relatively limited area.

Figure 9.10 Flooding in Austria, 12 August 2002.

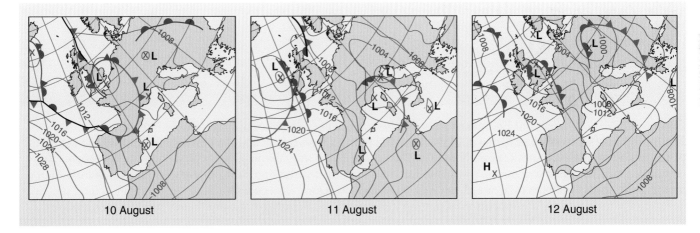

| 10 August | 11 August | 12 August |

Figure 9.11 MSL pressure charts for Europe at 0000 UTC on 10, 11 and 12 August 2002, showing the build-up of several slow-moving low-pressure systems over central Europe. By 11 August a complex low was over the Mediterranean. On 12 August a large area of fairly low pressure linked central Europe to the Mediterranean.

■ What will have been the consequence of the slow-moving cold front that swept through central Europe between 10 and 12 August, shown in Figure 9.11?

☐ The passage of a slow-moving cold front through unstable moist air would have led to persistent heavy rain.

Figure 9.12 shows the regions most affected and the pattern of rainfall in the worst-hit area. Records for Prague show that the precipitation during a 24-hour period straddling 12 and 13 August was seven times more than the normal August monthly total, so it is no surprise that the rivers could not cope. There was an anxious period of several days as the excess waters swept downstream, threatening other towns and cities. The flood surge reached Hamburg, some 500 km downstream, on 24 August.

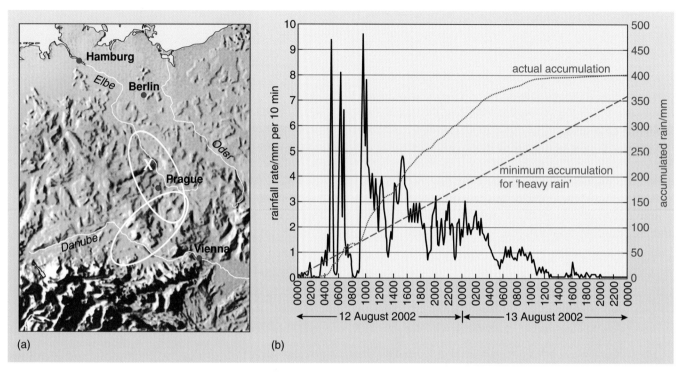

Figure 9.12   (a) The central European rivers that bore the brunt of the flooding following intense rain on 12/13 August 2002, with the regions of highest rainfall marked by white ovals. (b) Rainfall amounts in the centre of the region of intense rainfall (point X in (a)). The jagged black line, the scale for which is on the left, shows the amount of rain falling in successive 10-minute intervals. The dotted red line rising to the right, the scale for which is on the right, shows how the total amount of rain built up to 400 mm. Compare this with the dashed red line, which corresponds to the steady accumulation of rainfall that would occur during non-stop 'heavy rain'. Times are local.

The intensity of the rainfall was certainly heavy, and at times exceptional. 'Heavy' rain, which one would notice drumming loudly on a roof, accumulates at a rate in excess of 7.6 mm per hour or more, which in the units of the graph in Figure 9.12b is equivalent to more than 1.26 mm in 10 minutes. In this instance, the rate of accumulation not only greatly exceeded this, but did so for an exceptional length of time and that is what ultimately led to the flooding. The rivers and drains were unable to carry water away fast enough.

A contemporary report from the news service of the *New Scientist* magazine (Extract 9.2) captures the scale of the event and notes that major flooding calls for swift actions to mitigate health risks as well as generally clearing up.

Extract 9.2   Flood-stricken Czechs plan mass-vaccination

The Czech Government will vaccinate about 65 000 children against hepatitis A, following the worst flooding in the country in 200 years.

Flood waters are now starting to subside in the capital, Prague, but the mayor is urging the city's 50 000 evacuees to stay away until power and sewage services are fully restored. About another 150 000 people in the country have also been forced from their homes.

Hepatitis A can spread if sewage systems are damaged and infected faeces enter drinking water. Mass hepatitis A vaccination is thought to have prevented an outbreak after heavy floods in central Europe in 2001.

The Czech Republic's health minister has also asked the government to provide 3.5 million euros for other public health measures, including the testing of drinking water and the distribution of water disinfectants. Other potential killers in disaster-stricken regions include dysentery and cholera.

Millions homeless

But while the flood danger in Prague is decreasing, waters are surging through south-eastern Germany, threatening catastrophe. In Dresden, waters are rising at around 20 centimetres per hour.

There is also a state of emergency in Bratislava, capital of the Slovak Republic, where the level of the Danube is at its highest for a century. Romania and Russia are badly affected. And in Austria, where seven people have died due to flooding, Chancellor Wolfgang Schuessel told the BBC: "This is the worst natural disaster to have hit Austria in living memory."

Fears that much of Prague's 14th century architectural treasures could be devastated are easing with the falling level of the River Vltava. Defences around the Old Town have not been breached, but teams are continuing to work to stop debris damaging the Charles Bridge.

But floods outside Europe have been much more severe. About 800 people died and millions were left homeless following summer floods in India, Bangladesh and Nepal. And hundreds more have been killed in China, where thousands of people are killed each year due to flooding.

Emma Young, NewScientist.com news service, 15 August 2002

Question 9.2 (continued)

Use Table 9.1 to record the impact of the floods in central Europe in the summer of 2002. Put one or more of the code letters given in the table caption into the appropriate boxes.

Question 9.4

The central European flood of August 2002 was caused by rainfall that amounted to a total accumulated depth of 400 mm. Explain why streets in the cities were flooded to a depth several times this figure. (Hint: where does rain go when it falls on built-up areas?)

9.7   Wind, rain and flood

High winds start to be a problem on land when they lift small items left lying about, endanger high-sided vehicles, and damage trees. In times gone by, strong winds were a serious potential hazard for suspension bridges, though modern bridge design has adapted to cope with the problem, greatly aided by computer models of airflow around structures. Nevertheless, bridges are often closed when winds reach gale force. As winds strengthen further, they produce ever greater damage. Your answer to Question 8.4, in which you compared the Saffir–Simpson scale for tropical cyclones and the Torro scale for tornadoes, illustrated the impact of high winds, particularly on the buildings and structures that provide shelter and infrastructure for communications and energy supply.

Tornadoes are very destructive, but their impacts are localised. A tropical cyclone brings damaging winds to a much larger area and also produces very heavy rain. Damage from cyclones arises from the combination of wind, rain and storm surges.

As you saw in Section 4.4.1, the development of tropical cyclones requires an ocean surface temperature of at least 27 °C, and therefore they normally occur in summer and early autumn. In the Pacific and Atlantic Oceans north of the Equator, tropical cyclones are thus most likely between May and November.

Widespread floods delivered by tropical cyclones born in the Bay of Bengal are a common enough occurrence for the people of Bangladesh. The greater part of the country is little more than ten metres above sea level and its 600 km of coast is dominated by the Ganges–Brahmaputra Delta, at the top of the Bay of Bengal. When heavy rain, a storm surge and high tides coincide the effects are truly disastrous. The arrival of Tropical Cyclone Sidr, a Category 4 storm, on 15 November 2007 resulted in one of the most destructive events for more than a decade. The cyclone tracked from the southwest to the northeast across Bangladesh. Figure 9.13 shows satellite images at six-hour intervals on 15 November. The lowest recorded pressure was 944 hPa.

■   What conclusions do you draw from the fact that of the five IR images in Figure 9.13, the Indian landmass is darkest in the one taken at 0600 UTC?

☐   The landmass is warmer at 0600 UTC than at the other times.

India is 5.5 hours ahead of Greenwich Mean Time. As GMT and UTC are essentially equivalent, the 0600 UTC image will have been taken 30 minutes before midday, local time, when solar heating is near its maximum.

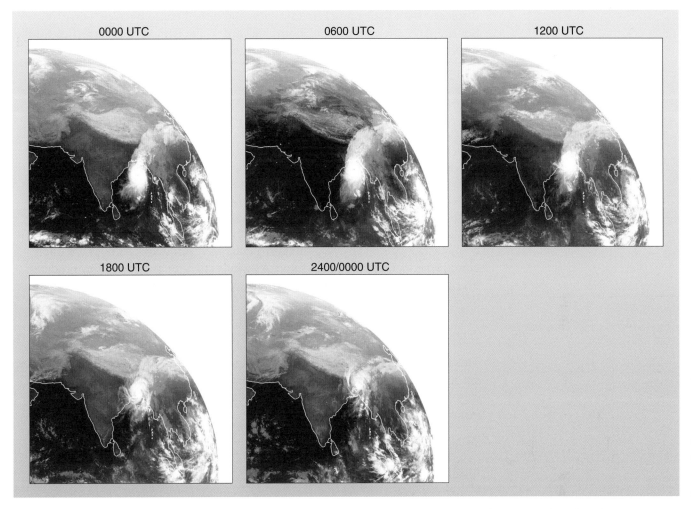

Figure 9.13 Infrared images from the Meteosat-7 satellite archive for 15 November 2007, showing the progress of Tropical Cyclone Sidr.

■ Roughly when did the tropical cyclone hit Bangladesh?

☐ From Figure 9.13, it appears that the cyclone made landfall sometime between 0600 and 1200 UTC (i.e. in the afternoon local time) and would have had its maximum impact between 1200 and 1800 UTC (i.e. in the evening local time).

In addition to the winds and rain, high tides contributed to a storm surge of more than five metres. The catalogue of impacts on the population was enormous. There was an immediate shortage of drinking water, shelter, food and medicines. Electricity supplies and the mobile-phone network were interrupted and crops were devastated. The frail wood and corrugated-iron houses, in which much of the population lives, were no match for the strong winds that lashed the country. The storm damage also extended across the borders into India. Initial reports suggested that around 3000 perished and over one million people were displaced from their homes, but the situation turned out to be even worse. Several days after the tropical storm had struck, the United Nations Office for the Coordination of Humanitarian Affairs summarised the devastation as follows.

Extract 9.3

According to the Government of Bangladesh, more than 7 million people were affected by the storm. As many as 3243 people have been confirmed dead to date, another 880 remain missing, and 34 708 were injured. There were also significant material damages caused by Sidr, a category 4 storm that made landfall in Bangladesh in the late evening of 15 November bringing torrential rains and packing winds of up to 240 kilometres per hour. More than 1 million houses have been damaged, 366 000 of which have been completely destroyed, and extensive damage to roads and public buildings, including almost 10 000 educational institutions, has also been reported. In addition, more than 1.8 million acres of crops were damaged and over 523 000 livestock have been confirmed killed.

ReliefWeb bulletin 27 Nov 2007

This is a typical example of the way in which the impacts of very severe weather are felt disproportionately in less well-developed countries, where buildings are often poorly constructed, the infrastructure is less able to cope and mass evacuations cannot be organised.

Question 9.5

Identify three observations from the account given above that support the classification of Tropical Cyclone Sidr as a Category 4 storm on the Saffir–Simpson scale. (You will need to look back at the details in Table 4.2, but in this context it is important to note that the damage scale is based on US building styles.)

Question 9.2 (continued)

Use Table 9.1 to record the impact of Tropical Cyclone Sidr on Bangladesh. Put one or more of the code letters given in the table caption into the appropriate boxes.

Study comment

Now that you have completed all the rows in Table 9.1, you can check your table against the answer to Question 9.2 in the back of the book. If your entries for any of the events are very different from those suggested, you might want to review the text that describes that event, although you may also have included impacts described in the video extracts.

9.8 Making an impact on the weather

The debate about links between human activity and climate change is beyond the scope of this course but this short section adds to the discussion of smog in Section 9.3, illustrating that the interaction between weather and society is certainly not all one way.

Figure 9.14 shows the results of a statistical analysis of rainfall off the east coast of the USA over a period of 17 years. Note that the average amount of rainfall for any particular day of the week is spread by bars of 'uncertainty' plotted above and below each data point, reflecting the spread of the original data. The researchers on this occasion have used the uncertainty bars to show the range across which 70% of the raw data were spread. The central dot then marks the 17-year mean rainfall for a particular day of the week. The amount of rainfall shows a significant dependence on the day of the week. But the weather cannot be naturally dependent on the day of the week! The researchers who carried out the analyses argue that the pollutants arising from vehicle exhausts on the heavily populated eastern coastal strip build up from Monday to Friday each week before tailing off each weekend. The pollutants act as condensation nuclei for cloud formation and therefore imprint an average weekly pattern of rainfall. Further analysis showed the rainfall pattern drifting across the Atlantic, with the 'Saturday peak' reaching mid-Atlantic in the middle of the following week. The strength of the pattern is masked a little by the uncertainties in the measurements but it is nonetheless there. The weather has an impact on human society and it appears that human society has an impact on the weather.

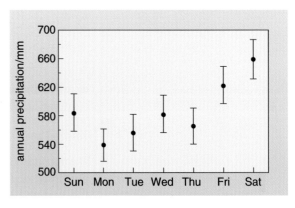

Figure 9.14   The patterns of rainfall over 17 years off the eastern seaboard of the USA, showing a significant weekly cycle.

9.9   The end of the course

Now you have completed the course you should be able to observe weather events with a greater understanding of some of the processes that underlie them. You should also have a better appreciation of some of the limitations of weather forecasting, which may help you to interpret pressure charts and forecasts more realistically. You may want to continue keeping records of your local weather or to hone your skills in cloud recognition. The weather is always there to be observed and it is endlessly fascinating!

S189 Learning Outcomes

Within the context of the topics covered in the course, you will have the opportunity to develop and demonstrate the Learning Outcomes listed below. On completion of the course, you should be able to:

Knowledge and understanding

Demonstrate general knowledge and understanding of some of the basic facts, concepts, scientific principles and language relating to meteorology and weather forecasting, in particular:

KU1   the main weather elements and relationships between them

KU2   patterns of circulation within the atmosphere

KU3   formation and evolution of high- and low-pressure areas, and of frontal systems

KU4   techniques used to gather meteorological data

KU5   computer models of the atmosphere and weather forecasts

KU6   interpretation of surface pressure charts

KU7   weather at different scales

KU8   the importance of the weather for human society.

Cognitive skills

CS1   Apply your knowledge and understanding to describe, analyse and interpret meteorological observations, information, data and charts, in familiar and unfamiliar situations.

CS2   Express course concepts in your own words in a factually correct way.

Key skills

KS1   Receive and respond to information presented in a variety of ways, including text, tables, graphs, diagrams, computer-based multi-media and websites.

KS2   Use information technology to retrieve and record data.

KS3   Begin to understand how to develop your own learning strategies.

Practical skills

PS1   Make, record and interpret observations and simple measurements relating to the weather.

Questions: answers and comments

Curly brackets { } enclose additional comments that you are not expected to include in your own answers.

Question 1.1

(i) At the North Pole the Sun is always very low in the sky, so the heating effect of the solar radiation is spread over a larger area than it would be at lower latitudes. {You could illustrate this with a diagram similar to that of Figure 1.5.}

(ii) The Sun's rays take a longer path through the atmosphere than they would if they were travelling perpendicular to the ground, so more of the solar radiation is scattered or absorbed by the atmosphere and less is available to heat the ground.

(iii) Snow and ice are very good reflectors of solar radiation, so only a fraction of the radiation that does reach the ground actually heats it. The rest is reflected back.

This question required you to express concepts from this chapter in order to explain observations in a factually correct (and concise) way. Being able to do this is an important Learning Outcome (CS2) of the course. To practise this skill, you should always write out the answers to numbered questions and compare your answer carefully with the one provided. The question stated that one or two sentences per reason was sufficient, and this kind of guidance is intended to help you produce suitably concise answers.

Question 1.2

(a) The high temperature occurred during an exceptional heat wave that lasted for only ten days, and would therefore be classed as a weather event.

(b) This temperature is typical in the area over a period of five months, so relates to the climate of Mecca, rather than to any short-term weather event. {Mecca, at latitude of about 22° N, has a hot climate all year round. May to September are the hottest (i.e. summer) months.}

(c) This pattern of rainfall is typical in the area over a period of seven months, so relates to the climate of Trinidad, rather than to any short-term weather event. {Trinidad, at latitude of about 10° N has a hot, humid climate all year round. Seasons are defined by rainfall: May to December is the wet season.}

(d) The series of bands of showers was established for a ten-day period only, so would be described as a short-term weather pattern.

This question required you to interpret four meteorological observations and measurements, only one of which, (a), had been previously described in the text. Demonstrating that you can apply your knowledge and understanding to interpret both familiar and unfamiliar situations is one of the most important Learning Outcomes (CS1) of the course and is a skill you will practise often as you answer numbered questions.

Question 2.1

There is no contradiction. The presenter was saying in a colloquial way that the average temperature locally for the month of August had the same value as the long-term average. The long-term average being used for the comparison will have been calculated for a 30-year period {probably 1961–1990, but possibly 1971–2000}. In 2002, the local average for August must have been lower than this long-term average, whereas in each of the years 2003–2006, it must have been higher than the long-term average. {A long-term average that includes the measurements from 2001 onwards will not be used for comparisons until 2011 at the earliest and probably not until 2021.}

In answering this question, you demonstrated that you could apply your knowledge of course concepts to interpret meteorological data, so it is particularly relevant to Learning Outcome CS1.

Question 2.2

(a) The way in which the relative humidity would change over the 24-hour period is shown in Figure 2.23b.

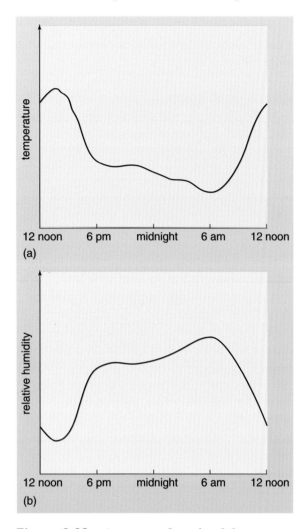

(a)

(b)

Figure 2.23   Answer to Question 2.2.

{The height of the peaks and troughs you have drawn doesn't matter, since there is no scale on the vertical axes, nor do any small 'wiggles'. The important point to have brought out in your sketch is that even though the amount of water vapour in the air has remained the same, the fact that the air temperature has noticeably varied will result in a substantial variation in the relative humidity. You should have shown that the relative humidity is at a maximum when the temperature is at a minimum and vice versa.

The air cools during the night, reaching its lowest level in the early morning; this corresponds to the highest relative humidity. The air temperature increases during the day and the relative humidity decreases. The air temperature reaches a maximum in the afternoon; at this time the relative humidity is at a minimum.}

(b) The best time to spray is when the relative humidity is high, as the evaporation from the leaves and the soil will then be minimised. The best time to spray over this 24-hour period would have been late evening, when the relative humidity was increasing; next best would have been very early morning, when the relative humidity was still high even though it had started to drop.

This question requires you to demonstrate your knowledge and understanding of relative humidity (Learning Outcome KU1). Part (a) also allowed you to demonstrate achievement of an aspect of Learning Outcome KS1, in that you are responding to information presented in the form of a graph.

Question 2.3

If there is an inversion, warm air overlies cool air. A parcel of air rising towards the inversion would be cooling and would continue to cool at the same rate if it were to rise within the inversion layer. So if it were to enter the inversion layer, the parcel would be getting colder even though the air surrounding it was warmer than the air just below the inversion. This would mean that the parcel would be more dense than the surrounding air and would sink back to a level just under the inversion. {An inversion therefore always results in a stable atmospheric environment.}

This question required you to demonstrate your knowledge and understanding of the relationship between air temperature (and specifically its variation with altitude) and air density (and specifically its relationship with stability). It is therefore particularly relevant to Learning Outcome KU1.

Question 3.1

(a) The ground on the island has warmed more than the ocean. Thermals can therefore rise from the land surface and air is lifted to a level where the temperature is below the dew point. Hence cumulus {i.e. convective} clouds form immediately above the island.

(b) The cloud base marks the level in the atmosphere at which rising air reaches its dew point. This temperature will be at roughly the same height above the ground right across the area shown in the picture. Hence the clouds will have a flat base. The level to which the tops of the clouds build depends on how strong the thermals are {and this will vary according to the nature of the land surface}. Hence different parts of the cloud build to different extents.

This question required you to demonstrate your knowledge and understanding of the relationship between several weather elements and associated concepts: clouds, dew point and the way in which air temperature varies with height. It is therefore particularly relevant to Learning Outcome KU1.

Question 3.2

If the air below the cloud has low relative humidity, rapid evaporation will reduce the size of the raindrops emerging from the cloud. The smaller drops will fall less quickly. If they spend long enough in the air, they will evaporate completely before they reach the ground.

This question is also mainly relevant to Learning Outcome KU1, requiring you to demonstrate your knowledge and understanding of the relationship between humidity and precipitation.

Question 3.3

(a) The five values add up to 351 mm. The mean of these measurements is therefore $\frac{351\,\text{mm}}{5} = 70.2\,\text{mm}$.

(b) The mean value of 70.2 mm is much more than the 47 mm average quoted in the caption. The 47 mm average will have been calculated from data spanning 30 years, according to the rules discussed in Section 2.1.2.

Question 3.4

The high-level clouds show the direction of the high-level winds to be southerly {i.e. from the south}. These winds will be blowing anticlockwise round the centre of low pressure. {The UK is in the Northern Hemisphere.} The kind of sketch you might have drawn is shown in Figure 3.17. It indicates that if the high-level wind is southerly at your location, the centre of low pressure must be to the west of your position.

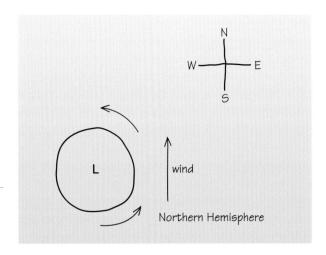

Figure 3.17   If the wind is observed to be southerly in the Northern Hemisphere, low pressure is to the west of the observer's position.

This question required you to demonstrate your knowledge and understanding of wind (Learning Outcome KU1). Because you were asked to back up your answer with a sketch you also demonstrated that you can understand information that is presented in the form of a diagram, which is an aspect of Learning Outcome KS1.

Question 3.5

The kind of sketch you might have drawn is shown in Figure 3.18.

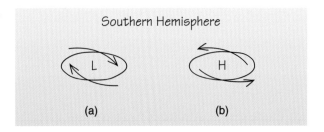

Figure 3.18   Surface-level winds circulating round (a) a low and (b) a high in the Southern Hemisphere.

{In the Southern Hemisphere the Coriolis deflection is to the left. Winds aloft therefore appear to circulate anticlockwise around areas of high pressure and clockwise around areas of low pressure. Near the ground, winds speeds are reduced by friction with the surface, and the deflection is smaller. Surface winds therefore spiral out of highs and into lows.}

The comments about the Learning Outcomes (KU1 and KS1) associated with Question 3.4 also apply to this question.

Question 4.1

The wind directions are likely to be:

(a) San Francisco: NW. Here there is no prevailing wind direction in January but winds from the northwest are the most common.

(b) Cape Town: SW. This is the prevailing wind direction in January.

(c) Perth: S. This is the prevailing wind direction in January.

(d) Tokyo: NW. Here there is no prevailing wind direction in January but winds from a roughly northwesterly direction are the most common.

To answer this question you had to interpret a map of the pattern of circulation of the atmosphere near the Earth's surface. It is therefore particularly relevant to Learning Outcomes KS1 and KU2.

Question 4.2

(a) Polar continental air is cold and dry, because its source region is over very cold land. As the air mass moves south, it will encounter warmer surroundings. Because its own temperature will then be lower than that of its surroundings the air mass will be very stable.

(b) The stability of the air mass means that it will not rise. Therefore a high-pressure area will become established in the region into which the air mass moves.

(c) This cold and dry air will bring very cold winter weather with largely clear skies (because the dryness of the air means that few if any clouds will form).

(d) In summer the air mass will be cool but will contain rather more moisture than in winter, because although the land in its source region will still be fairly cold, the snow will have melted and there will be evaporation from the surface. As it moves south, the air mass will bring this cool air to the central USA, but the ground over which it moves will be strongly heated during the day. The lower levels of the air mass will therefore warm up, and become less stable. The moisture in the air means that small convective clouds {fair weather cumulus} may form.

In answering this question, you have demonstrated knowledge and understanding of the motion of air masses within the general circulation of the atmosphere. Moreover, you have applied that knowledge and understanding to an unfamiliar situation (or a least one that has not been discussed in the text). This question is therefore particularly relevant to Learning Outcomes KU2 and KS1.

Question 4.3

Tropical maritime air is warm and moist, and therefore brings hot and humid conditions. As it moves over the hot land, it warms from below, making it less stable. It then rises and the high relative humidity results in the formation of deep convective clouds which can produce heavy showers or thunderstorms. The warming is greatest from the middle of the day and convective activity is therefore most vigorous in the afternoons.

Like Question 4.2 and for the same reasons, this question is particularly relevant to Learning Outcomes KU2 and KS1.

Question 4.4

(a) Cold front, cf. Figure 4.10.

(b) Warm front, cf. Figure 4.11.

(c) Occluded front, cf. Figures 4.12 and 4.13.

(d) Stationary front.

{The symbol for a stationary front has not been previously shown in this chapter, but you may well have deduced that because there are symbols on both sides of the line, (d) represents a front that is not moving, i.e. a stationary front.}

This question requires you to demonstrate some of your knowledge of the way in which frontal systems are represented and is therefore particularly relevant to Learning Outcome KU3.

Question 4.5

A hurricane system is driven by the latent heat associated with evaporation of water from the ocean surface and its subsequent condensation in the clouds. When the hurricane makes landfall, the source of water vapour is cut off and the storm quickly weakens.

This question requires you to apply your knowledge and understanding of the formation and evolution of tropical storms to explain a meteorological observation that has not been explicitly covered in the text. It is therefore particularly relevant to Learning Outcome CS1. Because there is no exactly similar example in the text on which you can base your answer, you have to express course concepts in your own words, so the question is also especially relevant to Learning Outcome CS2.

Question 4.6

A high rate of evaporation is required if there is to be enough latent heat for a tropical cyclone to develop. The evaporation rate is higher over a warm ocean, and a minimum sea-surface temperature of 27 °C is necessary. Tropical cyclones therefore develop in the summer, when the ocean surface receives the maximum amount of sunlight and warms up, and in the autumn, before the ocean surface has cooled down again.

Like Question 4.5 and for the same reasons, this question is particularly relevant to Learning Outcomes CS1 and CS2.

Question 5.1

The completed Table 5.1 shows some suggested advantages and disadvantages of various meteorological observing systems. You may well have thought of others. As there wasn't much space in the table for writing, you may have used single words or shorter phrases to express ideas.

This question requires you to demonstrate your knowledge and understanding of techniques used to gather meteorological data (Learning Outcome KU4). In compiling your own table of ideas, you have addressed another aspect of developing your learning strategies (Learning Outcome KS3). You have also demonstrated achievement of another part of Learning Outcome KS1, in that you have responded to information presented in the text, in figures and on the DVD, and reformulated it into a table.

Table 5.1 (completed) Some advantages and disadvantages of various meteorological observing systems.

Measurement platform	Advantages	Disadvantages
Surface stations	Cheap to build Easy to maintain Direct measurements with relatively simple instruments	Mainly concentrated in populated regions of land Restricted to near-surface measurements Concern whether measurements at different sites are made consistently
Satellites	Global coverage Rapid access to images recorded at the same time but at different frequencies Top-down viewpoint	Indirect, remote measurements Expensive to build, launch and operate Limited weight and power supply for instruments
Radiosondes and aircraft	Direct measurements made in the atmosphere Instruments can be manually operated (aircraft) Less restricted in weight and power than satellite instruments	Limited coverage and altitude range Restricted number of launch sites for radiosondes Aircraft limited to commercial routes or a few research flights

Question 5.2

The completed Table 5. 2 shows all the boxes completed.

Table 5.2 (completed).

	Ocean	**Land**	**Low-level clouds**	**Very deep clouds**	**Space**
Interaction with sunlight	absorb sunlight		scatter sunlight back into space		no scattering or absorption of sunlight
Emission of IR radiation	radiate IR strongly upwards into space		radiate very little IR		no radiation of IR along satellite line of sight
Visible image (positive) in daytime	black	various shades of grey	pale grey	white	black
IR image (negative)	black	mostly very dark	grey	white	white

This question requires you to demonstrate your knowledge and understanding of techniques used to gather meteorological data (Learning Outcome KU4), specifically with respect to the interpretation of images from weather satellites. Like Question 5.1, this question also relates to Learning Outcome KS1

Question 5.3

(a) A polar orbiter takes around a day to map the full globe, whereas a geostationary satellite sends back images of the same fixed view centred on a specific longitude every hour.

(b) The geostationary view is severely foreshortened in the polar latitudes, so much so that Antarctica cannot be seen with any detail.

This question requires you to demonstrate your knowledge and understanding of techniques used to gather meteorological data (Learning Outcome KU4), specifically the coverage provided by the different types of satellite employed for weather observations.

Question 6.1

On the assumption of persistence, the most likely daily mean temperature in New Delhi on 6 March that year would also have been 20 °C. Although 'tomorrow is often the same as today' in the record during the period covered by Figure 6.2, there is evidence of day-to-day temperature change of up to 5 °C, so there is a reasonable possibility that temperature that year might have changed over the course of five days. Based on the four years of data in Figure 6.2, the mean daily temperature has ranged from 17°C to 25 °C on 6 March. It would be sensible to assume that the mean daily temperature might vary over a similar range by 6 March in the year in question, so the daily mean temperature would probably have been within the range of 17°C to 25 °C.

{Note that this is just a rough estimate; there are too few historical data to be more confident. You might have noted that Figure 6.2 shows a small upward trend in temperatures in New Delhi during the whole of March and therefore have estimated a slightly higher mean daily temperature than 20 °C, but there is little evidence for a trend in the early part of March especially compared to the day-to-day changes.}

In answering this question, you demonstrated your knowledge and understanding of persistence forecast models. You also showed that you could apply your knowledge of course concepts to interpret meteorological data, and that you could respond to information presented in the form of graphs and diagrams. This question is therefore particularly relevant to Learning Outcomes KU5, CS1 and KS1.

Question 6.2

The mackerel sky indicates the approach of a warm front.

(a) The warm front has a slope of 1 : 150, so if the cloud base is at 5 km overhead, the front reaches the ground 150×5 km = 750 km away, to the west, in the direction from where the wind is blowing.

(b) At 30 km per hour over the ocean, the front will reach the observer at ground level in

$$\frac{750 \text{ km}}{30 \text{ km per hour}} = 25 \text{ hours.}$$

In answering this question, you demonstrated that you could apply your knowledge and understanding of frontal systems, so it is particularly relevant to Learning Outcome KU3.

Question 6.3

A model with large boxes will average over a greater surface area to find the surface height within each box. It will thus tend to underestimate the tops of high mountains, by including more of the lower ground around them, and underestimate the depths of deep valleys by also including more of the ground around them. A model with higher resolution should represent these extreme features more accurately.

In answering this question, you demonstrated your knowledge and understanding of computer models used in weather forecasting, so it is particularly relevant to Learning Outcome KU5.

Question 6.4

(a) There is a very high likelihood that the temperature will be 5 °C to within 1 °C either way, so a confident temperature forecast of 5 °C can be made.

(b) 5 °C is the most likely temperature, but the forecast is uncertain to within 5 °C either way, so a more cautious forecast of 'air temperatures probably above freezing, although a ground frost is possible' may be appropriate.

(c) The ensemble indicates that either a warmer, around 10 °C, or cooler, around 0 °C, situation is possible. It is most likely to be warmer, but there is a significant chance (around 30%, since 11 of the 32 members predict this) that the weather will in fact be freezing.

{Note that the ensemble has no members for which the predicted temperature is close to the mean of the ensemble, so reporting the mean of 5 °C as the ensemble forecast would be very misleading. This type of situation may occur when the airflow could be from two different directions, according to the precise position of a low- or high-pressure system in the forecast, bringing air of very different temperature in each case.}

In answering this question, you demonstrated that you could apply your knowledge of the use of an ensemble of model runs in forecasting and your understanding of the reliability of forecasts, to analyse a situation that had not been specifically described in the text. This question is therefore particularly relevant to Learning Outcomes KU5 and CS1.

Question 7.1

(a) You should have marked chart (a) with an L; (b) with an H; (c) with an L; (d) with an L in the bottom left and an H in the middle at the top.

{Two of the charts (b and d) contain an area of relatively high pressure bounded by closed isobars and with the pressure increasing towards the centre: these are the highs. Three of the charts (a, c and d) contain an area of relatively low pressure bounded by closed isobars and with the pressure decreasing towards the centre: these are the lows.}

(b) Pressure at A is 996 hPa.

Pressure at B is 1008 hPa.

Pressure at C is 1028 hPa.

Pressure at D is 1008 hPa.

{A and B both lie on isobars that have their pressures marked on them: A on an isobar marked 996 hPa and B on an isobar marked 1008 hPa. C and D also lie on isobars but these do not have the pressures marked. However, because the isobars are drawn at 4 hPa intervals, the isobar on which C lies must correspond to a pressure midway between 1024 hPa and 1032 hPa, i.e. 1028 hPa. Similarly, the isobar on which D lies must correspond to a pressure exactly midway between 1012 hPa and 1004 hPa, i.e. 1008 hPa.}

(c) Pressure at F is roughly 990 hPa.

Pressure at G is probably around 1019 hPa.

{The pressures at positions F and G lie *between* the values plotted on the isobars. The pressure at F is between 992 hPa and 988 hPa. As the isobars are fairly evenly spaced in that area, it is likely that the pressure changes uniformly between the isobars, so as F lies roughly halfway between isobars the pressure there is probably roughly halfway between 992 hPa and 988 hPa, i.e. around 990 hPa. The pressure at G is certainly between 1020 hPa and 1016 hPa, but is difficult to estimate more precisely because the irregular spacing of the isobars in that area suggests that the pressure is not likely to change uniformly between the isobars. However, you might reasonably have estimated 1018 or 1019 hPa, since point G is nearer to the 1020 hPa isobar than the 1016 hPa isobar.}

In answering this question, you have demonstrated that you can read MSL pressure charts to identify highs and lows and work out pressure values. It is therefore particularly relevant to Learning Outcomes KU6 and CS1.

Question 7.2

(a) The wind direction at P would be roughly northerly.

The wind direction at Q would be approximately south-southwesterly.

The wind direction at R would be roughly northeasterly.

{To answer this question you need to remember that lines of longitude run N–S and lines of latitude run E–W.

The point P marked on Figure 7.7 is close to a centre of high pressure. The winds would blow clockwise round the high, and slightly outwards from its centre. So the wind at P would be approximately northerly (i.e. from the north).

Q is close to a centre of low pressure. The winds would blow anticlockwise round the low, and slightly inwards towards its centre. So the wind at Q would be a little south of westerly.

At R, which is well away from both the high and the low, the wind would blow parallel to the isobars, and in a direction consistent with the air circulation round the high and the low, i.e. roughly from the northeast.}

(b) The isobars are more closely spaced either side of U than either side of T, so the wind would have been stronger at U.

In answering this question, you have demonstrated that you can interpret MSL pressure charts to work out overall wind directions and to give a qualitative statement about the strength of the wind in a region. It is therefore particularly relevant to Learning Outcomes KU1, KU2, KU6 and CS1.

Question 7.3

A high passing to the south will result in the wind backing.

{Figure 7.15 shows the kind of sketches you might have drawn to work out the answer. Your position is marked by the dot, and the approximate wind direction there is indicated by the arrow. The centre of high pressure is initially southwest of you, so you will experience the wind coming from the northwest. When the centre of the high is directly south of you, the wind at your position will be westerly. When the high has moved still further, so that it is southeast of your position, the wind will have shifted again and will be southwesterly. This sequence means that the wind will have changed direction anticlockwise. In other words, it will have backed.}

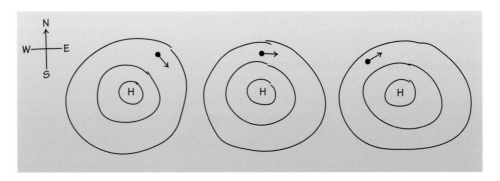

Figure 7.15 Answer to Question 7.3.

In answering this question, you have demonstrated that you can use information about patterns of MSL pressure in a region to work out wind directions. It is therefore particularly relevant to Learning Outcomes KU1, KU2, and CS1. You have also used a sketch to back up your answer, which is an aspect of Learning Outcome KS1.

Question 7.4

As the surface edge of an active cold front passes over, warm air at the surface will be undercut by cold air, so there will be a drop in temperature. The wind will veer. Air is forced to rise by the steeply sloping frontal surface. Cumulonimbus cloud will build up quickly and a fairly narrow band of (possibly heavy) rain will be experienced.

In answering this question, you have demonstrated your knowledge and understanding of frontal systems, and written a short description of weather events in your own words. It is therefore particularly relevant to Learning Outcomes KU3 and CS2.

Question 7.5

The UK is in a region that is well away from centres of high or low pressure. The airflow across the region will therefore be parallel to the isobars, and the UK and countries bordering the North Sea will experience a southwesterly airstream. Air masses approaching from this direction are moist and comparatively warm, so temperatures will be above average for early February. Because the situation is persistent, there will be an exceptionally mild spell.

In answering this question you have demonstrated that you can interpret an MSL pressure chart to work out wind direction, and apply your knowledge and understanding of patterns of atmospheric circulation to describe a meteorological situation that has not been previously described in the text. It is therefore particularly relevant to Learning Outcomes KU3, KU6 and CS1.

Question 8.1

(a) The voltage difference between charge clumps in a thundercloud is millions of volts and hence equivalent to the push of a million or so AA {1.5 V} batteries.

(b) The current in a lightning strike is tens of thousands of amps and hence hundreds of, or even a thousand, times what a vehicle starter motor draws.

(c) A single lightning flash lasts several millionths of a second. A camera flash of a five-hundredth (i.e. two-thousandths) of a second is therefore about a thousand times longer.

In answering this question, you have demonstrated that you have an understanding of some of the scales associated with weather phenomena, and the question is therefore particularly relevant to Learning Outcome KU7.

Question 8.2

Thunderstorms occur most often over inland regions, because land surfaces heat up more quickly than ocean surfaces. The thermals that are necessary for cumulonimbus clouds to build are therefore much stronger over inland areas than over the sea.

Solar heating is stronger in tropical latitudes than in higher latitudes, and this gives rise to stronger thermals.

By the late afternoon, the land has been heated for most of the day and is at its hottest. Air close to the ground has been heated by conduction and this initiates convection.

In answering this question, you have demonstrated that you have knowledge and understanding of the processes by which convective clouds form and build into convective storms, can apply this understanding to explain meteorological observations, and can express the ideas in your own words. The question is therefore particularly relevant to Learning Outcomes KU1, CS1 and CS2.

Question 8.3

Sea breezes bring onshore airflow over the Florida Peninsula from both the east and west coasts. This convergence gives rise to increased updraught compared to that which might occur solely from convection. This strong updraught drives the formation of deep cumulonimbus clouds. Precipitation processes in deep (i.e. cold) clouds involve ice crystals and as these rub past one other, static electricity is produced, leading to lightning and then thunder.

In answering this question, you have demonstrated your knowledge and understanding of clouds and precipitation and shown that you can apply this understanding to interpret meteorological observations, expressing yourself in your own words. The question is therefore particularly relevant to Learning Outcomes KU1, CS1 and CS2.

Question 8.4

The consequences expected of a T3 tornado are that some of the bigger trees are snapped or uprooted and that mobile homes are overturned/badly damaged. The consequences expected of a Category 3 tropical cyclone are that foliage is torn from trees and shrubbery, large trees are blown down and mobile homes are destroyed.

The two damage statements are indeed similar, confirming that the effective wind speeds must be also similar: 150–180 km per hour. However the two events differ in scale. The tornado will be initiated overland, and it will be localised (tens of metres across) and short-lived. All the damage will occur as result of the wind. The tropical cyclone will be born over a large area of tropical ocean, and affect an area hundreds of kilometres across, making landfall after several days. Damage will be done by wind, rain and its accompanying coastal storm surge.

In answering this question, you have demonstrated your knowledge and understanding of weather at different scales and compared information presented in the form of tables. The question is therefore particularly relevant to Learning Outcomes KU7 and KS1.

Question 8.5

The winter fog in the Central Valley is radiation fog: its chief characteristic is that it forms in cold weather after the ground has lost heat by radiation to the cold night sky. The moisture in the air comes from the preceding period of heavy rain.

The summer fog of San Francisco is advection fog: it forms offshore over a cold ocean surface and comes ashore on the wind. The cold ocean is a result of upwelling driven by winds drawn inland by thermals over the Central Valley. In this case, the moisture in the air results from evaporation of water from the ocean.

You may have structured your answer differently from the one given above, but that doesn't matter provided you have made the same points. In answering this question, you have demonstrated your knowledge and understanding of processes that can lead to the formation of fog and expressed yourself in your own words. The question is therefore particularly relevant to Learning Outcomes KU1 and CS2.

Question 8.6

The Chinook is a Föhn-type wind. It gains its warmth following a rapid 2000–3000 m descent from the Rockies (at 3000–4000 m) to the plains (at 1000 m). Heating is a result of the compression of the air as it flows down the mountain slope. The heat gained is typically 10 °C per 1000 m of descent, so even air that leaves the high Rockies at −10 °C reaches 20 °C by the time it gets to the bottom.

In answering this question, you have demonstrated your knowledge and understanding of katabatic winds at a synoptic scale and shown that you can apply this understanding to interpret meteorological observations, expressing yourself in your own words. The question is therefore particularly relevant to Learning Outcomes KU7, CS1 and CS2.

Question 8.7

(a) Figure 8.25a shows heavy rainfall on the north coast between October 2006 and March 2007. However, Figure 8.25b shows that the north coast then remained relatively dry through to September 2007. This six-month period of high rainfall followed by a six-month period of dry weather is consistent with a monsoon pattern (although data from many other years would be required to establish that this was a regular occurrence).

(b) The rainy season is therefore likely to be a consequence of intense solar heating, tracking southwards from the Equator with the ITCZ {northern Australia is just 'in the tropics' of the Southern Hemisphere}. Compared with the ocean, the land heats more rapidly. This causes strong thermals over the land between October and March, initiating a seasonal breeze from the ocean bringing in moisture-laden air. This air rises over the land, resulting in heavy precipitation. Between April and September, the airflow is likely to have reversed, bringing dry air from the interior of the continent.

In answering this question, you have demonstrated your knowledge and understanding of monsoon patterns of weather and the scale on which they operate, applied this understanding to interpret meteorological observations of an unfamiliar situation presented in the form of rainfall maps, and outlined an explanation in your own words. The question is therefore particularly relevant to Learning Outcomes KU7, CS1, CS2 and KS1.

Question 8.8

The map in Figure 8.31a shows conditions that are warmer than 'normal' in the eastern Pacific. This is an El Niño situation. The winds that normally drive the ocean current to the west have temporarily died down, closing down the upwelling of cold water on the eastern side and allowing the sea-surface temperature to become higher than usual.

The map in Figure 8.31b shows conditions that are cooler than 'normal' conditions in the central and eastern Pacific. This is a La Niña situation. Winds driving the ocean current to the west have set in to such an extent that the normal upwelling of cold water on the eastern side extends further out than usual into the central ocean, making the sea-surface temperature there lower than usual.

In answering this question, you have demonstrated your knowledge and understanding of large-scale ENSO patterns and used this understanding to analyse data presented graphically in an unfamiliar format. You have also summarised the main features of El Niño and La Niña events in your own words. The question is therefore particularly relevant to Learning Outcomes KU7, CS1, CS2 and KS1.

Question 9.1

(a) Getting drenched in a downpour could be avoided by simple planning, such as taking waterproof clothing or an umbrella, or rescheduling the walk.

(b) Suffering skin damage through exposure to the Sun is also best avoided by planning, such as wearing a hat and/or applying sunscreen lotion, although health insurance may cover the more serious consequences.

(c) The organisers and television companies would probably insure against a football match being obscured by fog, although fans planning to attend the game wouldn't.

(d) In most of the USA, it would be relatively easy to get insurance for wind damage to buildings, although in areas at high risk from hurricanes and tornadoes plans for precautionary measures (e.g. reinforced buildings and storm shutters) might be a condition of the policy.

(e) There is perhaps insufficient wealth in much of Bangladesh for either precautionary measures or insurance against damage by tropical cyclones to be put in place.

In answering this question, you have demonstrated that you have some appreciation of the importance of the weather for society, and can apply this knowledge and understanding in familiar and unfamiliar situations. The question is therefore particularly relevant to Learning Outcomes KU8 and CS1.

Question 9.2

Table 9.1 (completed)   Essential elements for a civilised society and weather events with potentially adverse effects. Key: H = heat; C = cold; F = fog; L = lightning/fire; W = wind; D = drought; R = rain (or other form of precipitation)/flood.

Weather event	Food/ water	Shelter	Energy	Transport/ trade	Communications	Health (illness, injury or death)
Europe, Jan 2007			C, R	C, R		C
London, 1952				F		F
Canberra, 2003		L (W)	L (W)			L (W)
East Africa, 2005–7	D					D
Central Europe, 2002	R	R		R		R
Bangladesh, 2007	R, W	W, R	W, R		W	R

In answering this question, you have demonstrated that you can analyse the impacts of the particular weather events described in the text. The question is therefore particularly relevant to Learning Outcomes KU8, CS1 and KS1.

Question 9.3

The Santa Ana is a Föhn-type wind: it is warmed by the rapid compression of the airflow as it descends from high country. In this case the descent is about 2000 m, so the airflow will have warmed by about 20 °C. The wind comes from the desert so it is also dry. In the early autumn, a Santa Ana is especially hot and dry. At this time of year, the vegetation in southern California is already likely to be dry and the Santa Ana will desiccate it still further, making it even more likely to catch fire. Once a fire has started, the wind will fan the flames.

In answering this question, you have demonstrated that you can analyse the impacts of the particular weather events described in the text. The question required you to apply your knowledge and understanding to describe a Föhn wind in your own words, and analyse the impacts it might have under given conditions. The question is therefore particularly relevant to Learning Outcomes CS1, CS2 and KU8.

Question 9.4

In cities the rain runs off buildings and hard surfaces into drains. It cannot soak away easily into the ground because streets and pavements are impermeable. The chief reason why the flood depth was much greater than the accumulated rain figure is that rain first flooded the drainage system, so it could no longer be carried away and then continued to build up at street level.

In answering this question, you have demonstrated that you can analyse the impact of a particular weather element on a given part of society. The question is therefore particularly relevant to Learning Outcomes CS1 and KU8.

Question 9.5

The minimum pressure (944 hPa) and storm surge (5 m) are both a good match to the high end of Category 4, and the structural damage of the rather flimsy dwellings is compatible with the US-based 'complete destruction of mobile homes'. The wind speeds of 'up to 240 km per hour' may refer to gusts rather than sustained speeds.

In answering this question, you have demonstrated that you can interpret meteorological observations in terms of information presented in a table. The question is therefore particularly relevant to Learning Outcomes CS1 and KS1.

Acknowledgements

Grateful acknowledgement is made to the following sources for permission to reproduce material in this book.

Cover image: © Royal Meteorological Society CloudBank collection at www.rmets.org/cloudbank.

Figure 1.1a: © TopFoto.co.uk; Figure 1.1b: Sipa Press/Rex Features; Figures 1.2, 4.1, 4.2, 4.5, 4.7, 5.4, 8.13, 8.23, 9.7, 9.9: © NASA; Figure 1.8: Terry Fincher. PhotInt/Alamy; Figures 2.13a, 3.1b, 3.7, 8.2: © Royal Meteorological Society CloudBank collection at www.rmets.org/cloudbank; Figure 2.13b: © Roger Coulam; Figure 2.13c: courtesy Tina Manthorpe/Flickr Photo Sharing; Figures 2.15, 5.12, 7.10, 8.25: © Australian Bureau of Meteorology; Figure 3.1a: © The Regents of the University of Michigan; Figures 3.3, 3.5b, 4.19–4.21, 5.3, 5.14, 8.11: courtesy NOAA; Figure 3.4b: © 2007 EUMETSAT; Figure 3.6: © Thomas Mueller; Figures 3.8 & 8.3: © Wikipedia; Figure 3.12: copyright University Corporation for Atmospheric Research; Figures 4.4 & 8.22: Perry, A.H. & Walker, J.M. (1977) *The Ocean–Atmosphere System*, Pearson Education; Figures 4.9 & 4.18: Ahrens, C. Donald (2003) *Meteorology Today*, Thomson Learning (EMEA) Limited; Figures 4.10–4.13, 4.15: © IOP Publishers Limited; Figure 4.17: Barry, R.G. & Chorley, R.J. (2003) *Atmosphere, Weather and Climate*, Taylor & Francis Books Limited; Figure 4.22: © Thomson Higher Education; Figure 5.2: Realimage/Alamy; Figures 5.6, 5.9, 5.11, 9.13: courtesy NERC Satellite Receiving Station, Dundee University, Scotland, www.sat.dundee.ac.uk; Figure 5.8: Tony McConnell/Science Photo Library; Figure 5.13: Michael Donne/Science Photo Library; Figure 6.3: © Cambridge University Press; Figure 6.7: climate*prediction*.net; Figures 6.8, 6.11, 7.1, 7.7, 7.11, 7.12, 7.14, 8.16a, 9.11: © Crown Copyright. The Meteorological Office; Figure 6.10: courtesy The Earth Simulator Center; Figure 6.12: Richardson, D. (1981–2006) 'Anomaly Correlation of 500 hPa Height', European Centre for Medium Range Weather Forecasts; Figure 6.13: Thorpe, A.J. (2005) 'Climate Change Prediction: a challenging scientific problem', Institute of Physics; Figure 7.3: Copyright © 1994–2008 Unisys; Figure 7.13: courtesy of Meteorological Service of New Zealand Limited; Figure 8.1: courtesy NASA and The Global Hydrology Resource Center at http://thunder.msfc.nasa.gov/images; Figure 8.10: © Australian Severe Weather at http://australiasevereweather.com.au; Figure 8.12a, 8.14 & 9.12a: Mountain High Maps ® Copyright © 1993 Digital Wisdom, Inc.; Figure 8.12b: © Richard T. Nowitz/Corbis; Figure 8.14: from www.islandnet.com. courtesy of Dr. Keith C. Heidorn; Figure 8.16b: provided by the SeaWiFS Project, NASA/Goddard Space Flight Center and ORBIMAGE; Figure 8.26a: © Royal Geographical Society; Figure 8.28: courtesy of www.oceanweather.com; Figure 8.30: taken from www.oceanworld.tamu.edu; Figure 8.31: © NOAA/ Climate Prediction Center; Figure 9.2: © South West News Service/Rex Features; Figure 9.3: © The Canadian Press (Jacques Boissinot); Figures 9.4 & 9.5: © Rex Features; Figure 9.6b: from www.bom.gov.au/info/leaflets/bushfire_weather.pdf. Copyright Commonwealth of Australia and reproduced by permission; Figure 9.6c: © Leo Meier/Corbis; Figure 9.10: © The Associated Press; Figure 9.12: adapted from Ulbrich, U. et al.

The S189 Course Team

Chair

Shelagh Ross

Authors

Nicholas Braithwaite
Stephen Lewis
Shelagh Ross

Course Manager

Isla McTaggart

Critical Reader

Barrie Jones

Production Team

Martin Chiverton (*Producer*)
Roger Courthold (*Media Developer*)
Emily Fuller (*Media Assistant*)
Sara Hack (*Media Developer*)
Rafael Hidalgo (*Media Project Manager*)
Chris Hough (*Media Developer*)
Carol Houghton (*Media Assistant*)

Jenny Hudson (*Course Team Assistant*)
Jason Jarratt (*Media Developer*)
Rob Lucas (*Image Bank Developer*)
Corinne Owen (*Media Assistant*)
Deana Plummer (*Media Assistant*)
Pamela Wardell (*Media Developer*)

Royal Meteorological Society Reader

Sylvia Knight

External Course Assessor

Professor Peter Read (*University of Oxford*)

The S189 Course Team would also like to thank David Grimes (University of Reading) and Michael Follows for their contributions.

Index

Page numbers in *italics* refer to information contained in figures or tables.

saturated air 30–2, 34, 36, 38, 44–5, 55

scattering of radiation 6, 8, 49, 117, 118, 125

sea breeze 42–3, 141, 172, 202, 207, *217*, 231

seasonal forecast 1–2, 152–3, 154

seasons 9, *10*, 11

secondary depression 96

shallow lows 169, *171*

shock wave 196, 231

Sidr, Tropical Cyclone 250, *251*, 252

sleet 58

smog 239, 240

snow 6, 57–8, 60, 238–9

snowflakes *57*

solar radiation
    and latitude 8
    scattering of 6, 7, 49, 117, 118, 125

solstices 9, *10*, 215

South Pole 8

Southern Hemisphere 8, 23, 31, 67, 68, 217

specific heat capacity 22, 216

specific humidity 31, 36

squalls 65

stability of atmospheric environment 43–7, 53, 54, 127, 187, 247

standard atmospheric pressure 15, 39

static electricity 190, 193, 231

Stevenson Screen 109

storm surge 103, *104–5*, 246, 250

stratocumulus clouds 50, *51*, *176*

stratosphere 25, 128

stratus clouds 50, *51*, 54, *55*, 57, 58, 90, *176*

streamlines 169

strong highs 169

sublimation 29, 38

subpolar lows 74, 76, 106

subtropical highs 74, 106

sunburn 6, 117

sunshine, average 23

supercells 188–9, 200

supercooling 30, 37, 56, 59, 187, 190, 237

synoptic scale atmospheric phenomena 141, 142, *153*, 160, 207, 209–12

temperature
    and altitude 25–6, 27, 43–7, 53
    apparent 34, *35*, 66
    averages 18–21, 22–3, 26–7, 108, 133–6, *213*
    and comfort 24
    extremes of 1, 12, 24, 236–9
    latitude, effect of 7–9, 22, 26
    measuring 14–17, 110, 123
    movement of molecules and 29–30
    sea-surface temperatures 225–7, 228, 230, 250
    wind chill 66–7

temperature charts 168

temperature inversion 26, 27, 55, 140, 173

thermal cell 72, 216, 227

thermal circulation 43, 106

thermals 52, 53, 61, 199, 200, 203, 205

thermo-electric effects 110

thermohaline circulation 224–5

thermometers 4, 14–15, 109, 127

thunderstorms 184
    development of 73, 185–9, 190, 231
    electrification 190–1, 194–7
    global pattern of 197–9
    lightning 184, 192, 195–7, 231, 240–2
    precipitation 190
    tornadoes and 199, 200, 231
    wildfires 242

timescales, meteorological 141, 148, 160

tornadoes 199–200, 231
    Fujita scale 200
    Torro scale 200, *201*, 202, 250

Torro scale *see* tornadoes

Trade Winds 74, 75, 76, 78, 106, 207, 217

trend-based forecast 138–9, 140

tribo-electrification 190, 193, 194, 196

Tropic of Cancer 9, 74, 215, 218

Tropic of Capricorn 9, 74, 218

tropical cyclones *40*, 97–100, *101*, 106, *124*, *155*
    damage caused by 250–2
    El Niño and 230
    monitoring 63, 101, *102*, 103, 171, 177, *178*
    naming 101, 103

Saffir–Simpson Scale 103, *104–5*, 202, 221, 250, 252

supercells 189, 200

tornadoes and 200

tropical depression 99

tropics 9, 31, 97, 197–8, 212

tropopause 25, 53, 73, 187

troposphere 25, 26, 27, 39, 53, 100

trough of low pressure 169, 218, 219

typhoons *see* tropical cyclones

UK Meteorological Office 1, *153*, 165

ultraviolet radiation (UV) 6, 117, 118, 125

uncertainty, in weather forecasting 152, 160, 162, 253

updraught 53, 58, 60, 61, 187, 188, 190

upwelling 205, 227, 228, 229

UTC (Coordinated Universal Time) 103, 110, 250

veering wind 65, 172, 175, 182

virga 61

visibility 55, 57

visible images *116*, 117, *118*, 119, 120, 125

voltage 191, 192, 193, 195

volts 191

warm clouds 58, 62

warm fronts 90–1, 93, 95, *96*, 139, *174*

warm occlusion 93

warm sector 95, 175, 177, *180*

water
    drinking water supplies 232–3
    three phases of 27–8

water molecules 27–8, 29–30

water vapour, concentration in air 4, 27, 38

water vapour images 122–3

weak highs 169

weakening highs 177

weather
    air masses and 85–8
    climate, distinction from 11–12
    models of 137–57, 215–20

weather balloons 4, 127–8

273